THE
PRESIDENTS

ALSO FROM C-SPAN

THE
PRESIDENTS

NOTED HISTORIANS RANK AMERICA'S
BEST—*and* WORST—CHIEF EXECUTIVES

BRIAN LAMB, SUSAN SWAIN, AND C-SPAN

Special Contributions by

DOUGLAS BRINKLEY · EDNA GREENE MEDFORD · RICHARD NORTON SMITH

PUBLICAFFAIRS

NEW YORK

PublicAffairs
Hachette Book Group
1290 Avenue of the Americas, New York, NY 10104
www.publicaffairsbooks.com
@Public_Affairs

Printed in the United States of America
First Edition: April 2019

Published by PublicAffairs, an imprint of Perseus Books, LLC, a subsidiary of Hachette Book Group, Inc. The PublicAffairs name and logo is a trademark of the Hachette Book Group.

The Hachette Speakers Bureau provides a wide range of authors for speaking events. To find out more, go to www.hachettespeakersbureau.com or call (866) 376-6591.

The publisher is not responsible for websites (or their content) that are not owned by the publisher.

Cataloging information is available from the Library of Congress.

ISBNs: 978-1-5417-7433-9 (hardcover), 978-1-5417-7437-7 (ebook)

LSC-C

10 9 8 7 6 5 4 3 2

With appreciation for the work of . . .
The storytellers who record our country's history;
The archivists who preserve it;
And, the historians and biographers
who help interpret it for new generations.

John Quincy Adams, a lifelong diarist, created a significant first draft of history. Here, Peter Drummey, the Massachusetts Historical Society Stephen T. Riley Librarian, examines an original diary page.

C-SPAN is directing any royalties from the sale of this book to the nonprofit C-SPAN Education Foundation, which supports the creation of history and civics teaching materials for middle and high school teachers and their students.

Contents

HISTORIANS' PERSPECTIVES ON PRESIDENT DONALD J. TRUMP

A Note to Readers on Style

Each of the following chapters is based on a single transcribed C-SPAN interview with a nationally recognized presidential historian or biographer. To achieve continuity for readers, questions were removed from the transcript, as were nonsalient portions, and the sequence of material has been frequently reordered. Double spacing between paragraphs indicates when text has been moved from another section of the interview.

Bracketed text generally indicates information that was conveyed during the questions posed during the interview and its inclusion was deemed important to telling the story. We also frequently added full names of historical figures and dates in brackets to enhance historical accuracy.

In the Complete List of Featured Books, we list the publication information for each of our highlighted authors. A website has been created to accompany this book, where you will find every chapter's interview in its entirety, so you can listen to each historian for yourself. You will also find many additional resources about each president, allowing you to continue your informational journey. The web address is www.c-span.org/thepresidents.

*   *   *

About the Rankings

Chapters in this book have been organized by each president's 2017 rating in C-SPAN's widely recognized Historians Survey of Presidential Leadership. In 2017, ninety-one presidential historians and professional observers of the presidency rated our leaders on ten qualities of presidential leadership established in 2000 by a team of presidential historians—Dr. Douglas Brinkley, Dr. Edna Greene Medford, Richard Norton Smith, and Purdue University political scientist and Executive Director of the C-SPAN Archives Dr. Robert X. Browning. Prior surveys using these same criteria were conducted with historians in 2000 and 2009. Contemporary presidents are not included in the survey until they leave office; President Obama received his first rating in 2017 and President Trump is not yet ranked. The president's overall ranking leads the chapter along with a summary of his results.

The historians who have participated in our surveys and the authors featured in this book overlap in only a few cases, making for interesting comparisons between the historians' rankings and the observations of the individual biographers.

The ten qualities of presidential leadership identified by our consulting historians are:

- Public persuasion
- Crisis leadership
- Economic management
- Moral authority
- International relations
- Administrative skills
- Relations with Congress
- Vision/setting an agenda
- Pursued equal justice for all
- Performance within the context of the times

The topline results for all three surveys are included in Appendix I of this book. Complete results and additional contextual information are available at www.c-span.org/presidentsurvey2017.

Our Special Contributors

These three nationally recognized presidential historians have long contrib-uted their scholarship to C-SPAN projects. For this book, their contributions include an essay, a featured chapter on a president, and participation in a podcast that formed the basis for our chapter on President Donald J. Trump. All three also served as advisers for C-SPAN's three Historians Surveys of Presidential Leadership.

DOUGLAS BRINKLEY is the Katherine Tsanoff Brown Chair in Humanities and professor of history at Rice University, a best-selling author of numerous books, CNN's Presidential His-torian, contributing editor to *Vanity Fair,* 2017 Grammy Award winner for his work with jazz at Lincoln Center for "Presidential Suite" (for Best Large Jazz Ensemble), and is the first-ever New York Historical Society's Presidential Scholar-in-Residence. Dr. Brinkley has a BA in American history from The Ohio State University, an MA in American history, and a PhD in military and diplomatic history from Georgetown University. Since 1993, Dr. Brinkley has been involved in numerous C-SPAN history projects, including its *American Presidents* and *American Writers* biography series.

EDNA GREENE MEDFORD is Interim Dean of the College of Arts and Sciences and professor of history at Howard University, where she has taught for over thirty years. Dr. Medford received her undergraduate degree in secondary education with a history emphasis from Hampton Institute (now Hampton University), an MA in US history from the University of Illinois, and a PhD in history from the University of Maryland. She has authored, coauthored, or edited four books and numerous scholarly articles on slavery, the Civil War, and Reconstruction. She serves on several national advisory boards and is a frequent contributor to historical documentaries and programs. Since 1994, Dr. Medford has been involved with several C-SPAN history projects, including its *Lincoln-Douglas Debates* and *American Presidents* series.

RICHARD NORTON SMITH is a historian and author specializing in US presidents and other political figures. He holds a degree in government from Harvard University. Between 1987 and 2001, Mr. Smith has served as the Director of the Herbert Hoover Presidential Library, the Dwight D. Eisenhower Center, the Ronald Reagan Presidential Library, and the Gerald Ford Museum and Library. In October 2003, he was appointed Founding Director of the Abraham Lincoln Presidential Library and Museum. He has written biographies on Herbert Hoover, George Washington, and Nelson Rockefeller and is currently working on a comprehensive biography of Gerald Ford. Since 1993, Mr. Smith has been involved with many C-SPAN history projects, and from 2006 to 2014, he served as C-SPAN's in-house historian, with a major role in series such as *The Contenders* and *First Ladies*.

Introduction

What are the leadership skills that make for successful presidencies? If you've recently found yourself thinking about this question, you're not alone. It's a topic that inspired us to open the C-SPAN Video Library and search for perspectives among our interviews with some of the nation's leading presidential historians, biographers, and journalists.

The result of this effort is this collection of brief stories from the lives of forty-four American presidents, each crafted from a C-SPAN interview transcript. These accounts vary as much as the men who have inhabited the office. Not intended as definitive biographies, the scholarship of our featured authors provides snapshots into life events that shaped US leaders, some of the challenges they faced, and the legacies they've left behind. We hope these stories will provide a starting point for your own exploration on presidential success.

As a further reflection on leadership, we opted to organize the book by the presidents' most recent scores in C-SPAN's widely cited Historians Survey of Presidential Leadership. In 2000, 2009, and 2017, our network asked presidential historians to rate all the chief executives on ten qualities of presidential leadership: public persuasion, crisis leadership, economic management, moral authority, international relations, administrative skills, relations with Congress, vision/setting an agenda, pursued equal justice for all, and performance within the context of their times. Nearly one hundred historians, listed on our website, participated in each cycle. Our chapters cite the president's overall score from our 2017 survey; Appendix I lists every president's topline results from all three surveys.

These ten leadership criteria were developed nearly twenty years ago with the guidance of three noted presidential historians who have lent their expertise to numerous C-SPAN projects: Douglas Brinkley, biographer of Theodore Roosevelt and Jimmy Carter; Edna Greene Medford, a specialist in the Civil War and Reconstruction eras; and Richard Norton Smith, biographer of Washington, Hoover, and, next, Gerald Ford. Brinkley, Medford, and Smith have featured chapters in the book and have authored a foreword or afterword for this project. They also participated in a lively podcast conversation about Donald Trump's presidency, which forms the basis for the chapter on the forty-fifth president.

The best- and worst-rated presidents won't surprise you: Abraham Lincoln consistently holds the number one position—as he does in most surveys—most recently earning 907 points out of a possible 1,000. Reliably, Pennsylvania's James Buchanan ranks the worst. In 2017, he earned just 245 points, a full 30 points behind the next-lowest, Andrew Johnson, the impeached Tennessee Democrat who took office following Lincoln's assassination. Aptly, Robert Strauss's featured biography of Buchanan bears the title *Worst. President. Ever.*

In between these two leadership bookends, we think you'll find many other fascinating stories. In our "Top Ten" section, Washington biographer Ron Chernow relates how George Washington, long before presidents were counseled about image-making, had an innate sense for the theatrical nature of leadership. During his first term, Washington traveled by carriage to most of the early states, but paused to enter towns on the back of a large white parade horse. Washington, an imposing figure, appreciated the public appeal of looking "good on horseback," says Mr. Chernow. In Dwight Eisenhower's chapter, biographer William Hitchcock describes the general-turned-president as a master of discipline while in office. "Plans are worthless," he would say, "but planning is everything." Notably, Eisenhower's overall survey rankings have advanced more than all other presidents in our top ten, moving from 10th to 6th to 5th.

In the well-populated "Men in the Middle" section, Amity Shlaes recounts that after Calvin Coolidge's sixteen-year-old son died from sepsis, the devastated politician found it within himself to campaign for reelection and then poured his energies into a successful "grand campaign" for tax legislation. For our chapter on Bill Clinton, we've selected journalist David Maraniss's seminal pre-presidential biography, *First in His Class*, in which he argues that past is prologue with Bill Clinton, that his life has been full of "recurring patterns."

In the section titled "All the Rest," you will find stories of presidents who consistently rank in the lowest tier of our leadership surveys. Scott Greenberger, biographer of Chester Arthur, tells of uncovering amazing letters from a young New York woman whom he believes coaxed Arthur's better angels into reforming a corrupt civil service system. Watergate figure John Dean, who knows a thing or two about presidential scandals, is our featured biographer of Warren Harding. He makes the case that the scandal-plagued reputation of the twenty-ninth president isn't entirely borne out by later research.

Although Donald Trump won't be rated by our survey until after he leaves office, we wanted to include him in this collection, so we asked historians Brinkley, Medford, and Smith to ruminate on some significant Trump-era themes that have persisted throughout 230 years of American history. Reading this chapter reminds one that US democracy has been a continually raucous, and frequently messy, process.

The Presidents marks the tenth book we have published with Public-Affairs using content from C-SPAN's archives. Our objective with all our books is to help tell the American story to interested readers. We also hope that this transcript-based format serves to introduce new audiences to the work of the many historians, biographers, and journalists who appear before C-SPAN cameras. To further these ends, C-SPAN structures our book contracts with PublicAffairs so that any royalties from sales are directed to the nonprofit C-SPAN Education Foundation, which funds the creation of instructional materials for middle and high school teachers and students.

The work of forty-three historians and biographers of varied political perspectives is included in *The Presidents*. We drew almost entirely from two C-SPAN content sources: *Q & A*, Brian Lamb's Sunday evening interview program, and *Booknotes*, its long-running predecessor series. In choosing the featured authors for the presidents, we focused on our most recent interviews; occasionally, we selected older books that were particularly significant or perception-changing. A few of the more obscure mid-nineteenth-century presidents necessitated reaching a little further back into our archives for interviews from *American Presidents*, a yearlong biography series we produced in 1999. As befitting the C-SPAN mission, these individual chapters and the ratings by the presidential historians are meant to stimulate your own critical thinking about US history and of the legacies of the men who have led it.

A website filled with additional information about every president is provided as a companion to this book, allowing readers to continue their historical exploration. You'll find it at www.c-span.org/thepresidents.

The starting point for each chapter is the transcript from our television interviews. Editing chapters from those transcripts is my task; it has become something of an art form I've been working on throughout all ten books. To facilitate storyline continuity, the sequence of the interviews have to be reordered, but every time text is moved, great care is taken to retain the author's original meaning. Every chapter of this book has been further reviewed by Brian Lamb and several other C-SPAN staff members: Katie Lee served as line editor; Rachel Katz checked for continuity; and Zelda Wallace and Anthony Davis fact-checked every chapter.

C-SPAN co-CEO Rob Kennedy, statistical adviser for our three presidential rankings, contributed the survey summaries. Rachel Katz wrote the authors' brief biographies and, as production coordinator, helped select the accompanying images.

As this book goes to market in the spring of 2019, C-SPAN will be celebrating its fortieth anniversary. On March 19, 1979, the US House of Representatives opened its chamber to television cameras for the first time and, as it did, a fledgling not-for-profit cable television network called "The Cable-Satellite Public Affairs Network," aka C-SPAN, also went live, committed to televising every House debate live and without editorial comment. Over the years, C-SPAN expanded to twenty-four-hour programming; added two more television channels (C-SPAN2 and C-SPAN3); and launched weekend programming blocks devoted to nonfiction books (Book TV in 1998) and US history (American History TV in 2011). In 1997, we debuted an FM radio station in the nation's capital (WCSP-FM), now widely accessible via a free smartphone app. C-SPAN's editorial philosophy is consistent for all of these services: no editing and no editorial comment from us. We see our mission as providing the public with real-time access to the workings of the federal government and to those who influence it, from all points on the political spectrum—hopefully creating a more informed citizenry.

In 1987, C-SPAN announced the creation of the C-SPAN Video Library. Today, this archive contains nearly 250,000 hours of C-SPAN content, a powerful resource that documents three decades of America's national political debate. The fully searchable digital content is available worldwide, free of charge, from smartphones or desktop computers.

Over the past forty years, more than 1,500 C-SPAN staff members have worked to create, assemble, transmit, and promote this unique brand of public affairs content to the public. During our busy anniversary year, we offer special thanks to the 265 folks currently onboard with us at our headquarters in Washington, DC, and our archives based in Lafayette, Indiana.

As C-SPAN transitions into our fifth decade, we want to thank two generations of elected officials, civil servants, think-tank leaders, educators, journalists, historians, and authors who have shared their expertise with our viewers and opened their organizations to our cameras. We applaud their commitment to openness and accessibility for the public.

Forty years into the C-SPAN era of televised government, the most common misperception about our network is that we are a government entity. In fact, C-SPAN was conceived and launched by an entrepreneurial group of early cable television executives who provided our seed money. These C-SPAN "Founding Fathers" and their successor cable CEOs have continuously supported us by serving on C-SPAN's board of directors, encouraging carriage of our networks, and offering strategic guidance in a rapidly changing media and telecommunications environment. For four decades, C-SPAN's operating funds have been provided by fees paid by our cable, satellite, and telephone company affiliates. These companies also provide our channels to their customers as a public service, without advertising support. It's no small understatement to say that C-SPAN wouldn't be here today without the civic-mindedness of these telecommunications leaders and their companies.

Susan Swain
Washington, DC

The Magnificent Lion
It's Not Your Grandfather's Presidency

Richard Norton Smith

As the then-director of the Herbert Hoover Presidential Library in West Branch, Iowa, I once received a letter from my counterpart at the James Buchanan Foundation chastising me for some none-too-generous comments I had made about his namesake on a C-SPAN broadcast. I should be careful, he suggested, to whom I applied the label of presidential failure. I sympathized with his position, if not his argument. As it happens, he has some distinguished company. The late, great Lincoln scholar David Herbert Donald liked to tell of his 1962 visit to the Kennedy White House, in the course of which JFK voiced unhappiness over the glib methodology employed by some historians in rating his predecessors as "Below Average" or even "Failure."

"No one has a right to grade a president," said Kennedy, "—not even poor James Buchanan—who has not sat in his chair, examined the mail and information that came across his desk, and learned why he made his decisions."

Whoever defined history as argument without end might have had in mind that great academic parlor game called "Ranking the Presidents." The reputations of some chief executives are literally carved in stone, as evidenced by the C-SPAN Historians Surveys that appear elsewhere in these pages. Most, however, are subject to endless second guessing, less because of new facts coming to light than to fresh ways of interpreting facts long established. Case in point—in recent years, no one in the presidential fraternity has fallen more steeply in popular and scholarly esteem than Andrew Jackson. Traditionally numbered among the "near-greats," not far below the holy trinity of Washington, Lincoln, and FDR, Jackson is the only president to have an age bear his name. Enshrined in public memory as the original populist, Old Hickory was seen as a fiery enemy of entrenched privilege as represented by the monopolistic Bank of the United States, and an indomitable nationalist whose defiance of South Carolina nullifiers set the precedent for Lincoln's breathtaking assertion of presidential powers a generation later.

Today, by contrast, the seventh president is widely stigmatized as a slave owner, an Indian killer, and an economic illiterate. Ninety years after his image first appeared on the twenty-dollar bill, many Americans want to replace Jackson's stern military visage with the face of a very different kind of hero, Harriet Tubman. (The same fate nearly visited upon Alexander Hamilton and the sawbuck until the runaway success of a Broadway musical setting his story to hip-hop rhythm made Hamilton as fashionable as Jackson was passé.) What happened to bring about such a dramatic change of attitude? In a word, the 1960s, a transforming decade in whose aftermath historians discovered vast numbers of Americans—women, African Americans, Native Americans, among others—whose stories had gone missing from its history books. Their subsequent inclusion in the national narrative is not without irony. For the more truly representative American society becomes, the more imperfect Jacksonian democracy appears.

Revisionism does not end at the Hermitage. Consider Jackson's Tennessee protégé James K. Polk. Dubbed "Young Hickory" by supporters, in his single term as president, Polk added more territory to the American nation—1.2 million square miles—than any chief executive before or since. While the threat of war and some skillful diplomacy were sufficient to obtain title to much of today's Pacific Northwest, Mexico was less easily persuaded to part with modern-day Texas, California, and the Southwest. Polk's conduct of the Mexican-American War, once celebrated as proof positive of America's Manifest Destiny to occupy the continent, struck many in the Vietnam generation as a shameful example of imperial conquest.

Offsetting the decline of Jackson and Polk is the improbable ascent of other chief executives long relegated to the historical basement. Recent scholarship has dramatically raised Americans' view of Ulysses S. Grant as the last American president for eighty years willing to deploy federal troops to protect black Americans in their most basic rights. A much smaller group of iconoclasts credits Warren Harding with pursuing naval disarmament and the first federal budget act. As for "poor James Buchanan," his mishandling of Bloody Kansas, his suborning of the Supreme Court over the *Dred Scott* case, and his fatally limited construction of presidential authority at a moment when the nation's existence hung in the balance—well, revisionism has its limits.

Theodore Roosevelt divided presidents into two categories: the Lincoln type and the Buchanan type. This was as prophetic as it was self-serving. The twentieth century would be dominated by TR and his heirs in both parties, activist chief executives who ushered the United States on to the world stage, entrusted a private economy to public planners, and belatedly committed Uncle Sam to the fight for democracy at home as well as abroad. What began with the first Roosevelt was reinforced by the second. First the Great War and the Great Depression, then World War II and the Cold War centralized power in Washington and personalized it as never before in the presidential office.

No one captured this trend better than Clinton Rossiter, the premier political scientist of his age. "The President is not a Gulliver immobilized by ten thousand tiny cords, nor even a Prometheus chained to a rock of frustration," he declared in 1951. "He is, rather, a kind of magnificent lion who can roam widely and do great deeds so long as he does not try to break loose from his broad reservation." Rossiter's ode to the heroic presidency was composed under the spell of both Roosevelts, Woodrow Wilson, and Harry Truman—assertive leaders boldly testing the limits of an office enlarged to meet the twin crises of economic depression and global war.

Presidential government arguably peaked in the decades from 1960 to the 1980s, when television brought the people closer than ever to the man in the Oval Office, even as it magnified the reach of his bully pulpit advocacy from Birmingham and Selma to the jungles of Vietnam and the collapsible Berlin Wall. Yet the lifejacket of one generation can become the straitjacket of the next. Ronald Reagan was the last president who could command an audience of sixty or seventy million for an Oval Office address with minimal competition from cable networks, and none from the internet. Three decades after Reagan's counterrevolution called into question the liberal consensus forged by his boyhood hero, Franklin D. Roosevelt, Reagan and his policies continue to evoke intense loyalty and no less fervent criticism. (Eighty years on, the same holds true for FDR and his New Deal.) Such controversy is the tribute posterity pays to the handful of presidential change agents who remake the political weather. Harry Truman said as much when he defined a statesman as a politician who has been dead for twenty years.

Everyone knows about the sign on Truman's desk asserting, "The buck stops here." Much less well known is the sign that Dwight Eisenhower kept on his desk . . . translated from Latin, it read, "Gently in manner, strongly in deed." Academic critics, accustomed to swashbuckling Roosevelts and their only slightly less energetic imitators, dismissed the old soldier as a grandfatherly duffer smiling his way through a bland decade. The first scholarly poll conducted after he left the White House placed Ike at number 22, just below Chester A. Arthur. Then, in 1966, the first of his White House papers became available for researchers to ponder. Soon students of the presidency were competing in their praise of what Princeton's Fred Greenstein calls Eisenhower's "hidden hand" leadership. Half a century later, historians are still peeking behind his artfully conceived defenses. According to the latest C-SPAN survey, most like what they see. As of 2017, Ike was ranked in 5th place, sandwiched between TR and Harry Truman.

Whatever their differences in style and political outlook, Truman and Eisenhower illustrate how ephemeral are appraisals based on real-time history. A nation addicted to Egg McMuffins and microwave pizza is unlikely to postpone judgment on its elected officials until such time as polarized emotions cool and sensitive papers become available. 'Twas ever thus. "If ever a nation was debauched by a man, the American nation has been debauched by Washington. Let his conduct then be an example to future ages. . . . Let the history of the federal government instruct mankind, that the masque of patriotism may be worn to conceal the foulest designs against the liberties of the people."

So declared the *Philadelphia Aurora,* the *Washington Post* of its day, in the twilight of George Washington's presidency. Laughable as its claims may sound to modern ears, the *Aurora* had nothing on the distinguished *London Times* in the autumn of 1864. "Mr. Lincoln will go down to posterity as the man who could not read the signs of the time," editors asserted, "who plunged his country into a great war without a plan, who failed without excuse, and who fell without a friend." Try selling this to modern-day Americans, millions of whom assume that Lincoln was born on Mount Rushmore.

Journalists, we are told, write the first draft of history. Unlike most first drafts, theirs gets published, part of a 24-7 news cycle that thrives on conflict and clickbait. While haste may or may not make waste, it most assuredly makes headlines. One by-product of this rush to judgment is the Clinton fatigue, Bush fatigue, and Obama fatigue resulting from breathless overexposure and editorial bias. Historians, by contrast, recognize that perspective is inseparable from detachment. It takes time for these to form, just as it does for useful comparisons to be made as successive presidents confront issues that may have stamped one or more of their predecessors with the taint of failure. A dozen American presidents have grappled with the tangle that is the Middle East, for example, some more successfully than others. Likewise, the Cold War tested the mettle of chief executives from Harry Truman to the first George Bush.

What all this points to is the difficulty of formulating some comprehensive or unified force theory of presidential performance. Forget apples and oranges—the nineteenth-century presidency bears as much resemblance to its modern-day counterpart as Franklin Pierce does to Franklin Roosevelt. When economic panic struck the young nation in 1819, James Monroe escaped blame because no one in that pre-Keynesian Eden assumed a connection between a remote and understaffed federal government and the inescapable sequence of boom and bust. Attitudes had begun to change by the 1890s, when Grover Cleveland was roundly criticized for laissez-faire policies, as expressed through his stubborn insistence that in hard times "though the people support the government, the government should not support the people."

Fast-forward to the 1930s. Following decades in which Washington's mandate had broadened to include the regulation of commerce, levying of income taxes, conservation of natural resources, and waging of foreign wars, it should hardly come as a surprise that those made homeless by the Great Depression should personalize their suffering by christening their improvised shantytowns "Hoovervilles" in bitter recognition of the president whose policies failed to arrest the economic death spiral forever after linked to his name. In little more than a century, the meaning of presidential leadership had been radically redefined, with profound consequences for anyone presuming to evaluate success or failure in the Oval Office.

Of course, some criteria transcend political or academic fashion. Character counts as much in the age of Trump as when George Washington, resolved to avoid entanglement in European wars, offered himself up as a punching bag to critics (among them a hostile newspaper scribbler on the payroll of Thomas Jefferson's State Department). Other factors perennially cited by presidential scholars include executive relations with Congress, crisis management, public persuasion, and administrative oversight. Organizers of the three C-SPAN surveys took all these and more into account. In an effort to better reflect contemporary priorities, we established a category labeled "Pursued Justice for All"—a subject of overriding importance to Andrew Jackson as to Lyndon Johnson, and one likely to produce drastically differing assessments of each man's time in office.

In addition, we created a catchall benchmark—"Performance Within Context of Times"—to convey the dynamism of an office in flux. Among the most frequently applied tests of presidential achievement is how the incumbent performs as leader of his party. Two centuries ago, John Adams blew up the Federalist Party in a self-sacrificing effort to avert a disastrous conflict with France. For this, his reward was defeat at the polls in 1800. By the standards of his time, America's first one-term president might be tagged a failure. Yet two centuries on, we revere Adams for putting his country's interest ahead of his own.

The same might be said of other leaders who courageously subordinated their personal ideological preferences to the national good—in effect, rising above principle in ways that posterity alone can appreciate. Successful presidents are opportunists. Forget their lofty inaugural rhetoric; pay attention instead to how they respond to the proverbial three o'clock in the morning phone call. Those who spend themselves in causes larger than themselves have a special place in collective memory. Thomas Jefferson worshipped before the altar of limited government, if no other. Yet he set aside his faith when Louisiana came on the market. "I stretched the Constitution so far that it cracked," conceded this strictest of constructionists.

In buying Louisiana for three cents an acre, Jefferson anticipated Richard Nixon's opening to Communist China, Bill Clinton's embrace of a NAFTA free trade deal, and George W. Bush's support for a government bailout of tottering Wall Street firms. All three men sacrificed ideological consistency to what they saw as the greater good. Not every patriot is a pragmatist. "If men were angels," James Madison famously wrote in defense of the new and untested Constitution, "no government would be necessary. If angels were to govern men, neither external nor internal controls on government would be necessary. In framing a government which is to be administered by men over men, the great difficulty lies in this: You must first enable the government to control the governed; and in the next phase, obliged to control itself."

Over the years, historians by and large have concluded that the cerebral Madison was a better theorist than wartime leader. In the latter capacity, he was judged the Un-Lincoln—a commander in chief sorely lacking in ruthlessness or strategic capacity. Certainly his practice of Jeffersonian frugality served Madison and his armed forces badly when war broke out with Britain in 1812. Having systematically starved John Adams's navy, the president of the United States was forced to entrust much of the battle at sea to privateers—as if a modern-day commander in chief were to outsource the war against ISIS to Bill Gates or Warren Buffet.

And yet . . . in the shadow cast by later conflicts, and assaults on civil liberties ranging from the incarceration of Japanese Americans after Pearl Harbor to more recent controversies arising from the current war on terror, Madison has come in for reappraisal. To admirers, he is a supremely *constitutional* war leader. No one went to jail for criticizing his administration and its conduct of the war. No Alien and Sedition Acts mocked his claims to the defense of liberty against Old World oppression. And if the enemy burned much of his capital to the ground, it is also true that his diplomats negotiated a peace treaty effectively confirming American independence. In the end, Madison, to employ his own criteria, not only managed to control the governed, he had also, amidst the passions unleashed by war, controlled his own government. No small legacy, that.

It should surprise no one that most presidencies, like most lives, combine elements of success and failure. (Think Wilson, LBJ, Nixon, or Clinton.) Conflicting judgments are unavoidable given the competing demands we make on this ceremonial/operational/educator/administrator/diplomat/legislative strategist. Wartime leadership requires qualities that may be ill-suited to the tasks of postwar reconstruction.

The high and holy work of abolition, the crusading vision of a League of Nations, the audacious vow to end poverty, or pursue foreign terrorists into their remote caves—historic as these may be, they have little in common with building an interstate highway system, the pursuit of regulatory reform, or debt reduction.

If after all these qualifications you are still seeking a basic formula for grading presidents, one likely to stand the test of time, you might well turn to the president against whom all others are measured. Abraham Lincoln topped all three of C-SPAN's surveys to date. His preeminence is acknowledged by Left, Right, and in between. The lowest scores accorded him by the network's scholarly jurors were three 4th-place rankings in the categories of "Relations with Congress" (2000 and 2017) and "International Relations" (2000). One might persuasively argue for Lincoln as the greatest man ever to occupy the White House. More important for our purposes, he is beyond argument the best politician ever entrusted with that most political of offices.

Law may have been Abraham Lincoln's livelihood, but politics was his life. To his friend Joshua Speed, the would-be congressman said in 1841 that he would be perfectly willing to die then and there. "But I have an inexpressible desire to live," he added, at least "till I can be assured that the world is a little better for my having lived in it." Yet another friend heard Lincoln confide White House aspirations almost as soon as the two met. "He never rested in the race he had determined to run," wrote Ward Hill Lamon. "He was ever ready to be honored; he struggled incessantly for place."

Even then, however, Lincoln's zeal for recognition was being diluted—some would say purified—through his involvement with the antislavery movement. Over time he morphed into that rarest of creatures, the political animal who dignifies ambition while rising above the grubby pursuit of office. As president, Lincoln embodied what Theodore Roosevelt's biographer Kathleen Dalton has called "the American spirit of self-improvement, change, and growth." It is part of American civic religion that these attributes are acquirable through the recitation of a thirty-five-word oath first sanctioned by George Washington on the balcony of New York's Federal Hall in April 1789. Certainly no one since has done more to validate Americans' faith in self-government than the prairie politician who owed his 1860 nomination to Republican delegates who were reluctant to endorse rival candidates less obscure than Illinois's favorite son, and therefore less electable in November.

In office, Lincoln grew in military competence and in the management of men. He grew in his mastery of public opinion and in his ability to communicate the tides of history. Most of all, by recognizing that a conflict over states' rights could only be justified as a war for human rights, he grew in moral authority. By the time he climbed into a carriage bound for Ford's Theater in April 1865, Lincoln had outgrown the racist society that produced him, as demonstrated in his public advocacy of at least some form of black suffrage. In the process, he bequeathed to America the most reliable of yardsticks with which to measure a president's character or gauge his legacy. On the eve of Emancipation, he said, "The occasion is piled high with difficulty, and we must rise with the occasion." Sooner or later every president can expect to be tested by adversity. How he or she responds—how far he or she rises with the occasion—will go far toward determining his or her place among Washington's successors.

A Brief History of Presidential Rankings

Douglas Brinkley

As secretary of the Continental Congress from 1774 to 1788, Charles Thomson kept meticulous journals documenting the swirling debates over the creation of the United States. At Independence Hall, he was the grand impresario—the record keeper—of the nation's founding. A true-blue leader in the Sons of Liberty movement, praised by John Adams as the "Samuel Adams of Philadelphia," Thomson's name appeared with John Hancock on the first published Declaration of Independence. But in 1800, when his friends John Adams (Federalist) and Thomas Jefferson (Democratic-Republican) ran against each other for president, giving birth to the two-party system, he feared that the young nation couldn't survive such brutal elections every four years. Defamation of character would destroy national unity. At the very least, Thomson reasoned, once the winning candidate was sworn in as president, the entire public needed to accept them as the *executive voice* of the nation.

To drive the point home, Thomson, in a strange act of conscience, burned his Continental Congress journals. He didn't want Jefferson or Adams to be tarnished in history by their sometimes petty and petulant 1775–1776 stances. Thomson believed that US presidents needed to be elevated to greatness by the aristocratic intelligentsia, irrespective of political party affiliation, cultivated as enduring heroes for the ages. From George Washington onward, he insisted, presidents needed to be honored for time immemorial. Once Parson Weems mythologized

George Washington in a popular book called *The Life of Washington,* then *voila!* The cult of the US presidency was born. To honor presidents, Americans have built monuments and put presidents' faces on currency. Presidents' Day is a national holiday. And, in recent years, the American way of grading past presidents' performances in office has become the historians poll. It's a marvelous new national tradition of great merit and engaged citizen fun.

In the eighteenth century, when the Republic began, ranking the American presidents was not much of a discussion. Washington was a demigod, and Adams acted like one, making him a bitterly controversial second choice. From 1800 onward, however, as more presidencies piled up, the debate expanded, but only in a cracker-barrel way. Someone would pose the question, "Who is the best president?" and answers would fly. Party loyalties tended to temper the rankings, as in an idle discussion recorded in print by a bystander in 1848. Typical for its time, it took place in a precinct office in Virginia between two men who were passing the time:

WHIG VOTER: Do you know who was the best president?

JOB APPLICANT: I do not. Some people say that Jackson was. Some that Polk was. Some that Jefferson was. I believe that Jefferson was.

WHIG VOTER: No! Washington was the best president, and the first, and he was a great warrior. And General Taylor will make as good a president as Washington was.

Needless to say, General Zachary Taylor was a Whig who would please that voter by winning the election that year.

James Bryce, the Irish-born diplomat, made a bold survey of the presidents in his 1888 book, *The American Commonwealth,* which was a hugely influential assessment of American government at all levels. He didn't quite rank the chief executives, but he did group them according to their abilities and achievements. His opinions were barbed, as when he dismissed most of the presidents between Andrew Jackson and Abraham Lincoln by making the point that "they were either mere politicians, such as Van Buren, Polk, or Buchanan, or else successful soldiers, such as Harrison or Taylor, whom their party found useful as figureheads. They were intellectual pygmies beside the real leaders of that generation—Clay, Calhoun, and Webster." Those three senators (Henry Clay of Kentucky, John C. Calhoun of South Carolina, and Daniel Webster of Massachusetts) are not household names today, but in the nineteenth century, they were indeed more revered than any of the contemporary presidents. In Bryce's viewpoint, Lincoln and Ulysses S. Grant belonged together and belonged, as well, to "the history of the world." For that reason, Bryce's top tier of presidents was composed of George Washington, Thomas Jefferson, Lincoln, and Grant.

In the early twentieth century, the ranking of the best and worst presidents was the stuff of school assignments, as young people took on a problem that most historians of the time sidestepped. To many scholars, the application of empirical parameters to a study as nuanced and yet thunderous as presidential history was inappropriate. Using numbers to bring order out of chaos might fit college football rankings or lists of the best movies of all time, but dozens of complicated administrations couldn't be nailed into a lineup so easily. In addition, hyperbole went against the grain of presidential historians, who felt that "best" and "worst" were strokes of a housepainter's brush on a canvas better penned with the finest nib.

The modern way of thinking met the field of presidential history when Arthur M. Schlesinger Sr. accepted an invitation from the editors of *Life* magazine in 1948 to conduct a ranking of the nation's chief executives. *Life* was a popular magazine, respected for its clean writing and excellent photography, but it was a far cry from the type of publications with which Schlesinger was normally involved. A Harvard professor of history, he served as an adviser for the *Journal of the Massachusetts Historical Society* and was a founder of the highly literate *New England Quarterly*. Schlesinger's own work tended to look for order within the tumble of events, as with his *Tides of American Politics*, published in the *Yale Review*, which traced alternating sixteen-year cycles of conservative and liberal leadership in America. When *Life* asked for a ranking, Schlesinger had the stature and the outlook to take a stab.

Life magazine understood the pulse of the nation, a fact that brought it continuous criticism from intellectuals who considered that it reflected all too perfectly the middle thinking of middle America. What *Life* perceived in the late 1940s, however, was that the common attitude about the federal government had changed. Possibly, the timing was significant. Franklin Roosevelt had changed the role of the president from a mere executive to a nearly daily presence in American homes, along with his active family. In both respects, FDR was not just the president. To many people, he was the federal government—omnipresent in ways that none of his predecessors had been. With Franklin Roosevelt, fascination with the presidency grew quickly. For better or for worse, Americans began to look at the history of their nation in terms of the presidents. Perhaps that was natural; the English, notably, had long looked at the life of their country in terms of the reign of one monarch or another, or even in terms of their prime ministers. The Chinese spoke in terms of dynasties rather than dates. Personification of more than 150 years of American history was apparently a fresh, yet time-tested, idea when *Life* scheduled its feature in 1948.

After Schlesinger conducted what he called an informal poll of fifty-five colleagues in the field of American political history, he separated his list into "Great," "Near Great," "Average," "Below Average," and outright failures. In his accompanying article, he used the rankings to look for similarities among the presidents sharing the various categories. The main thing that Schlesinger's ranking showed, however, was that there was a tidal wave of interest in this new way of looking at all the presidents simultaneously. In his memoir, he wrote of the bags of colorful letters he received afterward from all corners, many of them lambasting him for the results of the survey. At this point, only three years after the death of Roosevelt, his place among the "Greats" elicited the most ire. "I will agree that FDR was great," wrote one New Yorker, "if by that is meant great liar, great faker, great traitor, great betrayer."

Aside from those who made a new sport of disagreeing with the first ranking, there were many who saw otherwise forgotten presidents in a new light. James Polk, for example, was accorded fresh interest by his inclusion with the "Near Greats." James Monroe rose in standing.

While Schlesinger's ranking was fodder for many an after-dinner debate, it also made its way, slowly at first, into the thinking of academics. By the late 1950s, they were often making reference to the list—without mentioning, of course, its origin in *Life*, sandwiched between ads for Hunt's tomato sauce and Bayer aspirin. They were also increasingly fascinated by the truth behind Schlesinger's remark that "a judgment of historians is not necessarily the judgment of history, but at any given moment, it is the best available without awaiting the sifting process of time." He used that line several times in print. It pointed to the favorite aspect of any product in the postwar era: instant gratification. The apparent weakness in his defense of the ranking—that the judgment of historians locked in a certain date did not necessarily coincide with the sifting process of time—was also the strength of a new use for the ranking, as future academics would discover.

In 1962, Schlesinger conducted a second survey for *The New York Times Magazine*. He included seventy-five "students of history" on the jury and narrowed the scope of the exercise by specifying that the assessment be based solely on performance while in office. A fabulous general, for example, couldn't gain votes for battles won long before he entered the highest office. The notable change from the 1948 ranking was the drop of Andrew Jackson from "Great" to "Near Great." No president was as controversial in his own time, and ever after, as Jackson. The fact that Jackson was held in lower esteem in 1962 than in 1948 intrigued scholars, who embraced the idea of the presidential ranking as a dual measuring stick—first of the respect for the presidents, and second of the attitudes toward history, which were in flux to a greater degree than was realized.

As rankings proliferated, either fully enumerated or in the form of books with titles such as *America's Ten Best Presidents* (Morton Borden, 1961), the rankings themselves became controversial. "Is there any rationale for our comparing the administration of Chester Arthur with that of Franklin Roosevelt," inquired Curtis Amlund, a professor at the State University of North Dakota, "Coolidge with Kennedy; or Hayes with Truman?" Once again, a scholar grounded in detailed analysis was objecting to the process of labeling a president "strong" or "weak" and making a list based on those two words or ones like them. "The appropriate terms to characterize presidents are not 'strong' and 'weak,'" insisted Professor Amlund. "Rather, what the presidency most requires is adaptability."

Other scholars were as rigorous in their approach to the burgeoning field, as studies were made to learn whether the rankings were skewed by the political leanings of the respondents. No such evidence was found. Others argued that the snapshot aspect of the various rankings didn't allow for the rankings to become live, that is for them to give a deeper understanding of presidential greatness and even predict it in individuals.

That criticism and others like it inspired new approaches to the burgeoning field of presidential rankings. In 1982, Douglas Lonnstrom and Thomas O. Kelly II started something new at the Research Institute at Siena College, near Albany, New York. They designed a survey that included twenty different categories of assessment for the presidents. Sending it out in the usual manner to about 250 authorities, they planned it as a tracking survey to be administered on an exact schedule: in the second year of each new administration, in order to chart the rising or falling stars in the ranking.

The *science* in political science caught up to the field of presidential ranking with the work of Jeffrey E. Cohen, professor at Fordham University. He developed models using the statistics in previous rankings to determine with numerical precision the effect of scandal, such as that which plagued Bill Clinton's second term, on the lasting reputation of a president. Dr. Cohen also wondered, as did many others, about those authorities and experts who were surveyed, some of them repeatedly, for each new iteration of rankings. There were those who considered that people who made a living in the study of presidents might be insulated from the values of the general public. In the coarsest terms, they wrote books largely for one another, they listened almost exclusively to one another in conferences, as well as the faculty lounge, and they had at least a degree of the academics' disdain for views of the populace. To whatever extent such charges were true, it couldn't be denied that the type of experts invariably consulted for rankings didn't reflect the American citizenry at large.

The Gallup organization has occasionally polled Americans on the presidents, the results differing markedly from the academically based rankings. Four presidents were at the top of every one of the many previous academic rankings: Washington, Jefferson, Lincoln, and Franklin Roosevelt. In the 2011 Gallup poll, the top four were Ronald Reagan, Abraham Lincoln, Bill Clinton, and John F. Kennedy. While it may be that these were the best four, and the academics were wrong, the Gallup poll is noticeably tilted toward more recent times; of the fourteen presidents who received at least one percentage point, only three predated 1900. Only three of the thirteen presidents who served from 1932 to 2011 were left off of the list: Lyndon B. Johnson, Richard Nixon, and Gerald Ford. While Reagan may well have been the best president and Grover Cleveland may equally deserve a place in oblivion, the Gallup poll seemed to be skewed by a subfactor: which presidents the respondents had heard of. In seeking to temper the academics' rankings with a wider base of opinions, some means of identifying informed members of the public was needed.

C-SPAN has the means to blend the best of both worlds. A staple of intelligent television in the noisy cable era, C-SPAN televises extensive programming on individual presidents, both in studio interviews with authors and other specialists, as well as in on-site tours of places important to an understanding of each of those individuals. The audience for such programs came from all walks of life but had one thing in common: a serious interest in the full scope of presidents, including, but beyond, Washington, Lincoln, and Franklin Roosevelt. When C-SPAN embarked on a ranking of the US presidents in 1999, it duly engaged fifty-eight authorities in the field. Moreover, for ten days in late 1999, audience members could submit their own responses to the same survey. Just over 1,100 did so. When the responses of those who might be called caring amateurs didn't stray far from those of the professional historians, the question of elitism was put to rest.

Like Lonnstrom and Kelly at Siena, C-SPAN polled respondents on a variety of sub-values, rather than simply asking "who's the best?" Moreover, the specificity of the sub-values made the C-SPAN ranking invaluable to those looking for greater insight into the occurrence of greatness in the White House. Like the rest of us, presidents could be superlative in one area but abysmal in another, a fact clearly reflected in the C-SPAN style of ranking. The polls were repeated on an occasional basis, giving the nation a well-received barometer of the moving fates of the commanders in chief. It also gave social scientists a multilayered perspective on the American people and their history.

Jefferson, the third president, resisted the aggrandizement of the presidency overall and certainly that of the sitting president, especially when he held the office. He did oversee the building of a magnificent residence and office in Charlottesville, Virginia, as architecture was a pursuit he couldn't resist. He specially left instructions *not* to mention his service as US president on his cemetery tomb. Overall, Jefferson conducted himself with the humility of a village mayor. The difference between him and the current occupant of the White House, Donald Trump, is stark in their attitudes toward the presidency. Trump disdains the traditions of the White House, but he undoubtedly enjoys the spectacle and the spotlight that now accompany the US president at home and abroad. His awareness of history is in the framework of rankings, as when he asserts that "nobody's ever done a better job than I'm doing as president."

More than ever, presidents worry how history will view them, a trend that has intensified since the advent of rankings. Legacy matters. All modern presidents, quite naturally, when entering the White House dream of Mount Rushmore-worthy stature (or at least hope to make the top twenty in the up-to-date C-SPAN poll). On his first time out, Barack Obama landed a respectable number-twelve spot, but only time will tell if he holds it. So, Trump, upon leaving office, won't have the last word on where he ranks as president; C-SPAN's historians' poll will. And, while the space on Mount Rushmore is pretty crowded with Franklin Roosevelt, Dwight Eisenhower, and Harry Truman in waiting, President Trump should be wary of the presidential loser's club. William Henry Harrison, the ninth president, delivered the longest inaugural speech in US history on March 4, 1841, refusing to wear a winter coat in the bitter cold to enhance his rough-and-ready reputation. He died just one month later. And yet, five presidents—James Buchanan, Andrew Johnson, Franklin Pierce, Warren Harding, and John Tyler—are ranked *below* Harrison in the 2017 C-SPAN poll, which means that their White House tenure was a net negative. That is the sand trap the current and future presidents must avoid. There is nothing wrong with being in the middle, but being last is legacy *losing* writ large.

THE TOP TEN

ABRAHAM LINCOLN   16th President, 1861–1865

Overall Rank: 1

— ★ —

Total Score: 907

Abraham Lincoln holds 1st place among the historians in all three of our surveys, as he does in most presidential rankings. He has consistently received top ranks in crisis leadership, vision/setting an agenda, and pursued equal justice for all. In 2017, his lowest score was in relations with Congress, where he ranked 4th.

Party: Republican
b. February 12, 1809, Hodgenville, Kentucky
d. April 15, 1865, Washington, DC
First Lady: Mary Todd Lincoln
Age entering office: 52

Historian: **Harold Holzer**

Harold Holzer has authored and edited fifty-two books about Abraham Lincoln. His 2008 book, Lincoln President-Elect: Abraham Lincoln and the Great Secession Winter 1860–1861, *focuses on the four critical months between Lincoln's election and swearing in. It was recorded for C-SPAN's Q & A series on November 7, 2008.*

Lincoln President-Elect: Abraham Lincoln and the Great Secession Winter 1860–1861 explores the dangerous period that Abraham Lincoln faced between Election Day [of 1860] and Inauguration Day [in March 1861]. Election Day starts with cannon fire. . . . It's meant to rouse the people of Springfield, Illinois, to vote. Lincoln won his hometown by only about sixty-five votes—so, a close call and a potential embarrassment for him. And, [this story] ends with cannon fire: the artillery barrage that greeted Lincoln taking the oath of office and walking up the Capitol steps to his fate. Of course, it was not the last cannon explosion that would be heard in this fractured Union during his presidency.

People have underestimated his presidential election. I think they have regarded it as the Achilles' heel of his reputation because he didn't do visibly what he did [later] as a leader. He didn't speak publicly; he didn't cajole publicly. He stayed very quiet; he wrote private and confidential letters. But, I contend that he did an enormous amount to curtail the insidious spread of slavery and, in fact, built the pedestal for his presidency without which we wouldn't have the monumental Lincoln today.

. . . I wanted to see the secession crisis as Lincoln would have seen it, living in what was then a remote village in the West, far from Washington. [I wanted to understand how Lincoln managed] the press of daily business with people coming to see him—an open-door policy with visitors lining his staircase, asking for favors, begging for jobs and political rewards for supporting him; having to write an inaugural address and speeches for his inaugural journey; dealing with family business; the deep emotional challenge of closing up the only home he ever owned, renting it out, packing his furniture, relocating his family; getting rid of the family dog because he didn't want to take it with him; saying goodbye to his stepmother; and of appointing a cabinet—all happening concurrently, not neatly divided into sections. . . . I think the documentary evidence that I've uncovered by looking at all of the problems that afflicted Lincoln concurrently—by taking the approach that I wasn't going to look at cabinet selection, inaugural address challenges, political patronage all as separate issues; that I was just going to do his daily routine and examine the pressures and his response to the pressures—I think I've made a fairly strong case for the fact that he basically said "no" to the extension of slavery that might have prevented war from occurring in 1861. It might have postponed [the war], but, in the end, it might also have perpetuated slavery for another fifty years. In a sense he took a principled stand. He advocated it very cleverly, if privately. And, this deserves an airing.

Lincoln got under 40 percent of the popular vote in 1860, and, of that vote, almost all of it came from the Northern states. He won every Northern electoral vote, save for the votes in New Jersey. He won no electoral votes in the South. And, in those few Southern states where he was on the ballot—because most of the Deep South states didn't even give him a ballot place—he won 2 percent, 3 percent, 1 percent. Lost thirty and forty to one. It was the most lopsided victory in American history. And, like *Bush v. Gore* [in 2000, it was] even more nerve-racking for Lincoln. He wasn't sure that he was going to be a valid [president] or that there would be normal succession. He had to undergo two more elections: not just the casting of the electoral votes in February, which he was uncertain about, but the casting of the states' electoral votes in each individual state capitol in December. Lincoln was worried that some Southern states would simply fail to meet; would fail to ratify their votes, even though they were for someone else; or would fail to send the electoral results to Washington where they were destined to be opened by the vice president [John Breckinridge], a Southerner who had run against Lincoln for president. So, it was not a done deal in November. Lincoln said it was, but people knew that there was a scheme afoot to throw the results into disarray and, perhaps, throw the votes into the House of Representatives.

Seven [Southern states out of a total of eleven had seceded from the Union by the time of his inauguration]. South Carolina was first. Mississippi was second. [Then it was] Florida, Alabama, Georgia, Louisiana, and Texas. December 20 was the South Carolina secession convention, and about four states [held theirs] in mid-January. And then, in early February, Louisiana and Texas went out. And while that was happening, Southern senators made these flamboyant resignation speeches in the Capitol. A Confederate government was formed. An alternative president was elected, Jefferson Davis, and a rival inaugural journey was undertaken by Davis. People talk often about Lincoln's inaugural journey, but in fact, as Lincoln was conducting what he called "my meandering journey" from Springfield to Washington, Jefferson Davis was traveling from Mississippi to Montgomery, Alabama, to take over the reins of a rump government.

Lincoln didn't know Jefferson Davis, but he knew [his vice president, Alexander] Stephens. They were both originally members of the vanished Whig Party, and so they knew each other when Lincoln was in Congress in the late 1840s. In that secession winter, Lincoln carried on a correspondence with Stephens imploring him to try to put the lid on the secession crisis, to cool it down, to keep Georgia in the Union. He reassured him, privately, that he would not interfere with slavery where it existed. That was a concession he was willing to make because he knew that the Constitution made slavery legal by recognizing it in the Southern states. . . .

Later, he came close to offering Alexander Stephens a cabinet position. Lincoln's cabinet challenges were much more difficult than historians have acknowledged so far. And, even towards the end of December he was still weighing the possibility of offering a Southerner a job—to keep the Southern states from leaving.

[Hiring his personal] staff was pretty easy: it was one person originally, John George Nicolay, a German-born former assistant to the secretary of state in Springfield. Lincoln took a liking to him and hired him as a clerk and gatekeeper during the campaign. They took up residence in the governor's office in the state capital of Springfield on the second floor. The governor was not in residence, and the session was out. That became Lincoln's headquarters. It was a simple office, and adjacent to that was a reception room. Nicolay was the gatekeeper, correspondence secretary, and purveyor of good and bad news.

Ultimately, they hired a second secretary, John M. Hay, a young Brown [University]-educated law student who gave up the law to work for Nicolay and Abraham Lincoln. Later, of course, Hay went on to become secretary of state under McKinley and Theodore Roosevelt. He had a rather glorious career of his own, which poor Nicolay didn't have. That was it. Lincoln wasn't entitled to more White House staff than that. When he added a third secretary, William Stoddard, he couldn't hire him on the White House payroll because they didn't have room for a third staff member. He had to hire him as an assistant in the Department of the Interior, whose job was to sign Lincoln's name to land grant applications, and he was assigned to the White House. Not only does Stoddard wind up opening all of Lincoln's correspondence, hundreds of letters a day, he still had to sign those land grants.

The hotels [in Springfield] did a great business. There was a little bit of a break in December, and the hotelkeepers got nervous. But, then it started again in January. First of all, there were well-wishers; there were patronage seekers. There were family members who suddenly materialized, country cousins, most of them after jobs. But, Lincoln also summoned cabinet aspirants to Springfield, the first of whom was Edward Bates, the venerable Missouri leader who had been the first choice of many of the more conservative Republicans for the Republican nomination that year. . . . Bates came, and they discussed the cabinet. Simon Cameron of Pennsylvania came, representing a very big state, a very important state in the Republican coalition. He was tainted with this air of corruption in his past. He beat a path to Springfield to say, "Pennsylvania delivered for you, and you have to deliver for me." That was the hardest decision that Lincoln had to make. And, ultimately, one could say he made the wrong one because Cameron only lasted about a year and a half in the cabinet before Lincoln had to get rid of him.

Edward Bates was his first announced cabinet officer—the first man he saw, even though he twisted Bates around his finger a bit and said, "I'd love to make you secretary of state, but I probably have to make you attorney general. But, maybe it will be state. Go back to St. Louis and we'll see. . . ." But, Bates was charmed. He said, "All I want is for you to release a story to the newspapers that you have offered a cabinet position to me." Lincoln drafted it himself: "Mr. Lincoln has made it clear that Mr. Bates will join his cabinet." It was greeted with universal applause because he was a dignified, venerable statesman. A little bit conservative but reassuring to the people who felt Lincoln was too young and inexperienced.

Thurlow Weed . . . was the political boss of Albany, New York, and ostensibly a friend of New York senator William Seward. Weed came to Springfield to visit Lincoln and to try to get Seward not only to be secretary of state, but to have control over a whole bunch of appointments, which Lincoln resisted. At that meeting Weed must have said to Lincoln, "Who's organizing your inaugural journey from Springfield to New York?" And, Lincoln said, "I have no idea. I haven't given it a second of thought." Weed, I believe, recommended William S. Wood.

This fellow, Wood, came to Springfield and organized the journey. He put out memoranda and pamphlets—who was going to get which bedroom in which hotel; how the carriages were going to be lined up at each of the stops between Springfield and Washington. He got the Lincoln party roused in the early mornings to get them out. He organized the dinners. He did a pretty good job of it. When Lincoln rewarded him with an appointment as commissioner of public buildings in Washington, some things about Mr. Wood came out in the Senate confirmation hearings. After a few weeks, his name was quietly withdrawn, and he disappears from history. There are no descriptions, no photographs [of William Wood], just these wonderful, ornate brochures and time cards and schedules. "Mr. Lincoln will occupy the first car. Mrs. Lincoln will occupy the second car." They never were together; always the men and women were separate. And, "Mr. Lincoln will have to have a dining room table for at least eight. I need a room with my assistant. My own bedroom that needs to be no more than two or three rooms from the Lincoln room." He was a good organizer, actually. He didn't get enough credit.

Lincoln had been bleeding money [since returning to political life]. Everyone has written about how Mary Lincoln was a free spender on her clothes, and certainly during this period she goes off to New York and opens charge accounts in a lot of shops in New York City. She buys her wardrobe, buys dishes and things like that for the White House, and begins her infamous lavish spending. But, son Robert was a freshman at Harvard, and he was spending pretty well, too. Lincoln was sending him a few checks—twenty dollars here, ten dollars there, which was good money, considering that tuition was only a couple of hundred dollars in those days. Lincoln had really been off the earnings wagon for a long time. His law practice had all but evaporated after his nomination to the presidency, and he had no real source of income. He was nervous about it. He was a money lender. He lent money to his friends, to his relatives—at a pretty good interest rate. That was one of his sources of income. But, he was concerned. He rented out his house for a few hundred dollars a year. He had a yard sale. Got rid of all the furniture. Advertised it in the newspaper without his name: "Corner of 8th and Jackson, sale of used goods." He didn't charge for the dog. He just gave the dog to a neighbor. And, he took some of his last money out of the bank. In fact, before he left [on his rail trip to Washington], some of his neighbors saw him in the bank buying drafts, which was the equivalent of what we would do when we buy traveler's checks. . . . He bought these drafts to fund his trip. He didn't even have a finance committee to fund his inaugural journey.

[It's ironic that he was cash poor when] the big best-sellers in Lincoln's day were the *Lincoln-Douglas Debates,* which did not profit him, and his Cooper Union speech reprints, which profited the Young Men's Central Republican Union of New York. Fellon and Foster Cincinnati publishers made the money off of the *Lincoln-Douglas Debates* best-seller. . . . [About thirty thousand copies] sold back then. And, [it's nota-ble that these two best-sellers were based on] a guy who didn't campaign for president personally. He was silent from the time of his Cooper Union address in February 1860 practically until February 1861, when he gave his impromptu farewell address to Springfield. He then rewrote that speech on the train into a beautifully edited masterpiece. . . . So, he didn't profit from his writing, but he sure knew how to write.

Lincoln wrote his inaugural address above his brother-in-law's store in Springfield, Illinois, right across from the state capitol. . . . It was a tough, tough speech. It dared the South to leave, and it ended with these words, "It's your choice. Shall it be peace or a sword?" Then over the next month, he showed it to reader after reader, the German-American politician Carl Shurz, an editor in Springfield, and ultimately to Francis Preston Blair Sr. [a journalist who became a Lincoln adviser] and to [Illinois Democratic senator] Stephen A. Douglas. . . . I'm convinced that Lincoln showed Stephen Douglas his inaugural address so that it would get currency and approval among Northern Democrats. Why else did Douglas hold Lincoln's hat during the inaugural ceremony? Why else did Douglas make noises like, "That's right; that's a good one," dur-ing the speech? Why else did he go before the Senate the day after and say it was a great inaugural address? Because Lincoln had brought him into the process, and Douglas had invested in it. And, Lincoln made the speech more conciliatory as he went along.

William H. Seward was the experienced, expected candidate, the New York senator who had been defeated by this inexperienced charac-ter from Illinois. . . . Seward drafted the words for Lincoln to close the inaugural, and Lincoln executed them brilliantly. It came out with ele-giac perorations that are pretty famous today: ["We are not enemies, but friends. . . . Though passion may have strained, it must not break our bonds of affection. The mystic chords of memory, stretching from every battlefield and patriot grave to every living heart and hearthstone all over this broad land, will yet swell the chorus of the Union, when again touched, as surely they will be, by the better angels of our nature"].

. . . The final photograph of Lincoln in Springfield, Illinois, [shows him] proudly wearing his new beard that he'd grown beginning at the

On February 9, 1861, Christopher S. German took this final image of Abraham Lincoln before he left his Springfield, Illinois, hometown to assume the presidency. *Courtesy Library of Congress*

end of November. I devoted five pages [in my book] to it because there are three anachronisms about the beard: One is that he told the little girl who famously suggested that a beard would improve his appearance that it would be a silly piece of affectation if you were to begin growing whiskers at his late stage of his life. And then, he did. Two: Lincoln spent a few weeks growing a beard in front of all these journalists who wrote reports about the fact that Old Abe is putting on "airs"—H-A-I-R-S. This shifted the national conversation from a nervousness about policy to a fascination with the theatricality of what he was doing. [It created] a healthy, deep breath that you might get today when a president-elect takes a much-needed beach vacation. . . . It gives people a little bit of a rest, and that's good. And then, the third thing is that his beard decision was brilliant in another way. Lincoln was elected as honest Old Abe, the rail splitter. The self-made man who, with physical labor and hard work, rose above his prairie surroundings and was tough and had a heart. He needed a different image at that moment, and the bearded, avuncular, wise-looking statesman gave people reassurance. It was the dawn of the age of widely reproduced photography in the United States. People collected these new images of the newly bearded president-elect for their family albums. They bought the prints, which were based on the photographs, and hung them in their parlors. This wise-looking statesman looked over their homes the way religious icons did in previous generations. I think it offered a sense of reassurance. And, the final thing is that this is a guy who was allegedly very modest about his homeliness. He was famous for lines like the one he used in the Lincoln-Douglas debates: When accused of being two-faced, he said, "If I had another face do you think I would wear this face?" Meanwhile, when he grows the beard, he sits for photographers, he sits for painters, he sits for a sculpture—all in an effort to get his new image reproduced and out to the public. So, he had a very sure sense of the power of his image.

[Lincoln's pre-inaugural rail trip went from] February 11 to February 23—twelve or thirteen days. He made 101 speeches in lots of cities. . . . They were passing through town after town where people were lined up along the tracks. Even in the most rural areas, people were lined up waving flags, or, even by firelight, waving as the train went by at its robust 25, 30 miles an hour. Nicolay and Hay, the two secretaries, they kept thinking, where did all these people come from in these remote areas? And, each time the train stopped to simply get more wood and water, Lincoln was often called upon to do greetings or to introduce his wife. Then, ultimately, when he gets into state capitals like Columbus and Albany and Trenton, he makes very meaningful speeches. Some are wise. Some are unwise.

Lincoln had more security on that trip than any other president had had up to that point. His mailbag was just bulging with vile threats about poisoning, about poison ink, poison food, about being blown away when he got to his inaugural. And so, he built up this corps of uniformed and nonuniformed guards—really tough guys. His personal friend, Ward Hill Lamon, who was almost as big as Lincoln—some said bigger—was armed with brass knuckles and revolvers. [There was also] an officer named Bull Head Sumner. He got that name because a bullet once bounced off his head in battle. Elmer Ellsworth, who was a Zouave drillmaster—Zouaves wore colorful uniforms like Saharan foreign legion soldiers—David Hunter, John Pope—all of these guys became Civil War military figures. That was Lincoln's big corps of protectors, indicating the seriousness of the threats and the pervasiveness of the threats against him.

Lincoln gets to Philadelphia around the time of Washington's birthday, on the twenty-first [of February]. The next day he's scheduled to raise the flag over Independence Hall on his great icon George Washington's birthday. . . . After a fireworks display at his hotel, he's asked to go to a private meeting, and there he meets a Scottish-born detective, who's famous now, named Allan Pinkerton. Lincoln may have known him because he was a railroad detective [and Lincoln had earlier been a railroad lawyer]. Pinkerton says, "There is a plot against you when you get to Baltimore. You have to change trains." In those days the trains didn't go right through; you had to change in one part of town to the railroad that would go in the next direction, south in this case. Pinkerton said, "While you are changing trains, there's going to be a diversion outside. The police are going to rush to see what the commotion is. While that happens, you're going to be attacked by a group of pro-slavery 'Plug Uglies.' Don't forget, Mr. Lincoln, the same thing happened to James Buchanan in Baltimore four years ago. He was menaced by these 'Plug Uglies.' If it happened to Buchanan, who was favorable towards the Southern interest, it's certainly going to happen to you."

Lincoln said he'd take this under advisement. Then he goes back to his suite, where Robert Lincoln has let a relative stranger enter. Lincoln opens the door, turns on the gaslight, and sees a stranger there. Imagine how harrowing that was after that [Pinkerton] meeting. It was William Seward's son, Frederick, dispatched from Washington with a warning from his father. Enclosed in this was a message from General Winfield Scott, who had been warning about all sorts of menaces to Lincoln's arrival when he got to Washington. Inside that was a warning from somebody else where the same [Baltimore train] plot is described. So, in essence, Lincoln had it from two independent sources that there was a credible threat to him in Baltimore.

Lincoln said, "I'm still going to raise the flag outdoors." And, the next morning he says, "I'd rather be assassinated on this spot than to surrender [to these threats]." Everyone often says that [this declaration] was his presaging his ultimate sacrifice. But no, [he said it] because he had just been warned. Then he goes on to Harrisburg to make a scheduled stop. There was a young man named Andrew Curtin, a Republican, [who had] just been elected governor of Pennsylvania, and Lincoln feels he owes him the trip to Harrisburg. And he owes a trip to the [pacifist] Quakers to tell them they may have to arm; they may have to join the fight. So, it was very important. And then, he [changes his schedule and] agrees to go secretly from Harrisburg back to Philadelphia and then on the night train from Philadelphia to Baltimore [and on to Washington]. He later says it's the biggest mistake he's ever made because he's mercilessly lampooned, shown wearing a Scottish hat—a little twist on Pinkerton being [a] Scotsman—and a military cloak. But, it was probably . . . prudent for him to do this because there was no point in not reaching the federal capital. A show of bravado that ends in your own disability or death was not going to do the Union cause any good.

The descriptions from people who came to Washington, DC, with Lincoln was that the place smelled. People wrote constantly about the dust in the streets. . . . There was a spring thaw. Dust balls were blowing all over the place, and there was an army of people out there trying to get the dust out before the official inaugural activities were to begin on March 4. The sidewalks were made of wood for the most part. Not all the streets were cobblestones. Some of them were, but the side streets were still mud. The Washington Monument was unfinished. Abraham Lincoln, as a congressman, had been here for the dedication of the Washington Monument, but it had only risen about 40 percent of the way up, then funds had run out—and it was sort of a national embarrassment. It was a symbol, some said, of the fact that the Union itself was in jeopardy [that] the monument was never completed. Down on the other end of Pennsylvania Avenue, the Capitol was unfinished. But, here was a hopeful sign because the dome was rising beneath a web of scaffolding, the steel dome that we know today. Back then, it was a construction site.

[The Willard Hotel in Washington] played a big role in the run-up [to the inauguration], and it played a major role on Inauguration Day. It was Abraham Lincoln's first multiday headquarters after his election. . . .

The Willard is where he was ensconced from February 23 to March 4, 1861, doing all the business that a president-elect has to do, all the social and political things.

Henry Willard's establishment was the most bustling, best-known hotel—the best hotel address in Washington. An astonishing amount was going on when Lincoln got here. The [Hampton Roads Peace Conference]—an extra-governmental group of elderly, dignified gentlemen, most of whom had been in public service over the years—was meeting in this hotel in the ballroom. [Their goal was] to create and impose on the president-elect a plan for saving the Union that would have extended slavery all the way to the Pacific Ocean. Lincoln had to contend with that whole group when he got here. He came face-to-face with them in this hotel. So, to stand them down, he had a couple of meetings with them, but he would not back down [on his policies].

. . . Lincoln had a big public suite in the hotel where liquor flowed and cigars and hors d'oeuvres were served. There were bedrooms reserved for him and his family, and man did he run up a bill.

Washington legend is that this was the very hotel lobby where the term "lobbyist" was born, and maybe it happened on the night of February 23. Lincoln got here early in the morning. He went right out with William Seward to visit President James Buchanan down the way at the White House, to pay an unexpected call on the president. He made a couple of other stops, and when he got home at night, the hotel was filled with cigar-smoking, gin- and bourbon-drinking people who had things on their mind and things to expect. They wanted jobs. They wanted favors. They wanted diplomatic positions. They wanted postmasterships. Lincoln was told that the crowd was so thick and so angry and so demanding that one aspirant for a job had threatened to challenge another aspirant for the same job to a duel. Lincoln said, "That's probably not a bad idea—we would lubricate the process a little bit." He was eager for the aspirants to winnow down.

[What's new in my book] is the depth of Lincoln's commitment to preventing the spread of slavery. . . . The details of his journey [are new]; his preparation for his speeches is new. I would like to think that the other new thing is a challenge to those who believe that Lincoln selected his cabinet on the night he was elected. I think that's something he told those cabinet ministers later to make them feel they were his first and only choices. I'm convinced that he really didn't have the whole thing settled until a few weeks before he left Springfield. Even when he got to Washington, it was sort of a mess because he had problems with Simon Cameron and Salmon B. Chase and Seward—none of whom wanted to serve with the others. And, finally, the degree to which he wanted a Southerner in that official [cabinet] family is new.

[My goal with this book was to] really have a sense of recreating Lincoln's life [in the months before he took office], not only in his hometown of Springfield, but on his pre-inaugural trips to Chicago and to his mother's homestead on the prairie. [I also wanted to document] that whole journey to all the Northern state capitals and cities where he was greeted with parades and finally getting to New York, where he was treated coolly, and his passing through Baltimore incognito. And then, there is his coming to Washington and finding the capital so changed from the time that he had served there as a congressman and trying to redeem himself from his secret flight through Baltimore by making himself accessible and available in Washington—sort of taking the town by storm.

GEORGE WASHINGTON

1st President, 1789–1797

Overall Rank: 2

—★—

Total Score: 868

Historians have awarded George Washington 2nd position in the C-SPAN surveys since 2009, when he moved up from 3rd place, passing FDR. He is ranked 1st in economic management, moral authority, and performance within context of times. Like other slaveholding founders, his lowest rank is in pursued equal justice for all (13th).

No party
b. February 22, 1732, Westmoreland County, Virginia
d. December 14, 1799, Mount Vernon, Virginia
First Lady: Martha Dandridge Custis Washington
Age entering office: 57

Historian: **Ron Chernow**

Biographer and historian Ron Chernow joined C-SPAN's Q & A *on August 23, 2010, for a two-part interview on his 904-page Pulitzer Prize–winning biography of our first president,* Washington: A Life.

What we have done—in the very understandable, very laudable desire to venerate George Washington—is we've sanded down the rough edges of his personality, and we ended up making him bland and, dare I say, even a bit boring. People at the time saw Washington as this very dynamic and charismatic figure. I would love for contemporary Americans to share that excitement that Washington's contemporaries shared.

Washington, as a young man, has an amazing perseverance and doggedness about him—you could already see glimmers of a future leader. He is somebody who was pursuing money, status, and power. He's not a particularly attractive character in certain ways when he's younger, but he so transcends his past. He is someone who is so ennobled by circumstance that under the pressure of the Revolutionary War and then the Constitutional Convention, and the creation of the federal government—these monumental challenges bring out this greatness. This is a man who ends up so much greater than anyone would have predicted who had read about his adolescence or his early adulthood. It's a tremendously inspirational story at a time in our history when we all need a little bit of inspiration.

His was a difficult boyhood. His father dies when George is eleven. . . . Then he's left at the tender mercies of his mother, who is something of a holy terror. There was a lot of financial stringency at the time, which stayed with him—Washington was always very tense about the subject of money. That came from his boyhood. So, it was a troubled [youth], but he starts surveying, so it's also a period of great accomplishment.

Washington was a prodigy. By the time he is twenty-three years old, he's the head of . . . all the armed forces in Virginia. It's quite astounding. Virginia was the biggest, most populous, richest colony at the time. We still associate Washington with the Revolutionary War, but he had a whole other life as a young man in the French and Indian War [1756–1763].

He had dysentery in the French and Indian War during the famous defeat of General Edward Braddock on the Monongahela River. It caused diarrhea, and, not going into details, it was very painful for him to sit on his horse. It was an extraordinary example of Washington's bravery, riding in this battle. He was tall; he was a very conspicuous target on a horse. He took four bullets in his clothing—one in his hat and three in his coat. He had two horses shot out from under him. A Presbyterian minister, Samuel Davies, said afterwards that it looked like the heroic youth George Washington was being preserved by Providence for some important future service for his country, which was certainly one of the great calls of any sermon in history.

[His relationship with Martha Custis] started back in 1758. Washington was going to Williamsburg to consult a doctor. He had a friend, Richard Chamberlain, who knew this young widow, Martha Dandridge Custis, who was living, ironically enough, in a house on the Pamunkey River called the "White House." She was a wealthy widow. It was a whirlwind courtship. They met only two or three times before they decided to marry. I don't think it was the lustiest or most romantic marriage in history, but it was one of those marriages that ripened into a very deep friendship. Martha Washington is absolutely invaluable to George Washington. She gave him financial security. She gave him emotional support, and he really needed a confidante—he was a reserved character. She was a real social asset. She was a great hostess, a very good conversationalist. You have a sense with Washington—as often happens with single men—that once they marry, they go from having a rootless life to suddenly being settled. And God knows, Washington, who is going to achieve these monumental things, really needed a very settled home life in order to do that. Martha gave that to him.

[Their home was Mount Vernon on the Potomac River in Virginia.] Mount Vernon, which consisted of five separate farms, was eight thousand acres. On top of that, he had about forty or fifty thousand acres out west, which he was constantly trying to sell to pay off his debts. This sounds like a lot, but at the time there were a lot of people who were amassing large amounts of land. In fact, one of Washington's grievances against the British Empire is that at the end of the French and Indian War, they banned settlement west of the Allegheny Mountains. There were a lot of Virginians, like Washington, who were snapping up all of this land in western Virginia, and they felt that the British Empire was suddenly thwarting their ambitions—and there was no ambition that burned more brightly in the breast of a true Virginian than land. Everything revolved around land at that time.

At the height, [the Washingtons had] about three hundred slaves. Of those, about 125 were legally under the direct control of George Washington. That is important, not on a day-to-day basis, but important because in his will, Washington does something that no other founder does: he frees those 125 slaves. The other 175 slaves, who were known as the dower slaves, were brought to the marriage by Martha and pledged to the Custis heirs. . . . Washington legally could not emancipate those slaves. . . . He was always frustrated as a slaveholder. As illogical as it sounds, he always talked about them as if they were salaried employees, and he's paying them room and board, and why can't he get a full day's work in return? He can't understand that the slaves have no rational reason for performing well. So, he's constantly frustrated because he's a very efficient man, and he's always trying to introduce new scientific production methods at Mount Vernon. . . . If you're a slave, the best response is to be passive-aggressive. You do enough to get by, but there's nothing in it for you by performing with maximum intensity.

The Revolutionary War really starts in April 1775 at Lexington and Concord—"the shots [heard] 'round the world." . . . By Lexington and Concord, Washington has already . . . attended both the First and Second Continental Congresses. One of the reasons that he was such a successful general and president, he'd had long political experience. He'd been serving the House of Burgesses since 1758. He'd been very involved in the protest of the Stamp Act in 1765, the Townshend duties in 1767, and in opposing the Intolerable Acts later on. And so, this was a man who was very well versed in parliamentary government by the time that he is in a position of responsibility.

The Second Continental Congress appointed him [commander of the Revolutionary Army] by a unanimous vote. It was the first of four significant unanimous votes: Washington is unanimously appointed commander in chief; he was unanimously appointed president of the Constitutional Convention; and then both times that he ran for president, he was unanimously elected by the Electoral College. That's a record that we can safely say no one will ever duplicate.

Why did people want to follow him? Washington inspired a lot of confidence. In part, you want to give power to people who don't seem to be grasping at power. This was a lesson that Washington had learned very well. Also, when he was chosen as commander in chief, people were very impressed that someone of his wealth was going to risk all of it for the sake of the cause. Washington was a very good listener. He wasn't an egomaniac. There was a tremendous fear that whoever became commander in chief would then become the so-called man on horseback who would become very puffed up with his own power. There was a modesty and humility about Washington's demeanor, combined with a large degree of self-confidence as well.

The colonies were very fractious and very fractured throughout the contest. [For] most generals, their greatness is what they do on the battlefield. Arguably, Washington's greatness was as much what he did between battles, simply holding the Continental Army together. We tend to think of Valley Forge as the nadir of the Continental Army, when they're shivering and they're suffering and they're starving. Valley Forge in many ways was more the rule than the exception. This was an army that was constantly short of men, money, blankets, shoes, clothing, gunpowder, et cetera. George Washington not only had to hold this often-disgruntled army together, but he had to be a brilliant politician in dealing not only with the Congress but in dealing with thirteen separate states. Washington's story is a heroic story, and ditto for the Continental Army. But he got precious little cooperation from a lot of the states. His correspondence is one long jeremiad of complaint and grievance that nobody is helping him.

The Congress was constantly in arrears on paying people, to the point where at the end of the revolution there was a mutiny among the officers that they're owed so much back pay. . . . Money permeates the whole war. There's a constant shortage of money.

This is an important [experience] in terms of the development of Washington's political philosophy. The Continental Congress had no independent source of revenue. There was no executive branch at the time; there was just the legislature, the Congress. Congress could request that the states give them money, but Congress could not demand that the states give them money—so the states competed to see who could give the least money. For Washington, Hamilton, the other officers, this was really the beginning of their nationalistic philosophy. They realized that you needed a powerful federal government with a strong executive, that it must have taxing powers and independent sources of revenues. Washington's policies as president are a direct outgrowth of his frustrations during the Revolutionary War.

He goes up [to Boston] in July 1775 and takes control of the Continental Army. . . . It's a moment where the redcoats, the British, are bottled up in Boston. They're really under siege from the Continental Army, and Washington manages to drive them out of Boston, and he has his first great victory. It may be a little bit of beginner's luck because then he has an enormous amount of difficulty duplicating that feat.

He goes to New York, and that's where he suffers a string of disasters. In the Battle of Brooklyn, the British Expeditionary Force, the largest of the eighteenth century, is about to pounce on the Continental Army, not only to wipe it out, but wipe the whole revolution out. Washington evacuates his entire army across the East River overnight and flees up to northern Manhattan. Unfortunately, it's not the last disaster. Washington loses twin forts on opposite sides of the Hudson, Fort Washington and Fort Lee, and this begins this long bedraggled, demoralized retreat across New Jersey and across the Delaware River into Pennsylvania.

In Philadelphia, what happens is that because there's always a fear that the British are going to take Philadelphia, Washington and his troops first fight the British at Brandywine Creek hoping to stop them. It's one of the battles, unfortunately, that Washington blunders because of faulty strategy and intelligence. He was far from a faultless military leader. The British occupied Philadelphia until the spring of 1778.

Washington believed strongly in leadership by example. He made a point in every battle that he fought that he was right smack in the thick of the battle. He was often the most conspicuous target. Also, when they got to Valley Forge, precisely to avoid that situation where the generals seemed to be back in a warm house, Washington lived in a tent. He lived in temporary quarters, and then they started building huts. He wanted to show the men that he was sharing their suffering.

What he wanted was independence from England. Exactly what form the government would take was a subject that was postponed. He was gradually developing his nationalistic philosophy through his critique of the Congress. In terms of his military strategy, Washington realizes early on that he lacks what the British have in spades, which is sea power. He is up against arguably the greatest navy in the world. . . . They can rapidly move troops up and down the Eastern Seaboard. Washington doesn't see a way, nor do his generals, that he can defeat the British. And so, it becomes a war of attrition, an opportunistic war, where Washington tries to evade the British and, where opportunity presents itself, attack. . . . There are long stretches in the Revolutionary War where, in terms of battles, nothing is happening. Sometimes many months go by and there's no major battle. And then what happens later is that the war shifts to the south, but Washington stays in the north . . . [and] George Washington, the hero of the Revolution, is pretty much a distant spectator in the north. It's only when the French alliance started in 1778, culminating in the Yorktown victory three years later, that American land power, combined with

French sea power and the French army, finally bottle up Cornwallis at Yorktown, and that becomes the climactic battle.

Washington said that the bane of his life [as commander in chief] was that never in history had there been an army that was disbanded at the end of every year and then had to be reconstituted. At various times he had two or three thousand men under his command; at the time of Yorktown it maybe went up to fifteen or sixteen thousand. There are altogether twenty-five thousand Americans who died in the Revolutionary War, which sounds small compared to, let's say, the Civil War at more than six hundred thousand. But the [colonial] population was only three million, so that's a very significant number of fatalities given the population at the time.

. . . On November 25, 1783, Evacuation Day in New York City, George Washington and Governor George Clinton, at the head of eight hundred men, ride into Manhattan. As they are riding south into the city, the British are leaving onboard ships. Washington is greeted by delirious crowds. In terms of what was happening on the ground, that was the official end of the Revolution. Washington submits his resignation to the Congress in Annapolis in December 1783, a moment immortalized by John Trumbull in a great painting. At the time, that was in many ways considered the most important act that Washington ever took. Benjamin West, a portrait artist, told King George III that General Washington was planning on resigning his commission and going back to Mount Vernon. And George III says, "If he does that, he will be the greatest man in the world." This was considered unheard of for somebody not to try to parlay that kind of military success into postwar political power.

He's somewhat reluctantly drawn to the Constitutional Convention [in Philadelphia], but his position there is vital for a couple of reasons. Number one, the Constitutional Convention is conducted behind closed doors. In order to convince the public outside of those doors that some nefarious plot is not being concocted inside, the public is reassured by the presence of George Washington; they know that no evil cabal is going to form if Washington is the president of the Constitutional Convention. The other thing that's very important in the writing of the Constitution: given the fact that we had just fought a revolution against the uses of executive power, Article II—which details the powers

of the presidency—is far and away the most difficult part for these delegates to write; they kept fearing abuses of executive power.

Everyone knew that if he wanted it, George Washington would be
the first president, and so the delegates were emboldened to create
what turned out to be a very strong presidency because they imagined
George Washington, or someone like George Washington, holding the
office. They were well advised in that because Washington was quite a
brilliant president.

Washington didn't like to be touched. . . . When he had a reception as
president, he would go around the room and nod to people. Whether
this was borrowed from royal practice, because royalty didn't touch
people, we don't know. It was certainly alleged by his political enemies
that this was an aping of royal ways, which was a common criticism of
the opposition party while he was president. But he had this sense of
personal dignity that was very much part of his power and very much
a part of his mystique. Washington would never make it as a politician
today because he didn't press the flesh. He was not this glad-handing,
backslapping character that you have to be in politics today. There's
something very attractive about the formality and the innate dignity of
the man.

There are a lot of examples of Washington losing his temper. . . . For
me, it suggests all of these emotions boiling under the surface. Gou-
verneur Morris said Washington was such a passionate man, "he had
passions boiling in his breast almost too mighty for any human being to
control." This is very different from the way that we see Washington. But
the people closest to him sensed this tremendous intensity under the
surface that would periodically, like a volcano, boil over.

He was also prone to tears. The evidence is everywhere in his
story. . . . He was a highly emotional man, but he was somebody who
was always very reluctant to show those emotions and someone who was
always afraid of becoming a captive to those emotions. . . . He became
an almost overly controlled personality, emotionally muscle-bound in a
certain way. This was also a man who in his dealings with political associ-
ates, with military officers, could be, and often was, exquisitely sensitive
and courteous. I don't want to paint the portrait of him as tyrannical but
rather somebody who was very sensitive in dealing with people. He had
a tremendous sense of tact and courtesy. He was an exemplary figure

in that way. He was a very complicated man. This is a very tough nut to crack sociologically and psychologically.

During his first term as president, he decided that first he would visit all of the Northern states, and then he would visit all the Southern states. He traveled from town to town by carriage, but . . . he would always bring along a white parade horse, and when he was a mile or two outside of town, he would dismount from the carriage. He would get on the white parade horse and enter town. Why did he do that? He had a great sense of showmanship. He knew that he looked great on horseback. It's not coincidental that we have all these equestrian statues of George Washington. He had a theatrical sense, but he's a contradiction because, on the other hand, he feels so burdened by his own celebrity. This same man who rides into town on a white horse will then inform us in his diaries that, let's say, the following morning in leaving he learns that a procession of dignitaries would accompany him out of town at 7:00 a.m. Washington would write in his diaries, "I got up at 5:00 a.m. and left before this escort could accompany me because I'm tired of all of these adulations and the receptions." He constantly had to make speeches and make nice with people.

Washington had many virtues, but one virtue that he did not have was spontaneity. Nowadays we think of a politician as somebody who can, on the spur of the moment, come up with a funny anecdote, a few well-chosen words. George Washington was not like that. It was a torment to him; wherever he went, not only did people want to see him, but they wanted to lionize him. He got very, very tired of it. Whatever ambitions he had as a young man, and his ambitions were quite enormous as a young man, he had more than his fill as time went on. And then he began to feel oppressed by the whole thing.

The most interesting thing I learned about his presidency [is this:] sometimes it's portrayed that George Washington somehow floated above the fray, that he was a figurehead and that Hamilton was running it. Not at all. Washington was absolutely on top of everything that was going on. Even Jefferson marveled at the way that not only everyone was reporting to Washington, but that Washington wanted to review all outgoing letters. Jefferson marveled at the way that Washington was aware of absolutely everything that was happening in the administration. He was a much stronger president than people realized and very creative. Remember, he's forging the office of the presidency. He establishes a benchmark in terms of appointing people of brilliance and integrity. He is really the one who's defining the system of separation of powers and checks and balances. And then, most importantly, we're still living with George Washington's presidency. What I mean is that unlike the framers of the Constitution, Washington decides that the engine of foreign and domestic policy is going to be the presidency. It's not going to be the Congress.

Washington really forges the office of the presidency. Let me give you some examples: there's no mention in the Constitution of cabinet; there is a reference to reports from departmental heads. Washington creates the first cabinet. He chooses Alexander Hamilton as secretary of Treasury, Thomas Jefferson as secretary of state, and Henry Knox as the secretary of war. So, he establishes a very, very high benchmark for a talent and intelligence and integrity. The framers of the Constitution devoted Article I to the Congress because that was the people's house, and they expected that to be the most important branch of government. Washington, early on, discovers that Congress is really too large and unwieldy a body to shape policy. Washington decides that it is the president who is going to initiate policies that the Congress then reacts to. [That's] very important. We take this for granted, but in fact, it was not really the intention of the people who met in Philadelphia in 1787 to have that powerful of an executive. Washington really creates the office of the presidency that we have today.

He goes a long way to defining the relationship of the executive branch both to the legislative branch and the judiciary, where again, he makes a brilliant choice: John Jay becomes the first chief justice. George Washington appoints eleven Supreme Court justices, more than any other president. The Constitution mentions the Supreme Court, of course, but doesn't specify the number of justices, so the first court has six justices. Washington sends all six names to Congress at the same time. They all breeze through in forty-eight hours, which seems comical now where you can get one through in a process of many weeks and months. Washington said that he devoted more painstaking effort to the choice of judges than to anything else he did. He said that he felt that the independent judiciary was the cornerstone of the whole constitutional structure.

One of the things I loved about George Washington is that Washington always challenged people to match up to his high standards. He didn't stoop. He didn't bend. It's very interesting if you read Washington's farewell address, he's not flattering the American people; he's challenging the American people. I hope that people will see that George Washington was somebody who always, as a general and as a president, stuck to his principles. He never confused leadership with a popularity contest. He always felt the important thing was not to be loved but to be respected. Of course, if people respect you, in the long run, they would . . . love you as well. He was really an exemplary leader who had a vision of American greatness, but not simply a vision of America being strong and rich and powerful. He . . . also saw the country as an honorable country, a respectable member of the community of nations. Washington, from the time that he's commander in chief, is trying to mold the character of the country as well as the strength of the character. During the Revolutionary War, Washington as general is always telling them, "Don't swear. Don't drink. Don't pillage crops from the farmers. Respect human rights. Respect property."

In terms of the less attractive side of George Washington, any time he was dealing with money, Washington could be quite testy, quite acerbic. He was a very difficult and, at times, nasty person to deal with in a business situation. I also tried to get a very long and searching look at what it meant to be a benevolent slave master. There were good sides to Washington as a slave master—if one could say that—that he honored slave marriages, he honored slave families, that he made sure they got adequate medical treatment, et cetera. But, . . . he was intent on extracting a profit from these slaves. . . . After the Revolutionary War, he goes back to Mount Vernon, and it's the coldest winter on record in Virginia. It's so cold that he writes in his diary it was too cold for him to go out riding, and he was a very hearty specimen. Yet, he also was checking with his overseers to make sure that all of the slaves were out in the fields, draining swamps, pulling up tree stumps. This is really quite brutal work. You want to say to him, "George, if you can't go outside, is it really fair to expect that of the slaves who are doing this very heavy manual labor?" So, I love Washington, but it's not to say that I love him on every page of my book or in every phase of his life.

He was a scofflaw—I was quite shocked by that. One of the paradoxes of Washington, it's commonly said he was maybe the richest man

Gilbert Stuart's portrait of George Washington first appeared on the one-dollar bill in 1869. Until 2017, it was the most circulated US paper denomination, now overtaken by the one-hundred-dollar bill. *Photo credit: Leslie Rhodes and Ellen Vest, C-SPAN*

in the colonies. Whether he was, or he wasn't, one thing that I'm certain is that he was land rich, and he was certainly slave rich, but he was cash poor. I discovered that he had to borrow money to go to his own inauguration in New York in 1789. At the end of his second term as president, he had to borrow money again to take his family and slaves back to Philadelphia. So, this is a man who is constantly weighed down by concerns over money. It runs throughout his entire life. Unfortunately, like a lot of the Virginia planters, he was not only constantly in debt, but he was a real spendthrift. He was a compulsive shopper, George Washington.

[Washington stepped down from the presidency on March 4, 1797, and returned to Mount Vernon. He died there on December 14, 1799.]

[In today's world] I think he would not be surprised that things were as partisan as they have become because he was subjected to that himself. Things could be very nasty and partisan back in the founding era. In the founding era, even though the polemics were often quite vitriolic, there was a brilliance to the level of discussion. Even though people expressed themselves very vehemently, this was coming out of their own passions and their own political views. He would see a lot of mediocrity today—not everywhere; we have a lot of fine public servants, but the general caliber is lower than it was. It would disturb him to see people pandering to party. It would disturb him to see people pandering to lobbyists because he expected that politics derived from your personal principles and passions. One important thing to stress is that back in the eighteenth century, public service was honorable. . . . It would be wonderful, if maybe a forlorn hope, to try to revive that sense of public service that we had in the early days of the country.

. . . What I loved about writing about Washington was that he was somebody who had a real vision of the country. Not just a vision of American power and riches, but a real vision of American morality—what we stood for, what the character of the country was. Washington, like all great presidents, was one of those real leaders. He had this mythic faith in the public. He had this mythic connection with the country. Interestingly enough, although he was always optimistic about the country in the long run, he was frequently very pessimistic about the country in the short run. I keep reminding myself of that because Washington felt that the American public would often be misled for brief periods of time, but in the long run things would come out right. I hope that his faith is borne out.

FRANKLIN D. ROOSEVELT   32nd President, 1933–1945

Overall Rank: 3

— ★ —

Total Score: 855

FDR has ranked 3rd in the C-SPAN surveys since 2009. Historians have consistently awarded him the top spot in public persuasion. In 2017, he was also ranked 1st in international relations. He and Abraham Lincoln are the only two presidents to have been consistently ranked in the top ten in *every* leadership category.

Party: Democrat
b. January 30, 1882, Hyde Park, New York
d. April 12, 1945, Warm Springs, Georgia
First Lady: Anna Eleanor Roosevelt
Age entering office: 51

Historian: **Doris Kearns Goodwin**

Doris Kearns Goodwin is a presidential historian and author who has written seven books, including four biographies of US presidents. She was interviewed for C-SPAN's Booknotes *on October 25, 1994, to discuss her Pulitzer Prize–winning book,* No Ordinary Time: Franklin and Eleanor Roosevelt, The Home Front in World War II.

In 1921, when he was only thirty-nine years old, Franklin Roosevelt contracted polio. One of the things I understood more by doing this book than I ever had before was how much that paralysis was a part of his everyday life. I, like so many people in the country, had assumed that he had conquered the polio somehow and was simply left a bit lame. But, in fact, he was a full paraplegic. He couldn't even get out of bed in the morning without turning his body to the side of the bed and being helped into his wheelchair by the valet to get to the bathroom. He couldn't even really walk. He had thick braces on, and if he leaned on the arms of two strong people, he could appear to be maneuvering himself forward.

You almost wish that Roosevelt had had the courage to go to the public and say, "I'm crippled, and it's okay," because the public loved him so much, in part because of his courage and his strength. But only at the very end of his life did he ever give a speech sitting down. When he came back from Yalta [in February 1945], he was so tired that he finally excused himself and instead of standing on his braces, he sat down. For some reason, that speech made an enormous emotional impact on the country because they then saw that he was conquering this disability. But, at that time, nobody thought you could go to your country and tell them that you were a paraplegic; that they wouldn't allow you to be their president.

Franklin was not only an only child, but his father was a sickly man from the time FDR was young. His mother was a very young mother who was told she could never have other children after Franklin was born because it had been a tough birth. So, all of Sara's love, which was large, got focused on this child. She gave him probably the greatest asset a mother can give a child, that sense of unconditional love. But because he was so important to her, she never allowed him the freedom to feel like he could stand apart from her. You have the feeling that she hovered over him all of his life, even though maybe that's the source of his confidence. One of my favorite quotes by Churchill says that when you met Roosevelt, he had such inner élan, such confidence, such sparkle, that it was like opening your first bottle of champagne to be around him. I think that's a great gift a mother gives a child. If only Sara had known when to separate, I think he would have had an easier time with intimacy with other people.

When Franklin went to Harvard, Sara got a town house in Boston to be near him. When Franklin and Eleanor got married, Sara got two town houses in New York—one for her, one for them—and the doors went right in between. Roosevelt, seeing how uncomfortable Eleanor felt about having her friends in the big house at Hyde Park, suggested that he would build her her own cottage. It turned out to be this beautiful twenty-two-room house, about a mile and a half or so from the big house. It allowed Eleanor, for the first time in her life, to have a home of her own. She loved the place. After he died, she lived in that place until she herself died. The thing that's so striking in seeing the two separate places is how different they are. The big house of Sara and

Franklin's is so perfectly put together. The china all matches. All the furniture is gorgeous. Eleanor's house has all mixed-matched china. Every chair in the living room is a different size, so that a fat person and a tall person and a thin person and a short person would be comfortable in the chairs. You see how opposite their temperaments were. She liked to make people feel at ease, and he loved the elegance of that first place. So, in some ways, they were never meant for each other, but thank God for the country, and for themselves, that these opposite temperaments attracted when they were young and had enough to keep them going through this long marriage.

What I wanted to do in this book was to understand not only Franklin and Eleanor's relationship—which has been looked at in many, many other cases—but to understand the whole extended family that surrounded them in the White House. I came to an understanding that these two characters both needed other people to meet the untended needs that were left over as a result of their troubled marriage. What I came upon was a sense that the second-floor family quarters of the White House were really like a residential hotel during these years; there are about seven people living there, all of whom are intimate friends of either Franklin or Eleanor's. What a reader is going to get from my book is a sense of what it was like to be in the White House [from 1940 to 1945] because each of these rooms was occupied by somebody who was very important to either Franklin or Eleanor—their closest friends, and in some cases, romantic friends. I wanted everybody to see how close they were, to see that they could wander around in the middle of the White House corridors at night and actually talk to one another.

[At the one end of the second floor of the White House, you had Eleanor Roosevelt's bedroom, and right across the hall was Lorena Hickok.] Lorena Hickok had been a former reporter for the Associated Press, and, in fact, in 1933 she was considered the leading female reporter in the country. She weighed about two hundred pounds. She smoked cigars. She played poker with the guys, and she was really smart. She came to interview Franklin and Eleanor during the campaign in 1932, and Eleanor and she became really close friends. Lorena fell in love with Eleanor, and more importantly, she probably helped Eleanor become the activist first lady that she did. It was Lorena who came up with the idea of

Eleanor holding press conferences every week; only female reporters could come. A whole generation of female journalists got their start because every newspaper had to hire a female reporter. Lorena was the one who came up with the idea of a syndicated column that Eleanor wrote every day, missing only the day that her husband died. She really helped Eleanor transform the role of the first lady from a ceremonial to an activist one. And, in the course of that, she did fall in love with Eleanor. I don't think Eleanor fully reciprocated it, but they were close enough friends that she wanted her living nearby. Lorena Hickok lived in the White House the entire time during the war.

The person that I'm interested in for Franklin is not simply Lucy Mercer, who everybody assumes is the central romantic figure in his life because she had an affair with him back in 1918, and it almost broke up the Roosevelts' marriage. There's another woman that had an even more central role to play in his life, and that was his secretary, Missy LeHand. She had started working for him when she was only twenty-four years old in 1920. She loved him all the rest of her life. She never married, and everybody in Washington knew that she was really his other wife. When Eleanor traveled, which she did 200 or 250 days a year, Missy was the one who took care of Roosevelt. If he had a cold, she'd bring in the cough medicine to the White House. If he was grumpy during the day, she'd arrange a poker game at night. He had a cocktail hour every night, and somehow, she'd be the one to be his hostess. She really was, on a daily basis, the closest person in the world to him. That's the relationship I'd like to know more about.

Harry Hopkins [lived in the Roosevelt White House, as well. He] had been Roosevelt's chief New Deal man, in a certain sense. During the 1930s, he was the head of the Works Progress Administration. He had been a social worker, originally. But when the war broke out in Europe in May of 1940, Hopkins was staying overnight that night at the White House, and Roosevelt decided that he wanted him nearby; he didn't want him to go home. He needed somebody that he could talk to first thing in the morning, talk to late at night, and he made Hopkins his chief adviser on foreign policy. Hopkins went to see Winston Churchill before Roosevelt met him; went to see Josef Stalin before Roosevelt met him; it was really unprecedented. . . . He makes [Richard Nixon's envoy Henry] Kissinger look like a mild-mannered guy in terms of the kind

FDR, 1940, signing letters at the White House with devoted secretary Missy LeHand, often described as his "other wife." *Courtesy of the Franklin D. Roosevelt Presidential Library and Museum, Hyde Park, New York*

of power that Hopkins had, and he was incredibly loyal to Roosevelt. Hopkins was there from 1940 to the end of '42, when he got married. Roosevelt was sad when he [wanted to leave]. Hopkins eventually stayed there for about six months with his new wife, but then she finally wanted a house of her own.

[The White House's Rose Room belonged to Sara,] Roosevelt's mother, the indomitable mother. That's a pretty interesting room. First, whenever the mother came, she wanted the best bedroom suite, and that was this room, the Rose Suite. She would come to visit, maybe once a month, with her maids and her servants, and always being a duchess, in a certain sense, in the White House.

And then, also, Princess Martha [stayed in the Rose Room. She] was an interesting character. . . . She had come to Washington during the war years, in exile from Norway. Her husband was the crown prince, and her father-in-law was the king of Norway. She was beautiful; she was long-legged. Roosevelt always liked his women tall, or so it seems. She had a gay-spirited kind of conversation that he just enjoyed, and

Eleanor somehow understood that he needed that kind of companion-ship. Princess Martha would visit on weekends and keep him company at the movies, keep him company at dinners at night, often again when Eleanor was away, and this would be her suite. . . .

When Churchill came, no one else stayed in the suite. Churchill was an incredible character during this period of time. He would come and stay for three or four weeks at a time, and his habits were so exhausting that nobody else could sleep during the time he was there. He would awaken in the morning and have wine for breakfast. He would have scotch and soda for lunch; he would have brandy at night, smoking his cigars until 2:00 a.m. And when he would finally leave, after being in the suite for three or four weeks, the entire White House staff would have to sleep for seventy-two hours in order to recuperate from Churchill's visits.

[The Roosevelts' daughter, Anna, also stayed in one of the rooms on the second floor.] Anna had originally been her mother's daughter. When Anna was a young girl, an adolescent, Eleanor had told her the story of Lucy Mercer, and the fact that her father had had this affair with Lucy long ago. Anna had taken her mother's side. Over the years, the two had grown so close that they wrote each other letters two or three times a week, and they saw each other four or five times a year, even when Anna lived on the other coast. But, in the middle of the war, after Eleanor rejected Franklin's request to stay home and be his wife again, he got so lonely that he asked their daughter Anna to come [back to Washington] and take Missy LeHand's place. Missy, by that point, even though she was only in her early forties, had had a stroke, and she could never speak again. It was one of those devastating things for Roosevelt during the war years. . . . And then, in some ways, [Anna] became her father's daughter. Anna had long legs, she was tall, she loved cocktails, she could gossip at night with him—all the things that Eleanor never found it easy to do. After a while, Eleanor began to feel displaced by her own daughter, so it was a very complicated set of relationships that developed during this time.

Certain members of the press knew about Lucy Mercer. They knew that Missy LeHand lived in the White House. They knew there was an uncon-ventional set of relationships in the White House. They certainly knew that Roosevelt was a paraplegic, and yet there was, then, a sense that a president's private life is his private life, unless whatever he's doing has an impact on his public activities. I talked to one old reporter who said, "Who are we to judge? We're not angels ourselves, so it wouldn't be sporting to report on these unconventional relationships in the White House." As far as FDR's paralysis goes, what astonished me was that the majority of the people thought, as I did, that he was simply lame. The reason they were allowed to feel that way was that not a single newsreel ever showed him in his wheelchair, on his braces, being crippled. There was almost an unspoken code of honor on the part of the press that the president wasn't to be seen that way. . . . Sometimes reporters would see him being carried from a car into a building like a child, and yet they never took a picture. If a young reporter came along and tried to do that, an older guy would knock the camera to the ground. So, as a result, there was a dignity to the office of the presidency that is really missing now on both the sides of the press and the president. Roosevelt understood the importance of holding his private life secure. He would never have thought about talking about his mother's domineeringness or his feelings about Lucy Mercer. There was a reserve at that time that I suspect served us better.

Lucy Mercer had been a social secretary working for Eleanor. When he was assistant secretary of the navy, Eleanor and Franklin moved to Washington in 1913. Eleanor felt worried about the whole social circle of invitations . . . because you had to know which the "A" list and "B" list people belonged to. She hired this young woman, Lucy Mercer, who came from a blueblood family in Washington and yet needed money because her father had been an alcoholic. Lucy came three or four days a week and worked for the Roosevelts, and somewhere in that period of time, between 1914 and 1918, a relationship developed between Lucy and Franklin.

As far as we know, it lasted probably two or three years in that period of time, between 1914 and '18, but it came to an abrupt end when Eleanor happened to come upon a packet of love letters that Lucy had written to Franklin. Eleanor later said, when she opened these letters that the bottom fell out of her world. She offered Franklin a divorce immediately, but I'm convinced it was the last thing he wanted. I think he had never meant for the marriage to be over because of his relationship with Lucy. In some ways, Lucy's attraction for him was that she was confident, she was gay, she was easy; whereas Eleanor, during that period of her life, was still haunted by the insecurities of her own childhood. Her mother had told her she was ugly when she was a little girl, and her father was an alcoholic. Her mother-in-law, Sara, was being intrusive about their kids, and it was hard for her to develop a full sense of herself. I think Franklin felt attracted to this happy, young woman, Lucy Mercer, but when confronted with the thought of losing Eleanor, it was the last thing he wanted.

In the 1920s, after his affair with Lucy Mercer, and the Roosevelts decided to stay together, this gave Eleanor the freedom to go outside the marriage to find fulfillment. She became involved with a whole group of women who were activists—the League of Women Voters, fighting for reform causes, child labor laws. Sara Roosevelt always looked askance at these women. They would come into the Roosevelt house with their saddle shoes and their tweed outfits. They weren't the kind of fancy people that Sara was used to, so Eleanor didn't feel comfortable bringing her women political friends to the big house where Franklin, hence Sara, lived.

Hyde Park was the most important place for both of them. Franklin went during the whole presidency, something like two hundred times, to Hyde Park. He would get there by train. He would often get on the train in Washington, maybe at 10:00 or 11:00 at night, and it would reach Hyde Park by the morning. He'd sleep on the train. He loved traveling by train. He had his own compartment. Because of his polio and his paralysis, he didn't like fast-moving transportation. He hated airplanes, but he could feel grounded on the train. Eleanor was just the opposite. She liked to get places fast, so she only liked to travel by plane, but she would go [to Hyde Park] with him by train as well.

Lucy Mercer Rutherford had an estate in Allamuchy, New Jersey. FDR loved to figure out maps. He loved geography, so he figured out the railroad lines and knew that if he went along a different pattern—and he had to convince the Secret Service it was safe for him to do this—that he could spend an afternoon with Lucy. This was not until the last year of his life. Some people had assumed, and myself included, that he probably had known Lucy all of his life. I had heard about this affair, which started back in 1918. I knew he had seen her and was with her when he died, so I thought maybe it had happened all the way through that period of time. But the truth was that he had kept his pledge to Eleanor not to see her again, really until the last year of his life, after Eleanor had refused to be with him and be his wife again—after Anna had come back into the White House, and after he was diagnosed with congestive heart failure. In that last year of his life, I believe he knew that he was dying. He went to Bernard Baruch's plantation in March or April of '44 to recover, and it was there that he saw Lucy Mercer, essentially for the first time since 1918. She had just lost her husband, Winthrop Rutherford, who had been a very wealthy businessman, come from an old family, and so she was widowed. I believe when he saw her then that . . . it awakened in him a memory of what it was like when he was young, before polio. He had known Lucy three years before his polio attack, and now before his heart was giving way, he decided that he wanted to see her regularly.

After FDR came back from the Yalta Conference, and after he gave this major speech to the Congress in March of 1945, everybody could see that his health was failing. When he went to Warm Springs, Georgia, somehow there had always been this sense that he would recuperate by going down there; that something about the air, the beauty, the sim-plicity of the place [would invigorate him]. . . . So, they decided that he'd make an extended trip to Warm Springs. . . . He brought with him his two [unmarried] cousins, Laura Delano and Margaret Suckley, and they kept him company. He didn't have that much work to do when he was down there, and for the first week or so, it seemed like he might be getting a little bit of his bounce back, getting some weight back; he was losing weight tremendously in that last year. And then at a certain point, he invited Lucy Mercer to come and stay with him. She arrived about four or five days before he died. She stayed in a little guest house right across the way from his "Little White House." She brought with her a painter friend, Madame Shoumatoff, who wanted to do a portrait of Roosevelt. He seemed to be getting better. He took these little driving trips with Lucy. There was this favorite place, Dowdell's Knob, where you could see the whole valley in Georgia. Lucy later wrote that she'd never forget that day when he talked to her about all the plans he had after the presidency was over and what he hoped to do with the world. He still had idealism left about what the world would be like after the war was over.

Then on April 12, he woke up, and people surprisingly thought that he looked better than he had for weeks. His color was radiant almost. Probably it was, as doctors later said, that the embolism that later killed him was already beginning to be felt in his skin and in his coloring. But he nevertheless kept everybody company. He was a wonderful story-teller. All that morning he was talking to Lucy and Madame Shoumatoff. The two cousins are there, too. Suddenly, in the middle of talking to them, at about noon or so, he said, "I have a terrific headache," and slumped forward. One of the cousins went over to him, thinking he had dropped his cigarette or something, and then she realized that he had become unconscious. Immediately they called for doctors, they called for help, and they carried him into his bedroom. Lucy knew enough to leave at that moment in time, . . . so she and Madame Shoumatoff did leave. FDR died about an hour and a half later. He never regained consciousness.

They finally called Eleanor and told her. She was in the middle of giving a speech in Washington when she found out. She knew, she said, the minute the phone rang, that something had happened. She could just feel it. They didn't tell her that he had died, they just said, "You have to come back to the White House immediately." . . . She went to the White House and they told her that he had died. She immediately called for Harry Truman, the vice president, to come so she could give the news to Harry Truman. That's one of those celebrated moments in history. When Truman says to her, "Is there anything I can do for you?" and her first response is, "No, but is there anything I can do for you, for you're the one in trouble now?" Then she had the presence of mind to ask him, was it ethical for her to use a government plane to go down to Warm Springs to see her husband's body? Of course, Truman provided that for her. You can't imagine people even asking that today.

Eleanor gets down to Warm Springs, Georgia, and as you would do when there's a death like this, she asked her cousins who were there—Laura Delano, in particular—"Tell me everything that happened in the last twenty-four hours." Laura, I believe, had always loved FDR and probably always had been jealous of Eleanor. She maliciously decided to tell Eleanor that Lucy had been there. . . . And, then when pushed further, Laura Delano elected to tell Eleanor that Lucy had been at the White House that last year and that Anna, Eleanor's daughter, had been the one to make those arrangements.

I can't even imagine what it must have been like for Eleanor to have to present the strong face to the world that she did by getting on that train and going back with her husband on that famous train ride from Warm Springs to Washington, knowing inside this deep hurt that she felt. When she got to the White House, Anna was there. Her mother confronted her, really angrily, "How could you do this to me?" All that Anna said that she could say was, "I didn't know what to do. I loved you both, and I felt caught in a crossfire." Anna later said that she was sure that their relationship had been destroyed forever; she thought she had lost her mother.

I knew I didn't want to end the book at that point, even though a death is a natural place to end, because I just felt so sad at that conjury of emotions. I decided to follow that story through the summer and the fall of '45, after his death. Then, thank God, what I was able to find is that, as Eleanor traveled the country again that summer, everywhere she went people kept telling her how much they loved her husband. People that she had thought were her people—the poor people, taxi drivers, porters—felt that their lives were so much better off at the end of the war than at the start. She had been fighting Franklin all through the war; she wanted the war to be a vehicle for social reform on civil rights, for day care in the factory. She kept wanting more than he could provide. But now she saw, in the summer of '45, that the country was indeed a better place; that black people had worked in factories as they never had before, and they had done well in the military; that women had this great sense of mastery from having been 60 percent of the workforce during the war; veterans were going to college on the G.I. Bill of Rights; unions were stronger than ever before.

Eleanor said, as she heard all these tales, that she began to feel a sense of how much the country owed to Franklin Roosevelt. And, as she felt that, she was somehow, amazingly, able to forgive him for what had happened. Finally, in August of 1945, after the atomic bomb was dropped and the war came to an end, she was able to go to Anna, and forgive her as well, affording a reconciliation between the two of them that lasted for the rest of their lives.

I must say, as a biographer, when I learned that, my heart just felt so full in knowing that this woman had done something I'm not sure I could have done. Could I have the kind of spirit to forgive such a deep hurt like that? But it was so wonderful for her that she did. It meant that the rest of her life, those next seventeen years, instead of harboring bitterness toward her husband, that she loved him even more, in some ways, than in life. She was able to incorporate all of his strengths into herself. She had always been the idealistic one in the relationship, and he was the practical one. She always said she was the one who thought about what should be done, and he thought about what could be done. But now, somehow, after he died, she became more like him. She was a much better politician after his death than before because now she had to be both of them, not just herself. It was an amazing end to this story.

It makes you realize, if you looked at this story from the outside in, as the media would probably do today, they'd accuse him of infidelity; they might accuse him of harassment for his relationship with his secretary, Missy LeHand; maybe accuse Anna of betrayal of her mother. Yet, none of those labels would be right. I'm absolutely convinced these people never meant to hurt one another. They were simply trying to get through their lives with the best possible mixture of love and respect, through work and affection. It seems to me that the challenge is not to do what's so prevalent today in biography—to expose and to label and to stereotype. What I really wanted to try and do was to extend empathy; to understand why they needed all these relationships, and not to judge them harshly because of their own human needs.

THEODORE ROOSEVELT   26th President, 1901–1909

| Overall Rank: 4 — ★ — Total Score: 807 | TR has ranked 4th in all three C-SPAN surveys, trailing only Lincoln, Washington, and FDR. In 2017, historians ranked him 2nd in public persuasion, behind only FDR. He consistently ranks in the top ten in all leadership categories, except pursued equal justice for all, where he slipped to 11th in 2017. |

Party: Republican
b. October 27, 1858, New York City, New York
d. January 6, 1919, Oyster Bay, New York
First Lady: Edith Kermit Carow Roosevelt
Age entering office: 42

Historian: Douglas Brinkley

Historian and professor Doug Brinkley discussed his book, The Wilderness Warrior: Theodore Roosevelt and the Crusade for America, *which tells the story of Roosevelt's contributions to the early days of the conservation movement. This was a two-part interview for C-SPAN's Q & A recorded on April 30, 2009. Dr. Brinkley is one of three advisers for C-SPAN's Historians Survey of Presidential Leadership.*

What interested me in writing a book like *The Wilderness Warrior* is that Theodore Roosevelt really is the father of the US Fish and Wildlife Service. If John Muir is known as the creator of the Sierra Club, it's Roosevelt that realized that the federal government has an obligation to save species of birds and animals, to save plants and trees. The president has an obligation to make sure that we put aside for generations unborn our natural wonders, as Roosevelt did, like the Grand Canyon or Mount Olympus or the Petrified Forest.

Theodore Roosevelt was president mainly in his forties. He was our youngest American president, . . . so he was in the prime of his life, incredibly vigorous. There's a psychiatrist at Johns Hopkins University who wrote a book called *Exuberance*, . . . and she effectively argued that Roosevelt had a form of manic depression called exuberance, that he couldn't turn his mind off or his energy off. When you read a lot of Roosevelt, it's "Bully!" and "By Jove!" He would hike sometimes forty or fifty miles. He'd go into Rock Creek Park on horseback and ride all the time. As president, [he was frequently] disappearing into the wilds for days at a time without reporters. This was part of his need to act all the time. He was a person of pure motion, locomotion. Constant. If he entered a room, he took it over.

I've loved him since childhood, . . . but I really got interested in him in 1992 when I had a program called The Majic Bus, where I would bring students across the country, and I went to the Badlands of North Dakota. That's where TR spent his ranching days as a cowboy; it's where he did some of his hunting; [where] he wrote these incredible books—a book, that I particularly like, for example, called *The Wilderness Hunter*. . . . Roosevelt knew more about the Badlands than any person alive one hundred years ago. . . . I fell in love with that particular American landscape. Then I was teaching at Hofstra University with the late John Gable, who helped me realize that there had never been a book written on TR and conservation, on TR and the wilderness, of any magnitude. So, I had this great opening. I started realizing that between the Civil War and the Emancipation Proclamation of Lincoln and World War I with Woodrow Wilson, Roosevelt was using the White House to promote conservation and nature and what he called the strenuous life. [He did] more to save birds—his involvement with the Audubon Society and the eventual creation of US Fish and Wildlife—and our national monuments; it changed America. Anybody who opens up an atlas, there's America, and you see all of that green. You are looking at the Roosevelt reserves, Roosevelt monuments.

He put aside almost 240 million acres of wild America. Today, as people are talking about environmentalism and green movements, Roosevelt is becoming the key figure to understand. He was the only politician of his day who had absorbed Charles Darwin['s ideas], and who had understood biology, and understood birds' migratory patterns, and understood mating habits of deer and elk and antelope, and actually did something [with that knowledge]. He is a president who in his young days shot a buffalo, and then he's the president who created Wichita Mountains [Wildlife Refuge] in Oklahoma for buffalo.

Darwin's *On the Origin of Species* came out in 1859, and it didn't really hit America because of the Civil War. By the time Theodore Roosevelt goes to Harvard in 1876, majoring in natural studies, Darwin was the rage. And, it was a revolution. . . . People became Darwinian ideologues. In fact, I argue that Darwin is the central figure in Roosevelt's intellectual life. That's what some people don't like about Roosevelt's foreign policy—the survival of the fittest; the biggest navy; we are going to be the biggest power in the world. That's one side of him [that's Darwininfluenced]. He also erroneously ventured into social Darwinism quite a bit. But, domestically, he was spot on in his understanding of natural resource management and how to make sure you save species and [keep] entire environments intact. He was a great lover of the prairie. People don't realize Theodore Roosevelt felt more at home on a horse in Kansas, in Nebraska, than he did at sea. . . . He was our first president to go abroad as president. He went to Panama, and he went to Puerto Rico. And what is he writing about when goes down there? Birds. He was taking field notes of the wildlife of Panama. He saved forests in Puerto Rico and in the Philippines. There is his imperialism [following] the Spanish-American War—"I'm president now; we control these properties"—[but] he also had concerns of protecting ecosystems and species in those places we acquired.

Theodore Roosevelt's father was the founder of the American Museum of Natural History in New York, and young TR became a bird lover. . . . The first document we have with TR as a young boy is about birds, and the last article he wrote before his death at age sixty was about birds. I'm not saying that he just liked birds; he was one of the world's experts on coloration and variation, on inventorying what we have. He created these bird reservations—fifty-one federal bird reservations that are now the heart and soul of US Fish and Wildlife, [which] all began with Roosevelt trying to save egrets and spoonbills and pelicans on both coasts.

Women's fashion during the Gilded Age wanted feathers for women's hats; they wanted egret feathers or heron feathers, and so people would come and just gun them all down. They were massacring birds. There would be heaps of dead birds just for their feathers. We were losing species in wild Florida. You think that the West was wild; Florida was the last untamed place down around the swamps of the Everglades. These were a lot of ex-Confederates on the land, people that couldn't stand the federal government, with their Civil War memories. And their view was, "If it's a bird, I'll shoot it. There's money to be had."

Roosevelt's first [reserve] is in 1903 in March at Pelican Island, Florida. There are surveys from 1902 of Pelican Island, which is a dollop of land, a little island, but it was an incredible pelican nesting area. It's the first mapping we had of this part of wild Florida. These ornithologists that were friends of Roosevelt's—a man named Frank Chapman in particular, but others, William Dutcher being prominent—they eventually got to TR, who was a fellow birder and ornithologist, and said, "We could lose the birds of Florida. Can you do anything?" Roosevelt said he'd look into it a little, and then he famously said, "Is there anything to stop me? I so declare it a federal bird reservation." He just grabbed Pelican Island. It was the first time ever that land was set aside to be run and controlled for a species. This was now off limits, and there were signs: no trespassing.

Paul Kroegel . . . became the first game warden in Florida. [What ensued was known as the] "Feather Wars." Roosevelt's game wardens, out of his first four, two of them were murdered down there . . . because it was like a feather mafia going on for the women's fashion industry.

. . . The point is that conservation in the beginning of the twentieth century had two sides to it, just like there are now in land issues. It was nasty in Florida. And not only did TR create Pelican Island in 1903, but he created a "string of pearls" strategy of bird refuges all the way down Florida. It was TR saving them. We would not have these species living in Florida, we would have lost wild Florida forever if Roosevelt didn't act when he did.

TR's second big book was *The Naval War of 1812*, which made him the top, high-end naval strategist, and he became an assistant secretary of the navy [in the first McKinley administration. He resigned that post to fight with the Rough Riders in the Spanish-American War. In the 1900 election, he was selected as President McKinley's running mate.]

. . . Theodore Roosevelt becomes president in 1901 because President William McKinley was assassinated. TR gets sworn in, in Buffalo, and says, "I'm going to keep policies similar to McKinley." He doesn't. Immediately, after only two months as president, TR starts this aggressive conservation program. . . . In 1903, TR gets on the train and goes to Yellowstone with [conservationist] John Burroughs. Then he goes to the Grand Canyon; then he ends up in the redwoods of Northern California and then goes to Yosemite. Here is the president of the United States with John Muir, and they camp out. They spend three days in the wild. They camp under the redwood trees, which Roosevelt thought were our great cathedrals; he would use religious imagery about the redwoods. They slept in a snowstorm without a tent, and Roosevelt with his bully enthusiasm said, "The greatest day I've ever spent in my life, freezing in a snowstorm with John Muir." They would try to out-naturalist each other. Nobody knew birds like TR, but Muir was more of a botanist. Muir would talk about the plants and Roosevelt was out-playing him on birds, but they had a friendly competition. Roosevelt thought Muir was one of our great figures. They had some differences: TR was a hunter-conservationist; Muir thought that only in extreme cases of hunger should you shoot an animal. Roosevelt believed that was nonsense, that you had to constantly hunt, that hunters were the great conservationists. At one moment by a campfire, Muir says to Roosevelt, "When are you going to give up that boyish hunting thing of yours?" And TR uncharacteristically said, "I know I need to. I should." Of course, he didn't.

. . . Roosevelt, as president, collected for the biological survey for what is today's US Fish and Wildlife wherever he went. He would send specimens in, and he'd send skins in to get them analyzed. It's a key point in my book: after the Civil War, what the first people going West wanted was the geological survey; people wanted things mapped, and it was about money. Where are the mineral rights? Where is the copper? Where is the gold? Where is the zinc? TR, by the 1890s, is interested in a biological survey. He's saying, "I want to know what wildflowers we have, what native grasses. What kind of insects. What kind of songbirds. How many flocks. I want numbers." And so, TR, our only scientist-trained president, is applying what he learned at Harvard as a naturalist studies major, what he learned from his field observations, to the presidency— in his inventorying between 1901 and 1909, what [natural resources] we are custodians of in this country.

This bust portrait of Theodore Roosevelt was taken in 1904, the first year he campaigned for president in his own right. *Courtesy Library of Congress*

Mine is not just a Washington story of Roosevelt in the White House. There were foot soldiers for conservation everywhere, and TR was networking with these people. So, this isn't just a biography of Theodore Roosevelt; it's a book of TR and the conservationists and naturalists around him—Muir and Burroughs, men like Spencer Fullerton Baird, head of the Smithsonian Institute, who started caring about wildlife. . . . They are many. These aren't household names, and I wanted to inject them into mainstream history. . . . So, it's not just Roosevelt I'm writing about, but a circle of these people around him. I write about the cartoonist "Ding" Darling who joined his crusade. What Roosevelt was doing was creating a movement. It would be like Martin Luther King creating a civil rights movement. Roosevelt was spearheading the conservation movement for perpetuity. For example, many of our first rangers in the West were Rough Riders that served with him [in the war]. Roosevelt's concerns were to militarize, in a sense, natural areas because he was worried about poaching, people stealing petrified wood, people carving their initials, the garishness of commerce. He was doing law enforcement, saying we are going to protect our heirlooms. He called all these places—like Wind Cave or Yosemite or El Morro or Mesa Verde National Park, which he created—our heirlooms, and we are going to police them and protect them.

Roosevelt, as president, saw the last live passenger pigeon. There used to be a hundred million passenger pigeons in America; it's an extinct species now. Roosevelt wrote the last observation of one in the wild. People shouldn't think of Roosevelt's conservation as a policy as much as a passion. The foresight and prescience that he had [to understand] that we could not deforest ourselves, that we had to keep our rivers protected, that animals had to have habitats. Because he was influenced by Darwin, he believed that to lose a species, any kind, was like losing a masterpiece of old; that we had a moral obligation to make sure that we protected wildlife and species. To live without animals or wildlife, for Roosevelt, was to live in utter pain and a modern condition of commerce and not romance. He was a scientist, Roosevelt, but he got romantic excitement from the wild and from seeing species in the wild.

You look at a specific coast of Washington or Oregon—Roosevelt was saving these. . . . And early photography; Roosevelt was very interested in wildlife photography. He had a man named William L. Finley from Oregon. Finley would come to the White House and show him pictures of wild Oregon. Roosevelt went up to Portland and met him once, and it became a movement to save the wildlife of Oregon. Each of these states, particularly in the West and Florida, you can't write about these states without seeing the impact Roosevelt has had. And these weren't easy things to do. He saved the Grand Canyon. . . . Standing on the rim, he said, "It's for future generations. You cannot improve the beauty of it." He then was shocked to find that Congress was ready to mine it for asbestos and zinc and copper, meaning that Congress refused to make the Grand Canyon a national park. But Roosevelt had a weapon, the Antiquities Act, which he used like a club. Using the Antiquities Act in 1906, Roosevelt says, "I so declare it a national monument for future generations," overriding Congress. . . . But Congress, in particular Western senators and congressmen, was not really into the federal government grabbing an area like the Grand Canyon and closing it off.

Roosevelt's conservation can be seen as inspired by Lincoln's Emancipation Proclamation, [using] the power of the federal government. Roosevelt's heroes, incidentally, were very keen on protecting Yellowstone.

General Grant saved Yellowstone in 1872 as president. And Sherman and Sheridan, the Union generals, were hunters, but they wanted to create game reserves. Roosevelt is part of that tradition somewhat, but he is determined to use executive power to save wild America.

Roosevelt also created the modern global conservation movement. He . . . was calling for international conferences to save rain forests and redwood forests, old evergreen forests. It wasn't just localized to America for TR. He was evolved in the sense of seeing the problems of hyper-industrialization and the havoc it was going to wreck on wilderness areas, and he wanted the world to act. He could not be more relevant. His concerns one hundred years ago are now our true front-burner concerns today.

Roosevelt leaves office in March of 1909; he leaves the White House. In his last weeks, he put bird reserves and monuments everywhere. The Olympic National Park, Mount Olympus, he saved at the very last minute using executive orders. This was no lame duck president, TR. He then left to go for a year to Africa. While he was in Africa, President William Howard Taft fired [Roosevelt's] chief forester, Gifford Pinchot, . . . over an Alaska lands argument. Taft was trying to let commerce into lands that TR had put aside for preservation, for federal use. Pinchot goes to Italy, meets TR when he returns from Africa, and Roosevelt gets inflamed because Taft is daring to try to turn back even a portion of his conservation legacy. The Bull Moose Party is created, in a large part, on Roosevelt's anger at Taft for not being a warrior on the conservation front.

Roosevelt really believed in Taft during his presidency, and that's why he was his handpicked successor. TR could have won another term, easily. He's the only president, really, who just relinquished power because he had other things to do. It wasn't big game hunting that he had to do. TR left the presidency to explore and to collect. He was collecting for the American Museum of Natural History, and he went to Brazil to collect in what's today Rio Roosevelt.

. . . Taft [had fallen] in line as a conservation foot soldier, and it was one of the reasons TR felt comfortable with Taft. . . . But when Taft breaks on conservation with Roosevelt, Taft was finished. Taft preferred to be a Supreme Court justice to being president; his wife, Nellie, wanted him to be president. At the Taft inaugural in 1909, it was a blizzard—one of the worst weathers for an inaugural. In Roosevelt's typical fashion, he says, "History will know it as the Roosevelt Blizzard." And Taft said, "No, no, it's my blizzard." Already there was a clash of egos because Roosevelt was myth-making all the time. . . . Roosevelt turns it into the Heroic Roosevelt Blizzard for the media: "I'm going out in a blizzard." It was very hard for Taft to succeed that popular president.

Here's another example: TR famously has the teddy bear. Roosevelt had gone on a Mississippi bear hunt as president. They didn't get a bear there, so somebody caught one and roped it, had it tied against a tree. Roosevelt refused to kill it because that's unsportsmanlike; there was no fair chase. A cartoonist named Clifford Berryman did a cartoon of TR showing him not killing the bear, and it became the teddy bear. I saw the letter of a Brooklyn toymaker, a mom and pop toyshop: "Dear Mr. President, I'd like to make a bear called the teddy bear. I won't do it if I don't have your approval." Roosevelt writes back, "I don't think there's much of a market for a teddy bear, but you have my blessing to make it." Suddenly, the teddy bear became the most popular toy in the world; still is. Taft thought he could tap into that and created the Billy Possum and had companies make possum stuffed toys. The teddy bear stayed up; Billy Possum went nowhere. People thought they could take the magic that TR somehow had, but there were no coattails. And so, Taft became, has become, a very victimized person in history; ranks among the lowest of the presidents, and Roosevelt didn't help him any, even though he knew Taft was a man of integrity.

In 1912, Roosevelt was running as the third-party candidate, the Bull Mooser, against Woodrow Wilson and William Howard Taft. He went to give a speech in Milwaukee, and a crazed anarchist took a shot. TR was bleeding. Roosevelt had such bad eyesight that he had always carried bird glasses with him in his pocket, . . . and that's what the bullet hit. It wounded him terribly, but there is some thinking that if the bullet hadn't gone through those bird-watching glasses, he would have died.

But here he is bleeding, shot, and TR says, "It'll take more than that to kill a Bull Moose," and keeps going [with his speech]. Much like when Ronald Reagan was shot in March of 1981, it becomes a folklore moment in public opinion, the thought that the Bull Mooser couldn't be knocked down. He lost, obviously, as the Bull Moose Party, but it was the most successful third-party run ever. The folklore of Roosevelt, which he was always very conscious of, just grew with that story.

What Roosevelt believed was that [our natural resources] are what made the United States unique. He spent a lot of time in Europe, and yes, they had Westminster Abby, yes, they had the Louvre. But they didn't have the Grand Canyon; they don't have the giant redwood trees. He boasted that our natural beauty here was so spectacular that we had to save that for generations unborn and that the American character was going to be formed by having these intimate contacts with the wild.

Roosevelt's romanticism is a point I really want to make clear. He is a child of the post–Civil War era. He saw North fight South, the six hundred thousand dead. He believed the North messed it up, that the American Dream got messed up in the North because of hyper-industrialization. Philadelphia had sewage dumped in the rivers, and it smelled, and it wasn't healthy for you. The South was stigmatized due to slavery and racism. His Eden was west of the Mississippi River. He thought the new America was going to be reborn there. In order to do it differently than the South and the East, you had to have free people, but have cities like Boulder or Austin or Portland or Eugene that had greenbelts around them, that you don't want a metropolis. Los Angeles today would bother him. He wanted smaller-sized cities, where you have universities and businesses surrounded by wilderness, that you could go on day trips backpacking and feel replenished from the crunch of the very speedy, hyper-industrialization.

He was engineering the West a lot, and this angered a lot of people, and it was done with grandiosity. If you don't like a strong president, don't like Theodore Roosevelt, because he didn't even look at laws. He was running in saying, "I so declare it." That was his phrase: "I so declare it a federal bird reservation; I so declare it a national monument." Local people in commerce were outraged. How can Roosevelt be grabbing our land? TR, more than even FDR, is a believer in the power of the federal government, and he wants the federal government to protect American wilderness for future generations.

Do you know what would have happened with Yellowstone? This was back when he was a civil service commissioner. They were going to take the railroad, wanted to cut through the middle of Yellowstone, build it up as a commercial center, and allow people to build these contraption Coney Island–like sites in the middle of Yellowstone. Roosevelt and the Boone and Crockett Club went to Congress and fought tooth and nail to stop it, to preserve the integrity of Yellowstone. I think 90 percent of the Americans would say that's a good thing.

Now, on the contrary, the Left has had trouble with Roosevelt as a hunter . . . because he wanted to wipe out predators. He was the world's expert on cougars. He wrote many essays about them and would collect cougars, mountain lions; knew all about them, and also about different types of coyotes and gray wolves. They would do predator control, meaning they would use ways to eradicate wolves because he was mainly wanting to save the antelope, caribou, deer, and elk. Here's a factoid: the first book published by a president, ever, meaning a book with a byline by a president as he's in the White House, was Theodore Roosevelt's book, *The Deer Family*. He wrote, as president of the United States, about all of the deer populations in America using charts of where they lived and how to get them back.

. . . TR's sense of being a warrior wasn't just about the battlefield. He liked to have fights about everything that he believed in. And he was very bold. He was a warrior fighting to save wild America. To confront Roosevelt on wanting to save the Grand Canyon or Mesa Verde or Wind Cave or the bird refuges in Florida—you better be strong because TR knocked everybody over. . . . In an Alaska chain where he saved seal herds, Roosevelt heard that a group of Japanese seal hunters came within an American archipelago and killed American seals, and he was gearing up for war, if need be, with Japan over seals. So, when I'm using the title for this book, *The Wilderness Warrior*, this wasn't just a policy—it's not like doing conservation with Richard Nixon, or something. This was a whole other thing. You can't understand the essence of Theodore Roosevelt if you don't understand his relationship with Darwin, with ornithology, and with the big game of America.

I don't know any president that was as bold as Roosevelt. His hubris factor was so high that you can't comprehend it in the modern political spectrum. Nothing infuriates me more than when people say, "Bill Clinton is like Theodore Roosevelt." Or, they will say, "George W. Bush is like TR." They are nothing like Roosevelt. Roosevelt was a deep, intellectual writer who had such moral convictions. Theodore Roosevelt never lied.

DWIGHT D. EISENHOWER   34th President, 1953–1961

Overall Rank: 5

— ★ —

Total Score: 745

Dwight Eisenhower has moved up four spots since C-SPAN's first survey in 2000, the largest upward movement of any president in the top ten. His upward move was fueled by higher rankings in crisis leadership (from 10th to 6th) and international relations (from 9th to 6th). Ike's highest rank is in moral authority (4th).

Party: Republican
b. October 14, 1890, Denison, Texas
d. March 28, 1969, Washington, DC
First Lady: Mamie Geneva Doud Eisenhower
Age entering office: 62

Historian: **William I. Hitchcock**

William Hitchcock is a University of Virginia professor and historian specializing in twentieth-century American history, with a focus on the world wars and Cold War. He appeared on C-SPAN's Q & A series on May 3, 2018, to discuss his book, The Age of Eisenhower: America and the World in the 1950s.

The period from the death of Franklin Roosevelt to the death of John Kennedy—1945 to 1963—is a period in which [Dwight] Eisenhower's personality, his ideas, his values, and, of course, his presidency really dominated American public life. In that period, I think it's safe to say he was the most well-known, well-liked, popular American because, of course, of his record in the war years. But, even as he was emerging as a presidential candidate and then as president, he was overwhelmingly America's favorite public figure. His instincts, his values, his presence really became part of American life in the 1940s and '50s.

I call his the "disciplined presidency." Eisenhower, in the way he carried himself and the man that he was, was a disciplined man, a great
athlete when he was young, and an organized man in every respect,
very methodical. That's how he ran the White House, too. He was
extremely organized. A lot of people, especially the young senator
and future president John Kennedy, criticized Eisenhower's stodginess
for being so disciplined and organized and predictable. For Eisenhower, it meant that when crises came, he had a plan. He knew how to
respond. He knew who to turn to. He used to say, "Plans are worthless,
but planning is everything." So, you're always thinking, "What's over
the hill? What crisis might erupt? We should be thinking about it."
He was very systematic in the way that he governed. He met the press
every week; he met congressional leaders every week; he chaired the
National Security Council every week; and he had his thumb on the
government. He trusted the process. He believed the federal government could work well if it was well led. I think he still stands as a real
model to learn from.

Harry Truman loved Eisenhower in 1945, and even up through 1948,
he thought that Eisenhower would be a good president. He thought he
might be a Democrat, that's why. Nobody knew what party Eisenhower
was in when he was in the army. Truman thought maybe he could get
Ike to run, and Truman said, "I'll be your vice president." But in 1945,
he really did say to Eisenhower while they were touring Berlin . . . for
the Potsdam meeting, "General, I will do anything that I can possibly
do to help your career, and that includes your being president." He
admired Eisenhower so much, and that was a time when Truman had
just become president, so, I think he was still in awe of Eisenhower.

By 1952, you can tell there's a frosty relationship, and that's because
Eisenhower had been speaking out politically in 1951 and '52, criticizing
the New Deal, criticizing Roosevelt, criticizing Truman himself, criticizing the big federal programs of the New Deal. He ran as a conservative
in 1952, Eisenhower did. Truman [returned fire] saying, "Well, one day
he's a conservative, one day he's a liberal. You can't trust him." That's
like a lot of people who run for president. They tend to say different
things to different audiences. Eisenhower was just as good a politician
as anyone. But the relationship between these two men soured, and it's
really too bad.

. . . Eisenhower did say that he would go to Korea during the [1952] campaign. He wanted that to have the effect that [he] knew that it would have. When the former Allied commander of World War II says, "I'm going to go to Korea and see what's going on there for myself," as a candidate, he knew it would be a provocation. It would suggest that Harry Truman wasn't running the Korean War terribly well. He wanted to have that as a bombshell to drop in the campaign. He did drop it quite late in the campaign, in October, and he knew that President Truman would be offended. Truman was offended. He called it a "piece of demagoguery." After the fact, many people debated whose idea it was. [His press secretary, James] Hagerty, said at one point that other members of the [campaign] team had suggested it, but in fact . . . it was Eisenhower's idea. He said to Hagerty, "Just keep it quiet; we'll use this when we need to." . . . Americans responded by saying that the most successful soldier in American history is going to go to Korea to figure out why we're not winning this thing and maybe put an end to it. Everybody knew at that moment he had won the election.

[He went there in] December 1952, so you can imagine how cold it was in Korea. He hadn't become president yet. Civil and military relations are pretty tense at this moment. Truman had had to fire General MacArthur, the commander in Korea, in 1951 because MacArthur had said Truman was not handling the Korean War well. And here goes President-elect Eisenhower to Korea basically saying the same thing: that something's wrong; we'd better fix it; I'm going to go find out what's the matter. He did go, and it actually helped his choice of policy in Korea. He came back having seen the battlefield, having seen how difficult it was to fight in Korea, how stalemated it was, how mountainous it was. He came back determined, one way or the other, that he was going to end this war, but not necessarily through an armistice. For a while he thought he would increase the pace of operations in Korea until there was an opportunity to reach out for the armistice, which he was very happy to get, because he knew that this war wasn't popular. It needed to be brought to an end.

Eisenhower believed he had a great deal to do with [ending the Korean War] because he believed that he had rattled the nuclear saber, saying, "If we don't get this settlement, we might have to go nuclear in Korea." He believed that this had frightened the Chinese into putting pressure on the North Koreans to agree to an armistice. But we now

President-elect Dwight Eisenhower took the provocative step of visiting Korea in December 1952, which helped shape his efforts to end the raging war. *Courtesy Dwight D. Eisenhower Presidential Library and Museum*

know a great deal about what was going on with the other side. We know that the death of Joseph Stalin in March of 1953 had a big impact on both China and North Korea. Stalin was all in favor of the war, and when he died in March of '53, the new leadership in the Soviet Union said, "We would love to bring the Korean War to an end. It's dangerous. It might get worse. It might lead to a nuclear exchange. We don't want that." They urged the Chinese and the North Koreans to agree to an armistice. It was the pressure from the communist side, the changes going on in the communist bloc, that led to the breakthrough. They came to Panmunjom and said, "Let's have an armistice." But I will say, Eisenhower accepted the armistice, which he could do because he was a general. He was a Republican who had great credentials as being a military man.

His [1953] inaugural address opened with a brief prayer. . . . He didn't pull it out of the scripture. He said, "I'm just going to write something myself." A deeply spiritual man, he was raised in a family of deeply spiritual parents who were members of the River Brethren Church, an offshoot of the Mennonites. His forebears had come from Pennsylvania. They'd been essentially what we think of as Amish. His father read a piece of scripture every night in the family living room, and all the boys had to sit around and listen. He knew his Bible backwards and forwards. He did not enjoy attending church, and when he went in the army, he steered clear of organized religion. This is so interesting, so surprising, so important for Eisenhower: when he became president, he said, "I have to be seen as a public man of faith. I have to go to church every week, so I need a regular church." Mamie was a Presbyterian, so he went to the Reverend Edward Elson of the National Presbyterian Church here in Washington, DC, and he was baptized. A sitting president was baptized February 1953. He then used religion as a very important part of his public personality as president.

Eisenhower kept the United States out of Vietnam in 1954 as the French were collapsing in northern Vietnam. Their colonial war there was going badly, and the French begged the United States to get in. Eisenhower said, "No, we're not going to do it." So, we know that he stayed out, and we know what he said at the time, "It's the wrong war, in the wrong place, for the wrong purposes. We're not going to go to war to help prop up French colonialism." He then, though, invested a great deal of prestige and money in building South Vietnam into a democratic country. He believed South Vietnam could be a model to the rest of Asia. So, by 1961, the commitment we had made to South Vietnam was a very significant one. By 1965, when Lyndon Johnson sent hundreds of thousands of troops, the commitment was even greater. It's difficult to know if Eisenhower would have done the same thing. There's a good chance he might have because I think he believed what America was doing in South Vietnam was the right thing.

I have concluded that Allen Dulles, who was the CIA director for the entire time that Eisenhower was president, was a pretty dangerous man. . . . Eisenhower was wary about Allen Dulles, but I don't think he controlled Dulles sufficiently, and he gave him a little bit too much free rein. So, the CIA became quite reckless. We would learn later, when some of their secret records became available in the late '70s, just how far they had gone to overthrow governments, plan assassinations, sabotage, and the like. Much of that was known because the Congress started investigating the CIA in the 1970s. But there are a lot of concrete, specific things about how the CIA gathered intelligence, what they knew, especially through intercepts about the Soviet missile program, that we're only just now beginning to understand.

[There is a great debate as to whether President Eisenhower was aware of the CIA's activities.] Andrew Goodpaster, one of his closest advisers, always insisted that Eisenhower did not know about it, and he would not have approved it. I'm not quite so sure. I think that Eisenhower did know. I think that his national security adviser late in his presidency, Gordon Gray, kept him informed and they had an understanding not to talk about it. It was a wink and a nod sort of thing. But Eisenhower was unsentimental about these matters. As a lifelong military man, he felt these were bad, bad people, and if national interests required it, he would let [covert operations] go.

The *Brown v. Board* [Supreme Court] opinion of May 1954 was a huge milestone in civil rights. It told us that the segregation by race of public schools was unconstitutional. Some people thought maybe this was a bombshell that the Eisenhower administration knew nothing about and maybe even was hostile to. But there's ample evidence that Attorney General Herbert Brownell was working closely with the plaintiffs in the case, shaping the arguments in the court. . . . They filed an amicus brief in favor of desegregation. They, too, felt it was unconstitutional. So, this was a product of the administration's policies as much as [of Chief Justice Earl] Warren. Now, Warren shaped the opinion, which was so important, and it was a unanimous opinion. But this is a case where Eisenhower's reputation has been done wrong. He was often depicted as someone who was against the civil rights movement, or in some ways, a day late and a dollar short. But in that early period of his first term, he and Herbert Brownell really helped the cause. They did significant work pushing the ball forward.

What is interesting about Eisenhower is he blows hot and cold [on civil rights]. We see periods of significant activity, and 1953 and '54 is probably the period where he's really pushing. Then, he pulls back and says, "Wait a minute, I have a lot of friends in the South." And he did. He spent a lot of time in Augusta [Georgia] and thought they should be heard from too—that their views should be taken into consideration. So, he would then try to cool things down. And then, he would pick up again, and there would be a sudden period of activity. And we see that 1957 is such a period of activity—passing the Civil Rights Act of 1957, the [federal] intervention at Little Rock [High School]. After that, 1958, '59, he's quite loath to do anything really aggressive on civil rights. So, it's a picture of a pendulum swinging back and forth.

On press conferences, I think [his record is] quite remarkable. We've forgotten that presidents used to be much more available to the press than they are today. A press conference nowadays with the president is a highly scripted thing, it's very formal; you're not going to get a lot of mistakes or real news out of a press conference with the president now. The press secretary does it all. Throughout Eisenhower's presidency, he gave a weekly press conference for about thirty minutes. He stood there and took questions. Sometimes he didn't know the answer, and he would say, "I'll look into it. I'll get back to you." His press secretary, Jim Hagerty, was right next to him as he was doing all this and occasionally he would pass him a note or two, but Ike was [personally] available to the press. . . . The press admired him privately, but often in writing their reports they tended to condescend a little bit to President Eisenhower. I think this was part of the origins of the idea that he wasn't in charge, that he was a lightweight. I think that the [reporters] knew better, but it was a good joke. It became almost a punch line to say, well, here's old Eisenhower trying his best, but look how he stumbles over his syntax, and so forth. They could be kind of mean.

This sounds like a cliché, but it is true. . . . It's a personal characteristic, but it does influence him: he was a world-class card player. Not just a poker player but a bridge player. He loved to keep his enemies guessing, his adversaries guessing, the Chinese especially, and in the Cold War the Russians as well. He didn't want to go into public and say, "Well, here's exactly what our policy is," unless it served his interests. Sometimes it served his interests to say, as in Taiwan, "If there is an invasion of Taiwan, that will lead to war . . ." because it was a signal to the Chinese. But in general, he wanted to keep his enemies guessing, and who wouldn't?

The conventional wisdom was that Eisenhower didn't worry about the missile gap, didn't worry that the Russians might have had a lot of missiles, didn't worry about Sputnik because he knew because of the U-2 spy plane that the Soviets didn't have any big missile program at all. That's not true. The U-2 spy plane had started in 1955. They started running it over the Soviet Union in 1956. Eisenhower was always very cautious about using it because he was afraid one might get shot down and that would lead to an international incident, which it did in 1960. . . . So, there were very few U-2 overflights in 1957 and '58, and even into '59. . . . So what they know about the Soviet missile program is incomplete. . . . To say that, "Well, he just kicked back and said, 'Don't worry, there's no Soviet missile program,'" [there is no] evidence to prove that. The [administration was] actually quite anxious that the Russians were building some major ICBMs that could reach America. It wasn't until quite a bit later that we got the intelligence that proved that Russians were way behind the Americans.

Eisenhower had some health issues, there's no doubt about it. He smoked four packs of cigarettes a day when he was in the army in World War II, which means he basically was smoking every moment that he was awake. He quit in 1949, but I suspect it did take a bit of a toll on his health. He had quite a significant heart attack in 1955. . . . He had a chronic problem with his intestines, ileitis. That gave him all kinds of stomach pain throughout his life. It was finally diagnosed, and they finally operated on that . . . in 1956, in the summer he was running for re-election. And, he had a minor stroke later in his second term. It didn't harm him much, but it slowed him down for a couple of days and was a bit of a scare. These things, the mounting strain, the mounting toll of having been the Allied commander and then the president, started to show on him. He lived for ten years after he left the White House, but these were all signs of his constitution, which was very strong, starting to break down a little bit.

He had the first heart attack in Denver, so he spent a great deal of time at the Fitzsimons Army Hospital there recovering. He came back briefly to Washington in the winter. He chaired a couple of meetings and then went to Florida. Basically, he was pretty much out of Washington, out of the White House, for almost six months. He governed [nonetheless]. This is a topic that leads us into the question of his relationship with Richard Nixon. He did not turn over much leadership to Richard Nixon, his vice president. In fact, it was his chief of staff, Sherman Adams, who did a great deal of the day-to-day management of the presidency. It's odd that he did that, but I don't think he fully was confident that Nixon could manage the government in his absence. It's an interesting fact that he didn't turn over things to him and we didn't have the succession plan of the Twenty-fifth Amendment yet in place.

In 1956, Eisenhower wanted Nixon to step off the ticket, but he didn't like to confront people in this way. He didn't like to fire people. He didn't want to say, "You're off the ticket." What he wanted to do is offer Nixon a cabinet position, maybe in Defense, maybe Commerce, and make him feel as if he was getting some experience so that he could be more of a national figure. He said, "Dick, I think it's time for you to go and get some real experience running a big executive department. And that way, in 1960, you'll be a better candidate to be president because you'll have actually done something instead of just being vice president." Nixon thought about this and said, "Well, Mr. President, are you asking me to get off the ticket?" And Ike said, "Oh, no, no, I want you to get experience. I want you to be president one day." He couldn't fire Nixon. He couldn't direct him to do it. He just offered him the opportunity. They did a two-month back and forth on this. Nixon didn't want to leave the vice presidency because he knew it would be perceived as a demotion. He knew it would be perceived as having been dumped; he was very sensitive about not being taken seriously by Eisenhower. Nixon refused to accept the cabinet position. He said, "Mr. President, I will not go to the cabinet. If you want me to be off the ticket, just say so, and I'll step down." Ike wouldn't do it, so they went back and forth in this very curious way. Finally, Eisenhower gave up and said, "All right, well, you tell me your decision, Dick." Dick said, "I would like to stay on the ticket." And Eisenhower said, "OK."

[Eisenhower and Nixon won in 1956 by a landslide, carrying forty-one states to Democrat Adlai Stevenson's seven.]

. . . [Toward the end of his administration] Eisenhower and Allen Dulles did plan what became Kennedy's Bay of Pigs Operation. There's no doubt about it. We have a great deal of evidence showing that it was a yearlong process—thinking about how to invade Cuba with a group of Cuban exiles from Guatemala and overthrow Castro. But Eisenhower didn't pull the trigger on the operation. The reason is that it wasn't ready to go. It wasn't big enough. It wasn't strong enough. Eisenhower himself hadn't really done the careful planning that would have made it, potentially, successful. When Kennedy gets into office, he launches it right away. It fails. He invites Eisenhower to Camp David the next day, and Eisenhower says, "Well, did you do all these things: Did you ask all the tough questions? Did you go through the logistics? Did you go through the planning?" Kennedy says, "I just took the advice of the generals." Eisenhower says, "Well, that was your first mistake." Kennedy always resented that Eisenhower gave him this plan, in a sense, but then didn't take responsibility for it, which perhaps he should have done. But Eisenhower's view was, "You're the commander in chief, it's your job to ask the tough questions. If it fails on your watch, it's your responsibility." And, of course, publicly, Kennedy did take responsibility for it.

Eisenhower was very angry that John Kennedy [and not Richard Nixon had] won the 1960 election, no doubt about it. Kennedy had criticized Eisenhower in the campaign. Kennedy had said terrible things about Eisenhower. But by 1960, Eisenhower was a much more seasoned politician; he knew it wasn't personal. What he wanted was a good handoff to the new president. They met twice before the inauguration, and each time they met for a long time. They talked through world problems; they really discussed what was going on. Eisenhower said, "Look, it's a tough job, and I want to help you any way I can. Here's what I learned on the job. Here are a few pointers." Kennedy came away very impressed with Eisenhower every time he met him. He realized this man is a serious figure, which is not what Kennedy had said about him on the campaign trail. He'd said, "Oh, he's such a dummy; he's such a dunce. He's asleep at the wheel." But when he met him in person, he realized what a significant figure Ike was.

[Eisenhower's farewell address continues to be quoted today.] Isn't that interesting that a man stepping down wouldn't crow about all of his achievements but instead say, "There's still work to be done. I've left one big thing undone." The tone of that speech is a warning, which is that we've had to build the military-industrial complex in order to protect our freedoms. He said, "I regret we had to do that, but we have done it. We've created this enormous military power based on nuclear arms." And he said, "We now have to control it. We would love to get rid of it completely, but unfortunately the Russians won't let us. They're just as aggressive and dangerous as ever." He was saying, essentially, his preference would be total global disarmament. His preference would be peace. But he hadn't achieved that. What he had achieved was creating a defense system that would protect America, but it wasn't the same thing as world peace.

I spent the bulk of the time researching this book in Abilene, Kansas, at the Eisenhower Presidential Library. . . . Abilene is really where you have to go, not just because that's where Eisenhower's papers are located, the private papers, but because that's his hometown. The more time I spent in Abilene and the more time I spent in Kansas, the closer I felt I was getting to this man. He was a very famous, very successful, worldly cosmopolitan figure, but he really was from Kansas, and he never forgot it. He talked about it a lot. Getting to know . . . the town, feeling the landscape—which is so different from the East Coast—I started to get a read on this man.

He was a great internationalist. He believed firmly in the so-called free world, the free nations of the West, working together, working out their problems. [He believed] in displaying [collective problem solving] at the United Nations to the nonaligned, the newly independent nations of the world—all of those states that were just getting their independence in the 1950s—that this is how democracy works. He believed that the great states can come together at the United Nations and work out their problems together. He'd been the great coalition builder in World War II, and he was enormously effective at listening, hearing other people, working out problems. It showed in the coalition in World War II. He loved the UN for that very reason. It was, in a sense, a projection of American democracy on the world stage.

One thing I can say about Eisenhower is that the scale and scope of the US government, and, indeed, of the United States, was a bit more manageable in the mid-fifties than it is today. So, while I think Eisenhower can teach us some basic things about governance, and about humility, and about generosity, and kindness, moderation, the US government has just become so big. It's so difficult for any one president, no matter how gifted, to be in complete command. So, I think that it's dangerous to say, "Well this president is exactly what we should have today." But, we can be inspired by a character, and the character of experience, the character of knowing where you come from, the character of generosity, humility—those are things that Eisenhower had.

HARRY S. TRUMAN

33rd President, 1945–1953

Overall Rank: 6

— ★ —

Total Score: 737

Harry Truman ranked 5th in C-SPAN's first two surveys before being eclipsed by Dwight Eisenhower in 2017. His category ranks have been consistent throughout, scoring highest in crisis leadership (4th) and pursued equal justice for all (4th). His lowest ranks are in public persuasion (14th) and relations with Congress (14th).

Party: Democrat
b. May 8, 1884, Lamar, Missouri
d. December 26, 1972, Kansas City, Missouri
First Lady: Elizabeth Virginia Wallace Truman
Age entering office: 60

Historian: **Aida D. Donald**

Aida Donald, historian and former editor-in-chief at Harvard University Press and spouse and research partner of the late, noted Lincoln historian David Herbert Donald, was interviewed on October 23, 2012, about her book, Citizen Soldier: A Life of Harry S. Truman, *for C-SPAN's Q & A.*

Harry Truman had two big puzzles in his life, . . . and I worked very hard on the two puzzles, which turned out to be very important to his career. And it kept me working, it kept me very interested in this man from the Midwest, this man with a high school education who accidentally became president in a momentous time in our lives. The two puzzles were succinctly this: The first was, this is a man who got into politics having failed in many businesses as a young man, and the only way to get into politics in Missouri was to be part of a machine. There were two machines, and he hooked up with the Pendergast machine, which was unarguably the most corrupt and often vicious machine. I said to myself, how did this happen? How could he possibly work in this machine in local politics? That was the first thing I had to work out. The second [puzzle], of course, is what we all know about, and that is, how did he come to use the atomic bomb? What was behind the decision? What's the story about the atomic bomb before he became president and when the decision was on his desk? It's still a controversial story, and I wanted to know more about it.

Harry Truman was born in Lamar, Missouri, in 1884. He lived to be eighty-eight. He was the son of an improvident farmer and cattle trader who went bust and could never really support the family, and his father then ran farms. Harry had a rich uncle, and his mother inherited a farm, and so, Harry became a farmer. He couldn't go to college because his father went bust, so he had first started out in banking. He was a very good teller and manager of money. His father called him back and said, we now have these farms to run and we need you. He didn't want to go back; he hated farming. But, he did, and he became one of the best farmers in the area. He sent for books, and he learned how to rotate crops. He could do a straight furrow with the horses, and as he did, he would have a book in front of him. He said he read more books while the horses were doing their thing. He grew hay and oats and whatever local farmers were growing, but he says in one of his letters, "I never made a dime in farming." The Trumans were never successful, always poor with huge mortgages. He did that for ten years.

One of the reasons why Truman joined the army was to get away from the farm. It was the best excuse he could make. He could not just leave. His father died in 1914, and he couldn't just leave because he had a mother and a sister and a brother [to support]. But, if you joined the army, you were a patriot, and so that's what he did. They brought a handyman in to run the farm, and he got away from it and never went back to it. I have a whole chapter in my book on what a brilliant army career he had. He came out of nowhere. Who would have guessed that this young man, who says in his letters, "I was a sissy. I had no chums to play with. I wore heavy glasses, couldn't play football, couldn't rough-house, so I played with my sister and one of my two girl cousins." [That all changes.] He went into the army, and it made a man out of him. When he came out of the army he was so masculine, he was ready to conquer the world, which is what he ultimately did.

[He was in the army] about nineteen months, give or take. He got out in 1919. He saw a lot of combat. He was a battery artillery commander, and the records show he had commendations; the records show that he was excellent, and probably the best, in that whole series of sectors. He kept the guns so clean; he protected the horses. He took a rowdy bunch of what he calls "Irishmen" and turned them into a first-rate battery. And the men loved it. If they did not respond to his discipline, he threw them out. He said, "I'll court-martial you, so you must follow me." In fact, when he met them the first time and they saw this five-foot-eight thin guy with big glasses, they thought that this guy could be a real pushover. They had lost four captains because they were such a rowdy bunch. He looked at them and said, "I want you to know one thing. I don't have to get along with you. You have to get along with me. Dismissed until the morning." The next morning, he looked up their records, and he busted four right on the spot. He promoted a couple that showed promise. He brought in some new guys, and he started to polish up the team and make it really good. It was noticed what a good leader he was because he was sent on to artillery school, both in this country and then when he got to France, because he didn't know trigonometry, he didn't know algebra. He didn't know how to use the guns, how to raise them, how to turn them. All of that had to be learned in school, and he was a good student. He said it was the toughest thing he'd ever had to do, to go to those artillery schools. The one in France was Napoleon's artillery school. It was a very elite group. He was surrounded by these guys from Yale who looked down upon him as a high school graduate. He said, "But I showed them. I'm as good as they are."

I don't know what it was about Harry, who claimed at age six, "I fell in love with this blonde girl with curls and blue eyes [named Elizabeth "Bess" Wallace]. She sat in the class ahead of me and I never loved anyone else all my life." And he never did. He had no [other] girlfriends; it was just Bess. I don't know enough about the psychology of a man who will, all of his life, wait for a woman. He was thirty-five when he married her [in 1919]; she was thirty-four. She had [other] boyfriends, she had wealthy boyfriends, but she didn't marry them. I think what held her back was the possibility that they might find out after she married them about [her father's] suicide.

[Bess's father, David Wallace, had committed suicide when she was a teenager.] That had a great impact on Bess. First of all, she was so sad and so depressed, and her mother was so humiliated by having a husband who took his own life, because in those days it affected the whole family and their reputation. Mrs. Wallace took the family and went to Colorado for a year; she just escaped with the kids because the humiliation was so great. All of her life, Bess Truman was afraid that this story would get out because people thought if you committed suicide, you were insane, and therefore you carried an insanity gene, which children and grandchildren might inherit. When Harry decided to go into public life, she was very unhappy because she said this story might get out. He said, "I'll protect you as much as I can." In fact, they never told their daughter, Margaret, about this suicide until she was a grown woman. Margaret resented that, but she got over it. . . . And, it never came out; Harry protected her, and he went to his grave, as she did, and it was still not public knowledge.

Bess said no to all of [her other suitors] and was, for the times, quite old by the time Harry married her. Thirty-four years old back in the 1920s—you were really an "old maid." But, Harry never let go. . . . It might have been that he was such a romantic—and he was a romantic, he was a nineteenth-century figure more than a twentieth-century figure. It may be that his romantic side was so great he wasn't going to let go of Bess. And she was, by the way, a very pretty woman. She was athletic. She played tennis; she ran; she was more athletic than he was. She was quite a good catch, except for this dark dimension. I tried to figure out what it was [that attracted him so much], and I think it was just a combination of chasing something he probably thought he could never have, which psychologically must mean something, and then the romance. And he truly loved her, there's no doubt about that, all of his life.

[In 1922, following the failure of his haberdashery business, Truman got his start in local politics with the help of the local political boss, Tom Pendergast.] Harry Truman suffered from psychosomatic illnesses. Truman [had to learn how] . . . to cope with being part of the Pendergast political machine that was corrupt and sometimes violent, because his ethics, which he'd gotten from his mother, were very high. Yet, he had to do favors for the machine, which meant faulty contracts giving $10,000 to $50,000, or whatever the boss asked for, from time to time. The only way he could cope with himself was by being a divided self. He was, in his own eyes, an ethical man. He was always a poor man because he never took a dime. And so, what happened is that he developed illnesses—dyspeptic, migraine headaches, really terrible stomach trouble. So, he would hide at a hotel. He would sign in under an assumed name—usually [at] the Pickwick Hotel in Kansas City. He didn't even tell Bess where he was. And while he was there getting better, he started writing these memos about what was going on, how he had to be corrupt, and how it was hurting him, but he wanted a record kept. These were kept secret, these Pickwick papers, for many, many years. They were opened over time . . . and they were useful in the sense of who was getting what payoffs, what was going on. [With these notes] I'm able to plot Harry's illnesses and the times that he had to give in to Pendergast, which was not often, by the way.

. . . He was in local politics for a long time before he shot up to the Senate. Pendergast had to get rid of him; Truman was too honest, and [the boss] wasn't making enough money from him. Even though Truman wanted to stay home—after he was a county judge and the presiding county judge, which meant he controlled the flow of money for infrastructure, he wanted to be the collector of taxes—but the boss said no. Truman was too honest—you couldn't let him collect your taxes.

I read all [of Harry's Pickwick Hotel papers]. And . . . he said more than once, "Am I an ethical fool?" Everyone else was getting rich. During the time he was county judge, there were two bond issues in the county. First, there was a $10 million bond issue—and this is the 1920s and slightly into the 1930s, so, $10 million was a lot of money to spend on infrastructure. Pendergast says, "You'll never get it; [the public has] to vote for it." He got it. He went around [to the citizenry] and said, "We need it." And then the second one was $50 million. Harry Truman built 162 miles of concrete roads; before then, they were all dirt roads covered with oil. He built two beautiful city halls. One was in Art Deco style, which he chose, and one was in Federal style, which he also chose. He built culverts. No farmer was more than a mile or so from one of these very good roads because, in addition to the main roads, he built little spurs in concrete so the farmers could get their crops to market. And then, he wrote a little book about what he did—did not put his name on it, but he wrote it. It's a beautiful little book that you can still get. . . . So, he spent the money very wisely. Though, as we know from the Pickwick papers, every now and then some slipped away. He says in one of the Pickwick papers that if he had been a crook, he could have made a million and a half dollars, but, he said, "I never took a dime." He said,

"I was always poor, and I'll remain poor." And he was poor. He never owned a house. He always lived with his mother-in-law and her mother [at 219 North Delaware in Independence, Missouri], before she died. He did not own the house with Bess until all the old folks were gone.

[Truman was elected to the US Senate in] 1934. He was re-elected in 1940, for a second term, and was chosen for vice president in '44. [He was chosen as Franklin Roosevelt's final running mate for] a simple reason: as second place on the ticket, he would lose the least amount of votes of all the candidates who wanted to be vice president. People like Jimmy Byrnes from South Carolina and a host of others; Alben Barkley, senator from Kentucky. [The party was] at sixes and sevens, and Roosevelt was playing his usual game of toying with his aides, saying, "Oh, I like Jimmy Byrnes. Oh, I like Alben. Oh, I like this guy." They weren't getting anywhere until finally Ed Flynn—the boss in New York, a powerful machine politician—went down to Washington and said, "This has got to be settled right now. And what we've got to do is we've got to choose the man who will lose the fewest votes. So, it's got to be Harry Truman."

Everyone said, "Truman doesn't want it. He's been asked two or three times and he has said, 'I don't want to be vice president.'" And they said, "We don't care. Someone call him." Well, someone did, and Harry responded that unless the president called him, he wouldn't know it really was true that Roosevelt wanted him because Roosevelt didn't like him; FDR thought Truman was still a Pendergast [machine] crook. Truman was not FDR's kind, he was not an Eastern elite guy who went to Harvard or Yale and spoke with a broad "a" accent. This was a Midwest politician with a high school education. But, FDR got on the phone and said, "I want you to run with me." And Truman said, "Well, why didn't you say so from the beginning?" Then Truman started to curse. He had barnyard language when he was very angry, but only with men in the room, never with women. . . . So, he agreed to run. Bess was not happy, though by the time they got to the convention she was very pleased, and [their daughter] Margaret was delighted; they both jumped up and down.

[FDR was inaugurated for a fourth term on January 20, 1945, and died on April 12.] Truman was vice president for literally eighty-two days, and being Truman, he actually presided over the Senate [during those months]. Nowadays, the vice president doesn't bother with that

This June 27, 1945, portrait of Harry Truman was taken two months after he assumed the presidency following the death of Franklin D. Roosevelt. *Courtesy Library of Congress*

unless his vote is needed to break a tie. Truman was there every day, presiding. He said, "That's my job; I'm head of the Senate." . . . He was in [House Speaker] Sam Rayburn's office [on April 12]. . . . Truman got a phone call from the White House: "Get to the phone right away." And so, he picked up the phone, and at the other end they said, "Get to the White House as soon as you can." So, he grabbed his hat and dashed out to his car; they gave him a chauffeur when he became vice president. He went to the White House, was met and taken upstairs to the second floor, which was the family floor [where] he was met by Eleanor Roosevelt. And that's how he became president.

V-E Day [marking Allied victory in the] European theater ended [the fighting in Europe less than one month later on] May 8[, 1945. The Potsdam conference held in] July was attended by the Russians— the Soviet Union then—the Americans, and Clement Attlee, who had replaced Winston Churchill in an election. Truman didn't know anything. Truman had never learned anything from FDR or from his staff; it was a transition with zero knowledge. That doesn't happen anymore. The leaders decided that they wanted the UN to be supported by the big powers, and they wanted the Soviet Union to join in the war against Japan, with its enormous army and resources. Those were the two big things to be decided. But they were also jawing about what to do about East Germany, where you had areas of occupation. . . . Berlin was carved out into four [Allied-controlled] sections, but it was in the middle of the Russian area, so it was a kind of isolated enclave.

Now, it was the Japanese war they were focusing on. [In March 1945, the United States firebombed Tokyo] . . . destroyed the city, and about one hundred thousand people died. . . . The atomic bomb was dropped on August 6, the first one. And then, on August 9, the second one [was dropped on] Nagasaki. We killed or had causalities in Hiroshima of [around one hundred fifty thousand]. It was immense because some died of radiation later. In Nagasaki, maybe seventy thousand—a smaller number of causalities, but still immense.

What I learned [about Truman's decision-making process for the use of the atomic bomb was], number one, Truman was deadly serious when he said, "We've got to end this war quickly. That's why I'm going to use the bomb." Secondly, Harry Truman knew that the bomb had tremendous blast power, but he did not know, as far as I can tell, about radiation sickness. He did not know about gamma rays that may have killed, ultimately, as many people as the blast itself in both cities. He was not on top of that, nor was Secretary of War Stimson. This was something that the inner circle around [chief nuclear scientist Robert] Oppenheimer knew. There were two nuclear scientists who tried to reach the White House to say, "You really have to think about radiation." They never got to Truman but did get to General Leslie Groves, who was director of the atomic project. Leslie Groves said, "No, no, no, no, no." [Essentially] he said, "Radiation is not a problem. If we use the atomic bomb in Japan and decide to invade, our boys can be on the sands of Japan a half-hour later, and they would be perfectly safe."

It was nonsense. That area was toxic for how many years? The gamma rays were extraordinary. It's a bomb that was created by Oppenheimer to do the most damage possible to civilians. He knew what he was building. Truman [and the nuclear advisory committee he had assembled] threw aside the notion of testing it on an [uninhabited] island to show Japan the power of these "three suns," [to show] that we were making this bomb that would destroy the islands. He said, "That won't work." If you want to end the war, you've got to, in effect—Truman didn't use these exact words—deploy a "terror bomb," which is what we created. . . . [And, he decided that we must use it on] cities that had not already been convincingly bombed, so that you'll know that all of the destruction was the atomic bomb in each city. And that's how the war will end, Truman thought.

The Japanese emperor decided by August 14 that it was over. His clique, military, and otherwise, wanted to continue the war and, as a matter of fact, after the bomb was dropped on Nagasaki, the Japanese did not indicate they wanted to surrender. . . . What Truman did [after the two nuclear detonations] is to say, "OK, now we will return to conventional bombing. That's enough." People thought that was all we had. In fact, we had more bombs. . . . We had a third one on its way to Tinian Island to be put together, and we had as many as ten more being built. But, we went back to conventional bombing. On August 14, the emperor decided, "We'll all be in ashes," and he told his government that they were to surrender. His war minister was so upset he went home and committed hara-kiri. The clique around the emperor wanted to fight to the last man as they had in all the islands—Okinawa, Iwo Jima, you name it. . . . The Japanese people were told they were to fight even if they only had broomsticks. They must fight an invasion, which the United States had planned for November 1. The plan was to surround the islands with the navy, a total blockade and an invasion of American troops up to a half million, perhaps. The figures are tossed about; we're not quite sure. [They were to go] right onto the islands and then just keep moving up from one island to another until they collapsed and Japan decided to surrender.

Truman believed [that by dropping the atomic bombs] he saved at least a quarter of a million American causalities, which is a lot of American boys, and a lot of families if we had to invade and march through to Tokyo to get a surrender.

[Harry Truman's second war began in late June 1950 on the Korean peninsula when Communist North Korea sent troops into South Korea. Truman ordered US forces there in a military action, which lasted until July 1953.] I came to the conclusion, after I did all my research on the Korean War, that it was a mistake. In some places in my book, I call it [Secretary of State Dean] Acheson's war. This was an unnecessary war.

What happened was the North Korean communist government crossed the 38th parallel, which split Korea; this [dividing line] was agreed upon in the [World War II] peace treaties. And immediately, they started to overrun South Korea. Without consulting with the president, who was back home in Independence, Acheson went to the United Nations and said, "We've got to do something about this. We've got to stop it." He called Truman, . . . who flew back the next day. . . . We had the Truman Doctrine, which said that if communists try to take over countries, we will block them. We gave money to Greece and Turkey in 1947. We had an airlift to Berlin when the Russians blockaded. We had [established our] red lines, and the North Koreans had crossed a red line, and the president was furious. So, Truman backed Acheson and sent the US Army to push back the North Koreans.

[General Douglas] MacArthur was in charge, and he was told not to do several things, [particularly] not to do anything on the other side of the Yalu River. . . . [The Yalu River is] up in North Korea, separating China from North Korea. [MacArthur was told] not to cross it because it might bring China into the war. He was also told not to do anything to aggravate Russia because Russia was greedy for any colonies, anything it could grab. And [Truman also told MacArthur], "I'm not going to give you the atom bomb; you're not going to be able to use it." MacArthur said, "Oh, don't worry. The Chinese are not coming in." So, MacArthur got our army up to the 38th parallel, and the decision was made—and the White House knew—to cross the parallel to get into North Korea and destroy the North Korean army. This was an agreed-upon decision.

We did indeed push back the North Koreans, but it triggered the Chinese, who came rushing in [by the] hundreds of thousands. Truman said, "I was promised they wouldn't come in. Intelligence told MacArthur and MacArthur told me this wouldn't happen, and here we are fighting hundreds of thousands of Chinese." The Chinese pushed our army all the way back to Seoul, and beyond. MacArthur started to give press conferences where he asked for the use of the bomb. Truman said no. Truman didn't think he was going to be listened to, so instead of calling MacArthur back for a conference, he decided to fly to Wake Island—a famous flight, twenty-one hours. He sat down with MacArthur and repeated, "We don't want the Chinese in this war, but they're in it. We don't want to do anything to bring Russia in. And you're not going to get the atomic bomb. Now, what are we going to be doing?"

MacArthur said, "I can handle it. Give me the troops I need, and it will be all right." So, Truman thought, "OK, he understands what I, the commander in chief, have told him to do." Truman flew back home.

Then, MacArthur made a strategic blunder. We had an enormous and very good army. MacArthur split it in two, with a mountain range in between, [hoping to] get to the North Koreans to knock them out of the war and to get the Chinese. Well, this meant that if one [half of the] army was hit, the other couldn't help it. . . . As a result, both were pushed all the way back, and we were in trouble again. MacArthur wanted the bomb again, and Truman got very angry and said, "I warned you that I wasn't going to use the atomic bomb again." MacArthur had flouted the commander in chief, and [Truman decided he was] going to fire him.

There was a lot of discussion among his advisers. Some advisers said, "You should have fired him before Wake Island because this man doesn't take orders." Truman didn't want MacArthur to get wind of what he was doing because MacArthur would have resigned and come home as a hero. And so, Truman managed a way, quietly, secretly, to fire him publicly. And, of course, MacArthur was humiliated. He immediately came home and tried to make himself a hero. Congress thought he was a hero, and he had a parade down Fifth Avenue. But, Truman said that it was important in this stage in our history that the president is commander in chief and the generals have to listen to him; when he gives an order, it must be obeyed. And that was the lesson of MacArthur.

This was a very disturbing thing to learn: when the US Army withdrew from the North Korean side of the 38th parallel, we devastated everything from their capital to the parallel. We bombed them. We napalmed them. We shot them. No house was left standing. People were all killed—women, children. It was total devastation, and our army did that, under orders. Our American soldiers had been gently raised by their mothers, and this [destruction] made them sick. They came back from these bombing raids and from being [ground forces], and they just vomited. They didn't want to do this, but they were ordered to do it.

[Here's what I wrote in my book about the impact of this war: "The Korean War transformed the United States into a very different country. It soon had hundreds of permanent military bases abroad, a large standing Army, and a permanent national security state at home. We can add to that a huge nuclear force, a penchant for invading foreign countries, on little or no evidence of danger to the United States and a government not always protective of civil liberties."] I think this all started with Korea. It started with the kind of war we finally fought in Korea. Truman couldn't end it, as we know. He lost. He could have run again, but the war was still on; it was still dangerous. It was Eisenhower who ended it, but that's a different story. . . .

Truman [also] set up loyalty programs in this country because he was being accused of [having] communists in the government—[the charge was that] we had disloyal people, and that's why we were losing the war; people were sabotaging us. And so, Truman set up this kind of state [response], which we still have with us now. We don't have loyalty oaths anymore, but we have what Eisenhower later called the military-industrial complex, which runs half the economy, and which is very war-like. This makes us go into countries [even when] we don't understand their history; we don't understand their culture. If we think they're going to be communistic, we send an army. We get beaten badly, as we did in Vietnam. We withdraw, and then years pass, and we do it again. . . . It set a postwar pattern, postwar meaning post-Korea, that we are living with today. And it all started back then.

THOMAS JEFFERSON

3rd President, 1801–1809

Overall Rank: 7

— ★ —

Total Score: 727

Thomas Jefferson has held the 7th overall rank in all three of C-SPAN's historian surveys. He scores highest in vision/setting an agenda (5th in 2017) and relations with Congress (5th). His lowest rank is in pursued equal justice for all, where he has seen a steady decline in each of the three surveys and currently ranks 17th.

Party: Democratic-Republican
b. April 13, 1743, Goochland County (now Albemarle County), Virginia
d. July 4, 1826, Monticello estate, Virginia
First Lady: Martha "Patsy" Randolph (daughter)
Age entering office: 57

Historian: **Willard Sterne Randall**

History professor and biographer of leaders from the Revolutionary War period, Willard Sterne Randall was interviewed on Booknotes *for his book,* Thomas Jefferson: A Life. *The interview was recorded on October 29, 1993.*

If you start from when he's twenty-seven years old, [Thomas Jefferson's government service began as a] member of the Virginia House of Burgesses from the farthest west, the frontier county of Albemarle, Virginia. He was also the youngest lawyer to practice before the General Court of Virginia, which was also the supreme court of that colony. He was a delegate to the Continental Congress. He was in the Second Continental Congress, 1776, one year only, filling an unexpired term. He became a member of the first House of Delegates, was the Revolutionary governor of Virginia, and, in three years, literally rewrote the law of the largest state at the time, Virginia—126 new laws and a new criminal code. Then he went on to Congress again. He was the leading member of Congress for a few years then became the American minister

plenipotentiary, or ambassador, to France, replacing Benjamin Franklin, his mentor. Washington wanted him in his first cabinet, so he was
the first secretary of state. Jefferson found it hard to say no to George
Washington, as I think just about everybody else did. Then he became
vice president to Adams by three electoral votes in the first contested
presidential election. Then he defeated the Federalists and became the
third president of the United States. So, [on the federal level, he was]
our first secretary of state; our second vice president; and our third
president, for two terms.

Thomas Jefferson was born in Albemarle County, Virginia, the farthest
settlement west, the last ridge basically before you got into the frontier. His father had settled Albemarle County, one of the two original
settlers. He was a pioneer, . . . a great giant of a man, Peter Jefferson,
of legendary strength, sort of the Paul Bunyan of the Virginia frontier.
He helped draw the boundaries of Virginia. He rode out on expeditions with chains and surveyors. Jefferson worshipped him and learned
surveying and a love for books from his father, whose entire library was
only forty volumes, but compared to the libraries of most people on the
frontier at the time, that was quite a lot. Jefferson emulated his father,
but he's very much like his mother, who was a Randolph, very refined,
and he got his love of education from her.

There were so many [Jefferson children] that he basically had to
move out and go away to school. Our picture of a plantation at the time
is something more out of *Gone with the Wind* than was the reality. These
were small farmhouses with eaves and dormers, and Jefferson was a tall
boy. With . . . seven children at home with them by the time he was a
teenage boy, there just wasn't room for him, and he went off to school.
He was the older of two boys with a half-dozen sisters, and when his
father died, Thomas was only fourteen, and he became the man of the
family.

I thought that his relationship with his father and with his mother
was very important because there has been some spin put on his relationship with his mother since the 1960s and '70s. Modern scholars have
found that part of his early correspondence has been misdated, giving
the impression that he was twenty-nine or thirty years old and hated
women when he wrote certain things in his notebooks. It's been found
out recently that he was fourteen, and so when he wrote angry things

about women in Greek and Latin, he was actually railing at his mother, like many an adolescent boy does. But [he was] doing it in Greek and Latin, which she couldn't read, so he couldn't get in trouble. If you don't get that right, then you have a misogynist, because if you look at what he wrote, it's very angry. He had been turned into a woman-hater [because of that misdating, and] I don't find any evidence for that. In many ways, he was actually much more liberal than other men of his time. He saw that his daughter was wonderfully educated. . . . I think he gave women a higher place as life went on, although he was not ready to put one in his government, so he's also been attacked for that. I don't think he thought he had enough support from the public. There were some things that he remained confused about all of his life. One of those was exactly what to do with women. I think he was always awkward about that, but I don't think he was a misogynist.

Jefferson's father had slaves. They had been introduced into the family gradually. As the indentured white labor supply dried up, the Jeffersons, like others, bought more land and bought more slaves. When Peter Jefferson died, he left his family thirty-four slaves. Most of Jefferson's slaves came by inheritance from his father. And, when Thomas married [Martha Wayles in 1772], almost immediately his father-in-law died right after buying a whole shipload of slaves that nobody wanted and nobody could afford. So, Jefferson instantly became the largest slave owner in Virginia.

Six feet two and a half inches is the best estimate [of Thomas Jefferson's height that] I can come up with. He was thin, probably no more than 180 pounds. . . . A slave overseer who specialized in knowing the statistics about human beings said he was six two and a half, straight as a gun barrel, with a wonderful bearing. He didn't walk with a cane until the last few months of his life. He exercised and rode a horse until the last few weeks of his life. He was virtually a vegetarian, although not slavishly so. He always had a glass of red wine [with his meals] for about forty years that I can tell, and it was always a good one. He preferred country ham and French cuisine equally, but he believed in being outdoors as much as possible. So, he took care of himself. He died with a full head of teeth, which was extremely rare in those days, and he had a shock of red hair.

This engraving of Thomas Jefferson shows a more somber side of our third president, a redhead who stood over six feet tall. *Courtesy Bureau of Engraving and Printing*

Jefferson had migraine headaches. . . . They usually followed some serious loss. When his mother died, he had a migraine that lasted for six weeks. When his father died, there's a hint of this in his correspondence. Mostly they called in someone who bled you and purged you, which I'm not sure helped a headache or anything else very much. He had one period in Paris for six weeks when he was absolutely flattened and called in a doctor, who I don't think helped things very much.

[In researching this book, I learned that] Jefferson, the lawyer, was much more important than he's been made out to be. Other biographers have touched on his career, but in tracking him through his life, I very quickly learned that his legal papers and his casebooks and his record books still existed. They were out in a private collection in California. I was able to go out there and sit, and hold them, and study them, and see that the man had almost one thousand law cases on the eve of the Revolution, many of them in areas that mattered a great deal to him. He would represent slaves without fee to try to win them freedom. He was one of the first to think about divorce reform; divorce was illegal [then]. . . . Many of the areas that are considered quite modern, he had struggled with as a lawyer, and he had been shouted down by the slave-owning oligarchy and the British officials in Virginia. So, out of the law courts, we get Jefferson the revolutionary, on his feet, writing brilliant opinions, very articulate, a better speaker than most biographers have let on. That, to me, explained for the first time why such a good lawyer as John Adams would defer to him to write the Declaration of Independence and the key documents of the Continental Congress. That never made sense to me before. What I [previously] knew about Jefferson, basically, was at age thirty-three he dropped out of the sky in Philadelphia and wrote the Declaration of Independence; what I found out in this research is those early years [in law practice] were terribly important.

His closest friend was James Madison, roughly ten years his junior. He also had a number of young men [with whom] he ran the male equivalent of a salon. William Short was one; [David] Humphreys, and others who would be his aides for a while. Jonathan Trumbull was very close to him in Paris. He trusted Trumbull explicitly. Trumbull had been a soldier and was an artist, and he confided in him. He liked James Monroe. He picked him out when Monroe was a captain in the Revolutionary Army and brought him along. But these were always juniors; I don't find close friends of his own age. For a while, he was very close to Adams, and he was very fond of Abigail Adams, admired her greatly, but it wasn't until he was an old man and both Adams and Jefferson were out of power that they became close again. Jefferson could be very suspicious of people that he saw as potential rivals, and I think he trusted younger men more than most of the men of his own age.

He went to Paris when he was forty-one. His wife [Martha Wayles Jefferson, thirty-three,] had died not long before that. He was desolate. He thought his life was over. He went mostly because Franklin had asked him three times to come, and as long as his wife was alive and sick, he couldn't see his way clear to leaving her behind. She wasn't up to the voyage. But when she died, he went, at Franklin's invitation, to help negotiate the peace with the British. That was all done by the time he got there, but he became the apostle of the new country, publishing *Notes on the State of Virginia*, over there, trying to show the French what this new country was about. He was there for five years, a vital five years. He was very close to [the Marquis de] Lafayette, and a lot of the early stages of the French Revolution took place at his dinner table in the American mission on the Champs-Élysées, so this period was fascinating to me.

He was in Paris from 1784 to 1789. He was there when the Bastille fell. The rioting was going on outside his windows. He went out in his carriage for months to investigate. The crowds recognized him, and they would stop hitting the guards long enough to let him pass and then would let fly again at the Swiss Guards. He stayed there about three months after the revolution began and then came home.

I thought it was a good idea [to tell the story of Jefferson falling in love in Paris] because I thought that one of the things that happens to Jefferson and other leaders, especially the early leaders of this country, is they are turned into marble busts instead of human beings. In looking at Jefferson in love in Paris, we have quite a different slant on the man. It's not only Jefferson in love but Jefferson discovering the importance of women. In Paris, he learned to respect the intellects of the women of the salon who really ran the French government, not all that well sometimes, as Marie Antoinette could attest. Jefferson opened his mind in those years and had a wonderful time with Maria Cosway, an educated, brilliant painter, and it changed him into a much more sophisticated individual.

Maria Cosway was married to a British portrait painter, Richard Cosway, and he came to Paris with a commission to paint a duke. Jefferson was introduced to her by John Trumbull, the American artist who was living with Jefferson and painting Jefferson's image in the . . . famous Trumbull portrait, *The Declaration of Independence.* He took Jefferson around and introduced him to these painters, and they hit it off. Many times, they would all go off as a foursome, many times not. Jefferson saw Maria Cosway for the better part of six weeks before she went back to England, and then they corresponded for the rest of his life, less and less frequently, but until he was a very old man. Very fondly, he was the patriarch writing to her. She later became a nun and the headmistress of a girls' school in Italy. It was always this wonderful literary affair, if nothing more than that, between them. I don't think they ever did see each other again. He had several opportunities [to stay in Europe], but he decided to come back to America and go back into political life. I think those years in Paris healed him from the terrible years in Virginia during the Revolution when he lost his home, his farms, and when his political career looked wrecked as well.

Between 1784 and 1789, [while Jefferson was in Europe] things were not going so well in the United States, depending on your point of view. There was Shay's Rebellion in Massachusetts, that so shocked Washington and Adams and Madison that they called a convention. And then, there was a new US Constitution. Jefferson was [away] for that. He was in France, and if he'd been here, I think he might have objected to a lot of the new Constitution because he thought revolution was a good thing. He wrote long letters to Madison trying to influence Madison during that convention, but it took six months before the letters went back and forth, and Jefferson had absolutely no effect whatsoever on that convention.

Jefferson's daily expense records [for his travels in Europe] are in the Henry Huntington Library in California, [written] on the backs of envelopes and in foolscap. He kept meticulous day-by-day expense accounts. The man was obsessive about record keeping, so we can tell what he paid for a drink and what he paid the valet and how much to get the carriage fixed, et cetera, so you know his itinerary. . . . With those records we went off to France and tried to find the towns and the routes, many of which didn't exist anymore or weren't easily found. We were able to reconstruct his travels that way. . . . Jefferson actually went over the Alps in a mule train in the wintertime to try to find products in Italy that he could bring back to adapt to the United States to help its infant economy. Actually, he violated the laws of Italy and diplomatic immunity by stealing sacks full of unmilled rice because he thought the Carolinas needed not only a better grain of rice but one that didn't use slave labor, one that would grow in the hills where so many slaves wouldn't be killed from malarial insects. He risked his life going into Italy and smuggling out this rice. He also brought back ice cream, pasta, and several other things. He was always looking for new things to bring back to the United States.

. . . Jefferson was very good at operating behind the scenes. He appeared not to be running [for president in 1796], but as Adams and Hamilton and others found out, the appearance wasn't the whole story. He was very good at lining up support, bringing around state committees, very good at working in secret, something he learned as a diplomat in Paris. As a president, I have a very mixed view of him. He could be absolutely ruthless. While he founded the oldest political party, the Democrats, he trashed the Federalists, almost destroyed the two-party system for forty years, and brought the spoils system into politics. When he believed in something, he believed in it so completely he couldn't see the damage that he might do. I wouldn't like to see some of the things he did then done again.

. . . Jefferson was vice president [during the Adams administration, 1797–1801], but it was already obvious that he was going to oppose Adams when Adams ran for a second term. In those days, . . . the process was that the number one in the Electoral College got to be president; number two got to be vice president [which meant people from opposing parties could both be in the same administration]. Jefferson had miscalculated in his 1796 campaign, so he came out three electoral votes short, or he would have been president instead of Adams the first time. As a result of that election, the [nominating system] was changed, [and parties nominated tickets, where you would] . . . choose your own running mate. That didn't work very well either at first because both the president and vice president had the exact number of electoral votes. In 1800, Jefferson's vice president happened to be Aaron Burr, who said, "That doesn't mean I'm vice president; that means we're tied." So, there were thirty-six ballots in Congress to decide who the winner of that election was. It was a clumsy system at first before [the Constitution was changed in 1804, and] it came out the way it is now. . . . Jefferson served for two [terms as president]; the second time in 1804, he won very big.

The Alien and Sedition Acts [1798] were used, if not designed, [by President John Adams as a way] to stop Jefferson from forming an opposition party. It targeted newspapers in the Jefferson camp. Editors and writers were arrested; twenty-five editors and writers were indicted. They were imprisoned. The US Supreme Court justices rode around in carriages like hanging judges, reading their writings and rounding them up and having them imprisoned. When that law expired, Jefferson saw that it was not renewed. The Alien Act was intended to slow down the process of mostly French immigrants, exiles from the French Revolution, from becoming citizens. There were so many of them crowding into the country, and they were on the Jeffersonian side, or rather he was on theirs. The Alien Act passed in 1798, and immediately after that, the Sedition Act passed, which made it a federal crime to criticize the president, the presidency, the government, or the president's party in any way, punishable by a fine and prison.

I don't think Jefferson was in favor of the Sedition Act, but [as president] he shut down any criminal prosecutions that might have led to court testimony that was very unfavorable to him, so he did tamper with the courts. He didn't go quite the step of a Sedition Act, but he went after key Federalist judges and replaced them with his own people, and where that didn't work, cases all of a sudden dried up if they got too close to Thomas Jefferson.

Jefferson managed to keep himself open to a great number of constituencies. He also believed in equality among the officers of government. [As president,] he abolished normal seating arrangements, for example. Every department had to have an oval table so no one sat at the head, no one at the foot. He received visitors of all kinds, people from the hustings or diplomats, with almost no fanfare. He was approachable. I know that's very difficult today, but I think any president today would do well to try to keep himself open instead of just being surrounded by the old China hands, the palace guard. I hope there's a message in my book about that. But also, the inquisitive mind of Jefferson never stopped; he was always looking for new approaches and was not afraid to contradict himself frequently. He did rapid about-faces. He was a pacifist going into the presidency, yet he founded West Point and made war in Algeria, just for an example.

He was against a strong central government and was a strict constructionist on the Constitution. And yet, he used a congressional slush fund—not that I'm advocating that—when he needed to buy land because he thought that was the wealth and the future of the country, the Louisiana Purchase. So, the flexibility of Jefferson is one of the most important things about him.

I guess I'm expected to say, since he founded the Democratic Party that he'd be a Democrat [today], but I'm not sure what camp he would be in because a lot of his ideas would make him much more conservative today. He was a decentralizer, and I'm sure that Reagan Republicans would be happy to claim him for that. Civil libertarians claim him; Unitarians claim him. All sorts of people have claimed him based on what he did then and what is happening now, but I'm not sure what Jefferson would do now.

I had to confront the question of was this man ruthless or not, and he could be quite ruthless in pursuit of something that really mattered to him, and his years as president are the most controversial. He did bring in the spoils system in this country that became one of the great political evils for almost one hundred years. He did it in [a] casuistic way. He kept very careful records that said he had given half of the political jobs to the Federalists and half to the Democrats—yes, the bottom half to his opponents, the top half to his own people. So, he really did set up a winner-take-all form of election, and sometimes he hounded people out of office or into prison, such as Aaron Burr. They'd been very close, and Jefferson couldn't have gotten as far as he did without Burr's support in New York. Once he turned on Burr, Jefferson was completely out of line as president in publicly indicting and convicting Burr before he'd even had a trial. Luckily, Chief Justice John Marshall shut that case down. John Marshall was Jefferson's cousin, and he wasn't at all intimidated by him. Marshall was very close to Washington, was his first biographer, a staunch believer in the Federalists and thought that Jefferson and what he represented were very bad for the country.

[In 1974] . . . Fawn Brodie brought out *Thomas Jefferson: An Intimate History*, which made the case that Jefferson had a slave concubine at Monticello, Sally Hemings. . . . What fascinated me . . . [was how this story] came about: . . . Jefferson had a hack writer, James Thomson Callender, working for him attacking Hamilton and Adams for years. When Jefferson didn't give Callender a high political office when he became president and refused to have anything more to do with him, Callender switched sides and attacked Jefferson in print in a Richmond newspaper. I actually found the first paragraph [of Callender's article while doing my research] about Jefferson, and there is Sally, although she's not given a last name. Callender makes the charge that they had a son and that she had gone to France with Jefferson when he became the ambassador there, and that she named her son Tom. . . . Brodie's interpretation was based on an interview with one of Sally Hemings's sons when he was very old, after the Civil War, and had gone to Ohio to homestead. . . . There was also a Jefferson family story going back and forth in the private correspondence of biographers in the nineteenth century. The family's version of this, privately, was that there were indeed mulatto children at Monticello but that they were not Thomas Jefferson's, that they were the children of Jefferson's nephews.

The public opinion after Brodie's book was that Jefferson was a hypocrite: here was the man talking about freedom and that all men are created equal while he's got a slave mistress at Monticello. Thomas Jefferson['s reputation] was reduced to that, as far as what we should know about him. If we know one fact now, it wasn't that he wrote the Declaration of Independence or founded a university; it was that he had a slave mistress.

[Editor's note: In 1997, historian Annette Gordon-Reed published a Pulitzer Prize–winning book that changed the scholarship on the Jefferson-Hemings relationship, using records to support the Hemings's family claims. To help settle the long-standing controversy, a DNA test was done in 1998, scientifically linking the Hemings's descendants to Jefferson. In 2000, the Thomas Jefferson Foundation, the nonprofit organization that owns Monticello, announced that research suggested a "high probability" that Jefferson had fathered one of Hemings's sons and it was "likely" he had fathered all six of her children. Exhibits at Monticello have been updated to tell Sally Hemings's story to their visitors.]

I emphasize about six or seven different things in my book that [previous biographers hadn't]: Jefferson's legal career, his travels in Europe, his years in Paris, who his connections were there, and Jefferson the writer. I started out doing this [project being] fascinated that he was the writer of our Revolution, the closest thing [we had then] to a professional writer. [I learned] not only that he wrote the Declaration of Independence, but that writing is what he loved to do. The very last thing that he did when he lay dying was to sit up, and his hand moved in front of him as he tried to write one more letter. [Writing] was his favorite activity in life. As a writer myself, that fascinated me. He was a marvelous writer. He thought that the law should be in simple language so you didn't need lawyers like him. When he rewrote the laws of Virginia, he put them in laymen's language, got rid of the cobwebs. The Declaration of Independence is not only ringing rhetoric, but it's beautifully done, beautifully crafted. It follows an argument. Jefferson knew exactly how to craft an argument. You can hear the beat get stronger and faster, the excitement of the writing, as it goes on. I think he was a brilliant writer, and I think [his contemporaries] thought so, too.

JOHN F. KENNEDY

35th President, 1961–1963

Overall Rank: 8

— ★ —

Total Score: 722

John F. Kennedy has ranked among the top eight presidents in all three C-SPAN surveys. Historians have also given him consistent marks in each leadership category. In 2017, his highest rank was in public persuasion (6th). His lowest ranks were in moral authority (15th) and administrative skills (15th).

Party: Democrat
b. May 29, 1917, Brookline, Massachusetts
d. November 22, 1963, Dallas, Texas
First Lady: Jacqueline Lee Bouvier Kennedy
Age entering office: 43

Historian: **Robert Dallek**

Presidential historian Robert Dallek is also a lecturer at Stanford University's Stanford in Washington program. On January 2, 2014, he discussed his book, Camelot's Court: Inside the Kennedy White House, *on Q & A.*

Presidents come to office initially on a wave of enthusiasm and excitement, even if they've only won by the narrowest of margins, which was true with John Kennedy. He won by a sliver, and yet very quickly, he gained popularity and approval from the public.

What I find so interesting with John Kennedy is that during [the fiftieth] commemoration of his assassination, he had a 90 percent approval rating. . . . The question any historian has to ask is, why is this the case? After all, he was there for only a thousand days. His was the seventh briefest presidency in American history.

The answer is that, on the one hand, people don't much like his successors: Johnson with Vietnam, Nixon with Watergate, Ford's truncated presidency, Jimmy Carter's presidency, which people see as essentially a failure. The only one is Reagan. The two Bushes don't register that powerfully. . . . Bill Clinton, yes, but he had the Monica Lewinsky affair—the only elected president in the country's history to have been impeached. It's a black mark against his record. Kennedy, of course, dying so young at the age of forty-six, having only been there for a thousand days, it's a blank slate on which you can write anything. And he was so young. The country identifies with that. They have a sense of loss to this day over his assassination, but he gives people hope. What they remember are JFK's words: "Ask not what your country can do for you, ask what you can do for your country"; or, his famous peace speech at American University in June of 1963 in which he said to "think anew" about the Soviet Union. He and Khrushchev had come out of that Cuban missile crisis—a nuclear war so much on the horizon—both frightened and terrified by that experience. As a consequence, Kennedy wanted to move towards some kind of détente with the Soviet Union, and Khrushchev was receptive to that. That's how you got the Nuclear Test Ban Treaty signed in the summer of 1963. It happened very quickly. They had been hustling over that for years, and suddenly it occurred. . . . If Kennedy had lived, we would see the talks with the Soviet Union more quickly than it came about with Richard Nixon.

I love the anecdote that when JFK was first elected, Bobby Kennedy asked [historian] Arthur Schlesinger if he would like to be an ambassador. Schlesinger said, "No, Bobby, if I do anything, I'd like to be at the White House." A few days later, Schlesinger saw the president-elect, who said, "So Arthur, I hear you're coming to the White House." Schlesinger said, "I am? But what would I be doing there?" Kennedy said, "I don't know, Arthur. I don't know what I'll be doing there, but you can bet we'll both be busy more than eight hours a day." The point is JFK understood that being president was not a set-piece affair. He evolved, and he grew in that office. That, in many ways, was his greatest strength: Kennedy grew in the office.

[Kennedy's 1957 Pulitzer Prize–winning book, *Profiles in Courage*, is an important part of his biography. It's authorship is] a complicated story. He did write part of it. There were others who contributed. My research told me Kennedy would listen to tapes of the transcripts of the chapters, and he would edit them; so, it would be unfair to say that

Special Counsel Theodore "Ted" Sorensen with President Kennedy on March 12, 1963. As chief speechwriter, Sorensen was Kennedy's wordsmith. *Credit: Robert Knudsen, White House/John Fitzgerald Kennedy Library*

Kennedy was the sole author of *Profiles in Courage*. On the other hand, it would be unfair to say that he didn't have anything to do with it or had a ghostwriter do it because he was vitally involved. So, it was a combined effort, so to speak. But I think Mrs. Kennedy was a bit jealous of Ted Sorensen maybe trying to take too much thunder and too much credit. These are complex relationships that spring up in these White Houses. Ted Sorensen was the president's wordsmith. He was a brilliant speech-writer. He and Kennedy had a kind of symbiotic relationship. I don't mean they were friends. I don't mean that they socialized, because they didn't have that kind of relationship. But there was a kind of intellectual exchange between them and a kind of intuitive understanding of where this president wanted to go in his administration and what he wanted to say. Sorensen had the gift of being able to translate that into a language that is memorable. After all, some of Kennedy's speeches are going to last, going to be remembered.

[My research and writing also details JFK's serious health issues. John Kennedy had health problems, including Addison's disease, a possible fatal malfunctioning of the adrenal gland. He had chronic back pain that had led to major unsuccessful surgeries, spastic colitis that triggered occasional bouts of diarrhea, prostatitis, urethritis, and allergies that added greatly to the normal strains of his nationwide campaign in 1960.]

[After Kennedy died,] there's no question that Ted Sorensen was the keeper of the flame. . . . There was a three-man committee that controlled JFK's medical records, and [by 2002] two of the members signed off [on opening them up]; Sorensen was reluctant to do it. I went to see him in New York, met with him in his residence, and persuaded him to let me have access to the records. He didn't know what was in there, and when the records came out, the *New York Times* ran a front-page story about my findings and *Atlantic* magazine pub-lished an article about my book and on Kennedy's medical history. Sorensen was angry. When he'd see me, which was a few times after that, he'd say, "There was no cover up." But, of course, there was. They were hiding from the public the extent of Kennedy's medical history and difficulties. If people knew how many health problems Kennedy had, I don't think he even would have been elected in 1960—however unfair that may be, because he comported himself brilliantly during the presidency. I set his medical records down alongside the timeline of the Cuban missile crisis with the [White House] tapes we had. There were no concessions to his medical difficulties during that crisis. Now, [we have subsequently learned] it was medications that helped him get through it without stumbles.

[After these stories came out, Ted Kennedy and Arthur Schlesinger concluded] that my description of Kennedy's health problems enhanced, rather than undermined, his public standing, his reputation in history. How he managed to rise above his health difficulties and be an effective president was a very impressive achievement, and so they would take it with that. But, even Ted Kennedy did not know the full extent of his brother's health problems, and it is the measure of how much they hid it—Joe Kennedy, Bobby Kennedy, the president himself, and Jackie—they were the ones who knew, but it was largely hidden from the world.

[In the years after JFK's death, the public also learned about John Kennedy's womanizing while he was in office, which his White House press corps did not cover.] . . . I interviewed a number of journalists for my [2003 Kennedy] biography and asked them, "Did you know that Kennedy was womanizing?" They said, "Yes, we always suspected." "Why didn't you write about it?" "We didn't do it in 1960s; you didn't intrude on the president's private life in that way." And so, [Kennedy's womanizing] was hidden from the public.

When I first published my book and the story came out about [Mimi Beardsley, a nineteen-year-old intern with whom Kennedy had an ongoing affair . . .], I heard on the grapevine that a publisher offered her a million dollars to write her own book, a memoir. It wasn't until about eight years later that she finally did it. I never asked her why . . . she did it. Maybe she needed the money. I suspect [the tabloids] would have still been willing to pay her because it really was very much a tell-all book, and some of the details she reveals are somewhat shocking.

There are two ways you can look at this. On the one hand, it didn't have an impact on his conduct in the presidency, as far as I can tell. Was he going to be found out, was he going to be impeached? Not in 1962, '63. The . . . mainstream press, did not write about the president's private life in that way. But it says something about the man's character, about his personality, about the fact that there was some kind of deep-felt neediness that this man had, that he had to seduce this nineteen-year-old young woman. And it was not just [seducing her], but her description of some of the things that went on, that he encouraged her to give oral sex to Dave Powers, Kennedy's principal aide, and to his brother Ted. She resisted when JFK suggested that she perform oral sex on Ted Kennedy. But with Dave Powers, she did it, and she said that Kennedy watched. He later apologized to them. But, what word can you apply to this? Perverse.

The journalists I talked to, including [the longtime conservative columnist] Bob Novak, said they suspected. They had clues. They thought there were lots of women coming and going from the White House. In my first biography, a journalist told me the story that when Kennedy was on the campaign trail in 1960, he was in northern California, and there were [a] bunch of pompom girls from the local college. Kennedy points to one of them via his aide. He went up to this young woman and said to her, "The senator would like to see you in his hotel room." She went up there. The story the journalist told me . . . is that Kennedy looked at his watch and said to this young woman, "We have 15 minutes." What happened after that, the journalist didn't say. But the point is, sure, the reporters knew; at least they suspected [what was going on].

. . . In this day and age, it seems to me that it would be madness for a president to try and do this [in the White House] because it's a different world from what it was in the 1960s. It would be brought forward; it would be all over the press, all over the television, and probably destroy the man's presidency. But it was a different time in the 1960s. I'm not justifying it. It was terribly excessive, what he did with Mimi Beardsley. . . . On the other hand, I'm not a Puritan, and I'm not saying that, "My god, he should have just been loyal to Jackie." That was between them. Jackie knew about this; she knew he was a philanderer. There was an anecdote that the first couple was up in Canada, and they were in the receiving line standing next to a White House military aide. And [the first lady] said to him in French, this man understood French, "It's not enough that I come to Canada and stand in line?" One of these [young women] was in line to shake her hand, and she was furious at this situation. And who can blame her?

Kennedy was badly burned by the Bay of Pigs experience [in April 1961]. He had listened to the experts—the CIA, Joint Chiefs of Staff [and the operation failed]. Soon after, he went to see President [Charles] de Gaulle in France. He did that trip in May–June of '61. De Gaulle said to him, "You should surround yourself with the smartest possible people, listen to them, hear what they have to say. But at the end of the day, you have to make up your own mind." And Kennedy also remembered what Harry Truman had said, "The buck stops here." After the Bay of Pigs, he was absolutely determined to make up his own mind, hear what these experts had to say, weigh what they were telling him. But at the end of the day, he was going to make the judgment, and he was the responsible party. That was abundantly clear when you read the transcripts of all those tapes during the Cuban missile crisis [in October 1962]. He was his own man. He was the one who was making up his own mind. He held the Joint Chiefs [Chairman] Maxwell Taylor at an arm's length; the chiefs wanted to bomb, invade, and Kennedy didn't want to do it.

John F. Kennedy was very critical of the Joint Chiefs. Maxwell Taylor began with a kind of cachet because he was Kennedy's guy, and Kennedy made him the chairman of the Joint Chiefs. But over time . . . Taylor so much reflected what the [other] service chiefs were saying during the Cuban missile crisis and subsequently about Cuba . . . that Kennedy became skeptical of him. I don't know that Taylor would have lasted that much longer into a second term. There's an anecdote that after the Cuban missile crisis was ending, Kennedy held the Joint Chiefs at arm's length. He brings them in, and they say to him, "Mr. President, you've been had. Khrushchev is hiding missiles in caves." And, they leaked this [to the press]. . . . Khrushchev wrote Kennedy a note saying, "I don't live in the caveman age, and that means I'm no caveman." But the Joint Chiefs still talked about the need to plan bombing and an invasion [of Cuba]. Kennedy said, "You can go ahead and make plans because you never know what's going to happen." And, of course, they make all sorts of contingency plans. Part of that plan was to drop a nuclear weapon on Cuba; Kennedy thought this was crazy.

The chiefs told him that all the collateral damage [of dropping a nuclear bomb on Cuba], in essence, could be contained. What that would have done to the south coast of Florida, let alone to Cuba—which would've turned into a pile of rubble. And so, Kennedy thought they were kind of mad. But, giving them their due, one has to recall that the Joint Chiefs came out of World War II, and they remembered fighting Hitler, Mussolini, and the Japanese military, who fought to the bitter end. Their attitude was "bomb them back to the Stone Age," which is what they did in Germany and Japan, with the fire bombings of Tokyo, the Hiroshima and Nagasaki atomic bombings. So, this was their atti-tude. Thomas Power, head of the air force, had said, "What are all these concerns about nuclear weapons? If at the end of that war with the Soviet Union there are three Americans left and two Soviets, we've won." So, [Kennedy was dealing with] this kind of [attitude among the chiefs].

I knew [Kennedy's defense secretary Robert] McNamara a little bit. I interviewed him a couple of times. The first time I interviewed him [was prior to 1988, and] I began by asking about Vietnam. . . . Within fifteen minutes, all he could talk about was Vietnam; he was profoundly conflicted. During the Kennedy presidency, he was the biggest advocate of exercising muscle in Vietnam, asserting the authority of power. With journalists like David Halberstam who raised questions with him, he was dismissive, even contemptuous. So sure, McNamara eventually came around to the proposition that this was a military no-win situation in Vietnam, but he had been so arrogant about leading us into that war. I think that's what agitated him so much. . . . He eventually got out of the Johnson administration because Johnson saw him having almost a nervous collapse over his struggle over Vietnam. They sent him off to be president of the World Bank. McNamara was a man who was profoundly conflicted, but only over time. He was one of the architects of expansion of a larger war in Vietnam.

The biggest [advocate for Vietnam acceleration on Kennedy's team] was Walt Rostow. Rostow became Lyndon Johnson's national security adviser. Rostow, during the Kennedy presidency, was already talking about bombing Hanoi and Haiphong and putting ground troops there; and Rostow never gave up on that war. I knew Rostow, as well; talked to him, interviewed him, . . . and his attitude was, "We saved the other Southeast Asian countries. We gave them time to develop." That was his rationale [for prosecuting the Vietnam War].

Dean Rusk was Kennedy's secretary of state. Rusk [made the decision to] replace [JFK's undersecretary of state] Chester Bowles, who Kennedy didn't like having around and was trying very hard to get rid of. Finally, Rusk had to send Bowles on a mission around the world. . . . He replaced him with George Ball, who was much more of a team player. On the other hand, behind the scenes, Ball was candid with Kennedy about Vietnam, in particular. He told him at one point, "Mr. President, if you put two or three hundred thousand ground troops into those jungles of Vietnam, you'll never hear from them again." Kennedy said to George Ball, "You're crazy as hell," meaning, I believe, that, "I'm never going to do that." We will never know exactly what Kennedy would have done about Vietnam. . . . I don't think Kennedy ever would have done what Lyndon Johnson did in Vietnam; I don't think he ever would have put in 545,000 troops.

Dean Rusk's personality was such that it was very deferential to the president on making foreign policy. But I think there's a mixed assessment [of Rusk's effectiveness] in the sense that this is what Kennedy wanted. He didn't want a secretary of state who was going to vie with him and compete on the making of foreign policy. . . . The Kennedy administration was a foreign policy administration. Kennedy was very much a foreign policy president, and I don't think JFK wanted a secretary of state who was going to be aggressive about challenging what he wanted to do in the conduct of it. What Kennedy complained about was that Rusk didn't have ideas; he was not someone who came forward with suggestions that Kennedy might have used, that he had little imagination in dealing with the foreign policy. And that was a legitimate complaint.

. . . I think Kennedy felt a certain amount of guilt over the fact that [South Vietnamese president Ngo Dinh] Diem was assassinated [in a CIA-backed coup in November 1963] because he said privately, "Listen, whatever his failings, he had led his country for quite a few years and done constructive things and was a bulwark against the communist takeover." Kennedy was reflecting on his own recriminations about having allowed such a coup to take place. He was also [expressing] the concern that the United States was now going to have to take greater responsibility for Vietnam than it had taken in the past. Kennedy was keen to get out of Vietnam. He had a conversation with [National Security Administration senior aide] Mike Forrestal the day before he went to Dallas, Texas, and said he wanted when he returned a full-scale review about Vietnam, including the possibility of getting out. . . . I don't know what he would have done. I don't think he himself knew what he would have done.

. . . [As president,] Kennedy was not that interested, initially, in domestic affairs. He was dragged, so to speak, kicking and screaming into dealing with civil rights. When he dealt with it, it was quite courageous of him to put that Civil Rights Bill before the Congress in 1963. It could have jeopardized his re-election, since he knew he was going to be alienating Southern states and Southern voters, and they had put him across [the finish line in] 1960. He didn't know he was going to run against Barry Goldwater; he thought he might well be running against him, but he didn't know for sure. And so, it was courageous of him to do that. He felt that the time had come [to advance civil rights. So, I contend that] Kennedy grew, he evolved in that office, but he was very much a foreign policy president.

RONALD REAGAN

40th President, 1981–1989

Overall Rank: 9

— ★ —

Total Score: 691

Historians have moved Ronald Reagan up one position in each of C-SPAN's last two surveys, placing him in the top ten for the first time in 2009. His scores have increased most dramatically in crisis leadership (8th in 2017) and economic management (16th). Reagan ranks 33rd in administrative skills—one of the lowest category rankings of any president in the top ten.

Party: Republican
b. February 6, 1911, Tampico, Illinois
d. June 5, 2004, Los Angeles, California
First Lady: Nancy Davis Reagan
Age entering office: 69

Historian: **Lou Cannon**

Biographer and journalist Lou Cannon covered Reagan for the San Jose Mercury News *and was the senior White House correspondent for the* Washington Post *during Reagan's administration. He was interviewed for* Booknotes *on April 18, 1991, for a two-part series on one of his five Reagan biographies,* President Reagan: The Role of a Lifetime.

[I first met Ronald Reagan in 1965.] . . . He was going around the state giving little speeches. The speeches were the brainchild of his management team of Stu Spencer and Bill Roberts. Reagan, at that time, was planning on running for governor, and the Democrats thought he would be such a weak opponent that they wanted to get him nominated. Reagan was giving these speeches to show that he was not just an actor reciting his lines. Typically, he would give a very short speech saying what his views were—a lot of generalities and not much of anything really— but then he would answer questions. The purpose of these forums was to show that he, in fact, could answer questions, that he wasn't just a person who could not function without a script.

I never set out to write [multiple] books about him, but I found that there was more to Ronald Reagan than the surface, that beneath the surface you had a rather complicated character and a guy who wasn't quite what either his fans or his critics thought. He was a little sharper than his critics thought. He knew more; he saw further. But he had great gaps in his knowledge and great lapses that his fans didn't see. My effort in these books, and particularly this book, is to try to get beyond this and get some kind of a coherent whole.

. . . On some level, Ronald Reagan was much brighter than [critics] like to say he was, that he knew what he did. He understood the power of storytelling. I quote an authority on intelligence in the book as saying that Ronald Reagan made sense of the world narratively. He was not a good analyst. He didn't have a high intelligence in the way scientists and lawyers do—analytical, logical intelligence—but he had a great understanding of people and of the power of storytelling. Stories move us. Ronald Reagan knew that. He had the capacity to do that, and on some level, at least some of the time, he knew what it was he did. He got stories from everywhere. He got them from newspaper clippings. He had been on the road for *General Electric Theater* in the '50s. Ronald Reagan was afraid to fly, so he took the train. He would clip out the newspapers in the little towns across America. In those days, there was a lot more individualism among the American press than there is today. We were just at the beginning of television, and there were a lot of distinctive stories that happened in places that didn't get repeated on every wire service or in every paper in the world. He got the stories from people that he talked to. He had a terrific memory for anecdote and story. He remembered stories from his youth and refashioned them. He had been a sportscaster, and his specialty as a sports announcer was in recreating baseball games, which means describing a game that he never saw from information that had come over the telegraph. So, he invented stories, he retold stories, he recast stories, he remembered stories, and he read stories.

[I chose] *The Role of a Lifetime* as the subtitle of my book because Ronald Reagan valued acting. . . . Usually, the jibe that Reagan was only . . . a B-movie actor, it was one of these things that was said to run him down; that, as if somehow being an actor he was not worthy of being a politician, or certainly of being a president. Reagan was portrayed in his very

Ronald Reagan is seen here in a 1940s Hollywood studio publicity photo. Starting in 1937, Reagan appeared in fifty-two films and often credited his acting skills for his success in politics. *Courtesy Ronald Reagan Presidential Library*

first campaign as a guy who couldn't hold his own with a chimpanzee in [the movie] *Bedtime for Bonzo*. The point that I was trying to make, both with the title and in the book, is that Ronald Reagan is a person who values the performance and who thinks of himself as a performer. After he was elected governor, he was asked what kind of a governor he would make. He said, "I don't know. I've never played a governor." When he left the White House, he was asked about how acting had helped him be president, and he said, "I don't understand how anybody could do this job without having been an actor." So, Ronald Reagan didn't run away from the fact that he was an actor. He was proud of it.

It somewhat distorted his presidency in the sense that what he did best and valued most was the performance aspect of the presidency—what Theodore Roosevelt had referred to as the "bully pulpit" part of the presidency. I happen to think that is an important part of the presidency. Reagan believed that his immediate predecessors, President [Jimmy] Carter and President [Gerald] Ford, had not been particularly skilled in that aspect of the presidency. I agree with that, too, but I don't agree with the idea that the performance aspect of the presidency is so dominant that it should drive out other parts of the presidency the way that it did during many of the Reagan years.

The canard that Reagan was "only" an actor or "merely" an actor, I don't see, by the way. The acting profession seems to me as respectable as the professions from which most conventional politicians are drawn—the law, journalism, you name it. But the sense in which Reagan is run down as an actor is that he is speaking somebody else's lines, that somebody else prepared the script. [That is not so.] It was a script of his own devising. He came to the presidency wanting to do essentially three things: cut taxes, raise the military budget spending—which he thought had gone way down since the Vietnam years—and balance the budget. He accomplished the first two, and he didn't accomplish the third because of the first two, in my view. No economist has yet explained to me how you can cut taxes and significantly boost military spending and not come out with a huge deficit, which is what he did.

I think America was in Reagan. He had a view of this country's goodness and of this country's mission and an idea that America stood for something very special, particularly in its commitment to freedom. He always believed that, . . . and he expressed it very well.

[The source of Reagan's inspiration was less the Constitution than the movies.] It doesn't mean that he valued Hollywood more than he valued the Constitution of the United States. It means that the stories that he told and the way he viewed America was very much based in Hollywood, where he had spent, referencing the title of a great film, the best years of his life. He was grounded in movie stories, movie lore. There are many examples in my book where he tells stories which he thinks happened, in fact, which happened in a movie—the famous story about the B-17 pilot who rides the plane down with his wounded gunner, various other stories. . . . I don't think there is anything particularly sinister in this. Hollywood, when Reagan was a part of it, was a reflection of American values. It was the leading exponent of American mass culture. People went to the movies in the 1930s and the 1940s. Reagan was cast as a handsome, Midwestern hero playing the heartwarming role, to paraphrase [historian] Garry Wills, of himself. I don't think it is surprising, since he was in Hollywood from the time he was twenty-six years old to the time he was in his mid-fifties, that he would draw his stories from where he lived and from the craft that he practiced.

[Reagan famously carried his speaking notes on index cards.] I suspect it was more of a function of his eyesight. From the time of his childhood, he had a little problem with sight. He was nearsighted. . . . He also had a great developed shorthand where he could compress almost the whole of a speech, this basic speech he had that was often just called, "The Speech." He would write it out. I've looked at those cards in the Hoover Archives. On some of his early, early cards, you would see that he would get almost a whole speech on a card. I don't think the cards made people mad [per se]; I think what upset people is [him using the cards] after they got to know him. Congressmen are good examples. Congressmen who had known him for several years, . . . who had maybe been at the White House a dozen times, or if they were in the leadership, many more times—and here the president is reading to them from cards. That annoyed them because they thought he should be talking to them without notes. They also felt that he was too much a captive of those cards. They were a device for him. They were a comfort mechanism for him. They were like a cane is for some people or some prop that somebody uses that they feel comfortable with. They were security for President Reagan. I think he overused them, particularly in the last years of his presidency.

[Asked to name some of the defining moments of the Reagan presidency, I'd say] one of them was clearly the assassination attempt. This occurs on March 30[, 1981]. He is sixty-nine days into his presidency, and all at once he's wounded. America sees this rather gallant man quipping, telling stories, using one-liners that would have seemed artificial in many circumstances, except this is a person who could have died from this wound. We found out later that the bullet just missed his aorta. Doctors have told me that many people never really recover fully from gunshot wounds, and here this man is well advanced in life. At this point he's just had his seventieth birthday, and he bounces back in a hurry. He became a mythic figure in America when he was quipping to the doctors, "I hope you're all Republicans," and those kinds of lines. That was a defining moment in his presidency.

Another moment that was very important to him was when Congress finally got his tax and budget bills passed in that first year of his presidency. Dick Wirthlin, who was his pollster, showed that what people particularly liked about Reagan was that he was getting bills through Congress. There had been a long period where Congress and the presidency had been stalemated. Most Americans are not partisans. They like to see their government work. And here, paradoxically, under a person who denounced government, the government seemed to be working.

There are a lot of other moments in the Reagan presidency that are worth something. I'll just give you two or three: one is him standing in Berlin in front of [the Berlin] wall and saying, "Mr. Gorbachev, tear down this wall," which is a speech that still gives me goosebumps when I hear it. Another was Ronald Reagan in Red Square, where it seemed to me the mere fact of him being in Red Square—of him and Mikhail Gorbachev walking together, even though they both had their own propaganda impulses for this meeting—was a signal to the world: "Hey, this Cold War is really over."

Another, and a darker one, was Ronald Reagan in that speech he gave in November of '86, soon after the midterm elections, where he is explaining what happened—or thinks he is—in the Iran-Contra Affair, and he is so unbelievable. He's telling stories that turn out to be totally untrue, and you see a different kind of Ronald Reagan. People always believed Reagan. He's telling these stories, and he's essentially unbelievable, as every poll afterward said. People who had always trusted Reagan said, "Hey, this guy's lying to me." That was a new experience for Ronald Reagan—being criticized. [During his presidency,] he took many positions that a majority of Americans didn't agree with. The [support for the Nicaraguan rebel] Contras, for one. There was never a poll that showed a majority of Americans supported the Contras. That's fine. You go through life, and you are disagreed with. But people believed Reagan [and this event changed that impression]. . . . I remember watching that speech on television and saying, "I've never seen him look that bad."

As [then House Speaker] Tip O'Neill said on another day when the space shuttle Challenger had gone down—Tip had had a big quarrel with him that morning in front of a lot of other congressmen because Reagan had started in about how some of the unemployed were people who didn't want to work. Tip got angry and said, "You've been telling that story for years. I'm talking about people who were thrown out of work in the steel mills. They are not welfare cheats." Then, later in the day, you had the Challenger disaster, and Reagan gave that [famous televised] speech. Tip O'Neill wrote that he'd seen the best and worst of Ronald Reagan in one day. I think that was true. . . . You often did see Ronald Reagan's best and worst close together, and Ronald Reagan's gifts often rescued Reagan from himself.

Reagan kept himself to himself. On one level, he was always the most mannerly and courteous of men. He treated people well—the people who worked for him, the secretaries, the people who guarded him. He was never imperious. He never threw his weight around. He was never demanding. But he also didn't give of himself. He kept apart. Different people who've worked for him have described that it was like he'd [worked with] so many different directors, been in different casts, been in so many movies that it was like he didn't form lasting attachments.

[If you worked for Ronald Reagan] . . . unless you had a lot of self-security on your own, unless you had a lot of confidence in yourself and didn't need the approval of the sun king, you became disenchanted after a while. What you see running through the [Reagan-era] kiss-and-tell books is a disenchantment with Reagan, partly because the people involved never really felt that he took them to him. Somebody asked me just the other day, did I like Reagan? I said, "Yes, I liked him well enough." This person knew Reagan very well and said, "I don't dislike him, but to like somebody, he has to be a person who extends to you some kind of friendship." And Reagan didn't do that. He was the friend of the American people. He had a bond with the people. But up close, if you formed an attachment to Reagan, it was often one way.

As far as the [Reagan] kids are concerned, I quote all of the children in this book, either from things they've written or from interviews I've done, all of whom say in their own different ways that they don't really, really quite know their father. There's a particularly poignant story from Michael Reagan's book about how Reagan arrives at his prep school graduation in Arizona and introduces himself and says, "I'm Ronald Reagan." And he says, "I'm your son, Michael." Now, Michael was wearing a [gown and] mortarboard, but still.

[Two of his top cabinet members, Secretary of State George Shultz and Defense Secretary Cap Weinberger had an ongoing feud, which was interesting to write about] because these were two people of genuine accomplishment. They both had Reagan's ear, and they were both distrusted by different groups of people within the Reagan administration. Reagan once quipped at a Gridiron Dinner that the trouble with his administration is that "sometimes the right hand doesn't know what the far-right hand is doing." There was a lot of truth to that jest. There were the people who considered themselves the militant guardians of the conservative flame, who thought that people like George Shultz and [Chief of Staff] Jim Baker, who would by any standard of normal political measurement be considered quite conservative, were dangerously moderate or liberal. The moderates, the pragmatists as they were often called during the Reagan administration, many of them thought that the right wingers, as they called them, were raving, dangerous people. In this context you had Weinberger and Shultz who didn't like each other. Their feud went back, way back, . . . [but] the significance of their feud within the Reagan administration went way beyond their personalities. They were often on opposite sides of the fence, and they were successful in blocking the advocacies of others. Reagan's great fault as a president—which goes back to his childhood of wanting harmony in this situation where he had a home with an alcoholic father—Reagan craved harmony. He didn't like disharmony, . . . and the conflict between Shultz and Weinberger produced frequently a paralysis within the Reagan administration.

[Deputy Chief of Staff Michael] Deaver and Baker were often worried that Reagan would say something [off script]. They'd seen a lot of examples where he talked off his script, or he just would say what came into his head and get into trouble for it. The one that comes to mind during the campaign of 1980 was that he went to some religious conference, and a religious broadcaster asked him about creationism. Reagan said, "Well, maybe they could teach both. They could teach evolution and creation." I raise it only because Reagan just was offhandedly saying what occurred to him, and it created a huge furor that Reagan didn't believe in evolution. I think more was made of the reply than was warranted. But you never knew what was going to pop out of Reagan. What Baker and Deaver, particularly, were trying to do was to keep the focus on the economic program. . . . The people who were managing in the Reagan White House tried very much to get a particular theme and stay with it. They knew that if they just turned Reagan loose that he would talk about anything that came up, and pretty soon the White House would be enmeshed in some extraneous or ancillary controversy that had nothing to do with what they were trying to emphasize, and often, with what Reagan was trying to emphasize. It's odd because in some ways, the conservatives tended to overrate his abilities, and the people who were the more pragmatic faction tended to underrate his ability. But they all really, at some level, agreed that you just couldn't turn Ronald Reagan loose.

There were a lot of controversies between these three people [Baker, Deaver, and Attorney General Ed Meese] and among other people in the Reagan White House that didn't really withstand close analysis. By 1983, they were in such conflict that oftentimes something that Meese wanted to do, the Baker faction opposed just because it was Meese advocating it, and vice versa. Oftentimes the conflict was not based upon a different perception of Ronald Reagan as it was on a power struggle in the White House that went on. Reagan was oblivious to it. Reagan never paid any attention to these conflicts in his staff, and that allowed them to rage. . . . Reagan never took any action against this. Reagan would complain about leaks, but the leakers were all around him. And, he never banged heads.

Ronald Reagan could not conceive of someone being duplicitous. The idea that somebody would sit there and tell you something that he didn't believe in order to advance himself with Ronald Reagan, in order to get a job or promotion within the White House, in order to get somebody else demoted or fired or hurt—since Ronald Reagan wouldn't do these things, he didn't see that other people would do these things. Ronald Reagan was gullible, frequently, in dealing with people. Nancy Reagan observed this about him. She's not unique in observing it about him, but she was the closest to him of anybody on earth, so she saw it the most, and she felt it the most keenly. She felt that he needed protection from people who pretended to share his agenda or his objectives and, in fact, did him harm.

Nancy Reagan was the constant protector of her husband. She had a lot to do with who was chosen and who wasn't chosen for the White House staff. She was a large pain in the knee to a lot of the people on the staff. But Nancy Reagan often did not get her way on policy, or you wouldn't have had the Star Wars [missile intercept program]. You probably wouldn't have had the commitment to the Contras [in Nicaragua]. . . . Nancy Reagan thought that Ronald Reagan ought to get rid of Caspar Weinberger, yet Caspar Weinberger served longer as secretary of defense than all but one in the history of the country. She was very influential on the president's schedule. She was very influential in the immediate confines of the White House staff. But Ronald Reagan had a stubborn streak in him, and on policy he usually followed what he thought was right, which often was not what Nancy Reagan would have had him do.

Landon Parvin was one of my favorite people in the Reagan White House and an underrated guy. . . . He had been Nancy Reagan's speechwriter, and he did a lot of the Reagans' humor speeches. He did a lot of the Gridiron speeches, and he contributed to speeches by both Reagans. He wrote the AIDS policy speech and got really torn apart on that speech; I think he would have gone further—or, Nancy Reagan would have gone further—than Reagan was willing to go. Landon Parvin made a singular contribution during the long and difficult period of trying to bring Reagan out of the Iran-Contra morass. Parvin was the principal speechwriter on the 1987 speech where Reagan finally owned up to his responsibility, where he says, "My heart and mind tell me one thing, and the facts tell me another." This was as close as Reagan ever got publicly to admitting that he had, in fact, traded arms for hostages. . . . Landon once said that what Ronald Reagan was really saying was, "I didn't do it, and I'll never do it again."

I reprinted a memo from [former president Richard] Nixon [in my book]. . . . It shows that Ronald Reagan did, in fact, follow Nixon's advice on a number of things. Nixon would call Reagan from time to time. He called him in times of crisis. He called him after the Iran-Contra [scandal broke]. Reagan consulted with Nixon before he went to Moscow. Most of the Republicans who were part of the Republican establishment in Washington and who were part of Reagan's team had been members of the Nixon administration. Jim Baker had been, George Shultz, Caspar Weinberger. . . . Although Reagan marched to a different drummer, he certainly did pay a lot of attention and have a lot of respect for Richard Nixon's advice. We didn't really know about this during the Reagan years because at the outset of the Reagan administration, . . . we were quite close to Watergate. We were only six years away from the resignation, and the White House press office and others in the administration did their best to conceal Nixon's influence with Reagan. They didn't want it known. They never advertised it. But it was always there.

[Of his Supreme Court nominations, President Reagan] doesn't even mention [Judge Douglas] Ginsburg or Anthony Kennedy in his memoirs. For Robert Bork, he references that things were going bad. He didn't have anything to do with the selection of any of those people. Most of them were chosen at the Justice Department. But what he did have something to do with, curiously enough, was the selection of Sandra Day O'Connor, the first woman in the Supreme Court. Ronald Reagan had made a promise during the 1980 campaign that one of his first nominees to the court would be a woman. He chose to interpret that promise not as if he had said "one of the first," but as if he had said "the first." Of course, [Attorneys General William French] Smith and Meese and their people came up with the list of names, as they would for any president. You don't expect the president to be carting those names around in his head. But Reagan never interviewed anybody else for the O'Connor seat in the court other than Sandra O'Connor. He liked her, and he wanted to name a woman, and once he'd interviewed her, that was it.

Ronald Reagan was not power mad. He also said that he knew when it was time to leave the stage, and he was able to walk away from the White House in 1989. I don't think that [leaving] drove him crazy or that it even particularly bothered him. He felt, as he says at one point, cooped up, like he was in a cage in the White House, and all the more so after the assassination attempt. Obviously, there was a high degree of security. One of the qualities about Ronald Reagan that was, on the whole, a positive quality about him was that he became president and wanted to accomplish certain things. He didn't become president just to be the most powerful man in the world. He knew himself enough that he was able to walk away from it when the time was over and be happy with himself.

[Ronald Reagan's career as an actor] had prepared him for the presidency, but I do conclude that it hadn't prepared him fully and sufficiently. It had prepared him to be a performer. It had prepared him to be able to take center stage, dominate it, communicate to the American people, to know what his role was. But what it had not done is it had not equipped him analytically to be president. . . . [As for lessons for today from the Reagan presidency:] the world that Ronald Reagan comes from doesn't exist. Hollywood has changed. There are no re-creations of baseball games anymore. There's no Dixon, Illinois, as it was. Television has homogenized America. The world that Ronald Reagan came through, and came from, doesn't really exist anymore. All of Ronald Reagan's adversaries, as well as Ronald Reagan's friends, surely must know that he was one of a kind.

LYNDON B. JOHNSON

36th President, 1963–1969

Historian: **Robert A. Caro**

Pulitzer Prize–winning historian Robert Caro discussed his book, The Passage of Power: The Years of Lyndon Johnson, Vol. IV, *his fourth book in a series on LBJ that totals over three thousand pages. Caro appeared in a two-part interview for C-SPAN's* Q & A *on April 24, 2012.*

All his life, the one quality about Lyndon Johnson, above all, is his decisiveness, his willingness to act, to make decisions, and to try as hard as he could for everything. Lyndon Johnson has only one goal in his life—to be president. In 1958, he seems perfectly positioned to become president. He's been Senate majority leader. He has all the senators in his camp. He has passed the first civil rights act in history to blunt some of the Northern antagonism, too. In 1958, he calls seven or eight of his top lieutenants to his ranch. He says, "I am destined to be president. I was meant to be president. You all know that. And I'm going to be president." And then, they're waiting for the campaign to begin, and, suddenly, he doesn't run. He doesn't give any orders. He doesn't want to go and speak anywhere. He's terribly indecisive and he throws away his chance at this 1960 nomination.

People who knew him best [had a theory], like John Connally—who later became secretary of the Treasury, secretary of the navy, this great politician, [who] once had me down to his ranch for three days. Those interviews were fascinating because he was closer to Lyndon Johnson during his early years than anyone else. . . . I asked him [why Johnson didn't campaign in the primaries in '60], and he said, "The one thing about Lyndon Johnson. He was afraid to fail."

Why was he afraid to fail? His brother Sam Houston Johnson said to me, "The one thing that was most important to Lyndon was not to be like daddy." His father had been a politician for a while, a successful politician, and had failed, lost the ranch, and the family was plunged into not only bankruptcy, but into being the laughing stock of their town. Johnson, when he was Senate majority leader, had Bobby Baker as the man who counted [senators' likely] votes for him, and Baker says, "I learned never to let him fail on a [Senate] vote. Never." All the people who knew him best say that Lyndon was afraid to fail, to be like his father, and he was afraid that if he ran for the presidency he would fail. That's really why he didn't run in 1960, why he didn't run hard.

There's no question about it that Robert Kennedy tried desperately to get Lyndon Johnson to withdraw, or not to accept, the offer of the vice presidency [on his brother's ticket in 1960]. John Kennedy had won [the Democratic nomination] the night before with 806 votes on the ballot. The next morning at 8:00—this is in the Biltmore Hotel in Los Angeles—the two suites of the two candidates are in a back corner of the hotel. Johnson is on the seventh floor in 7334. Kennedy is two floors up at 9334. In the morning, either Jack Kennedy or Robert comes down the back stairs, because they don't want the reporters to see them, and has a conversation with Lyndon Johnson. Whenever there are only two people in a room, you really can't say, as a historian, what happened because one gives one version and one gives the other. But we know what happened after the meeting. Johnson calls in his three closest advisers: John Connally, Bobby Baker, and James H. Rowe Jr., who had been Roosevelt's adviser and Truman's adviser. And he says, "Jack Kennedy was just down here, and he offered me the vice presidency." Kennedy goes back upstairs where there's a group of Northern bosses who can count votes. They know that Kennedy has to have Texas and some Southern states. Dave Lawrence, for one, was there and says Kennedy walks into the room and says, "Johnson hasn't said he'll accept it, but it looks like he's going to." Lawrence, . . . a tough old Irish politician, reaches out his hands to Jack Kennedy, this young great, charismatic, handsome Irish politician, and they shake hands because Lawrence knows [Johnson] is the key to the election. What happens the rest of that day, no one can know. Everybody has different versions, but we do know that Bobby Kennedy came down those back stairs at least three times, and each time tried to get Lyndon Johnson to withdraw from the ticket.

The first time that Bobby Kennedy comes down, he meets with John Connally and Sam Rayburn. . . . Bobby is very upset. Rayburn says in a statement, "His hair was hanging down all over his face. He says we're going to have a floor fight. Labor and the liberals won't stand for Lyndon Johnson. They're going to put up their own candidate [for vice president], so we'd like him to consider, instead, being the chairman of the Democratic National Committee." Rayburn replies with a single-word epithet, and Robert Kennedy leaves. . . .

. . . At each of these three meetings, Robert wants to meet directly with Lyndon Johnson. Lady Bird is saying, "I don't think they ought to meet together," and Rayburn also knows they shouldn't meet together; there's simply too much antagonism there. The second time that Bobby Kennedy comes down, Connally says, "I've got to get Rayburn." Johnson said . . . that he had made [Connally] his campaign manager because he was the only man tough enough to handle Bobby Kennedy. But Connally knows that as tough as he is, . . . there's someone a lot tougher, and it's Sam Rayburn. Sam Rayburn is old. We know now he has cancer at the time. He's blind. But he's Sam Rayburn, this massive, unsmiling, grim figure who has ruled the House of Representatives for a quarter of a century. [He and Johnson were] almost a father-son thing. Rayburn loved Lyndon Johnson like a son; he would spend most Sundays in Washington at Johnson's home. He loved the two Johnson girls, and all during Johnson's Senate career, Rayburn is his rock. Rayburn is his support. Rayburn is the guy nobody can go around. And he's for Lyndon Johnson. Connally says to Horace Busby, Johnson's speechwriter, "Go in there and talk to Bobby Kennedy. Keep him occupied. I've got to find Sam Rayburn."

Connally comes back with Sam Rayburn, and Bobby Kennedy says that he wants Lyndon Johnson to withdraw from the ticket. . . . This old, blind man, so tough, says, "Are you authorized to speak for your brother?" Bobby Kennedy says, "No." Rayburn says, "Then come back and speak to the speaker of the House of Representatives when you are." Bobby Kennedy leaves, goes back upstairs, and there is yet a third time he tries to come down to get Johnson to withdraw from the ticket, and this time he meets with Johnson alone.

No one can really know [whether Jack Kennedy sent his brother down to entice Johnson off the ticket or if Robert was freelancing]. Robert Kennedy in his oral history says, . . . "Of course not. I was so close to my brother. What do you think I did? Go down and secretly try to get his vice president off the ticket?" However, one of the things we know is that all that day, Jack Kennedy did everything he could to get Lyndon Johnson to accept the nomination. At one point Jack Kennedy goes down the same back stairs to see Sam Rayburn alone. . . . Rayburn, in his description of this, says to Jack Kennedy, "I ask you two things. Will you keep Lyndon Johnson occupied and happy as vice president?" And something else: "And will you make him a real part of your administration?" Kennedy says, "I can tell you that [I will]." Rayburn says, "Then Johnson will go on. I agree that Johnson can go on the ticket." Johnson will not go on the ticket if Rayburn doesn't approve.

. . . People are saying to Johnson, "Don't take the vice presidency. Right now, you are a powerful majority leader. Don't take the vice presidency. You won't have any power." Johnson says, "Power is where power goes." Meaning, I can make power in any situation. Nothing in Johnson's life previously makes that seem like he's boasting because that's exactly what he had done all his life. He was a junior congressman; he got himself a position of real power. He took the job as the whip in the Senate. He took a nothing job, . . . a job no one wanted, and he made it have real power. He took the majority leader job. The majority leader didn't have much power, and he made that position. He thought he could do the same thing with the vice presidency.

. . . [The vice presidency was] one of Johnson's worst misjudgments because as soon as the election is over, it's as if the realization comes to him that "God, I have no power now." So, he's got to try to make some. He does it on two fronts. One was on Capitol Hill, where he tries to remain as the power in the Senate. Kenny O'Donnell, one of Kennedy's aides and his appointment secretary, says, "Johnson wanted to be both

Lyndon Johnson, here in a September 1955 photo by Thomas J. O'Halloran, served as Senate majority leader for six years before being selected as John F. Kennedy's 1960 running mate. *Courtesy Library of Congress*

vice president and majority leader." If he had succeeded, . . . think what you would have had: a president who had a vice president who had his own independent source of power. The Senate would be independent of Kennedy. But that bid fails. At the same time, Johnson submits this letter to Kennedy which asks for general supervision of various government agencies, something no vice president has ever had before. He asks for an office right next to the president's in the White House. He asks for his own staff within the executive wing. He thinks he's going to get these things. He's absolutely confident he's going to win on both fronts.

. . . This great reader of men, Lyndon Johnson, this man who thought he could read any man had read one man wrong—and the one man was John Kennedy. He doesn't realize how tough JFK was. . . . He gives this memo to Kennedy, and Kennedy handles it by utterly ignoring it and being very cool about it; and Johnson loses, fails.

[Behind his back, the Kennedy people called Lyndon Johnson names] among other things, "Rufus Cornpone," "Uncle Cornpone," "Uncle Rufus." They are, of course, mocking the fact that he has this Southern accent. They're mocking the fact that he is a big, clumsy Southerner. Beyond that, why did they treat him with a meanness—in fact, a cruelty, when you get down to it—for three years? . . . Among other things, they were afraid of him. They had watched Lyndon Johnson when he was majority leader running Washington. They had seen his incredible energy, his incredible drive. One night, John Kennedy, when he was still in the Senate, was leaving. He's been working until midnight or 1:00 a.m. He's walking out, and there's one light burning in the Capitol, and it's in Lyndon Johnson's office. He turns to his aide and says, "Nobody outworks Lyndon." [The Kennedys] were afraid that if they let Lyndon Johnson off a very tight leash, he will start to build up his own power in Washington.

[The strained Lyndon Johnson/Robert Kennedy relationship] had an immense impact, although that's going to play out in 1967 and '68 largely over Vietnam and, in a way, over civil rights, too. But the seeds of it all, the absolute antagonism, is when Bobby Kennedy is attorney general and has the power in the administration. Johnson is the vice president, and Bobby Kennedy just humiliates him, time after time. Every time Johnson wanted to use a plane, he had to get written permission from the Pentagon. That was Robert Kennedy. Every time he wanted to give a speech, every word had to be cleared. And Bobby Kennedy does more. . . . There are scenes between Robert Kennedy and Lyndon Johnson in my book that when you're writing them, you can hardly believe you're writing them. You keep looking down at your notes to see, are you exaggerating or not, because it seems you must be exaggerating.

Probably the hardest [part of the Johnson story] to write, the hardest to research, too, was Johnson's vice presidency because it was so poignant during this period to see this powerful man humbled, humiliated, day after day, that it was actually painful for me to learn about it. Horace Busby once said he couldn't go over to the White House on the rare occasions when Johnson was there and watch how the Kennedy lower-level people treated him because it was so horrible. Johnson's a very complicated character. You felt that this is a terrible thing to happen to any human being, but to happen to Lyndon Johnson? Somebody said it was like a great bull put out to pasture late in life. He doesn't know what to do. That's what happened to Johnson.

[The Kennedys] made sure Lyndon Johnson didn't even know about the Bay of Pigs [crisis in April 1961]. That whole weekend, Johnson is sent by Kennedy to introduce Konrad Adenauer, the German chancellor, around Texas. He has to introduce him to the legislature. He takes him to a country fair in Stonewall, Texas. . . . I'd have to say, probably, he never knew there was a planned invasion.

One thing after another that the Kennedy administration does, they don't tell him about. When Kennedy introduces the Civil Rights Bill in 1963, for a while they won't bring Johnson into the picture at all. Finally, aide Ted Sorensen is told to call Johnson and get his advice on the Civil Rights Bill. Johnson has to say to him, "I don't know what's in the bill. The only thing I know about it is what I read in the *New York Times*." This is the greatest legislator, the greatest parliamentarian of America in the twentieth century. . . . This was a man who could get things through Congress that no one else could get through Congress, and they haven't even consulted him on the bill or told him what's in it.

The Cuban missile crisis [in October 1963] is a more involved story. But at the end of it, Ted Sorensen would tell me . . . they were really frightened, the Kennedys, of what might happen if there was a similar crisis and Lyndon Johnson was president. That's how hawkish they felt that he acted.

The last half of my book is the assassination and what happens in the forty-seven days after that. I'm writing it, and I'm watching Lyndon Johnson take up the reins of power. It's so dramatic to see what he does. I don't regard this as just the biography of Lyndon Johnson; I want each [volume of the series] to examine a kind of political power in America. This is a kind of political power, seeing what a president can do in a time of great crisis, . . . what does he do to get legislation moving, to take command in Washington. That's a way of examining power in a time of crisis.

[On November 22, 1963, the day President Kennedy was shot,] Robert Kennedy is sitting by the swimming pool at Hickory Hill, his Northern

Virginia estate, and . . . he's talking to Robert Morgenthau, the great district attorney of New York who later is United States attorney, . . . and suddenly they see a number of things happen simultaneously. They see a workman at Hickory Hill . . . suddenly stop. He's holding a transistor radio to his ear, and he comes running down this long lawn toward the swimming pool where Kennedy and Morgenthau are sitting. Before the man with the radio arrives, the telephone rings and it's [FBI director] J. Edgar Hoover to tell Robert Kennedy that his brother has been shot, perhaps fatally. Hoover didn't like Robert Kennedy, and Robert Kennedy didn't like him. Robert Kennedy was later to say that Hoover didn't show any emotion at all. He just delivered the news. So, sitting on the other side of the pool, Morgenthau sees Robert Kennedy clap his hand to his face in shock and horror.

Lyndon Johnson calls Robert Kennedy from [Air Force One as they were bringing the slain president's body back to Washington] . . . to ask him two things: Should I take the oath of office in Texas, or, wait until I get back to Washington to take it? But Johnson has not really asked; he knows he wants to take it in Texas. He wants Robert Kennedy to agree that that's the best course. And, he wants the wording of the oath. Deputy Attorney General [Nicholas] Katzenbach said to me, "I was really appalled that he would call Robert Kennedy twenty-six minutes after he learns his brother is dead." The man [Robert] hates is now his brother's successor and is on the phone asking him for the formal details on how to take office.

The [next] forty-seven days, seven weeks, is a period unlike any other in Lyndon Johnson's life. He has all these forces within him. Lying is a big part of his entire career up to here. But it's like he rises to something else . . . because he knows he has to be a president. The country needs continuity. Their young president has just been struck down in an instant, and, although most of these conspiracy theories are disproved in a couple of days, that's not the headlines. As Air Force One is flying back to Washington, here are the headlines: "Suspect Arrested"; "Suspect Charged"; "Suspect Visited Soviet Embassy in Mexico City"; "Suspect Has Ties to Anti-Castro Groups." We had just come through, a year before, the Cuban missile crisis, a crisis of nuclear war. It would be very easy for the country to become worried. Let me strike that: the country was worried. There was a great anxiety in the country.

Johnson knows he has to step off that plane and be a president. And he is. He rises to it. And for the next seven weeks, he is the president. There are no rages. A big part of Lyndon Johnson's life is not just his lying, but his raging, his bullying of subordinates. There's none of that. Someone says it's like an alarm clock had always told him to yell at somebody every twenty minutes, and for seven weeks, this alarm clock didn't go off.

You had a Lyndon Johnson who before . . . the assassination was a certain type of man, bullying, ruthless, conniving. He has to rise above that to make the country know it has a president. He has to curb his temper. His secretary, Marie Fehmer, . . . gave me a brilliant insight when she said his very physical movements changed on the plane going back to Washington. She said he always shambled; suddenly he's walking disciplined, like a president. And that doesn't change; that's the way he acts [going forward].

He has to be humble with the Kennedy people, to ask them to stay on—people he knows despise him. So, he humbles himself. He says, "I need you more than Jack Kennedy ever needed you." He says to one of them, "Jack Kennedy understood things about history that I don't. But you understand them. You have to stay with me. You have to help me." So, he changes in that way. No more rages in that way. He walks with dignity. . . . He's not going to be able to [maintain] that very long, as we're going to see as soon as my next book opens. But as this book says, he had done it long enough.

[Johnson was willing to lie to the public, and he also threatened the media.] I don't think we've known this about Johnson. . . . In December 1963, he's been in office for a month, and he's defeated Congress. He's got Kennedy's civil rights bill started through Congress. He's got Kennedy's tax cut bill, which was stalled, started. . . . He flies off to Texas for a two-week vacation, during which he starts to create the War on Poverty, a wonderful thing. But he also has a number of conversations about how he's worried that the press is getting too close to the fact that he's accumulated a fortune during his life.

One story involves a man, Jesse Kellam, who comes out to the Johnson ranch and says, "There's a reporter, Margaret Mayer, from the *Dallas Times-Herald* who's sent me this list of questions. What do I do about it?" Johnson telephones the managing editor of Mayer's newspaper and says,

"You don't want to be investigating me because someone might investigate you." I don't know if he actually uses the words "tax returns," but it's pretty [clear what his meaning is]. . . . The managing editor, named Albert Jackson, is heard on the phone, saying, "Don't worry. We'll stop her. We'll stop Margaret Mayer. I'll talk to her next week." Johnson says something like, "Next week's not good enough. It's a Saturday. Call me back tomorrow morning." Tomorrow morning, Jackson calls back and says, "She will be stopped." . . . They made clear to her they didn't want the story. They didn't want her investigating it anymore. . . . Margaret Mayer covered Lyndon Johnson for years and years, and she knew she was stopped on this.

[Johnson's finances were supposed to be in a blind trust, but] the people involved say it wasn't very blind. There was a law firm called Morrison and Ferguson. Morrison was one of the trustees of the blind trust, and his partner, Thomas Ferguson, who was a judge in the Texas Hill Country, would tell me that it seemed almost every night Johnson was talking to Morrison and telling him what to do. There was a special telephone line in Morrison's house. You just picked it up and got the White House; there was a special telephone line on the desk of someone named Earl Deeth, who was the general manager of KTBC [Johnson's radio station] and several others. *Life* magazine had found out about this, . . . they had been investigating. They had started by investigating Bobby Baker and campaign contributions, but they soon found that it was leading to Lyndon Johnson. The very morning that Jack Kennedy is assassinated, at the same time that the motorcade is going through Dallas, there is a meeting in the offices of *Life* magazine to divide up the areas for a major series on what one of them calls Lyndon Johnson's money, and they're about to investigate. [Events, of course, forestalled this.]

The civil rights bill and the tax cut, to understand how Johnson got them moving again, it's like a lesson in politics. . . . You want to see what he does in this time of crisis and what he does with these two bills, which are effectively stalled, how he almost immediately comes in and gets them moving, and you say, wow! If you're interested in political power, Johnson has a gift, a legislative gift—it's a gift beyond a gift, a talent beyond a talent—that is genius. To see Johnson, in an instant, grasp the situation and know what to do about it, it's hard to figure out what he does, but when you figure it out, it's thrilling.

This book ends with the State of the Union address on January 8, 1964. In this period of time, Johnson takes Kennedy's programs, he gets them started, he makes the country have a feeling of continuity. But he does something more. He says to friends, "I've got to continue Kennedy's programs, but if I want to run for re-election and I want to do what I want to do with the presidency, I have to make a program of my own." And that Christmas, down at his ranch, he has his advisers create the War on Poverty. In the State of the Union address, he says, "Too many Americans live on the outskirts of hope," and he lays out the basic outline of the Great Society and the War on Poverty.

You get really angry when you follow some of Johnson's methods, some of the things that he did. In my first volume, when you learn about Lyndon Johnson in college, you say, this is really incredible, the things that he did to get campus power—stolen elections, blackmailing a woman student. You do get angry at him. It's disgusting. Each one of my books is supposed to be an aspect of political power. So, my second book is about a stolen election. Stolen elections are part of American political life. When you see him stealing this election and you see the negative campaigning he uses, you get angry at him. My third volume is probably the angriest I ever got because there's a section on Leland Olds, a liberal New Dealer, a member of the Federal Power Commission. Johnson becomes senator, and he's been financed by the oil and natural gas people; his job is to destroy Leland Olds, and he destroys him. Anyone who watches Johnson through my writing . . . destroy this man's reputation so that the rest of his life is just ruined, it's horrible. And when Johnson comes over to Olds in an interval of the hearings which Johnson is chairing and destroying his reputation, and says, "You don't take this personally, do you, Leland? It's only politics," you get very angry at him.

Power always reveals what you wanted to do all along. The cliché is Lord Acton's statement, "All power corrupts; absolute power corrupts absolutely." I don't think that that's always true. I think what's always true is that power reveals, because when you have enough power to do whatever you want to do, then people see what you wanted to do. This is particularly true in the case of Lyndon Johnson.

... THE MEN IN THE MIDDLE

WOODROW WILSON

Overall Rank: 11

— ★ —

Total Score: 683

Woodrow Wilson's overall rank has steadily declined, from 6th in C-SPAN's 2000 survey to 11th in 2017. Although historians have marked him down in all leadership categories over the three surveys, his most precipitous fall has been in pursued equal justice for all, with a decline from 20th to 35th.

Party: Democrat
b. December 28, 1856, Staunton, Virginia
d. February 3, 1924, Washington, DC
First Ladies: Ellen Louise Axson Wilson (1913–1914)
and Edith Bolling Galt Wilson (1915–1921)
Age entering office: 56

Historian: **A. Scott Berg**

Pulitzer Prize–winning biographer Scott Berg discussed his book, Wilson, *which details the human side of President Wilson. This interview was recorded for C-SPAN's Q & A on August 28, 2013.*

Of all the presidents of the twentieth century, Woodrow Wilson perhaps lingers the longest and the most. I think there are several reasons why: one is that so many of the programs Woodrow Wilson initiated are with us to this day. The foundation to our economy, the Federal Reserve System—that goes back to Wilson. Certainly, our foreign policy is rooted in a speech Woodrow Wilson gave in 1917, on April 2, when he said, "The world must be made safe for democracy." He was calling for American entry into World War I. All our foreign policy decisions since then, for good or for bad, are rooted in that [concept], so that's something. The other reasons I wanted to write about Wilson were for the ideals and ideas. Here's a man that was so high-minded. I don't think we've ever had a president quite so high-minded as Wilson, and I thought that was a good thing to remind ourselves.

Wilson entered Princeton as a professor in 1890, and then in 1902, he became the president of the college. From 1902 to 1910, Wilson was the president of Princeton. . . . He was then governor of New Jersey for a little less than two years, it's more like seventeen or eighteen months, and that being the case, Woodrow Wilson really did have the most meteoric rise in American history. This is a man who in 1910 was the president of a small men's college in the middle of New Jersey; in 1912, he was elected president of the United States. He had never run for office before he ran for the governorship of New Jersey, and he had a remarkable not quite two years as governor.

There's a lot of evidence that Wilson wrote all his own speeches [the last president to do so . . .], not the least of which comes from the fact that Wilson as a teenager learned shorthand and shortly after that learned how to type. . . . We have documents of Wilson's shorthand notes, of even the most important speeches he ever gave. That great April 2, 1917, speech asking for a declaration of war is originally written in shorthand. Then he types a draft, writes over that with pencil or pen, making corrections, and then you can see the subsequent drafts after that. So, there's plenty of evidence that he wrote all his own speeches. I should add that a lot of his speeches weren't really written—his campaign speeches, for example. He was a brilliant orator. He was a natural speaker, and when he did hundreds of campaign speeches he would go out there with a card with maybe five bullet points on it, and he would talk extemporaneously for an hour to an hour and a half. Somebody would then transcribe the speeches, so we have copies of them. In all those speeches, I almost never came across a grammatical error, a problem in syntax, a paragraph that wasn't fully and naturally formed. Every paragraph seemed to have some lovely metaphor to it. He thought oratorically.

Woodrow Wilson was a racist, by any definition of the word. This is not his greatest flaw, but it's certainly the biggest strike against him personally. For someone who was such a progressive thinker as he was, it was certainly the most regressive aspect of his thinking. In his defense,

Woodrow Wilson was governor of New Jersey when this c. 1912 Harris and Ewing Studio photo was taken. Wilson was sworn in as president on March 13, 1913. *Courtesy National Portrait Gallery, Smithsonian Institution; gift of Aileen Conkey; gelatin silver print*

and my job is not to defend him or to excuse him, rather really to try to explain him, he was a nineteenth-century figure born in the South. Woodrow Wilson was born in 1856. His first memory is being told that Lincoln got elected president, and because of that there was going to be a great war. He grew up literally remembering the war and Reconstruction. So, this was a man forged in the South and forged in the nineteenth century where slavery was part of life. He grew up with a father who was a preacher, who preached that the Bible supported slavery, that this wasn't an un-Christian act, so Wilson walks in [to the White House] with all this [baggage]. . . . I think there was probably, above all, a political reason for Wilson's racism, at least for its lingering. That is, he came to Washington with this great progressive agenda, and I think he knew he couldn't get anything passed unless he had the Southern bloc of senators behind him. There was no way he was going to get anything done unless he made some actions in their favor, and that meant introducing Jim Crow to Washington.

Wilson was so intellectual. He was our most academic, most educated president. He's the only president with a PhD, and as a result of that, most of the books that have been written about him have been academic in nature; they've missed the very human side of this man. He was a deeply emotional, passionate, romantic figure. He had two wives. When his first wife died, he courted and fell in love with a woman and married a second time. He wrote thousands of passionate love letters to each of these women. This was a real living, breathing human being, and I don't think we've seen that about Woodrow Wilson. This even connects to the racism, in a way, because what I learned about Wilson is nothing is quite black and white; even his racism, I don't think, was virulent. He really didn't want to keep the black man down, that was not the great issue for him. He just felt the country wasn't ready for the races to mix. And, that being said, he always kept the door open at the White House. Any African American petitioner—he saw them all. They were welcomed in the White House. So, it concerned him; he just didn't know how to deal with it. What he thought was wrong-headed, then, and certainly when you look at it a century-plus later, it's quite backward.

. . . He did believe that "separate but equal" might work, should work, had to work, for a while, because he didn't think the country was ready to integrate. That being the case, he thought if everything was equal, fine. During the years of his administration, he would get reports that, in fact, things were not that equal, that in segregating the Treasury Department and the Post Office, the conditions for black workers were quite different from conditions for the white workers. Here is where he is really guilty, which is that he did nothing about it. He looked the other way, and he let it be. And that's a shame.

[Woodrow Wilson played 1,200 rounds of golf, more than any other president.] It means that the White House was a little different in 1913 to 1921 than it is today. Wilson's doctor, Dr. Grayson, who met Wilson on his first day at the White House, recognized that this was a sick man. He didn't realize the full extent, but there was obviously some arteriosclerosis developing. . . . Everyone who dealt with him medically knew this was a man who needed to relax. This was a man who needed fresh air every day, just needed to walk. The doctor very cleverly, very early on, said, "You need to do some regular exercise." This [medical condition] was not known or covered [by the press]. And later on in Wilson's life, in 1919, when Wilson collapses and has a stroke in the White House, this was kept from the world for months and months, and only then did it dribble out a bit because an incautious doctor spoke to the press.

One hundred years later, some fascinating papers were discovered in a garage that belonged to Dr. Cary T. Grayson. He was an admiral who was Woodrow Wilson's personal physician and became a great confidant and political adviser. They found these trunkloads of Dr. Grayson's papers, and within them he kept meticulous notes, and he literally had his hand on the pulse of the president. He took notes, especially in the last years of the Wilson presidency when he collapsed and had the stroke. . . . [But he also took notes about Wilson during] the years after that, when he retired to Washington. You see [in Grayson's notes] all this humanizing detail, the most striking of which is that this was a very sick man, physically and, ultimately, mentally as well. A lot of this comes out in these Grayson archives. It's really quite something.

There were thirteen collapses of some sort, usually physical of varying degrees, going back to when Wilson was a young man. These were enumerated by Sigmund Freud, so take it with a grain of salt, or a whole sack of salt. Freud did a study of Woodrow Wilson based on information that an enemy of Wilson had given him. Freud was no great friend of Wilson either, but in going through it and reconstructing—or maybe deconstructing—Wilson's medical history, he did see these thirteen episodes in which he just shut down. They go right up to his presidency, not the least of it when his first wife, Ellen, his really beloved wife, died.

He met [Ellen Axson] in Rome, Georgia, where she was from. Wilson graduated from Princeton and was a diehard Princetonian all his life, but after college he went to law school in Virginia. Then he practiced law for a short time in Atlanta and realized he really didn't like it in Atlanta, and he definitely didn't like the law. While he was packing up his bags to leave Georgia and go on to graduate school at Johns Hopkins, he had one bit of family business to do. There was a family estate that needed some settling in Rome, and there he cast eyes on the daughter of the Presbyterian minister. He being a son of a Presbyterian minister, the two fell madly in love with each other—Wilson more madly and faster, but ultimately the two of them were deeply, deeply in love with each other.

There are thousands, I mean thousands, of love letters. . . . There's just one after another—you can't quite believe it. I don't know of a romantic correspondence in history that is as voluminous as the Wilson correspondence, and I'm not forgetting the Adams' and the Brownings'. These letters are just endless, and they got a little sickening after a while because there are only so many ways you can say, "I love you, dear," but he found thousands of ways of saying it.

Ellen Wilson is not only buried in Rome, Georgia, but she is sort of buried in history, I'm sorry to say. One of the things I've tried to do is to exhume her because she was a fascinating woman. She was mostly written off as a rather docile wife in the background, as was the nature of things in the late nineteenth century. The truth is she was an extremely talented painter and could have had a career as an artist. She was also a big reader. Wilson ran every speech, every article he ever wrote by her, and she was very quick to make very, very clever comments on things he did. He was always extremely beholden to her for all her suggestions. He trusted her implicitly in every way. When they got married, she basically gave up her art career. She did a little painting after that, and she painted a little in the White House for her one year there. She was a genuinely interesting woman. She was also the first socially active first lady that we had. We think of Eleanor Roosevelt as being out there in the trenches. Ellen Wilson was really the first to take on a social cause in Washington, which was the slums. She thought the way the African Americans lived in the [the capital] city was just appalling, and so she used to drag members of Congress through the alleys of Washington just to let them see what was happening. On her deathbed, she called out to Wilson, who had proposed some [alley rehabilitation] legislation, to say, "Have they passed the legislation yet?" And indeed they did, just moments before she died. . . . She died of Bright's disease, which is a kidney ailment. Today, with dialysis, she would have lived a longer and happier life, but she died a year after the Wilsons arrived in the White House.

[Wilson's brief courtship of Washington jewelry store owner Edith Galt is] an amazing story when you consider that the world is blowing up while all this is going on. The world has gone to war. It's the greatest conflagration the world had yet seen, and here the president of the United States is so despondent over the loss of his first wife he can barely get out of bed. It's only his sense of duty that gets him to work every day and the great responsibility that is on his shoulders. And then his doctor, Dr. Grayson, arranged a chance meeting with this widow in town—a young widow, rather attractive, not terribly well educated, loved nice dresses, and knew her jewelry. Wilson met her and fell instantly in love with her. Part of it is that Wilson really wanted not only to be in love but wanted to be married. He was one of those men who needed a woman by his side.

Edith wouldn't give him a "yes." He knew within a few weeks that he wanted to marry her, and he just forced himself upon her, and she kept resisting. . . . Her first marriage was relatively loveless. It wasn't unhappy, but it was a marriage without passion, so she had never really known love herself. There she was in her forties, and she had figured, "I will have a very happy long widowhood, and love will never come knocking on my door." Then it did in the form of the president of the United States, and that carries a whole lot of baggage because suddenly you are going to be known to the entire world. They kept the courtship as secret and as private as they could. Mostly that was Wilson's attempt to protect her until she was ready to commit. Within a year, they were married in her house, in the living room. He didn't think it was quite proper to do it in the White House, and he didn't want to make a big state wedding out of it, so it was a small family wedding.

"He kept us out of war." That was the slogan when he ran again in 1916. [However,] he definitely knew [that the United States would have to eventually join the war effort]. From the very beginning, Wilson did everything he could to keep the United States out of the war, as almost everybody in the very beginning tried to keep the war from even happening. This was [propelled by] an incident that should not have blown into a world war; it was largely about personalities as much as anything else. Over the next few years, from 1914 to '15 into '16, Wilson began to see the inevitability of American entry into the war. The Germans were torpedoing ships; American lives were being lost. We had to respond somehow. Wilson tried doing it diplomatically through a series of memoranda, and notes were going back and forth all the time, but at a certain point it was a question of honor.

Our entry into the war begins in April 1917, . . . and it ends on November 11, 1918.

This was an incredible [period]. The world had never seen anything like this. We got in it because Woodrow Wilson felt we had to get into it, at a certain point. . . . Woodrow Wilson felt that this really could be the war to end all wars, and that if, perhaps, we could adopt his fourteen points, the fourteenth of which was the establishment of a League of Nations—a kind of international parliament where every country could sit at a roundtable, a King Arthur's Court—it could solve problems before they exploded into wars. Ultimately, it was Wilson's rhetoric that pushed us in. That was his wanting to add a moral component, not only to US foreign policy but to the world at large, that we should be guided by some sort of morality. . . . A lot of the Republicans, especially Theodore Roosevelt, were pushing us into the war. Roosevelt thought, "We've got to get into this thing. There are these autocracies, and we've got to see the end of these rulers." Wilson really avoided that. He didn't want that. He put it off as long as he could, but when the [British ocean liner] *Lusitania* went down in 1915, American lives were taken, and Wilson began to see that the Germans were not going to let up. He saw that it was going to be inevitable, we were going to have to get into this war. You could see him starting to mobilize the country with matériel, but also intellectually mobilizing the country, getting them to think beyond our borders, to think beyond our provinces.

[Here's how I describe the outcome of the war in my book: "Four dynasties that had long dominated much of the world had fallen and the combat itself produced stunning statistics. Eight hundred and eighty-five thousand British soldiers died as had 1.4 million French, more than 4 percent of their population, and 1.8 million Russians. The Central Powers had lost more than 4 million soldiers. Altogether, close to 10 million soldiers died in the Great War and more than 21 million were wounded. Counting civilian deaths as a result of disease, famine, massacres, and collateral damage, somewhere between 16.5 million and 65 million people died."]

[After the war ends,] Wilson goes over to Paris, which was an interesting thing in itself, that the president of the United States decided to leave the country in December 1918. Except for one brief trip home between

December 1918 and June of 1919, the president of the United States was not here. When Wilson came back from Paris with this peace treaty that he had spent six months negotiating, everything was all tucked in, it was ready to go. The one thing Wilson hadn't fully considered was that peace treaties have to be ratified by the Senate. . . . It's not as if he didn't know his Constitution, but he didn't realize that in the six months he was gone, his Republican enemies had plotted a whole battle plan such that when he returned, there was no way anything he brought back was going to get passed.

It was really intense. What happened [politically], too, was that Wilson had won the Great War. Wilson was now the greatest hero on the earth. The Democrats had won the war, and the Republicans became convinced, "We can't let him win the peace. We have to negotiate that peace, not [simply approve] the Wilson peace." I think it was largely political, but there were certainly many members of the Senate who just didn't like the treaty. When he realizes the Senate was not going to ratify the treaty, Wilson decided, "I will go to the people." He began . . . a twenty-nine-city tour, but he collapsed in Pueblo, Colorado, just after he had given a speech. Dr. Grayson came into the train compartment. This is the dead of summer, and these un-air-conditioned train cars were just deadly. Grayson said, "The tour is over. You will be dead, Mr. President, unless we end this right now." And so, they went back to Washington, and a few days after their return, in early October of 1919, Wilson had a stroke.

[As the president convalesced from his stroke, Edith Wilson,] I would say, didn't reach for a power grab, except to the extent that she did not want anything to affect her husband's health. She didn't want to be the president of the United States, but she didn't want anyone to disturb the suffering president. A doctor rather quietly suggested to her, "Well, Mrs. Wilson, the president has been briefing you on everything; perhaps you should be running the White House." And so, for the last year and a half [of his presidency] nobody saw the president. No document went before the president's eyes unless it first passed through Mrs. Wilson.

The press covered it at first rather respectfully; he had banked a lot of goodwill, and the press basically loved Wilson. Wilson was the first president to have press conferences, for example, so they loved his openness. . . . And he was clever with them, and they liked that. They saw that he had been on this exhausting tour where he was changing hearts and minds in this country, and that the League [of Nations] probably would have passed, so they were very tender in the beginning. Then it was: "Where is the president? Nobody has seen the president in quite some time." And then, the Senate began to wonder, especially the Republicans: they figure, we hate to kick a man when he's down, but he is down so let's kick him.

He couldn't see them, in fact, and so after several weeks turned into months, the Senate was saying, "We'd like to see the president. Is he alive? Is he compos mentis?" They sent a small committee of two to go to the White House and see the president.

The question of the hour [was: Why didn't someone suggest that Wilson step down]? And, the main answer is because . . . Edith Wilson stepped forward and said, "If you take the presidency away, that is really going to kill the president." Dr. Grayson was going along with this, and not only were they complicit, but these two people really foisted a conspiracy on the United States government. Things were not clearly spelled out then. We didn't yet have the Twenty-fifth Amendment, which delineates presidential succession. It was all very vague back in 1919, and so it was really up to Mrs. Wilson and the doctor to make that decision.

. . . Yet another reason why they did this, with all due respect to Thomas Riley Marshall, vice president of the United States, . . . he was a bit of a joke in Washington. The rumor was that he had business cards that said, "Thomas R. Riley, vice president of the United States and toastmaster." He was a guy who really loved being vice president. It was a perfect job for him because it really required nothing. . . . He almost never saw Woodrow Wilson. He was invited to cabinet meetings in the beginning, but he, Marshall himself, realized he was sitting in the background. He wasn't asked to speak, and nobody was listening if he did.

[Despite his medical condition, Woodrow Wilson did serve out the remaining months of his presidency and, amazingly, even considered running for a third term. After his term ended on March 21, 1921, he and Edith moved to a home in Washington, DC, and he died there on February 3, 1924.]

Wilson has been with me since I was fifteen years old, and I'd been reading about him and writing about him ever since, so to be able to get it all out of me is a relief and a pleasure. The greatest thrill, pleasure, though, for me was to bring some humanity to this man. With all the good and all the bad about him, he is a fascinating human being.

BARACK OBAMA

Overall Rank: 12

— ★ —

Total Score: 669

Included in the C-SPAN survey for the first time in 2017, historians ranked Barack Obama in 12th place overall. He ranked in the top eight of all presidents in pursued equal justice for all (3rd), moral authority (7th), and economic management (8th). His lowest ranking was in relations with Congress, where he's ranked in the bottom five of all presidents (39th).

Party: Democrat
b. August 4, 1961, Honolulu, Hawaii
First Lady: Michelle Robinson Obama
Age entering office: 47

Historian: **David J. Garrow**

David Garrow won a Pulitzer Prize in 1987 for his biography of Martin Luther King Jr. He later spent nine years on his biography of Barack Obama, Rising Star: The Making of Barack Obama. He sat with us for a two-part interview for Q & A on May 12, 2017.

Once you choose to run for president of the United States and succeed, your earlier life, your biography, is a major part of American history. Barack Obama actually had a much more interesting, much more richly varied earlier life than we have, to a large extent, known up until now. People are aware that he grew up in Hawaii and lived a bit in Indonesia as a child. But the really transformative period of Barack's life, in his mid-twenties, came when he was living in Chicago for the first time, 1985 to 1988. He was working as a community organizer on the far South Side. His first immersion in an African American community is distinct from his multi-ethnic international earlier life. [He was] also living in a very intense private relationship with a young woman in Hyde Park[, Illinois], and it's during those years that he comes to define himself both as a black man and as someone who aspires to a political career and is aiming for the presidency.

[I spent eight hours with Barack Obama, off the record, for this project.] My first visit to see Barack in person was April of 2016, probably an hour and twenty minutes or so in the Oval Office. After that, I offered to let him read the typescript manuscript of the whole first ten chapters of this book. And he did that over the course of the late summer [in 2016]. I then went back for three-plus hours on two different Sundays in October of 2016, and then I believe December 4, 2016, after the election. Barack sat there with the marked-up typescript and we went through it chapter by chapter. [He did not read my epilogue, which] was still being composed and edited down during that fall. [He disagreed with some of what he read about my book.] I think what I can say without violating Washington ground rules, which are ground rules that don't match up pretty well with academic history, is that once someone has written their own account of how they remember their life, that when they're presented with other witnesses, multiple, multiple witnesses whose memories significantly differ, someone who's already written their version remains very firmly attached to their version.

Barack Obama is very deeply attached to the version of his life that he put forward in his book *Dreams from My Father*. That's a book that stops in 1988, when he's leaving Chicago before he goes to law school. In my book, only the first four chapters overlap with *Dreams from My Father* because I go all the way through Harvard, through all his years in Illinois politics and his US Senate campaign in 2004. My very purposeful intent with this book has been to produce a book of record that folks will still be using and relying upon twenty-five or thirty-five years from now.

I began reading about Barack in early 2008 when he won the Iowa caucuses and burst on to the political scene as a serious presidential contender. All throughout 2008, I was disappointed by the quality and the depth of journalism about his earlier life. I thought that the mainstream media was simply being insufficiently curious about him. On the other hand, we simultaneously had all of these wacky oppositional actions out there regarding where was he born. Was he really Muslim? And so, I came to this project with a professional belief that someone of my background and experience should tackle this and do the best, most thorough job I could as an experienced scholarly historian. . . . And now, nine years later, it's over one thousand interviews. And that's counting people one by one; no one counts four times just because I spoke to them four times. . . . One of the great strengths of this book stems from the fact that all throughout the 1980s, Barack Obama was quite a letter writer. There are many people who still have long hand-written letters from Barack.

. . . At the time that Barack is a young child in Hawaii, Frank Marshall Davis is living in Honolulu. Frank, earlier in his life, had been a very prominent black poet in Chicago. Frank had married a wealthy white woman in the late '40s, and they decided to move to Hawaii because they were going to experience a whole lot less racial discrimination as an interracial couple in Honolulu than in Chicago. By the mid-1960s, one of Frank Marshall Davis's best friends in Honolulu is Barack's grandfather, Stanley Dunham. Stanley and his wife, Madelyn, Barack's maternal grandparents, pretty much raised Barack in a very modest, small apartment in a building in downtown Honolulu. Stanley was an amateur poet himself, a man who enjoyed dirty limericks, and he and Frank Davis would hang out together. Stanley was very conscious of having a grandson who was half black, and Stanley went out of his way to introduce his grandson, Barry, back at that time, to Frank Davis.

For Barack, Frank Davis was the first adult African American male who he knew, someone the age of a grandfather. . . . Barack as a young man, when he's in high school, when he's in college, is writing poetry, or trying to write poetry some people might say. There's no question that Frank Davis did have some formative impact on Barack. But Barack no more knew that Frank Marshall Davis had actually been a communist in the 1940s than he knew that Bill Ayers, later a good friend in Chicago, had been involved in planting bombs. In neither instance is it a reflection upon whom Barack is, what people had done years earlier.

One of the most striking things with Barack's own memoir, *Dreams from My Father*, is the almost complete absence of women in that book. Barack himself, back in the 1990s, spoke with regret about how he pretty much left his mother [Ann Dunham] out of that book. . . . His Genevieve

[Cook] relationship, and especially his Sheila Jager relationship, were defining, transformative relationships, yet in his own telling of his life story, they are 99.8 percent absent. [The three women that I write the most about in my book besides Michelle Obama, his mother, and his grandmother are: his first college girlfriend, starting in 1981, Alex McNear; Genevieve Cook, whom he dated in 1984–1985; and Sheila Jager, who was in his life starting in 1986.]

Genevieve Cook, like Barack, was someone from a very rich international background. Her father was an Australian diplomat, a government minister. Her mother was a very prominent arts figure who, with Genevieve's stepfather, lived in Indonesia. Genevieve went to Swarthmore College, wrote a very erudite undergraduate thesis about young people who came from nowhere, whose homes were the world. So, the overlap between Barack's life—Hawaii, Indonesia, no father in the picture, his mother traveling the world—and Genevieve's life is very striking.

Genevieve Cook, whom Barack meets in New York after he graduates from Columbia and they became involved very quickly with each other, was just starting out teaching public school and was unhappy as a teacher. It's probably without question the most difficult period of Barack's life. Right out of college, he takes a job and stays in it for precisely 365 days at a financial publishing firm called Business International Corporation. Everyone else who worked at BI, as they called it, was quite happy there. They are a nifty set of people. It's now owned by The Economist Group. But Barack was entirely a fish out of water.

This is 1984, '85. He describes it in a letter to his mother as "working for the enemy" because Barack's private politics as of 1985 were certainly anti-capitalist in some fashion. At the end of 1984, when he hits the 365-day mark, Barack quits BI and is trying to find something else to do in New York. He works [briefly] for NYPIRG, New York Public Interest Research Group, a Ralph Nader–type group, up at City College in West Harlem. . . . But Barack found trying to organize undergraduates at a commuter school unfulfilling, and he leaves that as of May of '85. He is living in an almost hovel of a situation in Hell's Kitchen on the west side of Manhattan when he sees a job ad for a beginning community organizer in Chicago. That job ad is what begins his progression.

Genevieve Cook's journal for 1984, 1985, which she shared with me almost in its entirety, . . . documents and details just how much cocaine Barack was using with his best friends in New York—they are providing it; he is not spending his money—throughout the spring into the early summer of 1985. That's when it ceases. Let's get that point on the record: there's no drug use after that.

Genevieve [also] gave me copies of all the letters and postcards that Barack had written to her between 1984 and 1986. . . . The letters confirmed Genevieve's story: Barack asked her to accompany him to Chicago. She declined. But Barack continued to write her throughout his time in Chicago.

Sheila Jager, [the other important relationship from this period, is] half-Dutch, half-Japanese. On the paternal Dutch side of her family, her grandparents are honored in Yad Vashem, the Israeli Holocaust memorial, for helping protect Jews in the Netherlands during World War II. Sheila, likewise, had lived in Paris for a time [and] written a very erudite undergraduate thesis. These were all very impressive young ladies.

Sheila dates to the spring of 1986, and her testimony on this [period of Barack's life] is very powerful. With some of his community organizing buddies in 1987, '88, Barack would talk about being interested in a political career, becoming mayor of Chicago, because [of] Harold Washington, the first black mayor of Chicago, who ended up dying very tragically in the fall of '87. Washington was a very formative political presence for Barack even though they barely met each other. By 1987, a year and a half into being a community organizer, Barack has understandably concluded that organizing community groups is not going to produce transformational change. He concludes that he needs to pursue a political career. Now, with his male friends, he's saying, "Maybe I could become mayor." But with Sheila and with a second woman, a community activist woman to whom he was very close, Mary Ellen Montes, . . . [he was saying something more]. It's very powerful that Sheila has memories of Barack saying to her, "I feel I have a destiny and that I'm thinking I could one day become president of the United States." Mary Ellen Montes's memories of what Barack was saying to her in 1987, 1988 match up identically with Sheila Jager's.

Barack and Sheila begin living together in the early fall of 1986 after having been introduced three or four months earlier by one of Sheila's fellow graduate students, a Pakistani academic. . . . All through Barack's time in college during the 1980s, his really close friends were neither white nor black. They were mainly international South Asian young men, Pakistani or Indian ethnicity, from successful families. This is part of Barack's fundamental international grounding as a young man.

. . . It's a very intense relationship; Sheila takes Barack home that Christmas [1986] to meet her parents in northern California, and they are already talking about marriage. . . . Barack and her father argued. Sheila's parents didn't think a community organizer was the best potential husband material, and so nothing comes of the marriage issue right then. But Barack and Sheila continue to live with each other for another eighteen months in Chicago. By that time, Barack has made the decision to pursue a political career, to go to law school. He asks Sheila to join him at Harvard. Sheila says no because she wants to get on with her fieldwork, her own professional career as a scholar. But she does go to Cambridge, Massachusetts, and very privately, quietly, lives with Barack for a month or more even then. And they remain involved with each other [at some level] until early 1991.

In the spring of 1990, . . . Barack is elected president of the *Harvard Law Review*. [He is the] first black person to ever have [this role. That's] . . . very important.

Barack and his best friend during law school, Rob Fisher, co-authored a 250-page unpublished book manuscript that Rob and his mother have held on to. It's a fascinating document. Half of it is about race and racial policy, and the stance that Barack and Rob take in that manuscript about civil rights process and civil rights policy is a very significant window looking forward into Barack's political life. Rob is white. He's originally from southern Maryland, tobacco farm country. Rob is a little bit older than Barack, had a PhD in economics from Duke. He had taught economics at Holy Cross College in Worcester, Massachusetts, before starting law school at the exact same time as Barack. They meet on day one at Harvard. Scores and scores of their classmates whom I've spoken to, without exception, described Barack and Rob as the two brightest people in that Harvard Law School class of 1991. They had an amazingly intense intellectual friendship across those three years, taking almost all of their courses together and, in the third year, writing this long book manuscript together as part of a seminar paper process for Professor Martha Minow, later the dean of Harvard Law School.

First and foremost, the unpublished book manuscript that Barack and Rob Fisher wrote during their third year of law school at Harvard, the chapter that's about race and racial politics and racial policy, there's nothing in there that to me as a progressive Democrat, who knows race, finds surprising. But there's a lot of material in there that could have been used [during his presidential bid] in Republican attack ads to present Barack as a dangerous figure. If people are old enough to remember Lani Guinier, a well-known African American law professor nominated in 1993 by President Clinton for a Justice Department post, her nomination was abandoned because of critical reactions to some footnotes she had in law review articles. That's what I think could have happened with that book manuscript.

Barack's political aspirations and sense of destiny lead him to push Sheila Jager aside. During that time there was a well-known political figure in Chicago, a hugely respected man, [Illinois State] senator Dick Newhouse, whom everyone in black Chicago believed could never go higher because he was married to a white woman. So, it is in the political tradition of black Chicago in the late 1980s and in the early 1990s, that for a black man to aspire to represent black Chicago, it is necessary to have a black spouse.

[Barack, then twenty-seven, first met Chicago lawyer Michelle Robinson, twenty-five, when he served as a summer associate at her Chicago law firm, Sidley Austin, in 1989. They began dating and continued a long-distance relationship when he returned to Harvard.] Barack and Michelle joined Trinity United Church of Christ in early 1992 in order to get married there that October. Barack had first come to know Reverend Jeremiah Wright five years earlier when Barack was working as a community organizer. Reverend Wright's church was a little outside the geographical boundaries of Barack's neighborhood where he was organizing. But Reverend Wright began to have a big impact, in part a paternal impact, on Barack even in 1987, '88, before Barack leaves to go to law school.

I love Jeremiah Wright, and I'm proud to say that, but that comes from the part of me that is grounded in Martin Luther King Jr. because of my own previous book on Dr. King. Black liberation theology, which Reverend Wright represents, is a radical doctrine. One of my oldest and closest academic friends, James H. Cone, a theologian at Union Seminary, is the leading progenitor of black liberation theology. What Jeremiah's church came to represent was the living embodiment of what black theologians like Jim Cone, like Cornel West have championed. . . . Barack and Michelle were not there for [one] of Reverend Wright's most notorious sermons [about racial justice, which later became an Obama campaign issue], and I don't think Reverend Wright's preaching is in any way reflective of Barack Obama's beliefs. Trinity Church was a great church to be a member of if you were an aspiring young African American politician in Chicago. Many good things can be said about Reverend Wright, [and] I would say, too, that no one should be judged by history for the three stupidest things they've ever said. . . . The immense amount of good that Jeremiah Wright has done in his life vastly outshines how any of us might feel about a sermon like that.

. . . Everyone who knew Barack in high school, in college, in his first few jobs, before he goes to Chicago in 1985, thought he was a completely unremarkable person; that's the Barack Obama of 1985. Three years later, after the three years in Chicago on the far South Side living with Sheila, when Barack arrives at Harvard Law School in 1988, every classmate who meets him, without exception, thinks that this is someone who will be a public star. So, to my mind, the humongous contrast between what people who knew Barack before Chicago thought of him and what people at Harvard see in 1988, that is what really documents the self-transformation he experienced between 1985 and 1988. The Barack from the community years, Barack as a student and then editor of the law review at Harvard, a young lawyer, a law teacher, a state legislator in Illinois across the 1990s, I think he is a wonderful, compelling, impressive political figure. ·

One of my favorite moments comes on the floor of the Illinois State Senate [where he served from 1997 to 2004]. . . . Barack is recounting how at their condominium in Hyde Park, he's not allowed to smoke indoors. Michelle sends him out to the back porch. He's out there after midnight smoking a cigar, he says, and he watches an immigrant family

In 1995, Barack Obama embarked on his first political campaign, successfully vying for an Illinois Senate seat. Here, he gathers signatures in Chicago for his nominating petition. *Credit: Marc PoKempner*

coming down the alley collecting bottles and cans with their children in tow. He's telling this spontaneously on the Senate floor and the impact that it has on him of the challenges that this family is facing. That's a politician whom I thought was incredibly impressive.

This was on the Senate floor in Illinois in the aftermath of losing his year 2000 congressional challenge . . . [against] incumbent Democratic representative Bobby Rush. This would have been the [typical] Harold Washington career trajectory, to go from being a state legislator to then being a congressman. In the wake of that loss, Barack, in my judgment, makes the choice that he has to figure out how to win, that being victorious is essential.

You start seeing a series of changes. I'll give you two quick examples: when Barack first announces to run for the state senate back in the mid-1990s, he, by hand, fills out a questionnaire saying he supports gay marriage. It's relatively well known that that is something he backed off of very quickly, and very significantly. Similarly, early on, he was a very outspoken proponent of gun control. There was some significant backing away from that, too. So, in my very detailed chapter recounting his US Senate candidacy, 2002 to 2004, what my book presents in quite extensively documented detail is someone who is changing themselves in order to be a successful statewide politician.

Emil Jones Jr. was a longtime Chicago politician, who by 1997, when Barack enters the Illinois State Senate, is the Democratic leader of the then-minority caucus. Come November 2002, Democrats take control of the Illinois Senate. And now Senator Jones, a very traditional Chicago African American politician, is one of the three most powerful people in Illinois, has control of the Illinois State Senate, and has a pretty conflictual relationship with the speaker of the Illinois House, Mike Madigan. When Barack is first talking about running for the US Senate in the 2004 cycle in the spring of 2002, he goes to Senator Jones, now his majority leader, to ask for his support. This is really a defining moment in Barack's political rise because of Senator Jones's decision to support Barack. One of Barack's competitors is supported by Jones's rival, Speaker Madigan. So, Jones's decision to put all of his political weight and influence behind championing Barack as the Democratic nominee for US Senate, that is what makes Barack Obama a serious statewide contender in Illinois.

[My book ends with Barack Obama's successful run for the US Senate in 2004. In an epilogue I offer my observations about Obama's White House years. Its final sentence is this:] "But it was essential to appreciate while the crucible of self-creation had produced an ironclad will, the vessel was hollow at its core." [In other words,] the Barack Obama whom we saw as president was a very different person. The person we see today giving $400,000 speeches, hanging out with billionaires and Hollywood celebrities, is a radically different person than who Barack was from the 1980s up through 2004.

All of his life in Illinois with [Michelle], his daughters, during the 1990s up through his election to the US Senate, they were leading a very modest, financially challenging, middle-class life. Barack as an Illinois legislator is a very outspoken progressive, very tough critic of the Patriot Act, of the US intelligence community, a very tough voice calling for single-payer universal healthcare coverage. He was someone who did a superb job in Springfield in the state legislature, actively reaching across the aisle to deal productively with very conservative

Republicans—state Republican politicians more conservative than Mitch McConnell or Paul Ryan. The Barack who was so successful in Illinois in a Republican-controlled legislative situation for most of his time, and who was a very outspoken progressive voice, that's not the man who we ended up having as president.

What most surprised me was the extent of his transformation with regard to the intelligence community: that someone who had been so critical of the Patriot Act starting right in 2001 after 9/11, ended up instead as both a champion of the intelligence community and someone who, again and again, as has been very widely reported in our top newspapers, authorized more investigations and prosecutions of journalists than any president in American history. That was not who Barack Obama was prior to the presidency. And, even during the presidency, I was deeply puzzled by the extent of his social interaction with Hollywood celebrities. You don't see anything in Barack's life up through 2004 where he's aspiring to hang out with musicians or movie stars, nor is there any evidence of him seeking great personal wealth. Even the *New York Times* has criticized him pretty outspokenly for now going this route of $400,000 per appearance speeches. I find this very hard to square with whom he was up through 2004.

. . . I think the point to emphasize here is that over the course of Barack's presidency, there were scores and scores of people in Illinois who had known him in years earlier who were deeply disappointed with the trajectory of the Obama presidency and disappointed in two ways: number one, disappointed that Barack forgot many of the people, most of the people, who were essential to his political rise; I'm speaking of primarily African Americans, not white people. During the final six months of the Obama presidency, there was a retroactive effort to invite people to the White House to make up something that would have changed the feelings of [his old Chicago allies]—had it been done in 2009 or 2010. . . . The world in which Barack grew up politically in Chicago during the 1990s was a very progressive world. And so, a lot of the people who knew Barack well back then were disappointed with him as president; they have policy disagreements with him. They were not upset that they didn't get invited to the White House Christmas party, they were upset that someone who was a very outspoken critic of the Patriot Act ends up as a champion of the CIA and of Justice Department prosecutions of journalists.

People ask me nowadays, what do I think the Obama presidential legacy will be? I'm afraid that most of that legacy lies overseas in foreign policy—Syria, number one, then North Korea and Iran. When we look at President Obama's domestic legacy, there are two things that are very important that will have long-lasting good consequences for the United States that can be summarized in four words: Sonia Sotomayor and Elena Kagan, his two nominees to the Supreme Court. Both great justices; both justices who've done better than some professional critics expected when he nominated them. So, [I have written] a critical epilogue, but it's not a hostile one.

JAMES MONROE

5th President, 1817–1825

Overall Rank: 13

— ★ —

Total Score: 646

In C-SPAN's 2017 survey, historians upped James Monroe's rank to 13th position, moving him ahead of James Polk and Andrew Jackson. Monroe's highest category rank is in international relations (7th). Like other Virginia presidents who were slaveholders, his lowest rank is in pursued equal justice for all (25th).

Party: Democratic-Republican
b. April 28, 1758, Westmoreland County, Virginia
d. July 4, 1831, New York City, New York
First Lady: Elizabeth Kortright Monroe
Age entering office: 58

Historian: **John Ferling**

John Ferling is a former professor of history at the University of West Georgia who specialized in the American Revolution. He was interviewed for C-SPAN's Q & A on July 25, 2018, to discuss his book, Apostles of Revolution: Jefferson, Paine, Monroe, and the Struggle Against the Old Order in America and Europe, *his fourteenth book on the era.*

[James Monroe was a two-term president, fought in the Revolutionary War, was secretary of state. He was secretary of war for a while; a congressman, and senator. As to why he hasn't gotten more historical attention] I don't have an answer. . . . He is a major figure or plays a role in major events from the mid-1770s all the way down through the 1820s. He is friends with people like Thomas Jefferson and James Madison and the Marquis de Lafayette. In fact, he's the one that invites Lafayette to come back to the United States in the 1820s, and Lafayette comes to his house and visits Monroe. He owed Monroe a debt of gratitude because when Monroe was the minister to France, he liberated Lafayette's wife from prison. [Madame Lafayette's mother,] in fact, was guillotined while both of them were in prison. His wife, fortunately, escaped that.

James Monroe was from Virginia. He started at the College of William and Mary when he was about eighteen years old. Like Alexander Hamilton, who dropped out of college to go into the army in 1776, Monroe dropped out of college and joined the Third Virginia Regiment and soldiered during the American Revolution. The Third Virginia Regiment was training right outside of the room he was living in at the College of William and Mary; Williamsburg was aflame with revolutionary sentiment at that point, so Monroe got caught up in that. He soldiered through the Revolution. Then he met Thomas Jefferson, and Jefferson became his mentor and his law teacher. Monroe remained a satellite of Jefferson's through the rest of his career. In fact, his career bore an uncanny resemblance to Jefferson's, in the sense that each served in the Virginia legislature, then each was a governor of Virginia. Each served in Congress. Each was a diplomat, including secretary of state for both of them, and each wound up as president of the United States.

JAMES MONROE.

One of three founding fathers to die on July 4, James Monroe, seen here as a younger man, devoted his life to the developing nation. *Courtesy Bureau of Engraving and Printing*

Monroe was a very brave individual. He fought in a number of important battles—Trenton, Brandywine, Monmouth—during the Revolutionary War. At Trenton, he was severely wounded. He took a [musket] ball
in the shoulder, and it severed an artery, and fortunately a doctor was
there to patch him up. It was just one of those fortunate incidents that
occurred, because Monroe had been posted on a road leading out of
Trenton to keep anyone from going in or coming out before the attack
was made that next morning. The soldiers made enough noise that dogs
started barking, and the person that owned the dogs was irate. He was
awakened at 2:00 in the morning. He came out and was cursing the
soldiers. When he discovered what was going on, he said, "Well, I'm a
physician." Dr. John Riker is his name. He said, "I'll go with you." So,
he was at Monroe's side when Monroe was wounded, and he was able to
patch him up and save his life.

Monroe was probably twenty-four or twenty-five years old when he linked
up with Jefferson. I think that Monroe hoped—and he certainly wasn't
the only one who harbored these desires; Hamilton did, too, and probably numerous other people—that he might be the George Washington
of the nineteenth century. He was from Virginia, and Washington was
from Virginia. At an early age, Washington had gone to war in the
French and Indian War; Monroe goes to war at an early age in the Revolutionary War. Monroe stood to inherit a great deal of money from a
wealthy uncle of his who had no children, a man named Joseph Jones
who was a real power in Virginia politics in the colonial period; during
the Revolution, he served in Congress for a time. And so, Monroe felt
that like Washington, he might become a wealthy planter and maybe
a military hero and that he might be the next George Washington.
So, . . . he attaches himself to Jefferson, and this is around 1779, and
he's left the Continental Army because he cannot get a field command,
which was very much like Hamilton. Hamilton left the army, too. He
had been an aide-de-camp to Washington and had tried and tried to get
a field command, and it didn't come through.

So, Monroe leaves the army and becomes a law student under
Jefferson. Jefferson, by this time, is the wartime governor of Virginia,
1779 to '81. He probably had the toughest governorship of any wartime governor during the Revolution because the British are raiding
Virginia. Jefferson is chased out of Richmond twice by British armies

that are coming in. The British even ride up to Monticello and try to capture Jefferson; he narrowly escapes. Because of Monroe's military background, Monroe is not only studying under Jefferson, but he was carrying out some fairly dangerous and important military assignments. There was a war going on in the Carolinas, and Jefferson sends Monroe to North Carolina to see what kind of information he could gather on the British troops under Lord Cornwallis down there. [He's also asked to] establish relay stations to get important information back to Jefferson as quickly as possible. These are fairly risky undertakings, so I think that when Monroe does this in his mid-twenties, he's already thinking about a political career.

. . . At one point later on in the 1790s, Alexander Hamilton, in essence, challenged Monroe to a duel. Hamilton had a proclivity for doing that, and then the duels never took place. But when he challenged Monroe, Monroe's response was, "Go get your guns." He didn't back down. [What happened was that] some letters had been released and Hamilton had been accused by two scurrilous individuals of stealing money from the Treasury and investing that money privately. When word of this was transmitted to the speaker of the House, he got two congressmen— one of whom was Monroe—to go with him to interview Hamilton. They were satisfied that Hamilton was telling them the truth, that he not only had not stolen anything but that he was being blackmailed because of an extramarital affair he was having with a woman named Maria Reynolds. They promised Hamilton that nothing would come out and that the notes that they had taken on Hamilton's letters would never see the light of day.

Four or five years later, somebody leaked those letters, as oftentimes happens, and Hamilton was convinced that Monroe may have been the culprit. No one knows [for sure, but] I don't think Monroe was. Monroe was in France at that time, but he had been recalled by Washington as minister to France and was bitter toward Washington as a result of that. He also felt that Hamilton was probably the one whispering in Washington's ear to recall him. So, Monroe certainly had an axe to grind, and he may have surreptitiously contacted the person in Virginia who possessed the incriminating information. Hamilton certainly thought that was the case. Monroe retained Aaron Burr as his second [for the duel]. Burr, in essence, said, "Look, don't worry about it. Hamilton is always challenging people to duels, and they never are carried out. This one will never come about either." And it didn't. There was a lot of correspondence between the two, and it dragged on for several weeks, but they never fought a duel.

James Monroe held a number of [important] offices, [but he] didn't succeed in everything that he attempted. For example, he goes to France as the minister to France [in 1794] but has no experience as a diplomat. He blunders, in that he's probably too positive toward the French, at least from the standpoint of the Washington administration, which was shading more over toward England at that point. Monroe sees himself as sort of a shield protecting the relationship between the United States and France that had begun with the French alliance back in 1778. He feared that this alliance was going to break down, and [in fact] it did break down because of the [1794] Jay Treaty, which the Washington administration accepted. The Jay Treaty . . . attempted to work out a rapprochement with England and sought commercial benefits, a trade treaty with England. We really didn't get very much out of the Jay Treaty, but it did prevent a war with Great Britain, and in that sense, it was significant. A war with Britain in the 1790s would have probably been disastrous for the nascent United States. Monroe wasn't opposed to a treaty with England, but he was opposed to that particular treaty because he thought it was terrible.

When President Jefferson sent Monroe to England [in 1806] to negotiate a treaty on his own with Great Britain, Monroe desperately wanted to come home with a great treaty. . . . He knew that Jefferson respected Thomas Paine, and he knew that Paine was a great writer, the most famous writer of the nineteenth century. He knew that Jefferson had won great accolades for the Declaration of Independence. Monroe was hoping that this treaty with England would be his great prize that would equal what Paine and Jefferson had achieved. But he sends the treaty back, and Jefferson rejects it because the British refused to denounce their policy of impressment, of seizing American soldiers and American sailors and forcing them into the Royal Navy; they claimed that they were deserters from the Royal Navy. So, Monroe came away empty-handed in what he hoped would be his greatest success.

In the War of 1812, Monroe serves in James Madison's administration, and he serves simultaneously—it's a very short period of time—as both secretary of war and secretary of state. He was active in trying to save the militia soldiers and the other soldiers who were there when the British arrived in Washington and burned the city. But, until Monroe becomes president [in 1817], I can't point to anything that was an enormous success.

Of the three [founders] that I've dealt with [in my book], Monroe is the most difficult to get a handle on. He says very little about himself. He wrote memoirs, and it must be the worst set of memoirs that anyone has ever written because he just says what happened but doesn't expand on it. For example, he wrote, "I had dinner with Napoleon." End of the story. It would have been nice if he had told us something about what Napoleon said, or what Napoleon was like. And that's the same feeling that you get when you read his letters. What does come out is that he was a terribly ambitious person. He was a rather insecure person. He misinterpreted many things that happened. . . . When Jefferson refused to back his treaty [with England], he was convinced that Jefferson was stabbing him in the back so that he [Monroe] wouldn't get the credit for the treaty and that it wouldn't interfere with James Madison's election in 1808. I don't think that was the case at all, but that was the insecurity that characterized Monroe.

[James Monroe was not a gifted writer.] . . . Many times, Jefferson would turn to James Madison and ask Madison to write something, and Monroe would also jump in and begin writing. You can almost see Jefferson rolling his eyes at the thought that Monroe was writing. He just wasn't a very good writer and didn't leave behind anything that was particularly noteworthy. I'm not even sure whether he was the actual author [of his Monroe Doctrine] or whether it was written by John Quincy Adams, or someone else.

. . . James Monroe and John Adams and Jefferson and George Washington all waited until they were about twenty-seven or twenty-eight years old to marry. It's in the 1780s that Monroe marries. He marries a woman named Elizabeth Kortright from New York. Her father had been a wealthy merchant, but he had lost most of his money during the war, as happened to a great many other merchants at that time. Monroe was obviously in love with her; he didn't marry her for her money because she wasn't going to have any to bring to the marriage. They remained married until her death; she died about six months before he did. He passed away in the early 1830s when he was seventy-three years old.

Monroe was [frequently] in debt. . . . He was speculating heavily in western lands, much of it in what is now Kentucky. He was a lawyer, and he practiced law to some degree, but I don't know that he really enjoyed practicing law. One of the letters that struck me the most in researching the book was that Monroe wrote to Jefferson at one point— Jefferson was over in France, and Monroe was here—and he says, "I just really dislike practicing law. I want something else." His something else would have been a political office. Jefferson writes back to him, and he says, "Practicing law is not that bad," although Jefferson himself had not really liked practicing law when he had done so in the early 1770s. There are plenty of opportunities now in Richmond because several leading lawyers like John Marshall have gone to serve in the presidential administration. . . . Jefferson also says, "Practicing law helps break the boredom of farming." Jefferson is, of course, the great champion of farming, and in most of what Jefferson wrote he depicted farmers as the chosen people and farming as the best possible kind of life. So, I was surprised when I read that comment by Jefferson.

Those [early political leaders] who favored the French [over the British] probably had twin motives: on the one hand, the French had really saved the United States during the Revolutionary War. They provided loans. They provided gifts of money to the United States. And they also sent over first a navy in 1778 and then an army in 1780. Without that army and navy, the Americans would have never triumphed. So, there was a sense of loyalty toward the French. . . . Many of the people who sympathized with France, like Jefferson, like Monroe, like Thomas Paine, believed that the American Revolution was the spark that had triggered the French Revolution. They believed, at least at the outset, that the French Revolution was going in the same direction as the American Revolution. In fact, almost all Americans, including George Washington, supported the French Revolution in its first couple of years. It's only when the revolution really becomes bloody, starting with the September massacres in 1792 then the Reign of Terror in 1793 and '94, that they began to turn against the French Revolution. But Jefferson never really turned against it, Paine never really turned against it, and Monroe never really turned against it.

In fact, with Jefferson's victory in the election of 1800, Jefferson calls his victory "The Revolution of 1800" and "the Second American Revolution." And [Jefferson, Monroe, and Paine] thought they had defeated everything that England stood for, at least in the United States.

Thomas Paine was six years older than Jefferson. Thomas Jefferson was fifteen years older than James Monroe. Monroe is the one that, of the three, that I had the most difficulty figuring out what he was really like and I'm not sure, even now, I really understand what he was like. But he obviously was someone because he keeps moving into important positions; people looked upon him as a trustworthy individual, somebody who was a competent individual. He certainly seems to have been a compassionate individual when, [as minister to France], he liberates Paine from [France's] Luxembourg prison in 1794. He brings Paine home to live with him, and Paine lived there for about eight months. At one point, Monroe and his wife Elizabeth hadn't had a chance to do any sightseeing, and they left to go on a sightseeing trip throughout France. They'd only been gone a couple of days when they learned that . . . Paine was near death. And so, they cancelled their vacation and came back to Paris and cared for Paine.

[After he left the White House in 1825, Monroe once again] was afraid of losing everything that he had because of his indebtedness, and twice [in 1826 and in 1831] Congress did come to his rescue and provided money for him so that he didn't have to worry about indebtedness. When Lafayette came over and visited him in the mid-1820s, Lafayette offered to help. He said, "I'll give you the money to get you out of debt." Monroe would not take it, but he did ask Congress for money, or rather, friends of his went to Congress and intervened for him.

[Two years after Thomas Jefferson died, James Madison and James Monroe go together to Jefferson's Virginia home, Monticello.] That was one of the more touching things that I ran into in the course of my research. Monroe and Madison are like satellites around Jefferson, to some degree. Consciously or unconsciously, they're competing with one another for Jefferson's favor, so that at times they had something of a tempestuous relationship and didn't speak to one another. . . . But now, Jefferson is gone. They're both elderly. . . . Monticello is already beginning to fall into disrepair, the grass is overgrown, and they walk around and talk about Jefferson and they laugh together, telling stories. They are like two old brothers who have been reunited. Given the tempestuous relationship that they sometimes had, I found it a touching moment.

Monroe lived for four or five years after that [and died on July 4, 1831—the third president to die on Independence Day]. Madison lived for a decade or more after that. . . . Monroe did not liberate his slaves. It fluctuated around over the years, but he owned somewhere between twenty and fifty slaves; some of those he had inherited from Joseph Jones.

[. . . The last line of my book reads, "Jefferson, Paine, and Monroe might welcome another Age of Paine."] What I was suggesting is that many of the things that Thomas Jefferson, Thomas Paine, and James Monroe fought against during their political careers have now come about, especially there are signs of oligarchical control in America. That's what Jefferson feared would be the result of Alexander Hamilton's economic policies. . . . If they could come back—and all of them thought there was an afterlife—and see America today and see that the most important play on Broadway for the past several years is a play that lionizes Alexander Hamilton and vilifies Jefferson and ignores Paine, . . . [if they could] see the maldistribution of wealth in the United States and the amount of money that suffuses American politics today, they would fear that many of these things that are going on in the United States today bore an uncanny resemblance to the England that they had revolted against in 1776. [Perhaps] they would think the time had come for change and reform—maybe not a revolution in the sense of 1776, but a time for great change.

JAMES K. POLK

11th President, 1845–1849

Overall Rank: 14

— ★ —

Total Score: 637

James Polk fell two places in the 2017 survey after ranking 12th in 2000 and 2009. Polk's overall rank is hampered by low category ratings in moral authority (27th) and pursued equal justice for all (36th). He ranks 9th in both crisis leadership and administrative skills.

Party: Democrat
b. November 2, 1795, Mecklenburg County, North Carolina
d. June 15, 1849, Nashville, Tennessee
First Lady: Sarah Childress Polk
Age entering office: 49

Historian: **John Seigenthaler**

John Seigenthaler was the founding editorial director of USA Today *and founder of the First Amendment Center. He was interviewed on C-SPAN's* Booknotes *on December 9, 2003, to discuss his book,* James K. Polk, *on the four objectives Polk had as president.*

I knew that James K. Polk was a Tennessean [because] I'm a Tennessean. I knew that his grave is behind the [state] capitol. . . . His old homeplace in Columbia is preserved, and I'd been there many times, . . . but I knew virtually nothing about him and almost nothing that was good. What was done to him during his presidency over the Mexican-American War left him a bad reputation, a reputation as a warmonger. The attacks on him in Congress in the latter days of his administration reminded me a great deal of the attacks on Lyndon Johnson at the end of his administration over the Vietnam War; there are similarities there.

He was president from 1844 [to 1849], a one-term president by his choice. He said, "I will not run for re-election," and he would not accept any suggestion—and many Democrats pushed him—to run again.

About the week of his inaugural, he told his friend George Bancroft, who was to be his secretary of the navy—a great historian, by the way—he said, "Bancroft, there are four things I want to do that will be my great measures: One, we will lower the tariff, a controversial issue; two, we will create an independent treasury. We'll take all the government's money out of these corrupt private banks, which pay us no interest, and we'll put those funds in private vaults to pay the bills, meet the payroll; three, we will take California; and [four], we'll take Oregon. That will make us [a nation] from sea to shining sea." He said he would do it, and he did it.

[Some of the words I use to describe him are perfectionist, microman-ager, workaholic, a brooder, humorless, angry, arrogant, unforgiving, strait-laced, and "a little prig from Tennessee."] The truth of the matter is that when I got through with this book, I was not in love with him. I admired him for what he did. He was a tough-minded president, and he gave us a continental nation, and a dozen states exist because he took us westward. But he's not the sort of fellow I would have enjoyed hav-ing lunch with, and certainly not dinner with. You wouldn't want to go around the world on a tandem bike with him or even around the block, probably. But nonetheless, I did come away with great respect for him, and while not affection, but admiration, because he did great things.

James K. Polk was born in Mecklenburg County [near Charlotte, North Carolina]. He had a very agrarian upbringing. He went to sort of sea-sonal schools. When he was eight, his grandfather had moved to Mid-dleton, Tennessee, and found, really, a paradise, and so Sam, his father, and Sarah, his mother, went over the mountains and settled in Mid-dleton, Tennessee. He was a very sickly child—so sickly that he was not able to do all the work in the fields that other children were expected to do. At one point his father wants to make him a merchant, and, as a young boy, puts James in a store. It doesn't work. What James really wants is an education, and . . . his father finally sends him for a formal education. First, he went to a little seminary school near where they lived in Columbia, Tennessee, then to Murfreesboro, where there was an academy, and finally to the University of North Carolina, where he entered as a sophomore and graduated first in his class and spoke at the graduation. He was talented from the outset. He was fortunate in that

In this 1844 Philip Haas lithograph of President-elect James Polk, there is a barely visible map of his home state of Tennessee. *Courtesy Library of Congress*

he fell into the arms of the great Tennessee lawyer Felix Grundy, later attorney general of the United States and United States senator. Grundy mentored him in law. In those days, lawyers trained in the chambers of a distinguished lawyer.

[When he was seventeen years old, he had a painful and risky operation.] There were documents that were left by Dr. [Ephraim] McDowell, a Danville, Kentucky, specialist, one of the great surgeons in the history of this country. He left papers which were relied on to demonstrate that this was really a urinary stone operation. It was a brutal operation. Here's a seventeen-year-old young man, constantly, almost chronically, ill with lower-abdomen pains. Finally, Polk's father, who's wealthy, decides the best man in the country is Dr. Philip Syng Physick in Philadelphia. They put James in a covered wagon with a bed, and this ambulance, horse-drawn, heads north to Pennsylvania. It gets up around the Green River in Kentucky, and Polk has violent attacks, and they rush him to Danville, where this other surgeon, Ephraim McDowell, operates.

The operation was brutal: no [anesthesia]; they only could give him brandy. They didn't have any antiseptic to stop the poison. They held him down. His uncle was with him. . . . They used what was called a gorget, and if you look at the gorget, it looks like it sounds, a vicious knife. They went between the scrotum and the anus, right through the prostate. How he ever survived is remarkable, but he did. After he became speaker of the House, Polk corresponded with the doctor. There were just a couple of physicians [in the country at this time] who were capable of doing this surgery. Sam Polk, his father, really made a search before he decided he wanted Dr. Physick to do this. But McDowell had also been on his agenda, so it was just fortunate that McDowell was as close to Polk as he was, and they got him there. There's no doubt in my mind—and this is why I think the operation was important—that he and Sarah were childless as a result of this operation. I created a panel of about nine doctors—whose names are acknowledged in my book—some specialists, some general practitioners. [They] all thought it was very risky, but all concluded after they looked at it that there was not much doubt that he was either left sterile or impotent, or both.

[James Polk was admitted to the Tennessee bar in 1820 and began his law practice.] Polk was elected once to the Tennessee legislature [in 1823], seven times to Congress [beginning in 1824], once as governor [in 1839], and once as president.

. . . He's the only speaker of the House who became president of the United States. Nobody else has been able to make that springboard, . . . but Polk did it. As speaker, he presided over a hostile House. Members of that House constantly were trying to bait him into duels. A man named Henry Wise from Virginia, who was called a dead shot, and a man named Bailey Payton from Tennessee, both despised him. Both constantly harassed him from the House floor and insulted him. At one point they meet him at the door [of the House chamber, and wagging his finger] Wise said, "You were very insulting to me today on the floor, and I [took it personally]." . . . [But] Polk was against dueling, would not accept the duel, would not challenge in return for an insult. Andrew Jackson was the great dueler who wouldn't take any insult. Polk was Jackson's protégé, and everyone said that Jackson would be critical of Polk because he took those insults. But on the contrary, Jackson said he admired Polk's pacific attitude and courage in accepting leadership and not responding, as many did in that day.

[In the 1844 election, there were 2.5 million votes cast], all white men. No women. No black [people]. The difference in the vote between Henry Clay and Polk was 1.4 percent—thirty-eight thousand votes. The Electoral College—specifically, thirty-six votes in New York—really gave the election to Polk. Had New York gone for Clay, Clay would have been the president. There are echoes from this time to ours. James K. Polk failed to carry his home state of Tennessee, which reminds us that in 2000, if Al Gore had carried his own state of Tennessee, he would have been the president. Everything that goes around, comes around.

Today, we would call Polk a "yellow dog" Democrat. He was perhaps the most partisan president in history. Harry Truman, another very partisan president, once listed his eight great presidents, and Polk was one of those. . . . Truman said Polk knew exactly what he wanted to do; he said what he was going to do, and he did it, and that made great hay with Truman. Polk also was very critical of his generals, as Truman was of General Douglas MacArthur. And so, there's that similarity, too. Polk would have been right at home in today's acidic Washington political environment. He would have been up to the needles and the digs and the knives that are wielded; he would have waded right into that environment and been right at home.

Putting Andrew Jackson in context while writing about Polk really gave me new insights to Jackson, about whom I knew a great deal. Just, for example, Jackson's greatest problem during his presidency had to do with his inability to get along with the vice president, John C. Calhoun, and the Calhounites that were part of his cabinet. The marriage of John Eaton, member of the cabinet and his good friend, to Margaret O'Neill was a major scandal. . . . Polk was in Congress [as House speaker] looking at that. Jackson wrapped his arms around Martin Van Buren and named him vice president—really ordained him for the vice presidency in the second term, primarily because Van Buren was nice to Eaton and Mrs. Eaton. So, the whole Jackson cabinet is wiped out; Eaton resigns, and others are forced to resign. Polk comes into office, and I think one of the reasons he didn't dump James Buchanan was because he didn't want that same sort of image that had haunted Jackson. He didn't want anybody to leave the cabinet over a controversy. . . . Polk is watching from Capitol Hill as this debacle occurs over this scandal in the Jackson cabinet. The country was almost paralyzed, the government was not functional during that period, and President Jackson was old and couldn't function. Polk really loved Andrew Jackson, admired Andrew Jackson, but he didn't want to make the same mistakes that Jackson had made.

[I admire] his effort to finish the bank war that Andrew Jackson had started—Jackson, his role model, his hero, his mentor, the man who really made him president. He really tried to model himself after Jackson, and yet there were attributes of Jackson's character that turned him off. [But] I don't think Polk was a very likable man; among other reasons, he was duplicitous. Two or three times a week they'd open up the White House to everybody. His worst enemies would come down from Capitol Hill. He and [first lady] Sarah Polk, this lovely, congenial woman, would welcome them. He'd make them feel like they were king for a day. And that night, he'd go upstairs, and congeniality and collegiality went out the window. He would sit down with his diary and just rip them to shreds. He used that diary almost as a purgative, and obviously, it hooked me. It was the bait that led me to do this biography. It's fascinating reading.

Polk's diary is four volumes, and each one's about four hundred pages. It's a long read, but it's conversational and he was a good writer; he knew how to write a simple declarative sentence, and that's what the diary is. His line, "I know I'm the hardest-working man in America," reflects his egomaniacal instinct that occasionally emerged. He said, in another occasion in the diary, "I haven't had the cabinet here for six weeks. I've learned I can run every department of the government without their help." And then he says, "I'm the hardest-working man in America." The truth is, he probably was. He was a workaholic around the clock, early morning, late at night, and was very, very sickly during much of his administration.

. . . I cannot, for the life of me, figure out why Polk kept James Buchanan as his secretary of state. The two were constantly at war. Polk could control him, but he couldn't keep Buchanan from popping off, or telling him he was wrong, or even lecturing him. They fought about foreign policy. A good example: the British and the French are constantly meddling in US affairs. They've got interests in the middle of this country. And then, there is Mexico having this ongoing conflict with the Republic of Texas. So, there was a good deal [about which] to formulate policy. When it comes time for war with Mexico, Buchanan says in a cabinet meeting, "I really need to let the French and British know that in this war with Mexico, we don't have aims on California." Well, of course, Polk had aims on California, so, he says, "Do not do that. I do not want you to tell them that." Buchanan said, "If you don't, you may have war with both of them." Polk replied, "I'll go to war with them and fight to the last man before I'll say that we have no designs on California. . . ." And so, Buchanan was silent on the subject.

The Oregon Territory, which was Washington and Oregon, belonged to us jointly with Great Britain, and Polk considered it part of the natural right of the American nation to take that contiguous territory. He threatened to go to war with the British over it. He bluffed them and said he was prepared to go to war over it, and at the last moment, the British capitulated. California, he had hoped that he would be able to purchase. Both Henry Clay, when he was secretary of state under John Quincy Adams, and John Tyler, who was president immediately before Polk, had tried to buy California. The Mexicans were insulted by both offers and rejected blandishments by Polk to give them the territory for money. And so, Polk went to war with Mexico and took California.

. . . When it came time to take Oregon Territory away from the British, the issue was, at what parallel would we get the territory? If we went to war, we would get the 54th parallel, which is [where the slogan] "54-40 or fight" came from. That was the cry in Congress. The Tyler administration had left Polk with a proposal to the British to draw the line at the 49th parallel, and the British turned that flatly down. This infuriated Polk, and he told Buchanan, "You go back and tell the British we want it all—up to the 54th." Buchanan says, "You know this will mean war." Polk said, "I don't care. You tell them the old offer is off the table. We want the 54th parallel. We want as much as we can get." As always, Buchanan had a fallback position. Buchanan says, "Mr. President, you know we're about to have trouble with Mexico. Why don't we put this off?" Polk replies: "No. Tell them now. . . . We'll do our duty by both Mexico and Great Britain. We must look John Bull in the eye."

Reluctantly, Buchanan goes over and delivers the message and then comes back to the next cabinet meeting and says, "It was the wrong thing, but I did it." Right in the president's face! And believe it or not, Polk comes right back and says, "We did the right thing." And he leaves it at that. It was a constant fight between them; it was a constant war. I question, in my own mind, . . . why he didn't dump him.

The Mexican War starts in 1846. The conflict was started over the Mexican border. Eight years earlier, we had the Alamo and [the Battle of] Goliad, and then Sam Houston, Tennessean and friend of Polk, defeats [Mexican general] Santa Anna. They get him to agree that the line between the two countries, between the Independent Republic of Texas and Mexico, will be the Rio Grande River. The Mexican parliament doesn't accept that, but, of course, Texans do. . . . There comes a time when Mexico declares war on the United States because the United States is going to annex Texas. In 1845, Polk is coming into office, and Polk really wants Congress to get the annexation of Texas started before he takes over, and he works with Congress to get that done. The Mexicans react angrily.

Polk sends General Zachary Taylor down, and he says, "If the Mexicans come across and attack, consider it an attack on the country, and go into Mexico and take as much as you can." And so, that is what happened. A small party of Mexicans ambushes a small party of US soldiers, and Taylor goes in and takes Palo Alto, takes Resaca de Palma, and the war is on.

At the same time, Polk is having a terrible time with General Winfield Scott. Scott doesn't want to go to Mexico. Zachary Taylor is on his way. Scott says, "I'll go down in September," which was three, four months off. And Polk calls in his secretary of war, William Marcy, and says, "Get him on the way." Scott writes a letter in which he says, "I don't want to be shot at in the front by the Mexicans and in the rear in Washington." Polk at that point grounds Scott and takes his command away from him. Scott gets his command back by proposing a plan in which we attack Mexico across the Gulf [of Mexico]. Scott's attack comes across the Gulf, and he goes through to Mexico City while Zachary Taylor is going north. At the same time, General [Stephen] Kearny is going to [the West] to take California. So, it was really a three-pronged attack.

Polk despised both Zachary Taylor and Winfield Scott. They did nothing but win battles [for him], and against great odds, and yet every night in his diary when Polk gets news of another great victory he says, "They are both incompetent. They are unqualified for command." It was purely partisan [on Polk's part].

Abraham Lincoln stood up on the floor of the House in 1848 as Polk is about to go out of office. He was a freshman congressman, and he stood up on the floor and virtually called James K. Polk a liar [over his Mexican War policy]. . . . Lincoln wants to be sure where the first drop of blood [of the war] was spilled and demands, literally issues an interrogatory for the president to respond to, which he doesn't. It echoes a little bit of today with President George W. Bush's concept of preemptive defense: they're at war with us, and if they attack us, we're going in.

[James Polk and his Mexico policy is at the center of a great deal of history: Abraham Lincoln is criticizing Polk on the House floor and he later becomes president. General Zachary Taylor becomes a candidate for the Whigs and wins the White House in 1848. And, General Winfield Scott becomes the Whig's nominee in 1852;] I'll tell you, anybody who was anybody in [this era of] history intersects with the life of James K. Polk.

Polk died ninety days after he left the presidency. He went home to die. He left the presidency worn and sickly. He probably contracted cholera, either on the way home or after he arrived. It was a long trip. He went all the way south to New Orleans and came up the Mississippi and then across the Ohio and down the Cumberland River, arrived home, and was welcomed by Tennesseans. His old friend from Congress, Aaron Brown, was now governor, and they welcomed him home. He had ninety days of bad health and died.

Polk was fifty-three years old when he died. He was, at that time, the youngest president in history and died [of natural causes] younger than any president in history.

James Polk owned more than forty slaves, and he owned them on his Mississippi plantation and his property in Tennessee. In his will, he left all his slaves to his wife for her lifetime, then they were to be freed. She lived until she was eighty-seven years old [dying in 1891], and so Lincoln had freed the slaves long before Sarah Polk died. Polk said slavery was a common evil. You would think that as a one-term president not planning to run for election, he might have taken some steps to provide some leadership on slavery [even if] you can understand why he didn't do that during the political campaign—because you couldn't take that position and be elected.

James K. Polk was a man for his time. There's very little you can say that he left [undone]. His administration was between the only two Whig administrations in our history, and both of those administrations—the Harrison administration and Tyler administration—were interrupted by the deaths of those two presidents, and so those administrations did very little. Polk's administration is sandwiched between those, and he did a great deal. So, it's surprising to me that only historians [and not the general public] recognize him.

WILLIAM J. CLINTON

42nd President, 1993–2001

Overall Rank: 15

— ★ —

Total Score: 634

Bill Clinton entered the survey ranked 21st overall in 2000, and had jumped six places by 2017. Historians have consistently ranked him among the top ten in economic management (3rd in 2017) and pursued equal justice for all (6th). Clinton's rank in relations with Congress has improved from 36th to 17th, which is the largest increase in a category ranking by any president.

Party: Democrat
b. August 19, 1946, Hope, Arkansas
First Lady: Hillary Rodham Clinton
Age entering office: 46

Historian: **David Maraniss**

David Maraniss is a Pulitzer Prize–winning journalist and associate editor for the Washington Post. *He was interviewed on March 27, 1995, on C-SPAN's* Booknotes *for his book,* First in His Class: A Biography of Bill Clinton, *which details his years on the road to the White House.*

I thought Bill Clinton was a great story. That was really the underlying motivation [for my book], that whatever anyone thinks of Bill Clinton's presidency or his ideology, his life is a great American story. It's a narrative that I thought revealed a lot about ambition, and the clash between ambition and idealism—[his] coming out of nowhere, dealing with a troubled family, rising out of Arkansas from the point where he shook John Kennedy's hand in 1963, to actually living in the White House himself. That's just a great story.

Bill Clinton's early childhood . . . is probably the least-known part of his life and the part I had the most frustration trying to recreate—starting with his birth and up through probably his first ten years, dealing first with a young man without a father and then an alcoholic stepfather. Although I got a lot of people talking about that part of his life, I really don't know what it was like for young Bill Clinton to be in that household and I thought I'd really like to see how it affected him.

I moved to Hope, Arkansas, where he was born, and spent a few weeks there interviewing dozens of people who knew the family. I talked to a lot of his aunts and got a lot of the letters of that era and tried to recreate what it was like in that small town in the South during the late 1940s and the early 1950s. Then I moved up to Hot Springs, where his stepfather was from, and stayed in the same hotel that Al Capone used to hang out in, the Arlington Hotel up there, and tried to talk to as many women of his mother's generation—many of whom also dealt with the same problems that she did in terms of [not] being treated as equals with men and being abused by their husbands. So, I spent a lot of time trying to recreate that generation.

Essentially, he had two mothers. His own mother, Virginia, had left Hope when he was less than two to go down to New Orleans to study to be a nurse anesthetist. And so, he lived with his [grandmother Edith] "Mama Cassidy," who was a very rigid character. Bill Clinton is such a contrast of people; he has a certain discipline, and yet he's very undisciplined. His discipline comes from that grandmother, who would wake him at a specific hour, whether he was ready to awaken himself or not, and fed him constantly on a pattern. So, he had two mothers, one mother who was sort of rebelling against the life in Hope and wanted to get away from it, and this grandmother who was teaching him the discipline of that time and place.

Many of their relatives told me the stories of how Mrs. Cassidy would scream and yell at her husband, Eldridge Cassidy, who was probably the best-liked man in Hope. He was the local iceman at first. He would deliver ice on a horse and wagon and then eventually got a truck. But he was known as a very, very friendly man, and she thought he was too friendly with some of the women in town and would let him know.

His [maternal] grandparents didn't have a lot of money, but they weren't poor by Hope's standards. They certainly weren't rich; his grandfather never really cared about money, but he did run a store, and [Bill] lived in a nice white house. So, I wouldn't say that's poverty. Roger Clinton, his stepfather, was terrible with money and was always losing it—wasting it on alcohol and women and gambling. Roger Clinton's brother, Raymond Clinton, was a wealthy auto dealer in Hot Springs and belonged to a country club, and young Bill Clinton had a car in high school and played golf at a country club. So, I wouldn't say that that's poverty. I think [the stories that Bill Clinton built himself up from a life of poverty is] a little bit of the Clinton mythmaking.

[Virginia's] first husband was Bill Blythe, who is Bill Clinton's biological father, most likely. It's a very sensitive subject. But in my book, you'll notice that the time when Bill Blythe got out of the military in World War II does not quite correspond with the point in time that Virginia, Bill's mother, always claimed that he got out of the military. So, there's some question about when Bill Clinton was conceived. I had never heard that before. I heard it from people in Hope who would raise questions about it. I'm not trying to disparage Bill Clinton's mother, but as a historian I had to look into that, and, unfortunately, I wasn't able to totally resolve it. But there are some discrepancies on the dates. Bill Blythe had been married at least four times before he met Virginia Cassidy. She knew about none of those marriages. And, it's possible that there were even one or two others. It was hard for me to trace them all out throughout the small courthouses of the South. . . . I went to six courthouses: in Madill and Ardmore, Oklahoma; Oklahoma City; Sherman, Texas; in Shreveport, Louisiana; and in Texarkana. I found five [marriage records]. I was looking for W. J. Blythe—that's the way he was known. I was looking for divorce and marriage records and birth records.

Virginia had never been married before. When she did marry, she first married Bill Blythe, and then she married Roger Clinton; then she married Jeff Dwyer, and then she married Dick Kelly. So, she'd been married to four men, but five times. She married Roger Clinton twice. Roger Clinton married Virginia when Bill Clinton was four years old, and they divorced when Bill was fourteen, fifteen, but only for three months. . . . She didn't love him anymore. He was an alcoholic who had abused her. Their divorce records are full of cases: one time he took her high heels and beat her on the head with them, and he accused her of a lot of things which were untrue. It was not a very comfortable marriage, but she remarried him because she felt sorry for him.

I think young Bill Clinton saw a lot [of violence growing up in Roger Clinton's home]. That's not to say that every day in that household was a terror or that it was terrifying. I know from recreating Bill Clinton's life through his letters and conversations with some of his friends that it did not dominate the exterior of his life. His friends didn't even know that his stepfather was an alcoholic or abusing his mother, but I think that there were many occasions when it got pretty nasty inside that house. And, I think that's what drove him in a lot of ways.

. . . Bill Clinton was in constant search of father figures. He never had a father, and I think that later in his life it was his minister in Little Rock, W. O. Vaught, who was as unlike Bill Clinton as anyone could be in the world. He was a short, wiry, bespectacled, rigid man who taught only from Scripture, was very conservative in his political beliefs, but ran the largest Southern Baptist church in Arkansas. Bill Clinton took to Vaught and really looked to him not only for spiritual help but political advice. Vaught helped him work out his positions on abortion and the death penalty, but Vaught died before Clinton ran for president, and I think he missed him a lot during that tumultuous era.

Bill Clinton's whole life has a measure of calculation in it, which he has tried to diminish for a lot of reasons, one of which is that raw political ambition in America is often seen as a bad thing. You would never say that about someone who wanted to grow up and become the best ice skater in the world or the best pianist, but, if you wanted to become president at an early age, people would see that as a negative. And so, he always wanted to couch that, even though he had that burning desire in him. Part of the way to temper that [image] is to make it look like a lot of those things happened by accident. The prologue in my book is his handshake with John Kennedy in 1963, the iconic transfer of ambition from a president to a future president. As my prologue shows so clearly, that was no accident, that handshake. He was the one on the bus ride down [with other Boys' Nation participants] who kept asking the chaperon whether they could get pictures taken, and once the bus got to the White House, he race-walked his way to the best position in line to get the handshake. So, there was always that calculation.

[Bill Clinton graduated from Hot Springs High School in Arkansas and was accepted into Georgetown University in Washington, DC.] The watermelons of Hope, Arkansas, [also became part of Clinton's image-making]. He used to describe how the railroads would come through Hope in southwest Arkansas and stop there. The porters would get out, and there'd be fresh watermelons cut on these trays outside the train, and they'd bring them back, and the people would eat them on their way back to Texas. It was a way for Bill Clinton to talk about that he was from a place other than where his friends were from. He left Arkansas when he was seventeen years old, went to the East Coast, and was away for nine years, and he was dealing with a totally different culture. He was the Southern Baptist at Georgetown University, full of upper-middle-class Catholic kids from the East Coast. The sons and daughters of presidents of El Salvador and Saudi Arabia and the Philippines were in his class. Unlike so many of the kids of that era who would try to forget their past, shed their past, Clinton used that past almost as a defense mechanism. Rather than being embarrassed about coming from a small town, he played it up. One way he did that was by constantly talking about the watermelons.

He was never first in his class academically, but he was close. He was fourth in his high school class; he was Phi Beta Kappa at Georgetown. At Oxford he never got a degree, and at Yale Law School he graduated with the law degree, but he was never in class. But [my book's title], *First in His Class,* means that he's the first member of his generation to become president.

[Bill Clinton was out of sorts his second year as a Rhodes scholar at Oxford in 1969, because of] the draft, largely. About half of the thirty-two Rhodes scholars went to England their first year with sort of unofficial, but clear, Vietnam War deferments that they didn't deserve. President [Lyndon] Johnson had just eliminated graduate school deferments, but most of the local draft boards considered these guys local heroes, and they didn't want them to get drafted right when they'd won this great prestigious honor. So, they went over to England with deferments that they didn't really deserve. And in the spring, finally, of his first year, Clinton got his draft notice. He came back to Arkansas that summer of 1969 in agony trying to figure out what to do. He didn't want to fight in Vietnam. He was against the war. Who knows whether he was afraid of dying, but I think most young men are. There's a whole mixture of feelings that he was going through. He wanted to be in politics.

He believed in the established way. So, he was trying to figure it out, and he eventually manipulated his way into an ROTC post that he never served in and went back to England feeling guilty about that.

[His next stop was Yale Law School. When he was there, he made a point of sitting with the black students at their table.] It was at a time of black power, black separation to a certain degree, or at least a cultural identity that separated the races in college campuses. Clinton's friends, his roommates, all told me they were afraid to go sit at that table, even though they were, perhaps, further to the left politically than Bill Clinton. They just said they were uncomfortable being over there, and it was clear to them that the black students didn't want them to be there. Clinton just sort of barged his way into the table and would tell jokes about himself, self-depreciating jokes, jokes about the South, jokes about sex, jokes about anything. He really was very comfortable in that milieu, just a natural thing that he had. He is very good at adapting to different cultures and milieus and is particularly good at connecting with black people on that level, and almost every black person that I had interviewed for the book told me that in one way or another.

I found that in almost every era of Clinton's life, there's at least one story that had become mythologized. Sometimes it's totally innocuous, and it's just probably bad memories. . . . Sometimes there was definite psychological or political reason for the mythologizing. For instance, another one of the myths that Bill Clinton would tell was about how he accidentally got his job as a professor at the University of Arkansas. He says he was just driving back from Yale Law School and stopped at the side of the road on the interstate and called the dean and got the job. In fact, he had tried to get the job for many months and had gone through the normal patterns of using friends and contacts to get that job. I think that that myth was established by Clinton because he was going back to a place that all his Yale Law School friends thought he was crazy to go to. And so, [in his retelling] it was sort of like, "It was just easy; it was an accident. I didn't try to do it." The reason was that he knew in his mind he was going back to Arkansas to run for Congress; and so the idea that he had worked so hard to get hired as a professor when, in fact, he had really not much interest in being a professor—that's why he would create this myth that it was just sort of a fluke.

Bill Clinton, thirty-two, became Arkansas's second-youngest governor at his January 9, 1979, swearing-in ceremony in Little Rock. *Courtesy William J. Clinton Presidential Library*

[At age] twenty-seven, Clinton is running for Congress in Fayetteville, Arkansas. He had just moved back from Yale Law School to be an assistant professor at the University of Arkansas in Fayetteville. In 1974, he was running against [Republican incumbent] John Paul Hammerschmidt, his first race there—which he did well in, but lost. [Two years later he was elected Arkansas's attorney general and then ran for governor in 1978.] . . . In 1979, . . . he was inaugurated as the youngest governor in America since Harold Stassen; Clinton was then thirty-two.

[The relationship between Bill and Hillary Rodham Clinton, whom he married in 1975, is] always changing. I think that it was built on a shared passion for policy and politics and books and ideas and intellectual life, and also a sense of humor. When he married Hillary, he told his friends that he was going for brains over glamour. I think that she knew what she was getting into when she married him, in the sense of his enormous appetite for life. They've had several tumultuous parts to their marriage, but it's a pragmatic, political partnership with some extra spice to it as well. Absolutely.

To understand their relationship, you have to understand it's gone through . . . stages, basically. They met at Yale Law School, and from that point in the early 1970s until 1980 when he was defeated as governor, although they saw that they could get to their ultimate goal together, they were really leading independent lives in the sense that she was building up her own life and career. [She worked] first as a law professor and then as a lawyer and then working in Children's Defense Fund issues. Then he got beat, and she came to the realization that he could only recover with her more profound help. From then on, she was his key financial person, his key political adviser, his pro bono lawyer on ethical issues, and his main policy person. [He won back the governorship in 1982 and Hillary became] the head of his task force on education reform, which was successful, and which made his name in Arkansas. This established his career for the 1980s and helped him become a national figure. They carried that policy partnership into the White House almost without even thinking twice about it, and so then when the [Clinton administration's] health care plan was defeated, it forced them to reconsider whether she should be in that out-front policy role [as first lady].

[Political consultant Dick Morris has a key role in the Clinton story.] It was 1978, and Clinton was attorney general of Arkansas, and he was preparing to run for governor. Morris was really starting out in his career and was very aggressively pursuing candidates around the country. Clinton was one of those that he latched on with, but he drove Clinton's other aides crazy during that first campaign, and they essentially fired him until Clinton was fired as governor after only two years. Then Hillary called and said, "Come on back. We need you again." Then Morris stayed on for the rest of the '80s.

Dick Morris's advice was often very astute, and that's why Clinton, and even more so Hillary Rodham Clinton, really relied on Morris. [After Clinton lost his re-election bid in 1980,] Morris is the one who told Clinton to apologize to the people of Arkansas for his first term. It proved to be very effective saying that he understood that he'd made mistakes, almost like the prodigal son saying, "Let me back." It worked very effectively, and it was a technique, a sort of humble admission, that Clinton and Hillary remembered for the future and used again and again over the years.

This happened in 1981 when he was preparing to run again in '82. They taped a TV spot where Clinton essentially said, "I'm sorry. I learned my lessons. It will never happen again." At that point, Clinton was the youngest ex-governor in American history. He was really depressed; he fit that ironic description of the Rhodes scholar, which is a bright young man with a future behind him. Morris really pulled him out of it and told him, "Apologize; go forward." It worked. And then he developed what I call the "permanent campaign," which was essentially to go around the established media, the newspapers, and television; as you're pushing your legislative agenda, use your own public relations apparatus to sell your agenda. It's something that Clinton did from then on, to use polling constantly, not just to find out what the people were thinking about an issue, but how they would respond specifically to rhetoric. Clinton loved that. It isn't just pure Machiavelli. Clinton really did love to connect with people—he always had—and to have a scientific way of doing it really intrigued him. And he did that for the rest of his career as well.

[Longtime aide] Betsey Wright came down to Little Rock about a week or two after Bill Clinton was defeated in 1980. She lived in the governor's mansion for a while, piecing back together all of the detritus of his life, of his political career. She put into computers all of the thousands of note cards that he had of his key political allies and contributors. Then, when he won re-election, she became his chief of staff from 1983 through 1990. Her relationship with Clinton is one of the most interesting that I encountered. There's a real sisterly-brotherly, love-hate relationship going on all through their time together. She is both fiercely loyal to him and yet is angry at him all the time.

. . . There's a scene in [my] book where Betsey Wright and Bill Clinton meet at her house, and they go over a list of the women who might be problematic for Clinton if he were to run for president in 1988. When the book came out, she issued what I call a non-denial denial, saying that David Maraniss might have "misinterpreted what I had told him." But I hadn't; she knows I didn't. It's very clear to me and my editors at the *Washington Post* that for two weeks before that incident I'd read to her all of the parts of the book that referred to [his sexual interactions with women]. We have documents about it. I don't think Betsy Wright was mad; I think she was under a little bit of pressure to try to deny it, but no one has said a word about it since, or challenged any of the other parts of the book.

. . . Clinton has always considered himself an education politician, and he has so many degrees himself, but he was under court pressure to reform the education system in Arkansas. To get the money that he needed—he realized through polls that Dick Morris did and through discussions with the major business leaders in Arkansas who had helped fund his education reform effort—that he had to make the teachers accountable in some dramatic, clear way. And so, he imposed competency tests on the teachers. They hated it, but the public loved it. It helped Clinton politically so much to use the teachers as sort of a fake enemy. He set himself up in opposition to them in order to help himself politically and to get across this broader program, which he thought had a lot of merit. I don't think he ever really wanted to use the teachers in that way, but they were just convenient for him. So, for about six years of his governorship, he and the teachers were at odds. Yet, when I was covering the [presidential] campaign in 1992 and went up to New Hampshire, there standing next to me was the former head of the teachers' union, who used to denounce him all the time, campaigning for him. Clinton has a way of winning people over again.

In 1990, no one, including even his wife, knew until minutes before, and even maybe as he made the announcement, whether he was going to run again as governor for Arkansas. People in Arkansas who covered that race were trying to figure it out as well. It was stunning to me that one of Hillary's friends called her and said, "Do you know what Bill's going to do?" Here she is, his [wife and] main political adviser, and there was just enormous uncertainty about whether he would run again that year. Maybe that was a period when they weren't as close as some other periods. He told the people when he ran for governor in 1990 that if he were elected he'd serve out four years. Someone asked him that question at a political forum, "Will you serve out your term if you're elected?" In classic Clinton style, without even thinking, he said, "You bet." Just like that, and then he had to live with those two words and break them.

[When he ran for president in 1992, he got 53 percent of the vote in Arkansas.] There's a joke in Arkansas that they voted for him to get rid of him. That's not it, obviously, but most of them think that Clinton is always asking for forgiveness of one sort or another. People in Arkansas are often willing to give it to him, and they knew all along that his goal was to be president. By the time he made that decision [to seek the White House], people in Arkansas knew him so well that those who were for him were for him no matter what; those who were against him hated his guts and didn't care. There were no undecideds about Bill Clinton in Arkansas by that time; they'd known him for so long.

My book ends the day Clinton announced [his bid] for president. . . . This book is not about the 1992 campaign, and it's not about Bill Clinton as president. I would argue that although the book ends the day he announced for president, everything that happened since is in the book, because his campaign, in essence, was his life coming back to him, and his presidency . . . [has] largely been recurring patterns of his career coming back to him.

There's something in [my Bill Clinton biography] for everybody. There's certainly a lot of material for Clinton's enemies, as well as for his friends. I think they can find parts of his life where he was duplicitous, where he manipulated his way out of things and didn't tell the truth about them later, and there are parts of the book where you can see that he's a caring, compassionate, interesting person.

. . . The number-one question I get about Bill Clinton: What does this guy really believe the most? In a general way, I can say that I think he went into politics to do good and that his life and career have been that clash between idealism and ambition. If you're looking at one issue, as a progressive coming out of the South, race relations always meant the most to him, was the burning issue of his childhood and youth, and that Vietnam really, in a sense, got in the way of what he wanted to do in terms of his political career and for civil rights; and then again, so did his ambition. So, there are two or three points in his career where you can see him making decisions on issues relating to civil rights that are controversial.

The hardest thing was to decide in my own mind what I felt about this guy. I'd go back and forth violently because there were chapters in his life where I liked him and chapters where I didn't. So, I would beat myself up, saying, "Make up your mind; you've got to decide." Then I realized—he is a dual person, and that I had it right.

WILLIAM McKINLEY

25th President, 1897–1901

Overall Rank: 16

— ★ —

Total Score: 627

Ranking 16th overall in both the 2017 and 2009 surveys, William McKinley has received consistent marks from historians in all three C-SPAN surveys. His highest ranks are in relations with Congress (10th in 2017) and economic management (11th). His lowest rank is in pursued equal justice for all (26th).

Party: Republican
b. January 29, 1843, Niles, Ohio
d. September 14, 1901, Buffalo, New York
First Lady: Ida Saxton McKinley
Age entering office: 54

Historian: **Robert W. Merry**

Bob Merry is a longtime political journalist and author who most recently was the editor of The American Conservative. *He appeared on C-SPAN's* Q & A *to discuss his book,* President McKinley: Architect of the American Century, *on November 1, 2017.*

The most important thing going on [between 1897 and 1901] was that the country was burgeoning. It was expanding and poised to move dramatically into the world. America is an expansionist country, always has been. . . . What William McKinley did was push out—into the Pacific and into the Atlantic, into the Caribbean—in a way that no president had done before. That didn't just happen; it happened because America was building an industrial base; was building economic growth and economic wherewithal; was building a navy. McKinley had a lot to do with it, but it actually began before him. The country was gaining more and more interest in building a canal across Central America. When we ended up with conflict—serious conflict—in the Caribbean with the Spanish empire, which controlled and owned Cuba, it was inevitable that we would not only go to war with Spain, but that we would basically kick Spain out of the Caribbean. We would pick up significant numbers of their possessions, and we would become an empire.

McKinley was a tough nut for me to crack. . . . I thought I was pretty good at bringing people to life; McKinley was not easy to bring to life. For one thing, he didn't keep a diary and, of course, he wrote no memoirs because he was killed in office, but he also hardly wrote any letters. There's very little written record of what he was thinking, or how he was feeling, or what he thought about this guy or that person. I was really struggling with the book. My friend, David Ignatius of the *Washington Post*, who was reading my manuscript, touched on it. He said this guy is a mystery because he was a very consequential and a very effective president, and you can't quite figure out how or why he was able to accomplish what he accomplished because he was indirect. McKinley was an incrementalist. He was a manager. He was not a man of force. It turns out that even without that force, he had amazing capacity to manipulate people into doing the things that he wanted them to do while they thought it was their idea. Once I captured that, then you could see what he was doing, . . . and I think there was a silent, quiet drama that emerged out of the tale.

[Since] there wasn't a lot of documentation in terms of what he was thinking, I had to go to people that were around him. He had a wonderful assistant—called a secretary, but it would be almost like a chief of staff—George Cortelyou. He kept a diary, so you got a sense of what McKinley was saying and what he was thinking; other people kept diaries, too. There were some interviews done many years ago with people who were around then—[like Ohio political kingmaker] Mark Hanna who was very close to McKinley—and those interviews yielded up some pretty good anecdotes and stories. Newspaper articles, you had to scour everything there was that he had anything to do with and piece it together. But ultimately, it did come together.

William McKinley grew up in small-town Ohio, first in a little town, Lisbon, Ohio, and then in Poland, Ohio. He went to college in 1860, got sick in his freshman year, and went back to Poland. By the time he recuperated—the illness was mysterious, we never quite knew what it was—he had to go to work because the family was stretched, as families were in the economic downturn. He got jobs as a postal clerk and a schoolteacher, doing both, and he was doing that at age eighteen when the Civil War broke out. His family was always highly, strongly, passionately abolitionist; they hated slavery, and he grew up in that climate. His mother [Nancy Allison McKinley] was very bright and a reader, and they got the weekly *New York Tribune,* run by Horace Greeley, who was one of the leading abolitionists in America. So, the McKinleys ingested all of that [antislavery] commentary.

He gave himself a couple of days to think it over, but he pretty quickly enlisted in the US Army as a private. He spent four years in the service during the Civil War. He rose up to brevet major, most of his promotions coming as a result of battlefield heroics. He was truly a heroic guy. He didn't seem to have any sense of what fear might be or how it might be used to keep you out of crazy situations.

One quick anecdote: He was a quartermaster sergeant, and he was at the Battle of Antietam, the bloodiest day in American history. He was away from the battle, from the action; he was making sure that everybody got food and other provisions. There was a unit that had found itself isolated and couldn't get out of this situation it was in. This particular unit had been fighting since early in the morning and had no breakfast, no lunch, had run out of water long since, and this was late afternoon. These people were in extremis, and that unit was not going to be in fighting fitness at all. McKinley got it into his head from three miles away that he was going to load up a wagon, and he was going to get that wagon to these troops. He found a guy to volunteer with him, and he loaded up the wagon and started moving to the woods towards the clearing where the battle was going on. He ran into two officers who told him to get back, he can't possibly get there, forget it. He ignored them after they left and went through the clearing, got the back of his wagon shot off but managed to get a fair amount of provisions to the troops. Old, wizened veterans said, "God bless the lad." He became a commissioned officer as a result of that crazy deed and then continued to rise up as a result of similar experiences and similar battlefield actions.

After the Civil War, McKinley got back and immediately decided he wanted to become a lawyer, and I think he pretty much knew he wanted to become a congressman. His great mentor was his commanding officer [and future president] Rutherford B. Hayes, who became an Ohio congressman even before the Civil War ended. Hayes loved young

William McKinley. He thought he was one of the greatest young men he'd ever met.

Hayes was also from Ohio, and so McKinley wanted to follow in his footsteps. Hayes told him no. Hayes said, "I think you can make a lot more money; you'd be very rich by age thirty or forty if you went into industrial activity." There was, of course, going to be an industrial explosion, and Hayes knew it. [He advised McKinley to] go into the railroad business, or something, but that was not what he wanted. McKinley carefully preserved the letter but discarded the advice. So, he became a lawyer and moved to Canton, Ohio, which becomes his hometown and where his sister had been teaching school, and immediately emerges as a civic leader.

He joined everything. He was in veterans' organizations. He joined the Methodist Church. Everything that he seemed to join, he rose up into leadership positions. Chamber of commerce, well, he became the president of the chamber of commerce. The church, well, he became the superintendent of the Sunday school, and on and on. So, it wasn't surprising that he was well-known in his community, and when a vacancy emerged in the House of Representatives [in 1876], he went for it and won it.

William met [his wife, Ida Saxton,] before he went into politics. In fact, he even offered not to go into politics [for her]. This is a poignant story; in fact, it's a very defining story about McKinley. He was maybe one of the finest human beings who's ever made it to the White House. He was a genuinely fine guy, although he was more calculating than he let on. He met Ida Saxton, who was the belle of Canton. Her father was very well-to-do. Her grandfather had brought a printing press from Pennsylvania and started a newspaper that was very successful in Canton. Her father built on that business and got into banking, mining, development, and other things. They had multiple servants in their house, Saxton House it was called, on the main street of Canton.

Ida was a scintillating young woman. She was smart. She was petite and attractive. She was effective. She was clever. Everyone wanted to woo her, of appropriate age. She picked McKinley. She liked his stolidity and his good manners and his ambition and his ability to bring people to his side. They were married; it was a storybook thing. There were one thousand people at their wedding according to the Canton newspaper—which was owned by her father, so I don't know if that was true. McKinley was gravitating towards running for Congress at that time. They had a daughter within a year of their marriage, Katie. Then a year later she was pregnant again. Then, things began to go awry in a rush, in a crunch that almost makes it seem like there was a terrible fate that was befalling this young woman and her husband.

During her second pregnancy, she learned that her mother was dying; she was very close to her mother, and she took it very hard. That may have contributed to a troublesome pregnancy. . . . The baby was born, another daughter, named after her, Ida. The baby was not particularly healthy and died five months later. Ida was inconsolable as a result of that and went into a deep depression. It wasn't clear that she was going to come out of it until her sister said, "Well, William just decided she had to come out of it." And he just wooed her out of it. Then she had some kind of carriage accident during this period. . . . I suspect she might have had some spinal injury of some significance. Her mobility was affected, and she had a hard time walking throughout the rest of her life. It was intermittently different, at times it was sometimes worse and sometimes better. Even in the White House, she can get down the stairs easy enough; going up the stairs, they had an elevator, which was a new thing. It didn't work often, so he would have to carry her up the stairs. . . .

Then another thing happened—the development of epilepsy. Ida would have these epileptic fits, which in those days was considered a kind of mental disease; people ended up in institutions. William never wavered in his devotion to her, even as she became a totally different person. . . . She became sedentary. Her thinking became inward. She became somewhat peevish. He just accepted all that and never wavered. So, it's quite a poignant story, and it became a pretty famous story across America. McKinley gained a lot of political points for being as devoted as he was to this woman who sometimes struggled through life.

There was [press coverage] in terms of her being an "invalid." She was always in a wheelchair, and she didn't seem self-conscious about that. But the epilepsy was kept very much under wraps. They didn't want that to get out, and it never did. The press, the newspapers, didn't go into great detail, and no one really knew what was going on. But she was under a lot of medication, and that might have also affected some of her behavioral traits.

[Politically, McKinley's time in Congress] was a very precarious situation. Ohio was on an ice edge of politics. There was a great parity between Republicans and Democrats. We talk about redistricting today and gerrymandering and all the problems attending that. . . . In those days it was just axiomatic that if the Democrats controlled the legislature, they were going to mess with your district, and that happened. In one instance after his . . . second term, he lost, but he only lost after a recount that took . . . almost a year because it was so close. . . . So, he lost the seat, then went back and regained it, and continued to have it. [Altogether] he was in the House for fourteen years.

He became the greatest protectionist in America. [By 1889,] he was chairman of the Ways and Means Committee, and he crafted a highly protectionist tariff bill with high tariffs to help various industries. He soon found himself on the outs because we were beginning to move into a recession, and businesses took the occasion to raise prices. . . . The Democrats went after Republican incumbents. It was a terrible year, 1890. . . .

McKinley lost his seat in the Congress in 1890 [and the Republican Party lost nearly half their seats in the House], and he refused to believe that this was in any way a reflection on his views on protectionism. He wanted to be president, and so he didn't know where to go. When you lose a seat, you lose political momentum. He thought about waiting two years and then running for a congressional seat again. But, he decided that maybe the governorship was the best stepping stone, so he ran for governor. There was an incumbent Democrat [James Campbell] who was an effective and a popular politician, so he had to roll over that gentleman, which he did. McKinley served two two-year terms [as Ohio's governor].

The McKinley Tariff was not popular because of how prices were raised. Everyone said, "Well, this isn't working." Grover Cleveland, who [was re-elected president in 1892] . . . was a free trader, being a Democrat; he brought down the tariffs marginally. And then McKinley [who was elected president four years later in 1896] promptly put them back up; but in the meantime, McKinley had crafted this concept of reciprocity. That was not unlike what we might call "fair trade" today, in the sense that he advocated bilateral agreements with countries in which both countries would reduce their barriers to foster trade across those borders. This was a result of his recognizing that we needed to be able to develop markets overseas in order to ensure the continuation of prosperity.

[Under] the McKinley Tariff of 1890, the percentages were in the neighborhood of 50 percent on a lot of goods, and they were placed on a lot of goods. But the interesting thing about McKinley was that as he became president, he discovered that his views were changing. The reason was because he understood that America was becoming an explosive producer of goods, both agricultural and industrial, and it was clear that the huge market of America was not going to be sufficient to absorb all the goods that this amazing country, going through that amazing transformation, was going to be able to produce. In order for prosperity to continue, it was going to be necessary for America to sell goods overseas, and you can't sell goods overseas in any significant way if you have major barriers from goods coming in because you don't have anything to trade.

[The Republican Party selected William McKinley as their presidential candidate at their convention] in 1896. He basically had it; it was a coronation. He didn't have any significant opposition once the convention began. He ran against Democrat William Jennings Bryan. That year was the big currency issue, the big questions were about the "cross of gold" and whether we were going to have the free coinage of silver to expand the money supply. A lot of farmers and rural people in the West and South felt like they were being beleaguered by the bankers of the Northeast who were constricting the money supply. . . . McKinley stayed with the gold standard and launched what you might call the first educational presidential campaign in which he realized he was going to have to explain these issues to the American people. And he won by a significant margin.

Cuba was very, very significant [at this point]. . . . The Cubans, like the Mexicans earlier and others, had wanted independence. There was a ten-year insurrection that had occurred about two decades before McKinley was elected that was devastating to the island and to Spain. And now another insurrection was in progress as McKinley was elected.

Spain's number-one colony, since it had lost throughout the nineteenth century most of its colonies in Latin America, Central America, and South America, was Cuba. Spain also had the Philippines, it had Puerto Rico, it had Guam, and a few other islands in the Pacific. McKinley's predecessor, Grover Cleveland, didn't have sympathy for the Cubans. He called them the "rascally Cubans." He basically was a status quo guy. He thought that the best thing to happen would be for Spain to remain in Cuba, but that was becoming increasingly untenable. McKinley comes in, and he takes a different view. He has much more sympathy for the Cubans. He doesn't want to go to war with Spain, but he wants Spain to either . . . negotiate an end of the war, enter into more of an autonomy arrangement, or get out. Spain said, "You can't tell us that." McKinley wouldn't yield. He sent the battleship *Maine* into Havana harbor . . . to help Americans who might get caught up in the chaos, and [on February 15, 1898] it exploded at a time when there was a lot of passion in this country as well as in Cuba and in Spain. [Two hundred sixty-six Americans died in that explosion.]

War became inevitable after the explosion and McKinley knew it. So, he sent Admiral George Dewey, who had the fleet near Hong Kong, to the Philippines where we promptly destroyed the Spanish fleet. . . . And then McKinley sent his Atlantic fleet to intercept the Spanish Atlantic fleet and destroy that fleet. Then, he ordered the army to land in Cuba near Santiago and take Santiago, which they did [on July 2, 1898]. That's the famous Teddy Roosevelt ride up—people say the San Juan Hill, but it was the San Juan Ridge—and he marched up. TR led his troops up there in a very delicate time, a very difficult time, quite heroic—foolhardy, one could argue—but nevertheless, it succeeded. Roosevelt became a national hero along with George Dewey. That led to Spain suing for peace.

. . . McKinley was very, very tough in the negotiations. He wouldn't even enter into any talks unless it was clear that the Spanish would leave Cuba. He made it very clear from the beginning, and there was some legislation to this effect, that we had no desires on Cuba, but he said we were going to get Puerto Rico and we were going to leave the Philippines in our hands . . . and that we needed an island in what was called the Madrones at that time, which is the Marianas today, and that would be Guam. The Spanish were devastated. [The Senate approved the final treaty with Spain in February 1898.]

[The annexation of Hawaii . . .] happens around the same time. And again, it's a distinction between him and his predecessor, Grover Cleveland. Cleveland didn't want to annex Hawaii, but McKinley understood, and while he wasn't a man of vision, . . . he had a way of seeing events clearly and understanding their implications and therefore what he needed to do. He realized that the Hawaiian Islands were one of the two or three most strategic spots on the whole globe. From those islands you can control a huge amount of territory, and not just oceans, but also land along the waters. . . . The Polynesian peoples were the indigenous peoples of Hawaii, but because it was such an amazing spot in the middle of the North Pacific, people came there [from all over]. The whaling ships came. Americans came for various reasons, and then the sugar plantations emerged. Sugar was an amazingly high-margin business. You can make huge amounts of money, so Americans flocked in there to run these sugar plantations and got very, very rich. And in getting rich, they felt like they should have more political power, so they wrested the political power from the Polynesians. It was a monarchy. The Americans took over the island and said, we want it to be part of America. We just annexed it [through a joint resolution of Congress, which McKinley signed on July 8, 1898]. The main thing to be recognized here is that if we hadn't taken those islands, Japan would have. Japan had a very significant claim on those islands because those plantation owners had brought in lots and lots of Japanese workers for the fields and they weren't being treated very well, Japan felt. They were agitating for better treatment of their indigenous Japanese working in the islands. . . . Germany also wanted colonies anywhere it could get them in those days because it wanted to be like England. So, if we hadn't had gotten those islands, probably Japan [or Germany] would have gotten them.

I'm not quite sure when McKinley met Teddy Roosevelt for the first time, but he knew him vaguely when he became president. Many top Republicans were agitating to have Teddy Roosevelt be appointed assistant naval secretary. McKinley wasn't sure he wanted to give that man that job because he had heard that Roosevelt was always agitating everybody; he was a man out of control much of the time, and McKinley was a control freak in a lot of ways. He didn't like chaos. He told some of his friends that he wasn't sure that Roosevelt would behave himself in the office. But Roosevelt had so many admirers and friends, and his

This photo of William McKinley was taken September 6, 1901, just eight days before he was assassinated at the Pan-American Exposition in Buffalo, New York. *Courtesy E. Benjamin Andrews*, History of the United States, Volume V

friends loved him, and they really went to bat for him. The result was that McKinley finally acceded to their request and allowed Roosevelt to become the assistant navy secretary. [And, in 1900, the Republicans chose Roosevelt as their vice-presidential nominee when McKinley ran for re-election.]

[McKinley beat William Jennings Bryan once again in 1900, this time . . .] even bigger. By that time, McKinley's presidency had been so successful in terms of economic growth and the emergence of prosperity and the ending of the Panic of 1893 . . . that he managed to take the sting away from William Jennings Bryan's silver advocacy.

[Six months after McKinley was sworn in for his second term], Leon Czolgosz killed McKinley, in September 1901. He went into a receiving line where McKinley was greeting people at the Pan-American Exposition in Buffalo, New York. He had his hand in a kind of sling or a bandage as if it had been injured. McKinley reached to shake his other hand, whereupon he put a pistol to McKinley's chest and fired. That bullet didn't penetrate too much, but McKinley stepped back, and the second bullet entered his abdomen and was never able to be removed. Ultimately, McKinley developed an abscess or sepsis infection and died [on September 14, 1901. Vice President Theodore Roosevelt, forty-two, was sworn in as president that day in Buffalo].

It's hard to say, but if you look in our lifetime's terms, William McKinley would probably be a moderate Republican, maybe not quite a Rockefeller Republican, but maybe a Mark Hatfield Republican, the senator from Oregon. [He'd be] a moderate-to-liberal Republican with strong views about economics, free enterprise, but probably somewhat more liberal views on racial matters and on social issues.

William McKinley was a man of mark. He was a man of force, much more than he gets credit for. And therein lay a very interesting human story: How did this guy—with this easy temperament and this pleasant way about him and this incrementalism of management—how did he do all the things he did?

JAMES MADISON

Overall Rank: 17

— ★ —

Total Score: 610

James Madison has consistently ranked lower as president than the other Virginia co-founders (Washington, Jefferson, and Monroe). Like the others, his ranking in pursued equal justice for all is relatively low (18th in 2017). But unlike the others, historians give him "mid-range" rankings in several categories, including international relations (22nd) and crisis leadership (19th).

Party: Democratic-Republican
b. March 16, 1751, Port Conway, Virginia
d. June 28, 1836, Montpelier estate, Virginia
First Lady: Dolley Payne Todd Madison
Age entering office: 57

Historian: **Noah Feldman**

Harvard law professor and Bloomberg Opinion *columnist Noah Feldman was interviewed for his book,* The Three Lives of James Madison: Genius, Partisan, President. *The interview was recorded on December 19, 2017, for* Q & A.

I wanted to write about James Madison because I write about constitutions, that's my stock in trade, and ultimately for constitutionalists—Madison is our Einstein. There's nobody more influential, more significant, or more formative to the field.

The three lives of James Madison are these: the first life is the one that's most famous. That's where he invented the Constitution as a true constitutional genius, not only the greatest in our country but probably the greatest constitutional genius in the world.

In his second life, he discovered that the Constitution wasn't perfect. He thought he had provided against political parties, but he discovered that he actually had to found a political party, the Republican Party, in order to fight Alexander Hamilton and the Federalist Party. He became a partisan, very much against his own wishes, but a very intense partisan nevertheless.

And then in his third life, he got to be secretary of state for eight years and president for eight more. He had to take on the kinds of decisions that you have to take on when you're actually running the show, including fatefully taking us into our first declared war, the War of 1812, very much against his principles of a lifetime, which were against a standing army and against a navy.

Madison didn't have his name on a single authored document in the way that the Declaration of Independence was essentially written by [Thomas] Jefferson. He didn't have Jefferson's love of the crowd, and he didn't have Jefferson's incredible gift for expression. Jefferson was a true genius of expression, utterly brilliant; he loved a pithy, sharp formulation, and the Declaration is an amazing monument to that. They were very close allies throughout their careers. A lot of the time, Madison was moderating Jefferson's enthusiasms, and that was his own perception of what his job was. Madison never wanted to over-shadow Jefferson. He loved Jefferson very much. Jefferson was probably the person, other than Dolley, that Madison was closest to in his entire life.

Madison was very different from most of the other founders. He was "all in his head" is how we would put it today. He was deeply committed to reason and logic. He hated public speaking. He hated arguing. He hated disagreement. He was much smaller than the others. He was maybe five feet, six inches, and he even may have been a little bit shorter according to some accounts. He was very cautious about his health. You could get very sick in those days, and he didn't want to get sick. As a consequence, he never took a sea voyage anywhere. He repeatedly turned down offers to go to Europe, including offers from Jefferson to visit him in France. And last but not least, he was susceptible to serious attacks of what we probably today would call migraines, intense headaches that were almost physically paralyzing and debilitating. They only happened a few times in his life, but they happened at crucial stressful moments, and each time he powered through. He would be taken to bed for a few

President James Madison was an unusual political figure among the founding fathers for being more of an introvert who didn't like conflict. *Courtesy Library of Congress*

days, and he would get up, force himself back into the saddle, and go on with whatever he was doing.

One of the things that I could see up front, certainly, is that he was book smart in the traditional sense. He was usually the best prepared founder, which is a big reason for his success. His response to any deep policy problem was to dig down and try to learn as much as he could about it. One really good example of this is when he was first elected to Congress under the Articles of Confederation. The big problem facing the country was . . . a shrinking money supply. Instead of just mouthing off about it, he borrowed books and buried himself at Montpelier and tried very hard to read everything he could and to write notes for himself about this topic. You can see through his notes a mind . . . at work. The big challenge for Madison throughout his life was translating that book-smart learning into real-world political judgment, and there he proceeded like the rest of us, by trial and error. He would advocate a policy that was creative and made sense in light of what he knew; if it didn't work, he would try to do it differently. And, he sometimes admitted his mistakes, which is also not very popular for politicians today.

James Madison's estate, Montpelier, is [about ninety minutes south of Washington, DC. The staff there . . .] were especially helpful to me researching slavery in the Madison household, which is an important theme in Madison's life. That's a reality of Madison. He was essentially born into the arms of a slave, and a slave closed his eyes when he died. Slavery was a constant and ever-present aspect of his life, and one that has to be taken seriously and has to be encountered. The family had more than one hundred slaves when he was born; there were fewer than that when he died. Ultimately, Dolley Madison sold those slaves in an attempt to support herself financially, so by the end of her life she didn't have any slaves left. But that was not because she was freeing them for moral reasons; it was because she needed the money.

[James was forty-three and Dolley was twenty-six when they got married.] Extraordinarily, they were introduced by Aaron Burr, the same person who went down in American history, in infamy, both for attempting a rebellion of the western states and also for killing Alexander Hamilton in a duel. Burr was a very sociable guy, and especially in Philadelphia, which is where they met; Burr was famous among the young women of the city. It was a Quaker city, and Quakerism was very socially conservative. Young women of Quaker background weren't supposed to learn to draw; they weren't supposed to play instruments; they weren't supposed to learn to read music. Burr, a little bit mischievously, liked to help them overcome these strictures. Dolley Madison wrote about this later in her life, that many young women in Philadelphia had Aaron Burr to thank for their learning these accomplishments.

Madison was walking with a congressman called Isaac Coles, who was a distant cousin of Dolley's. He saw her on the street and was immediately smitten and deeply interested in her and wanted to meet her. He went to Aaron Burr because Burr knew everybody. Burr, in fact, told Dolley, "The great little Madison," as he referred to him, "wants to meet you." She wrote to a friend about it, which is how we know that this happened. . . . And then, within a matter of weeks, Madison wrote her letters and then asked her to marry him. And she said yes.

She had an enormous impact on him and, indeed, an enormous impact on the country. A reasonable argument could be made that Dolley Madison was the most important first lady that we've ever had. . . . She got sixteen years to be first lady, essentially, because from 1800 to 1808 when Madison was secretary of state, Jefferson was the president, and Jefferson was not married; his wife had died. . . . Consequently, most of the time Dolley functioned as the de facto first lady. She sometimes hosted events at the White House. She also hosted a lot of events at her house and Madison's house, which functioned as though they were White House events.

This is also the time, starting in 1800–1801, when Washington, DC, became the capital. . . . This was the moment when all Washington protocol was being set and where the manners and social style of a republican foreign policy were being created. Dolley was the person who set that. Jefferson had no interest in socializing, wasn't very graceful at it. Madison didn't like to socialize because he was shy. So, Dolley really ran the show.

She had an enormous impact on the nature of our national debate and our national way of expressing ourselves publicly. She also really influenced Madison because she was able to express concern, opinion, and emotions that he was not. . . . You see her expressing his opinions on his behalf, as it were. I think that really mattered for them interpersonally; it was the cement of a really wonderful and rich relationship. Madison and Dolley Madison preferred always to be together. In almost a half century of marriage, they were only apart for a couple of months, and then only because Dolley was sick and had to be taken care of by a doctor in Philadelphia. And in that period, they wrote to each other three times a day. You can see their incredible closeness. They were a deeply close and loving couple. It's a shame we don't have a written record to fully bear that out.

Madison was not especially close with his actual brothers and sisters, which is really fascinating because Madison was very, very close with a succession of men his own age. Edmund Randolph, who was also a protégé of Jefferson's, James Monroe, who was also a protégé, and, of course, went on to be president after Madison—those were crucial relationships in his life. They were like sibling relationships, and they apparently substituted in some way for actual sibling relationships.

Personal relationships are . . . the whole story for someone like Madison, precisely because Madison wasn't a guy who liked to be out there on the front lines waving the flag. He liked to be the person making things happen from the back room. The way he did that was through these very intense, very close, personal relationships, these friendships. Occasionally, his friendships became relationships of enemies.

In the case of George Washington, Madison went from being a very close ally of Washington's—helping to convince him to come, for example, to the Constitutional Convention. Washington was originally very skeptical about coming to [these sessions] because he was worried that it might not go anywhere, and he wasn't sure he should lend his reputation to something like that. Eventually Madison and Edmund Randolph brought Washington around and got him to come.

When Washington became president, Madison was his man in Congress. In fact, in the very first exchange between Washington and the Congress, Madison ghostwrote Washington's address to Congress, then he ghostwrote Congress's reply to the president, then he ghostwrote President Washington's reply to Congress. So, Madison was literally talking to himself and producing these state documents that he knew were of long-term historical value. That shows you how close he and Washington really were. They eventually fell out over Washington's policy of favoring England over France in a period of deep tension between those two countries [1792–1802]. Madison believed, in a fundamental way, that the United States had signed a treaty of friendship with France and owed it to France to stay with it in France's war with England, especially because the United States had previously fought a war with England.

Washington was more pro-British, and ultimately he declared neutrality in the war, which . . . was perceived by Madison and by others as a pro-British position rather than pure neutrality; this was neutrality that served the interests of the British. Madison criticized President Washington and went further than criticizing the policy. He ultimately made the argument that Washington was overstepping his constitutional bounds by declaring neutrality. Madison wanted to argue that in the same way that only Congress could declare war, only Congress could declare neutrality. Washington cared a lot about his reputation. He was deeply committed to the Constitution, and he deeply resented the idea that Madison was suggesting that he might have overstepped his constitutional bounds.

Alexander Hamilton was in the background egging on Washington at the same time. . . . Washington could not forgive what he took as a stain on his reputation created by Madison, and they just stopped speaking. After Washington died, Madison introduced in the Virginia legislature special legislation in honor of Washington and helped to put money aside for a monument. Yet, . . . he and Jefferson believed that Washington had become a partisan Federalist at the end of his career. They did not look on Washington's last years in a good light. In fact, they thought that Washington's famous farewell address, that we all love so well, was a totally partisan performance and not something that should be valued for the ages.

[Madison and our longest serving chief justice, John Marshall, had] . . . a very complicated ongoing relationship. For one thing, Madison succeeded Marshall in the position of secretary of state. Marshall was secretary of state under Adams before he was chief justice of the United States. And, in fact, it was the succession that led to the famous case of *Marbury v. Madison* [1803] because when Marshall was still secretary of state, he was supposed to deliver a commission to Marbury, which he never quite managed to deliver in the closing days of the administration. And then Marbury sued Madison demanding that he, as secretary of state, deliver the commission. Madison refuses, and that led to the case. Remarkably, Chief Justice John Marshall wrote the opinion in the case; he did not recuse himself, even though the case arose because of his failure to deliver. So, that shows you how things were a little different in those days.

Marshall was an unusual person. He was a Virginia Federalist. He was from Virginia just like Madison was, and most of the Virginia gentlemen strongly supported the cause of the Republican Party, that is, they were a little bit skeptical of too much central, or federal, power. They believed to a moderate degree in states' rights. That was not the position that Marshall took. Marshall was a maximalist on federal power to a very great degree and a loyal Federalist. So, in that sense, he and Madison were political opponents. From the bench when he was chief justice, Marshall kept up a steady stream of indirect critique of the Republican administration as best as he could. Looking back across a couple of hundred years, Marshall and Madison probably agreed on more than they disagreed about. They ultimately both took a central middle ground on the question of federal and congressional power. In what is probably his most important case, *McCulloch v. Maryland* [1819], Chief Justice Marshall stood for the idea that the powers Congress needed to . . . fulfill basic tasks laid down in Article I, Section 8 of the Constitution, it had. It's the so-called Necessary and Proper Clause, which had the effect of allowing Congress to do things. That is basically what Madison also believed, but . . . [both] said there are still some limits to what Congress can do.

. . . The federal Constitution had been ratified [by Virginia] at the dramatic Virginia Ratifying Convention [the final vote, 89 to 79, was June 26, 1788], where Madison had gone head-to-head with the great Patrick Henry. In Patrick Henry's last big public performance, Madison won and Henry had lost because Henry opposed ratification. . . . In the end, Governor Henry still controlled the Virginia State Legislature . . . and so [when Madison declared his intent to run in the first-ever congressional elections in 1789], Henry gerrymandered the districts in Madison's home area of Virginia to produce a district that was full of anti-Federalists, people like him, who had opposed ratification. Then he convinced James Monroe, who was one of Madison's best friends in the world and his business partner—they had invested in some land in upstate New York together—[to run against him]. Henry just seduced Monroe, probably by telling him, you'll defeat Madison and you will be greater than Madison. This is right after Madison had essentially drafted the Constitution. Monroe made a serious run for it. I find it extraordinary that he would have done this against his close friend. They had this very dramatic race against each other. It was the heart of winter, and they went town to town and participated in public, and usually outdoor meetings, where they would debate questions of the ratification of the Constitution and the policies of the era.

James Madison pulled it off, but just barely [final tally: 1,308 to 972]. In an incredible letter, Madison wrote to Jefferson saying, "You will be sorry to hear that I had a misfortune of running against another close friend of ours, Monroe. But it's over now, and our friendship is unaffected, at least on my side." Jefferson believed him; even more amazingly, Madison actually meant it. He was able to forgive Monroe. Of course, had Monroe won, Madison's whole career would have been over.

Extraordinarily, thirty-odd years later, the whole process was repeated again. Monroe, who had been serving as ambassador to Britain and then to France, was convinced this time by other Virginians in the United States that he should come back and run for president against Madison. Madison was supposed to essentially inherit the presidency from Jefferson in 1808. And again, a second time, Monroe went and ran against his close friend. Again, he lost. And, again, Madison forgave him. A little later, at the beginning of his second term in the presidency, Madison actually asked Monroe to become his secretary of state. It was probably because he badly needed a good secretary of state. I also think he genuinely missed Monroe. Once again, he genuinely forgave him for trying to upstage him and put him off course. That's a remarkable sign of Madison's character. It's a true sign of his capacity, to be seeking after friendship and to be forgiving.

The War of 1812 [fought between June 1812 and February 1815] was almost an incredible disaster. It began because the United States was excluded from trading with European ports, both British and French-controlled ports. In this period of time, the French and the British empires functioned like the European Union or NAFTA. They were free trade zones. When the United States seceded from Great Britain, the thirteen colonies, when they became states, lost access to British ports. That was a huge ongoing challenge for our trade. The United States needed to use leverage to try to pressure Britain and France to allow us to trade. Not only did Britain and France resist this, they begin to use their navies to seize American ships once the British-French wars really got heated up. . . . So, the War of 1812 was fought as an effort by Madison to coerce the British and the French, although primarily the British because they were the immediate target, to change their policy and stop seizing US shipping.

The strategy to do this was to invade Canada. The idea was by invading Canada, the United States would put pressure on Britain because it wouldn't be able to support its own colonies in the West Indies, especially Jamaica. That might conceivably have worked had we successfully invaded Canada. But unfortunately, Madison relied on militia because our Constitution was designed not to have a standing army. And militia, as it turns out, are very bad at invading. In a crucial moment of the first invasion of Canada, three thousand New York troops stood on the Niagara River, ready to cross into Canada, and refused to go. Maybe it was cowardice, maybe it was a constitutional principle that they expressed, namely that the president couldn't order them to cross and invade. . . . Madison thought that was constitutionally wrong. . . . So, we failed to invade Canada.

And then we failed to invade Canada again. Britain, which had been very occupied in fighting Napoleon, got a lucky break because Napoleon marched into Russia with six hundred thousand troops. The winter came. They froze. And he marched out with less than twenty thousand troops. Now, Britain had matériel, time, and effort to turn to the United States, and boy, did they turn with a vengeance. It was in that period [August 1814] where the city of Washington, DC, was burned to [the] ground by an invading British force. Suddenly, the United States was very vulnerable, and all Americans could feel it.

What saved Madison, what saved the United States, from total destruction and indeed the possibility that we would lose the war outright, was that the British were stopped in Baltimore. They tried a sea landing, and militia blocked the troops from entering Fort McHenry. That's the famous bombardment that Francis Scott Key captured in his poem that became our national anthem, *The Star-Spangled Banner*. That battle was actually a turning point in US history. We tend to forget this. . . . We forget that if the flag of the United States on Fort McHenry had been brought down, that could have meant the end of the republic as we knew it. By withstanding that, the Americans convinced the British that it wasn't worth continuing their efforts to conquer the United States. The British pulled back. They agreed to a treaty.

Nobody won, nobody lost. And that was perceived as a win, precisely because things had gotten so bad. Madison ended the war as a hero because he had survived. He had fought the second war of independence. We had stood up to Great Britain, the greatest naval power, in the world, and we hadn't lost. So, not losing was winning in that period of time. By the time Madison left office [in 1817], he was wildly popular, and his presidency inaugurated what was called the Era of Good Feelings, which was a period of essentially one-party government that lasted through several presidential terms after that.

[Madison died on June 28, 1836, at the age of eighty-five.] He wasn't profoundly sickly. He was just sickly enough to be worried about his health, and it turns out that's actually a pretty good strategy, especially in a world where they didn't understand anything about infection. They just knew that it was out there. Several really important decisions in Madison's life were based on avoiding places where he thought there would be yellow fever, and he was usually correct. . . .

. . . James Madison did have an influence on . . . all constitutions in the world in a couple of different ways. One, crucially, was the idea of federalism, which we today think of as a normal aspect of many different countries but was pretty innovative in the US Constitution. That's the idea that you have a central government that does have direct legal authority over citizens, but then you have state governments that themselves simultaneously enjoy power over individuals. That's a complex compromise that came out of our Philadelphia Convention in 1787. . . . So, there is one direct form of Madison's influence. Another is a basic commitment to freedom of speech and religious liberty, which is . . . an example of a provision that goes right back to the US Constitution, which is very important to Madison.

If Madison were here right now, I would definitely want to ask him what we should do about our own descent into partisanship in this particular historical moment. His own view was that you should only be a partisan in order to put an end to partisanship. His Republican Party was supposed to be the party to end all parties, and it wasn't, of course. It did briefly put an end to partisan division because the Federalists, more or less, shrunk to nothingness in response to his onslaught. But he didn't clearly understand exactly how to sustain a long-run, deeply divided republic, and I would want to hear his thoughts about that because it's a very great challenge that we're facing today.

The Constitution is Madison's monument. In that way, the Constitution is all around you when you come to Washington, DC. The whole three-part structure of government, the way that the government interacts, the way people speak to each other, the exercise of free speech, all of that is Madison's monument. . . . If you seek Madison's monument in Washington, DC, look around you, and you'll see it everywhere.

ANDREW JACKSON

7th President, 1829–1837

Overall Rank: 18

— ★ —

Total Score: 609

In 2017, Andrew Jackson's rank fell five places from the 13th position, which he held in the 2000 and 2009 surveys. It was the largest drop of any president in 2017 and was fueled by declining ranks in administrative skills and relations with Congress. Historians ranked him 38th in pursued equal justice for all, above only the antebellum presidents and Andrew Johnson.

Party: Democratic
b. March 15, 1767, Waxhaw, North Carolina/South Carolina
d. June 8, 1845, Nashville, Tennessee
First Lady: Emily Donelson (wife Rachel's niece)
Age entering office: 61

Historian: **Mark R. Cheathem**

Mark Cheathem is a history professor and co-editor of The Papers of Martin Van Buren project at Cumberland University. He was interviewed about his book, Andrew Jackson, Southerner, *for Q & A on April 10, 2017.*

Andrew Jackson was elected in 1828. He took office in March of 1829. At that point, he was just about to turn sixty-two, so he was a relatively older man. He had a long military career but a shorter political career, as he was someone who wanted to retire in the early 1820s and live out his life as a farmer and as a husband and as a father. He was coaxed into politics by some of his friends in Tennessee and wound up becoming president.

When Jackson came to Tennessee, to Nashville, in 1788, he was twenty-one years old. Nashville was on the edge of the western frontier at that point. Jackson started to rent a room from a woman by the last name of Donelson. She was the widow of one of the cofounders

of Nashville. Her daughter, Rachel Donelson Robards, was living in
the area as well, and Andrew and young Rachel apparently struck up a
friendship. Now, what's interesting is that Rachel was married. . . . Her
husband, Lewis Robards, was not happy, as you can imagine. There are
a lot of accounts of him being jealous and perhaps of even being abusive
toward Rachel. In any case, Andrew and Rachel continue their friendship. Lewis leaves town, abandons her, and Andrew and Rachel go down
to Natchez, on the Mississippi River. When they come back, they say
that they have been married. A few years later they find out that Lewis
Robards has just now filed for divorce, so Andrew and Rachel had been
living in adultery. And Rachel was a bigamist, legally, because she was
still married to Lewis and was saying she was married to Jackson.

The divorce does [eventually] go through, and Andrew and Rachel
do legally marry in early 1794. At the time it's not that big of a deal,
outside of probably Lewis Robards and a couple of other people. But
looking ahead thirty years, it is a big deal when it comes to the presidential election of 1828.

Andrew Jackson was wealthy, but it was a wealth that he built up over his
lifetime. Jackson isn't given anything in terms of wealth growing up. His
father dies around the time that he's born; his mother and two older
brothers die when he's a young teenager. He has extended family, but
he leaves them very early on in his mid-teens. Jackson had to build up
his wealth by himself, and slave ownership was one of the ways that he
did that.

When he became president, he had around 160 African Americans living in bondage at [his estate], The Hermitage. Over the course of his
lifetime, he probably owned close to three hundred enslaved people.
That was a large part of his wealth because to be an elite Southerner,
which Jackson was, you had to own slaves and you had to have them
work whatever crop it was you were growing—cotton, corn, sugar, rice
. . . in order for you to become wealthy and to stay wealthy.

Jackson was a typical Southern slave owner. If you think of slave
ownership as being on a spectrum, you have some slave owners who
were extremely violent, sadomasochistic, they raped enslaved women,
and so on. Then you have other slave owners who, even though they
owned other human beings, we would consider them rather benign in

terms of their ownership. Jackson was in the middle. There are times when he expresses concern about his slaves; if they are sick, he'll send a letter asking about their well-being, and he will make sure that they're given gifts. But at the same time, in 1804 there are two runaway slaves, and one of them was captured and brought back, one is not. Jackson offers extra money if they're given one hundred lashes. That tells you that Jackson saw the value of keeping slaves in line; if one slave runs away and you don't do anything about it, what's to keep other slaves from running away? [He believed that] you have to maintain control over your slave population, and if that means that you have to discipline one slave—or even kill a slave in order to keep the other ninety-nine in place—then that's what you have to do to protect your property.

The Hermitage was built in 1819; it partially burned in the mid-1830s when Jackson was president and then was rebuilt. Most of what you see of The Hermitage today was built during the peak of Jackson's wealth. . . . And it wasn't just The Hermitage; The Hermitage was approximately 1,200 acres of property that Jackson owned in middle Tennessee, but he owned other plantations in Alabama, in Mississippi, and west Tennessee, so his land holdings were extensive. All of those land holdings had to have enslaved people because white people weren't going to work that land and make a profit in the same way that enslaved people would.

In 1806, Jackson was involved in a duel with Charles Dickinson over a horse race. . . . Jackson loved to race horses; that was one of the signs of his wealth. As he was growing up, he saw people around him who owned horses. That was one of the indications of their wealth, and so he loves to race horses as he gets older. He . . . was betting on a horse race, something happens, and the other person had to pull out. There was supposed to be a penalty that this person paid, but Jackson didn't like the way that they paid it. This Charles Dickinson character comes in and inserts himself into that feud for some reason. He and Jackson have words and that leads to a duel, and Jackson shoots and kills him on the dueling grounds.

. . . Dickinson fired first and shot Jackson in the chest near his heart. Jackson was able to summon the fortitude to fire back. He shot Dickinson in the stomach, and Dickinson bled out later that day. After he shot Dickinson, he collapsed and was bedridden for a while. The bullet was so close to his heart that doctors couldn't remove it, and so he carried that bullet with him until he died. Bullets were made out of lead; that lead probably poisoned him over the years, but suffering from lead poisoning was better than risking extracting the bullet and piercing his heart.

[He was wounded one other time.] In 1813, Jackson gets involved in a street brawl in downtown Nashville with a couple of brothers by the last name of Benton, one of whom goes on to become Senator Thomas Hart Benton, one of Jackson's closest allies; they have a change of heart later in life. But again, there's a duel involved, and Jackson supports one of his friends in the duel; Benton doesn't like it, and so Thomas Hart Benton . . . and his brother Jessie Benton are roaming the streets of Nashville looking for Jackson. Jackson and his friends go down to downtown Nashville, they bump into each other, there are some words exchanged, and a gunfight ensues. Jackson is shot, falls down a set of stairs, and is bedridden. That episode occurs in the middle of the War of 1812. Jackson had already gone to battle one time and had come back. He's bedridden from this brawl, but he summons his fortitude to recover and then to go fight the majority of the War of 1812 against the Creek Indians and against the British. They eventually did extract [that bullet] from 1813. Jackson gave it to Thomas Hart Benton as a souvenir of their former relationship once they had reconciled.

Jackson helped save the United States—or at least that's what people thought—at the Battle of New Orleans [January 1815]. The interesting thing about that battle is that the treaty negotiations between the United States and Britain had already taken place in Europe. Both sides had agreed to declare the war a draw, to go back to the status quo antebellum, the way things were before the war. That news doesn't come to the United States immediately; it takes a while to get here. [Ironically] the battle that Jackson is most famous for actually occurs after those negotiations are over. But psychologically, most Americans hear the news about Jackson's victory first; then they hear news about the war being over. . . . The mythology about Jackson reinforces that the battle was so crucial to the United States staying together and being able to defeat the British; in reality, it's important, certainly, but it wasn't as critical as many people, then or now, think.

. . . Jackson had a national reputation [when he ran for president the first time] in 1824, and that's why his friends wanted him to run. He was seen from their perspective as a second George Washington. Here was a man who could replicate what Washington had done as the father of the country: Jackson could restore the country to its former greatness. By 1824, there had been two political parties, and one of those parties had essentially disappeared at the national level, and you had the Democratic-Republican party that was left. This was the party formed by Thomas Jefferson in the early 1800s. What happens when you have one political party in charge is that you don't have unity. . . . You start to divide into factions. That's what had happened during the second term of James Monroe's presidency, . . . Democratic-Republicans started to splinter into factions based on personality. Jackson and his supporters look around and think, this is no better than what we were during the early years of the republic. We need to find a way to bring the country back together and to make it great again, to use President Trump's phrase, and the way to do that is to elect Andrew Jackson.

The "corrupt bargain" was really the culmination of the election of 1824. Jackson won the most popular votes; he won the most electoral votes; he won the most states; but to become president, you have to win a majority of the electoral vote, and Jackson doesn't. He only wins ninety-nine, and so the election—according to the Constitution—had to go to the House of Representatives. The top three vote-getters in terms of electoral votes—Jackson, John Quincy Adams, and William H. Crawford—had their names submitted to the House. Each state delegation in the House would get one vote per state for who would become president.

Jackson goes into that House election thinking: I should become president. I won the most states if you were to tabulate the states, and in the House, I should win with a majority. But what happens, according to the Jacksonians—and there's no smoking gun [to prove their theory]—is that Henry Clay and John Quincy Adams got together [to affect the outcome]. Henry Clay had run for the presidency in 1824 and had not been one of the top three, but he's the speaker of the House and he has his eye set on the White House. [Jackson supporters believe that] he and Adams get together and allegedly decide that Clay will work the House, will make sure that Adams wins the presidency. In return, Adams will appoint Clay to be secretary of state. That was important because several presidents prior to John Quincy Adams had been secretaries of state before entering the presidency [including John Quincy Adams].

So, essentially, Clay is setting himself up to become John Quincy Adams's successor once Adams decides to leave office. And, that's exactly what happens in the House—the House votes for Adams to become president. Jacksonians jump on that alleged "corrupt bargain" and use that as their main campaign theme in 1828.

In 1828, Henry Clay, who was secretary of state at the time, and John Quincy Adams, who was president, used the Jackson marriage as one of the angles to try to derail Jackson's [second] presidential campaign against Adams. They besmirch Rachel's character and honor by insinuating that she was a bigamist, that she was an adulterer, that she was a whore. It's something that enrages Jackson, and his friends have to constantly tell him just let it go, it's not that important, focus on the big prize of the presidency. There are times when Jackson is ready to fight duels. He's ready to go back to his youth, when he was a little bit more violent, and to do something [physical] with Clay or with others, but his friends convince him to let it go, it's not that important.

Jackson believes [that Adams and Clay are behind these scandalous charges]. In fact, there's one newspaper editor in Cincinnati, Ohio, by the name of Charles Hammond who is doing most of the mudslinging in that regard. He is one of those who spreads rumors about Jackson's mother being a prostitute, about Jackson being the offspring of Jackson's mother Elizabeth and an African American slave. Hammond seems to be the central person who is involved in the mudslinging, but Clay and Adams don't do a whole lot to stop it. It is kind of interesting that even though they're not actively propagating these ideas, they had the power to stop them and they don't.

Jackson won substantially in 1828. He wins all the regions of the country except for New England. . . . It was considered a landslide. He wins a fairly large majority for the time. . . . Between 1824 and 1828, there's nearly a doubling of the number of voters in the United States. For Jackson to win after having lost in '24, and to win big, solidifies within himself and within his coalition this idea that he is the choice of the people. He is the one that the people have given a mandate to effect change in the United States.

The Eaton affair occurs between 1829 and 1831. This was a scandal involving Jackson's very close friend, Senator John Eaton, whom Jackson appointed secretary of war. John Eaton was from middle Tennessee near where Jackson lived. John Eaton had been good friends with Margaret O'Neale Timberlake and her husband, John Timberlake. John Timberlake was a navy purser—he would go out and be an accountant for the US Navy. He would be gone for months on end on ships, keeping track of wages and that sort of thing. While he was gone, John Eaton and Margaret O'Neale Timberlake would go to social functions together and rumors started to spread that they were having an affair. Then John Timberlake committed suicide, and the account was that he had slit his own throat because he found out that his wife and his best friend, John Eaton, were having an affair. Timberlake did kill himself; whether it was because of the alleged affair, we don't know. Margaret O'Neale Timberlake is now a widow, and less than a year after her husband commits suicide, she marries John Eaton, the man she was allegedly having an affair with. All of this happens before Jackson becomes president.

Jackson appoints Eaton to be secretary of war, and Washington society is aghast that Jackson has appointed this man who was having an affair with this woman they consider a "whore"—and they used that word. Jackson . . . defends Eaton and Margaret over the next two years to the point that he will call cabinet meetings to discuss whether or not John and Margaret had an affair, and he will provide evidence that shows that they did not. What historians and biographers of Jackson see is a president who lost his wife in December of 1828, a wife who had been accused of adultery, a wife who had been accused of having an affair. Many of Jackson's biographers, including myself, see Jackson projecting psychologically onto the Eatons what he must have felt about his own marriage.

He couldn't defend Rachel anymore—she's dead—so he's going to defend one of his best friends and his best friend's wife in order to salve his conscience about Rachel. This continues for two years, disrupts Jackson's cabinet; he spends an inordinate amount of time defending the Eatons, defending their marriage, calling witnesses to show that they're innocent. It all culminates in Martin Van Buren, who's secretary of state under Jackson, and John Eaton saying, we will resign in order to end this, and that will allow you as president to call for the resignations of your other cabinet members. You can appoint a new cabinet, start fresh, and we can move on from this entire episode. [And, in fact, all of Jackson's cabinet members, except Postmaster General William

Barry, did resign and Jackson reconstituted his cabinet and weathered the crisis]. . . .

Jackson was a two-termer. He lost a little bit of the percentage of popular vote during his second election in 1832, but the voting base had expanded, so he has more votes than he had in 1828. He was fairly popular with the people, but he was not popular with some of the Washington politicians. And, in fact, that one-party system that had helped elect him disintegrates into a two-party system during his second term; the Whig Party emerges as the opposition party. The Whig Party was made up of a variety of different factions, but the one thing they had in common was they hated Jackson. He is the force that binds them all together.

Jackson was a great hero at a number of points in his life . . . [and] I think that as president we could consider him a hero. In 1832, 1833, he stood up to South Carolina and the nullification movement there and kept the Union together. Nullification was the idea that a state, if they considered a federal law unconstitutional, could nullify, or void, that law and thus protect the people of that particular state.

Congress had passed two tariffs, the Tariff of 1828 and the Tariff of 1832, and South Carolinians thought that those tariffs were unconstitutional because they adversely affected Southerners as compared to Northerners. From their perspective, Southerners were going to pay more for imported goods, which is what a tariff is, a tax on imported goods. But there was also this other interesting facet to this, that South Carolinians and other Southerners were afraid that Congress would use the revenue generated by tariffs to emancipate slaves—to fund either compensated emancipation or colonization, which is sending enslaved African Americans back to Africa. So, there was a lot going on with nullification, but the tariff was really the focal point. When South Carolina passed a nullification ordinance saying that these two tariffs were unconstitutional, Jackson stepped in. He issued his own proclamation that said that this is treason, and we cannot allow this because it will destroy the Union. He threatened to send the military into South Carolina to keep the Union together.

[One of Jackson's greatest political battles as president was about] the Second Bank of the United States. . . . It was formed in 1816 and had a twenty-year contract to 1836. What Jackson saw the bank doing was manipulating the American economy and using government money against him personally. Shortly after the 1828 election, some of Jackson's advisers came to him and told him that Nicholas Biddle, president of the US Bank, had used bank money to help fund John Quincy Adams's campaign in New England. Jackson thought that was horrible that the people's money was being used for political purposes, and this just added to his suspicion about banks. . . . Based on that and based on the fact that Henry Clay was a strong supporter of the bank and tried to push the bank's recharter through in 1832 as an election year issue—all that coalesced Jackson's hatred of the bank. When Nicholas Biddle tried to start a recession as a way of getting back at Jackson's interjection into the bank's business, that just made clear what Jackson had to do: he had to destroy the bank. [Jackson shut down the bank in September of 1833; Congress retaliated by censuring Jackson in 1834.]

Andrew Jackson's image, placed on the twenty-dollar bill in 1928, has become a subject of debate as contemporary historians reassess his legacy. *Photo credit: Leslie Rhodes and Ellen Vest, C-SPAN*

[Jackson appointed five justices to the Supreme Court. One of those], Roger B. Taney, is one of the most controversial Supreme Court justices. He's mostly controversial for what happens in 1857 with the *Dred Scott* decision, which essentially says that enslaved African Americans are property and gives the Supreme Court's endorsement of that idea. Jackson puts him on the court as a reward for Taney's help during the bank war. . . . Taney was a strong supporter of Jackson's banking policy. He had been secretary of Treasury, and Jackson rewarded him for that loyalty [on December 28, 1835,] by making him chief justice of the Supreme Court right before he left office.

Andrew Jackson was seventy-eight when he died in June of 1845. He died of a number of different things: lead poisoning and the medical treatments that were trying to address the lead poisoning; Jackson had suffered from dysentery, which is a severe form of diarrhea, during the War of 1812, and that still plagued him. He had a number of health problems over the years.

I think I'm fairly even-handed [about Jackson's legacy]. I'm definitely critical of Jackson, which we have a right to be. Even living in the twenty-first century, we have a right to be critical of the stances that he took on certain issues during his lifetime. But, at the same time, I think we have to be fair and understand that the times he lived in are different from the times we live in. One of the things I tell my students is that you should always take a two-pronged approach to history: you should look at the people in their times, understand them within the context of their times. And in Jackson's case, that meant that white supremacy, racism, his attitude toward Native Americans, all those things were really part and parcel of the American character at the time. But we also have to look at them from our perspective, and we can be critical of them. So, when we look back at Jackson's racism, when we look back at his treatment of Native Americans, we should be critical of him, just as people during his lifetime were critical of him.

Thousands [of Indians died because of Andrew Jackson]. . . . During the various battles of the War of 1812, thousands of Native Americans, mostly Creek, are killed fighting American forces. . . . If you add the removal of Native American groups during Jackson's presidency, and even afterward as his policy is implemented under Martin Van Buren, certainly thousands, if not maybe ten thousand [dead and wounded] Native Americans are Jackson's responsibility.

. . . There were people [in his day] who opposed the removal of Native Americans, but particularly within the white South, Jackson is the norm. His view of Native Americans is that they were inferior, that they were uncivilized, that they stood in the way of American progress—that was white progress at the time—and so they needed to be removed. That was the norm. People were critical of him at the time and certainly that is the major criticism of Jackson today is that he removed Native Americans from their land.

If you look at the present-day states of Mississippi, Alabama, parts of Georgia, most of Florida, Jackson is really responsible for opening that land up for US expansion. You could argue that Texas is also partly his responsibility. After he leaves the presidency, he wants to see Texas become part of the Union, and he is instrumental in trying to convince the Texas government to join the United States in the mid-1840s. He doesn't personally go to Texas and talk to Sam Houston, one of his old friends who is president of Texas, but he sends one of his nephews out there through a diplomatic appointment to talk to Houston.

Jackson also keeps the Union together with nullification, and that is what most people look back on as his greatest triumph. If you want to pick the one thing that Jackson did that was best for the United States, it was keeping the Union together instead of having a civil war take place in the early 1830s.

JOHN ADAMS

Overall Rank: 19

— ★ —

Total Score: 604

Of the first five presidents—the founders—John Adams has consistently had the lowest overall ranking. Like the other founders, historians assign him a high rank in moral authority (11th). He scores relatively high in pursued equal justice for all (15th), but his overall rank suffers from low rankings in administrative skills (21st), public persuasion (22nd), and relations with Congress (24th).

Party: Federalist
b. October 30, 1735, Braintree (now Quincy), Massachusetts
d. July 4, 1826, Quincy, Massachusetts
First Lady: Abigail Smith Adams
Age entering office: 61

Historian: **Gordon S. Wood**

Gordon Wood is a professor of history emeritus at Brown University and the winner of the Pulitzer Prize for his book, The Radicalism of the American Revolution. *He was interviewed for* Q & A *on November 15, 2017, about his book,* Friends Divided: John Adams and Thomas Jefferson.

[Living in Massachusetts] made me a fan of John Adams because he was a good old Yankee. [I hadn't heard of him] until probably high school, but I didn't know very much about him until college. And I hadn't gotten to see his home until after college, so it was really a long time before I got to know him. Now, because I did three volumes for the Library of America of his writings, I really got to know him. I think I know him better than I know most of my friends. And, he's really something.

First of all, he's an old Puritan, although he's not a Congregationalist, he's not a serious Puritan, but he came out of that tradition. They kept diaries. He needed to write out his emotions, his feelings; he put everything into that diary as a young man. He said things about himself that most people would not say even in their diaries. He talked about his own vanity, and he talked about every intimate feeling he had; really expressed himself. That's not something Thomas Jefferson would do. Jefferson was very reserved. . . . He had a very different temperament. They couldn't differ more in temperament.

. . . Adams came out of a middling background, and whatever wealth he acquired, he acquired through his law practice. He did not inherit much from his father, who was not a wealthy man. Adams never became one of the rich men of Massachusetts, and he always resented that because he was always regarded as having a middling background, and he suffered a little bit of contempt from some of the wealthy Massachusetts men for that reason.

Adams would always be talking and razzing people; he had a sharp sarcastic tongue. Thomas Jefferson was restrained, reserved. He kept his arms folded in front of him when he talked, which is a sign of his reserve. Adams made mistakes because he said what he thought, and he offended a lot of people. Jefferson was the opposite, very polite— obsessed by politeness. . . . Part of being enlightened was to be polite; civility was very important to Jefferson. Adams knew about this [concept], but he just couldn't help it. He said, "I don't have the gift of silence," which is what Washington had or Jefferson had.

. . . Adams grew up in Braintree, Massachusetts, with . . . none of the connections that Jefferson had. Jefferson's mother was a Randolph, one of the most prestigious families in the whole colony of Virginia. He had, in a sense, a silver spoon from the outset, whereas Adams did not. So, there's a big difference in their backgrounds. And, of course, Massachusetts was a relatively egalitarian state compared to the hierarchical state of Virginia. There were a few slaves in Massachusetts, but nothing comparable to the 40 percent of Virginia which was enslaved. So, the worlds they grew up with could not have been more different.

They were both smart, bright, right from the outset. Jefferson probably knew more about more things than any single man in North America, and I include Benjamin Franklin in that, who would be his only rival. . . . John Adams was smart, but he did not have the breadth. He had some depth in history and in law that Jefferson didn't have; Jefferson just wasn't as interested in the law as Adams. In fact, although Jefferson became a lawyer, he really didn't think of it as a career, and he

Outspoken John Adams's love of the law and other bookish qualities are depicted in this c. 1825–1828 lithograph by Gilbert Stuart. *Courtesy Library of Congress*

came to hate the law and hate lawyers. Adams loved the law, the mystery of the common law, and he was a superb counsel. He was one of the best lawyers, and certainly the busiest lawyer, in the colony of Massachusetts.

Adams is eight years older. . . . When Jefferson joined the Continental Congress in 1775, Adams had already been there, and he was in the lead in pushing for independence. Jefferson saw him as his senior, and

Adams certainly saw him as his prodigy. Adams took Jefferson under his wing, this younger man. There's only eight years difference, but that can be a lot when you're young. That is how Adams and Jefferson played that role. In other words, Jefferson listened to Adams's opinion and probably said the right things to him because Jefferson was very keenly aware of people. He was always sensitive to people's feelings. I think that's where the friendship started. He deferred to Adams, and that was important.

Adams was a realist; he did not believe that all men are created equal. He thought all men are created unequal. He did not believe in American exceptionalism. We Americans are no better, no different from other nations; we're just as vicious, just as corrupt—these are the things he's saying. This is not the American myth; this is not the American dream. He took on every single dream or myth that Americans live by. We couldn't live by Adams's message. It would be too much to bear. Jefferson said what we needed to hear, in some respects, because you can't have a nation based on the notion that we're all unequal from birth. In other words, Adams . . . didn't know about genetics or DNA, but he believed that people are unequal from birth. He was all into nature, not nurture.

Jefferson was the opposite. He's into nurture, and that is what most Americans believe. . . . In other words, we're all born equal, and the differences that emerge are due to different experiences, different environments. That's why education is so important to us Americans, as it was important to Jefferson. Now, Adams didn't disparage education because [he felt] that it's not going to make that much difference. He told Jefferson in their later years, "I went to a foundling hospital in Paris, and I saw babies four days old, and already they were unequal. Some were smart, some were dumb, some were beautiful, some were ugly." He says those differences were right there at four days. That's not an American message. I think that's why we honor Jefferson in the way we do because we certainly honor the two men very differently. Jefferson has a beautiful memorial on the Tidal Basin in Washington. There's nothing [in Washington, DC] for Adams. Jefferson's Monticello is a World Heritage Site visited by hundreds of thousands of people from all [over] the world. I don't know how many people come to Quincy, Massachusetts, to the Adams's home, a very modest house relative to Monticello. He's got a fraction of the visitors.

Adams was not in the same league, in the celebrity league if you will. . . . Their friendship broke up, but they came back together in 1812, and they exchanged about 158 letters, with Adams writing three to every one of Jefferson's. But that's understandable because, at one point, Adams says to Jefferson, "How many letters do you get in a year for yourself? How many do you receive?" This is about 1820. Jefferson says, "I get 2,000-something." Adams says, "I only get 200." Ten to one, and Jefferson felt obligated to answer them. Jefferson is corresponding with [Alexander von] Humboldt, the great naturalist; he's corresponding with the czar of Russia; he's corresponding with all sorts of great people. Adams is not in that league at all. So, Adams says, "I'll write more than you because I know you're busy writing to other people." They were in a different league then, . . . and they still are, in our consciousness. There is no way that Adams can compete with Jefferson because Jefferson stands for America. Now, unfortunately, he's a slaveholder and that has tainted him very badly in these days.

Adams had been in the First Continental Congress; Jefferson didn't make that one. I think he became ill, but he sent along instructions, which got printed as a pamphlet. It was a review of the contest between Britain and their colonies, and it established his name in 1774. This was a very radical pamphlet, as radical as any pamphlet written until Thomas Paine because he takes on the king in his pamphlet. This is 1774, two years before the Declaration, and it anticipates the Declaration because he goes through a series of things that the king and the government have been doing. Jefferson comes to the Second Continental Congress in 1775, where Adams already had been in both congresses, and he's already in the leadership. Adams is serving on about twenty-some committees and is the chair of many of them, including the committee on the war. When the Declaration of Independence committee is formed, Adams and Jefferson are both on it. Adams is happy to have this young guy take on the drafting of the Declaration because he's so busy doing, in his mind, more important things, like running the war against Great Britain. Little did Adams realize . . . how important that Declaration would become. Later, of course, Adams becomes quite jealous of the fame that Jefferson is getting.

[During the Constitutional Convention in 1787 in Philadelphia, both men] were abroad—Jefferson as minister to France and Adams as minister in London. Adams had a profound effect on the Constitution, on the kind of government [it created], because he had written the Massachusetts Constitution in 1780. There, he'd set forth a kind of structure that gets copied by the federal government—a strong executive with veto power. What Adams had wanted was an absolute veto over all legislation, but he had to bend to his colleagues, and they gave a limited veto. The reason . . . all of our governors have limited vetoes, including the president, is because of Adams. . . . [Because] the two of them are away, they don't know about the outcome until about two months later. Adams loves it because it seems to fit his own description of what good government should be. Jefferson is appalled by the power of the president [in the Constitution]. He thinks it is much too great. He sees the president as a version of a king that was elected for life, he has served for life, and then he would die, and the aristocrats will elect the new king. That's how Jefferson thought the president of the United States would be.

. . . Adams was obsessed by oligarchy, he had a kind of iron law about oligarchy. He believed that there inevitably will be oligarchs who . . . attempt to run things. He feared the aristocracy more than he feared a monarchy or a single ruler. He was willing to give much more power to a president or to a governor than Jefferson [wanted]. Adams says at one point, "You fear the one, Mr. Jefferson; I fear the few." He is obsessed by aristocracy, although he has emerged himself as an aristocrat. Jefferson's notion of an aristocrat would be the talented and the virtuous man like himself. He assumed that the people, once educated, will elect people like himself. Jefferson was confident of the populace. He did not fear that demagoguery would take place. Adams is much more doubtful of democracy. Adams comes to doubt American elections. He thought they would soon become so corrupt, so partisan, that we would have to adopt the British technique—we would have to adopt, first, a lifetime tenure for the president, and for the Senate we would eventually have to make them hereditary. The question is: Have we reached that point yet in our elections? Because Adams would certainly [say], "I told you so. This is what happens when you have too much democracy." Jefferson had none of those doubts, none of those fears.

Jefferson had contempt for organized religion. . . . He mocked Christianity and thought that the Trinity was a joke. He would say this in private to his friends, that he didn't really care much about organized religion at all and he didn't think religion was all that important to people. John Adams believes quite the contrary, although he is a Unitarian like Jefferson, that is to say they did not believe in the divinity of Jesus. But, Adams has tremendous respect for religious feelings and for religion. He thinks it's useful, it's necessary, that people need to have religion. He never mocked it; he never made fun of it. So, he's very different in that respect from Jefferson.

The French Revolution was a momentous event, and Jefferson sees it as being influenced by our Revolution. He sees a worldwide revolutionary wave, beginning with us, that's going to spread eventually and revolutionize the world. Ten years later [than ours], you had the French Revolution, and that seemed to be the first of what's going to be many revolutions. Jefferson's a complete ideologue; he's so caught up in the French Revolution. At one point his successor as minister to France writes to him, this is 1793 right in the middle of the terror, and says, "Mr. Jefferson, your friends are being guillotined by the thousands." Jefferson writes back, "Well, so be it." He said, "If only an Adam and Eve are left alive but left free, it will be worth it. . . ."

That's how Jefferson appears in letters. Now, it's very doubtful he would have behaved that way because he tended to exaggerate, but that's the feeling he had about this revolution, that it was worth so many deaths. . . . He was as far in the vanguard of radical thinking as you could be and still be an elected official.

[By contrast] Adams is committed to the English constitution from the beginning, [which he thought was] the finest in the world. He wants the American republican government to be a republican model of the English [system]. He's completely taken with the English. Of course, when the revolution breaks out, England and France are in a titanic struggle for supremacy over a ten-year period of warfare. Adams's sympathy is totally with England, and Jefferson's is totally with France. That's the source of their ultimate break because the two parties that emerge—the Federalists are pro-English, and the Jeffersonian Republicans are pro-French. And, the two men are caught as leaders of these two parties by the end of the 1790s.

The Federalists of New England are frightened of democracy because when they see it in operation, people [they support] are not being elected. In Virginia, you've got all these slaveholding aristocrats who are the leaders of the Republican Party. . . . It's a paradox seemingly, but these [aristocratic] people have more confidence in democracy because there are none of the problems that the leaders are having in Massachusetts. [In] Massachusetts, the more egalitarian society, the so-called aristocrats are more vulnerable to challenge; it's easier to enter the aristocracy in New England. And so, they are much more frightened of democracy even though they're more democratic.

[In the presidential election of] 1796, there are only three electoral votes that separate [Adams and Jefferson]. Adams was appalled by that. He had been vice president to Washington, and he expected, "I should be acclaimed like Washington," who had gotten every single electoral vote. Well, it wasn't the same with Adams. He squeaked in by three votes, and if it had gone the other way, then Jefferson would have been the president and Adams would have been the vice president. Adams said he would never serve under Jefferson. He's not happy. He feels he's been humiliated by that close election. Then, when it comes to the election of 1800, he loses—and that is just beyond belief for him.

John Adams was the only president in our history who was defeated who did not stay around . . . to attend the inauguration of his successor. [The year] 1801 is the inauguration of Jefferson. It was 1812 [when the two of them finally resolved their grievances]. That really occurred only because of Dr. Benjamin Rush, who worked two years at it. He knew . . . Adams much better, and he felt that the nation needed to hear these two men talk to each other, that posterity required their correspondence. He used that argument over and over to each of them. Rush played it beautifully because he would report back to each. He would say to Adams, "Jefferson said he loves you," and then he goes to Jefferson and says, "Adams says he loves you." He really set them up—and it took him two years to do it. Finally, they break through. Then, once the correspondence starts, Adams, of course, is much more blunt, and he says things; he's razzing, he's sarcastic, he jokes, he's facetious. . . . He's pushing a little bit too much. Some more sensitive soul [than Jefferson] might have said, "Enough is enough. I'm not going to put up with that."

I have a chapter in my book entitled "The Great Reversal" because in their correspondence Adams develops a kind of confidence; . . . he just feels better about himself and about the country. Jefferson is going the other way. Adams's son, John Quincy, becomes president in 1825.

Jefferson congratulates Adams, but deep down he thinks that it's a mistake. He's frightened to death of what John Quincy is proposing because Quincy is coming in with internal improvements, infrastructure, if you will. The federal government is going to build bridges, canals, do all that kind of stuff. Jefferson and his fellow planters, slaveholders, are frightened to death because if the federal government can do that, then they can encroach, and they can get involved in slavery. He becomes a "fire-eater." He's concerned about the federal government's power to do something about the nature of the institution of slavery.

All of these founders who lived into the nineteenth century are appalled by what they've wrought. They are disappointed by the revolution; they are scared. It hasn't worked out the way they thought. It's too democratic. It's too wild. And certainly, Adams and Jefferson both have second thoughts. Not that they want to reverse it, but they just say, "This is not the world we wanted."

GEORGE H. W. BUSH

41st President, 1989–1993

Overall Rank: 20

— ★ —

Total Score: 596

Historians have ranked George H. W. Bush in the top half of presidents in all three C-SPAN surveys. In the 2017 survey, his highest ranks were 8th in international relations and 12th in crisis leadership. His lowest ranks were 23rd in public persuasion and 27th in vision/setting an agenda.

Party: Republican
b. June 12, 1924, Milton, Massachusetts
d. November 30, 2018, Houston, Texas
First Lady: Barbara Pierce Bush
Age entering office: 64

Historian: Jeffrey A. Engel

History and international relations professor Jeffrey Engel serves as the founding director of the Center for Presidential History at Southern Methodist University. He joined C-SPAN's Q & A on August 29, 2018, to discuss his book, When the World Seemed New: George H. W. Bush and the End of the Cold War.

[If I had to describe George Herbert Walker Bush to someone who had never met him,] I would say he was a gentleman. I would say he's a person who came up with traditional American values but also the values of being part of the elite. When we think about the term "noblesse oblige," that really describes George Bush. He's a person who was born well off, had the best education, had the best of training, and yet spent his entire life trying to work in public service to give more back. He really was just a gentleman of the kind that we really don't see much anymore in American politics.

It started with his mother, . . . who constantly told him that your responsibility as a person to the manor born was to give back. She always stressed that the team was more important than the individual, which is very important for Bush, who was really into athletics throughout his life. He played baseball in college, and no matter how many times he would say, "Mom, here's how I did," she would say, "Yes but how did the team do?" I think it really infused in him a sense of the broader success being more important than the individual.

[Prescott Bush, his father, served in the US Senate from 1952 to 1963.] In George Bush's life, it really demonstrated an example, if you will, of this kind of service that his mother had been describing her entire life, . . . the kind of service that his father exemplified, which was a service of compromise, service of negotiation. Prescott Bush was no firebrand. He was what we would call today a classic Eisenhower Republican. He was one of Dwight Eisenhower's favorite golfing buddies. Eisenhower said, "I like to work with Bush. I like to play with Bush because he's one of the only people that won't let me win." When you're the president, you get a few mulligans. . . . And so, we really have extraordinarily little legislation that was authored by Prescott Bush but an extraordinary wealth of tales of him going behind the scenes, getting the two sides to come together in a way that's very difficult even to conceive of today.

George Bush . . . spent a few years in the middle crucial years of his life in World War II in the South Pacific. Upon graduation [from high school], he and his friends, before they got drafted, all rushed to volunteer [for the military. This was] despite the fact that George Bush's parents—and even the high school graduation speaker who was none other than Secretary of War Henry Stimson, a close family friend of the Bushes—encouraged Bush and those like him to go to college, spend a year or two getting a little bit more seasoning. The expectation was that these types of people would become officers, and a good officer would have a little bit more understanding of the world. Bush and his comrades had no interest in that. The United States had just been attacked a few months before, and they want to get into the fight before it was over, ironically not realizing quite how long it would go.

George Bush was eighteen, and here's a good place where his family connections pay off. Having been unable to keep him from enlisting in the navy, his family was nonetheless able to get him a really coveted spot as a naval aviator. In fact, he ultimately becomes one of the youngest naval aviators in the entire Pacific theater, . . . remarkably young for having that sort of responsibility. He spent several years in training and then got sent off to fly torpedo bombers off an escort carrier. Also, as an officer he takes care of the men under his command, and it's remarkable that at this point he's only nineteen, twenty years old.

It was a searing lifetime event for him, in particular, the fact that he was shot down on September 2, 1944. He and his crew were on a bombing mission over the island of Chichijima. They were trying to take out a radio tower that they had attacked the day before unsuccessfully, and his plane was hit by enemy flak. Bush was able to hold the bomber aloft and keep it on track for the bombing run. Then, after dropping the bombs, he moved out to sea and told his crewmen, "Now, it's time to bail out, time to go, hit the silk." Then he himself jumped out and hit his head on the tail as it came by.

He parachuted down and realized as he was in the water all alone on the Pacific Ocean that there were no other parachutes. He realized at that moment that he was the only one of his crew that survived. That thought haunt[ed] him . . . [all of his life], I would say. He [told me] there was not a day that [went] by that he [didn't] think about his two crewmembers under his command and why he was spared and they were not. . . . It's largely one of those things that's impossible to answer with full certainty. It's pretty clear from the evidence that we have that they were most likely killed by the enemy shrapnel as it came in and that they were not able to get out.

He was in a small raft on the ocean, bobbing up and down, had taken in a tremendous amount of seawater, was vomiting. He writes home to his parents, subsequently, that he was crying profusely—the adrenaline having left his body at that point. And then he noticed something particularly bad, which is that his raft was beginning, with the current, to move towards the island. That was really not a good place for an American pilot to go.

We subsequently found out that other pilots who had been shot down on that island were not only killed by the Japanese, but there was some cannibalism that went on as well by the Japanese troops there. Bush, not knowing that but knowing capture is not a great thing for

Lt. George H. W. Bush, c. 1942–1945, sits in the cockpit of an Avenger. Bush flew fifty-eight combat missions in World War II, was shot down over the Pacific, and was awarded the Distinguished Flying Cross. *Credit: George H. W. Bush Presidential Library and Museum*

an American, paddles furiously the other direction, and ultimately an American submarine, the *Finback*, picks him up. He spends the next month underwater with the crew doing submarine missions until they could get back to base.

[He was in the military until] 1945. He had rotated back, had some more training, had fifty-eight combat missions. After he was shot down, he could have taken a break at that point, but he decided not to. Instead, [he went] right back to his unit to keep the fight up and not let his comrades down.

In 1945, he had just married Barbara Bush, and news comes out that the war is over. The atomic bombings of Hiroshima and Nagasaki brought the war to a quicker end than people were expecting. And within three months, he was out of the service and onto his next step of life, which for him was Yale. . . . They gave [returning veterans] an accelerated program of studies, so he was able to graduate Yale in three years. He graduated Phi Beta Kappa in economics and was part of the Skull and Bones Society, the single most prestigious [Yale] society.

He also was there with his wife and then, ultimately, with his small son, George. One of my favorite discoveries of the entire book is that Barbara Bush and George lived in an apartment complex that was next door to the official residence for the Yale president, who very kindly came over one day and asked her to stop putting out the laundry with [young] George's diapers when he was having parties. So, it really gives a sense of how a person could go within six months from the terror of World War II into the bucolic life of New Haven in the '40s.

. . . At the end of 1948, having just graduated from Yale, he had the opportunity to go to New York to work in his father's investment house. And he instead decided: "I need to go and make my life on my own, make my own fortune, make my own way." He hops in a Studebaker, a brand-new one, and drives across the country and winds up in Odessa, Texas. He had a friend of the family who had an oil company out there, and he began to work as a salesman for the oil company. Barbara and little George come a little bit after. I think this is a great moment for trying to understand who George Bush is on a profound level because, on the one hand, he's a person who is able to take the leap of faith to say, I'm going to try something new and not rest on the laurels of my family to succeed. On the other hand, he goes out to Texas with a very large check from some investors back home, friends of his father's, and he's working for a family friend. He knows if Texas doesn't work out, there's always a job back in New York for him. So, it's in a sense an adventure, but there's a very large net beneath them, if you will.

[His national political career began in 1967 when he spent four years in the US House of Representatives.] The most important thing about that moment in his life is the time that he stood up to his constituents. He voted for the Fair Housing Act—something which was remarkably unpopular in his district back in Texas—even though he expected that this would perhaps ruin his political career. Ultimately, he went back to his district and explained that he had just come back from visiting American troops in Vietnam and couldn't stomach the idea that an African American or Hispanic American . . . who would put their lives on the line in combat couldn't come home and buy a house. He voted for that bill out of conscience, and it really demonstrated that at the end of the day, he did oftentimes see a higher purpose to service.

[In March of 1971, he became the UN ambassador for twenty-two months.] They were, perhaps, his happiest years of his life. He found that he really loved diplomacy. He had run for the US Senate from Texas. He had given up his very safe House seat in order to do so. He was expecting to run against a relatively liberal candidate on the Democratic side. Instead, he found himself running against Lloyd Bentsen, who one can safely say was more conservative than George H. W. Bush. . . . He lost that election. But he had in the back of his pocket a promise from President Richard Nixon that if he did this run for Senate, and if it didn't work out, the next administration would take care of him. . . . They found a . . . position for him at the United Nations, at which point it was pointed out that George Bush had zero diplomatic experience, and his international experience had largely come during World War II. Bush very wisely turned that into a virtue. He explained to the White House staff under Nixon that since he didn't know anything, he would do exactly what Henry Kissinger said. That's exactly what Henry Kissinger, the secretary of state, wanted to hear.

[On January 19, 1973, he began as the chair of the Republican National Committee for twenty-one months, in the middle of the Watergate scandal.] He did it because the president asked. . . . The time at the RNC was arguably the worst time, politically, in his professional life. . . .

It became difficult, of course, [because] Bush had the unenviable job of being forced to go out on the stump every day and defend the president, a president who he increasingly over time came to believe, and then know, had been lying to him. So, like other Republicans at that time, the moment they realized not so much that they had been lied to, but they had been made to lie for Nixon, that was a moment that he and others encouraged Nixon's resignation.

[On September 26, 1974, he went to China as the US liaison for fourteen months.] Gerald Ford sends him there, the president who comes after Nixon, essentially as a reward for the good service he had done for the Republican Party. . . . He thought that going to China would be an adventure, much like when he first went to Texas. It would be something that was completely brand new, something completely foreign, and something completely exotic and exciting. If there's one conversation in his life I wish I had been a fly on the wall for, it's when he came back and informed Barbara that they were going to [be posted in] China. . . .

[Next, he served as the director of the Central Intelligence Agency for 357 days.] That came about as a long-term vestige of the difficulties of Watergate and Vietnam. The CIA was under tremendous pressure from congressional investigations at this point, and Gerald Ford decided to shake things up and move people around within his cabinet. He called Bush home in order to be CIA director. This was [an assignment—chief spy—that] Bush thought was going to kill his political career.

. . . When President Carter wins in 1976, Bush asked him if he could stay on at the CIA, but Carter wanted his own CIA director. So, Bush spends the next three years essentially prepping for his run in 1980. He goes back to Houston but really spends most of his time on the road meeting people in all the different states. Nineteen eighty is when he finally ran against Ronald Reagan. It was ultimately the best first challenge against Reagan in the sense that Bush managed to win the Iowa caucuses. Ronald Reagan at that point had assumed he was going to steamroll to the convention . . . and really didn't put too much time into Iowa. Bush made a point of visiting every single county in Iowa and shaking hands there. He wins the Iowa caucus, but frankly it's downhill from there once Reagan gets his full attention in the campaign. . . .

Bush winds up being the last man standing against Ronald Reagan and gives us some of our most important historical phrases and criticisms about Ronald Reagan. Bush, for example, is the one who comes up on the campaign trail with the term "voodoo economics" to describe trickle-down economics, or supply-side economics as Reagan would have preferred. We still use the term "voodoo economics" today, and we forget that it ultimately was Reagan's vice president who used that as a criticism against him when they were both going for the top job.

The 1980 convention was a weird one, historically, because there began to be talk that perhaps Ronald Reagan would choose Gerald Ford to come back and be his vice president. They would essentially be co-presidents, and these negotiations got very close before both sides realized this would never work, that somebody had to be in charge ultimately. Reagan then had to turn and find someone to be vice president, and the logical choice was the one who had been last man standing in the campaign, George Bush. It's a testament to both men, both their sense of opportunism and also their basic characters, that they were willing to look past the criticisms [during] their primary campaigns to work together over the next eight years.

[George Bush ran to succeed Ronald Reagan in 1988.] . . . One of the remarkable things about the Republican primary in 1987 and '88 is just how far most of the candidates on that field are trying to run away from the legacy of Reagan. We think of Reagan through the lens of history as someone who was remarkably popular. But at the end, he was personally popular, but his policies were not, especially his policies vis-à-vis the Cold War, and he still had the taint of Iran-Contra, as well. Most of the candidates were trying to criticize Reagan's legacy. Given his experience in 1980, had Bush not been a member of the administration, he would have been first in line to criticize Reagan in 1988.

Bush has a remarkable ability throughout his career, especially when he'd gotten to national-level politics, of being able to surround himself with people who would do the dirty work that needs to get done for an election, as he saw it. Lee Atwater, Roger Ailes, people who would play politics . . . as tough as possible—OK, I'll use the word "dirty." Bush would always have a sense of remove that he could say, "I did not order that," "I did not know about that plan," "I didn't know about Willie Horton," for example, despite the fact that his campaign clearly knew that the Willie Horton ad was going to run; Willie Horton being the famous racially charged advertisement that the Bush campaign ran in 1988. There was always somebody around him who could be the hitman. Ailes and people like Atwater played that role for him.

. . . I've seen documentation from people like Lee Atwater, in particular, who said, "We made a point of not discussing such things." This is not to alleviate Bush of any complicity or guilt in these situations. He was in charge. Ultimately, he is responsible for what happens with his campaign. But it does give a sense of the tone that he wants to set, that he told his people, "We're going to go for the win; we're going to do whatever it takes to win. We're going to play dirty, and in many ways, both play the race card and try to emasculate Michael Dukakis," their campaign opponent. He wanted those things done, but he wanted somebody else to do it. [In 1988, Bush trounced Michael Dukakis, 53 percent to 45 percent, winning 40 states and 426 Electoral College votes.]

. . . No president has ever been as prolific as a letter writer, as a note writer, as a person who maintained personal contacts across his entire life. I understood that at its height, the Bush Christmas card list was over twenty-five thousand people. Once you became a friend of George Bush's, you remained that way. He really believed that the personal touch was built over time. One of the most amazing things that we were able to get declassified and pull out of the Bush library to write this new history was all of the transcripts of phone calls that President Bush had with foreign leaders around the world. Every time he picked up the phone to talk to a foreign leader, we have that transcript. What's amazing is how little talking he did. He oftentimes would call people up, the [prime minister] of Australia or the president of Zimbabwe, and say, "What's going on in your world? What do you think about the situation?" And, he'd just listen.

My book is fundamentally about the end of the Cold War. It's silly to think that any one person is responsible for ending the Cold War, but if you had to choose somebody who was more responsible than anyone else, it would be Mikhail Gorbachev. He is really the central catalyst that gets the entire democratic explosion started. His desire to reform the Soviet Union—not to eradicate it; he was a true Soviet believer—but [he wanted] to reform and revitalize it, not set in motion the democratic revolutions that brought down his country's empire.

Bush had a tremendous responsibility for making sure that Gorbachev's reforms continued to go peacefully. Bush walked a tightrope throughout his entire first year in his administration knowing that if he pushed too hard on the Soviets, that could cause perhaps a counterrevolution, a conservative revolution against Gorbachev and the other democratic revolutions in Eastern Europe. If he was too easy on Gorbachev, well,

then perhaps that, too, could cause a counterrevolution. Then Gorbachev's opponents, and he had many, might say, "You're clearly too
close to the Americans; you must not have our interests at heart." That's
the macro influence that Bush had on the immediate evening of the fall
of the wall.

[The fall of the Berlin Wall on November 9, 1989,] was a surprise. It
was actually a mistake. East German spokesmen read the wrong memo
on television, giving the wrong information, giving people the impression that they had the right to cross the border. When tens of thousands of people saw that on TV and rushed to the gates, the guards
there made the wise choice that they should open them up rather than
mow the crowd down, rather than having, [as China did] a Tiananmen
Square[-type massacre]. No one [inside the Bush administration] had
any idea. It wasn't supposed to happen. It was an absolute mistake. I
have a wonderful memo from about two days before the wall fell from
Bush's National Security Council that says, and I'm paraphrasing, "We
should think about the fact that there might be a change in the border
status. We should start planning how we might want to put together a
committee to start thinking about how we should react." That's a typical
bureaucratic start to something that you expect is not going to happen
for six months, or a year, or maybe never. Most of the people who saw
the Berlin Wall fall on November 9, 1989, had the same reaction, which
was this was something we never thought we'd see in our lifetimes. . . .
And then, suddenly it happened, to everyone's surprise.

[The 1991 Gulf War was another defining time in Bush's presidency.]
The most important things about Iraq are threefold. The first is just
how much Iraq was—for Bush and those around him—not about the
Middle East, but about the end of the Cold War. They understood the
Berlin Wall had fallen. The Soviet Union is transforming rapidly. They
understood that the world had changed, and however the international
community chose to meet the threat of violence, the first time after that
change would set the pattern for decades to come. Iraq mattered, but
ultimately what mattered more was the post–Cold War sentiment that
they were trying to create and precedent that they were trying to create.

The second thing that was really fascinating about the Gulf War was
that Bush was fully prepared to go to war in January of 1991 with five
hundred thousand American troops in the region, and war planes, and

ready to go, even if Congress on the eve of that battle had voted against giving him authorization. It was a remarkably close vote; only a few votes tipped the balance. Bush wrote numerous times in his diary, and I have this confirmed by many people within the upper levels of his administration, that even if he lost the vote, he was still going to use his authority to send American troops in the combat. He recognized this would be a clearly impeachable offense, but he had an interesting rationale about it. First of all, he thought it was the right thing to do. He thought Saddam Hussein had to be taken out at that point. But secondly, he thought, "We're going to win this war, and frankly we're going to win this war quickly. Presidents who win wars quickly are very popular, and I would like to see Congress try to impeach me when I have a 90 percent approval rating." So, he thought that before impeachment hearings could possibly get moving, the war would have already been over by several weeks. And, he was willing to take that political risk.

[The third point about the war was the decision not to remove Iraqi leader Saddam Hussein in 1991.] Every member of the Bush administration will give you the same answer, which is also borne out by the documentary evidence. . . . No one in 1991 in the Bush administration, including [then Defense Secretary] Dick Cheney, thought it was a good idea to go on to Baghdad.

The reasons they gave are really haunting for us today: they suggested that the Iraqis would treat us like a foreign occupying force; they suggested that it would create ethnic and religious tension that would potentially lead to civil war; they thought it would put tremendous strain on the Israeli-Palestinian issue, which is the center of so much of Middle East politics. And frankly, Bush recognized that if you own Iraq, metaphorically speaking, you are responsible for it. That was a responsibility that the United States either shouldn't take, or perhaps wouldn't even be able to be successful at. And, we didn't need to because our expectation is that . . . Saddam Hussein is most likely going to die from a coup from his own officers. That was really the most likely bet at that point [which proved wrong].

I had the great privilege of going down [to Texas] a couple of times and reading chapters of the [finished] book to him and Mrs. Bush before [they] passed. . . . It was a remarkable opportunity that very few historians ever get, to read their work to their subject.

President Bush [was] remarkably supportive in a way that should be an example to other people who formerly held power. He always stated and always understood that the job of people who make history and the job of people who write history are fundamentally different and have to be separate; that his job was to answer every question as truthfully as he could, and my job was to assess things as truthfully as I could.

I found many things, which I explain in my book, where I think President Bush was misinformed, where he had mistakes in judgment. Overwhelmingly, I come away extraordinarily impressed by the job he did, especially as a diplomat. Even an All-Star hitter strikes out from time to time.

JOHN QUINCY ADAMS

6th President, 1825–1829

Overall Rank: 21

— ★ —

Total Score: 590

J. Q. Adams ranks two spots below his father, John, a differential that has existed in the last two C-SPAN surveys. JQA is the only president serving before Lincoln with a top-ten ranking in pursued equal justice for all (9th in 2017). However, very low rankings in public persuasion (33rd) and relations with Congress (32nd) result in his middle-of-the-road overall ranking.

Party: Democratic-Republican
b. July 11, 1767, Braintree (now Quincy), Massachusetts
d. February 23, 1848, Washington, DC
First Lady: Louisa Catherine Johnson Adams
Age entering office: 57

Historian: **James Traub**

James Traub is a journalist, contributing writer for The New York Times Magazine, *and a member of the Council on Foreign Relations. He was interviewed for* Q & A *on August 9, 2016, for his book,* John Quincy Adams: Militant Spirit, *where he used Adams's extensive diary and letters to tell his story.*

John Quincy Adams came from a world that revered public service. He was very close to the founding of the republic. If you would ask him, why were you qualified to be president, he would have said, "Because I have served the republic selflessly since I was a young man." And that was true. He'd been a diplomat, he'd been a congressman, he'd been secretary of state, and his own sense of service, of sacrifice, even of heroism, all had to do with the idea that "I am here for the republic. That is my purpose." I think he would be saddened and sickened by the disgust with which people today talk about the idea of service.

In his day, politics was not a route to wealth; quite the opposite. When he was a young man, he ran for the state legislature of Massachusetts.

Most of his friends, who were all lawyers like him, wouldn't do that because the theory was, first you make dough as a merchant or a lawyer or whatever; then, when you are comfortable, you can afford to go into politics because no one ever made a nickel out of politics.

Congressmen in those days would get nine dollars as a per diem, and so, Adams struggled economically his whole life, but he thought that it was right that he struggled. Part of his sense of public service is that you accept the fact that you're not going to make money doing it and you'll die poor. Indeed, the presidents who preceded Adams—Jefferson, famously, but also Madison and Monroe, not so famously—had terrible economic problems once they stepped down because they'd never made any money at all. Adams was haunted by the fear that he would die destitute. Actually, he was a pretty good investor, and he was able to invest enough money to bail out many impecunious family members, as well as to keep his own family going. But he would have thought profiting from politics was immoral.

He was not a likable person, and so I tend to use the word "admire" [about him] more than "like." . . . He was a forbidding figure. His son said he "wore an iron mask," and it's really true—he had a grim visage, bearish, chilly. I can imagine listening to him talk. He was an astonishing talker because he knew everything about everything and he'd forgotten nothing. But in the end, I do not describe him in my book as a likable man, and I give full measure to his unlikable, indeed, really unpleasant qualities—bad husband, bad father, but a great son, a reverent son.

. . . What I admire about him is this deep sense of an obligation beyond himself. He was never in a war; he never saw battle, but he was fearless, and he was prepared to risk his life in the name of public service. In the last part of his life, when he took on what he called the "slavocracy" in Congress, he started getting death threats. I've read them all because he kept all the letters, and there are dozens of them. The death threats were not things like, "You deserve to die." No, they were things like, "I'm in Covington, Kentucky. I am leaving now, and I am coming for you, and I will cut you down on the street." They were extreme. Sometimes he would get letters from people saying, "I'm halfway there. I'm still advancing towards Washington." Very credible threats. What did he do? Nothing. He didn't tell federal marshals. He didn't even tell his wife. He just lived his life; he would have thought it was shameful for him to have done otherwise. That's heroism.

I [was helped greatly, as his biographer, when I] discovered that he had kept a diary. Not an episodic diary like some public figures, but a diary like no public figure has ever kept, every day of his life from the time he was eighteen. He began when he was eleven, but from the time he was eighteen he hardly skipped a day until he was physically paralyzed and close to his death. That's an astonishing record. . . . We know what he thought. He tells us what he thought, so that's an astonishing weapon [for a biographer]. No diary is ever, of course, truly a transparent record. It's a record of what that person thought, not of what actually happened. And there are elements where Adams goes silent about things you wouldn't expect. . . . But the thing that does come through so powerfully is the personality of a man with a deep Puritan iron in his soul, self-accusatory, harshly self-accusatory: "I must wake up earlier. I'm falling short of my own standards. I must read more. I've reread my diary. It's all banal. It's nothing."

[In his diary I found some] things that are startling. He loved Lord Byron, and Byron was the most bad of the bad boys; mad, bad, and dangerous to know—everything Adams would have deplored. But Adams's literary taste was not just a dependent variable of his morals because he loved poetry and literature. He loved Voltaire, whom he also thought of as a libertine. The breadth of his personality also comes through [in his diary]. I was never bored. Well OK, I guess [I was somewhat bored] when I got to the thousandth iteration of his trees. He was fascinated by dendrology, . . . the study of trees. He planted trees, he grew trees, he loved trees, and there are moments, I know that my eyes scanned over [his text] and I thought, "Oh, more trees; I can skip this passage!"

He was born in a place that was then called Braintree, which we now call Quincy. He was the second child. He had an older sister, Abigail, nicknamed Nabby, and there were two more boys who were born after him. He was the second of four, but because he was the oldest boy, he was always treated as number one. . . . They must have seen pretty early on that he was an exceptionally gifted person and also very disciplined, which his two younger brothers were not. . . . And he always bore the weight of his parents' hopes, their expectations, their disappointments. It was a heavy burden to bear.

His youth was fascinating because his father, John Adams, took him to France in 1778 and then again in 1780 when John Sr. was a diplomat, and so this young man had an upbringing in Europe that was really like that of very, very few Americans. He also wrote in his diary . . . about the time he spent, maybe a year, as the thirteen- and fourteen-year-old secretary to America's then ambassador to Russia in Saint Petersburg. The ambassador wasn't received by Catherine the Great, and so Adams [used his time to] read Hume's five-volume *History of England*. His youth was very, very interesting.

Adams was a fantastic talker. People have testified that this man knew every word of Shakespeare, but he knew . . . everything about everything. He was an amazing talker, but he was not a public speaker. He was convinced that he was a terrible public speaker, and he tried very hard to learn. In 1805, he'd been a diplomat, and he was back in Boston earning a living as a lawyer. Harvard approaches him and says, "We would like you to be the first Boylston professor of rhetoric and oratory"—a chair, by the way, that still exists to this day. It's the oldest continuous endowed chair in America. Adams had long studied Cicero and the other great rhetoricians, but now he became obsessed. Every time he went to church, which he would do twice on Sunday, he would note the verbal ticks of the preacher. He would listen to what worked and what didn't work. He put himself through this education in order to make himself a better professor but also better at [public speaking]. Ultimately, Adams became a great speaker, as an older man. . . . I would say that at the end of his life, those last twenty years when he was in Congress, he then became [an effective] public speaker. In those days [listening to speeches] was the great entertainment that people would have. Adams became in demand because of the whole slavery [issue], and he would deliver speeches in New England. One time he was asked to deliver a speech in Cincinnati, which is the farthest west he ever went. Adams became one of the great speakers of the age of great oratory.

[His long career in political service began as the minister to the Netherlands from ages twenty-seven to twenty-nine; he was minister to Prussia, ages thirty to thirty-three; he was US senator for Massachusetts from ages thirty-five to forty; and minister to Russia from ages forty-two to forty-six. This is in the early 1800s. He served as minister to Great Britain, ages forty-seven to forty-nine; secretary of state, ages fifty to fifty-seven; president of United States from 1825 to 1829, ages fifty-seven to sixty-one;

and then he was a member of the House of Representatives until he died, from sixty-three years old to age eighty.]

[He served in the Senate from 1803 to 1808.] In those days, senators were not elected directly. They were chosen by state legislatures, so it wasn't surprising [he was selected, since] he was the son of a president and he was a very highly regarded diplomat. Through a series of retirements, he wound up [being offered] the job. The thing that distinguished him from the moment he got to Washington was that he was a member of the Federalist Party, his father's party, which is the opposition party. Thomas Jefferson was the Republican Party, . . . the antecedent of what is today's Democratic Party. . . . However, Adams always took the position, "I'm not here as a party man." Adams didn't believe in party. This was a very, very important question [for the founders]. George Washington didn't believe in parties. Most of the founders thought "party" meant "faction"; it was bad; it was selfish association instead of national patriotism. Adams absolutely absorbed that idea.

When Jefferson was doing things that were seen by [most] Federalists as being a disaster for their own party, they opposed them. For example, the Louisiana Purchase was going to hugely expand the magnitude of the country into areas such as the western parts of the South. Some of [this territory] would clearly be slaveholding areas, and all of it would be new men who would see old New England as antiquated. That was clearly bad for the Federalists. [However] Adams said the purchase was a good thing for America because he had a vision of America as a continental nation, as many did at this time. So, he supported it, although with a million weird caveats that nobody else believed in except him. On the one hand, he was an eccentric who had his own intellectual views and would follow them no matter what. On the other hand, he was indifferent to party and prepared to accept whatever consequences came of that. This was ultimately how he left the Senate.

In the run-up to the War of 1812, . . . the English were attacking American shipping. . . . Jefferson said this was unacceptable. Ultimately, Jefferson says we're going to establish an embargo—no transatlantic shipping. This is a catastrophe for New England; that was its economy. All of New England opposed the embargo except Adams, who said, "We can never be supine before a foreign foe"; that was a far more important principle. He knew this would be a disaster for him politically. Adams wasn't even sure the embargo would work, . . . but he couldn't bear the idea of allowing the British to get away with these depredations on American shipping. His friends said to him, "Are you crazy? You can't do this." He said, "I will do it." Ultimately, in 1808, Massachusetts chose his replacement before his Senate term had come up. Adams understood perfectly well what that meant. He said, "Fine, I will resign as of today." It was an episode that from the outside looks humiliating, but Adams considered it one of the proudest moments of his life.

JQA was secretary of state under James Monroe. This was a period [1817–1825] of peace. America was no longer at war, and so diplomacy was already a different kind of profession. America's great object then, in its foreign policy, was really what we would today call domestic policy. It was about territorial expansion. . . . Adams's great achievement was negotiating with Spain over territorial expansion. . . . He ultimately got the Spaniards to concede, literally, to a line to the Pacific Ocean. . . . Nobody expected it to happen, but Adams kept pushing for more territory. Even at some point, Monroe and the cabinet would say, "All right, fine, we have enough. Stop." Adams would say, "No, I can get more." And so . . . he got areas that went up to the eastern edge of Texas and then [Spain consented to] this [boundary] line to the Pacific. Samuel Flagg Bemis, the diplomatic historian, said Adams's negotiation was the greatest diplomatic achievement by one man that America has ever achieved.

[He ran for president in 1824. When none of the four candidates won a majority of electoral votes, the election was thrown to the House of Representatives. John Quincy Adams was elected by the House but was accused by Andrew Jackson of winning through a "corrupt bargain" with Henry Clay, whom Adams then appointed as his secretary of state.]

Adams is a politician; he has held elective office. He's done whatever you need to do to win. Yet, the thing that strikes you is that he's so solitary. When you ask why his great literary achievement is a journal, the answer is because he was most at ease speaking to himself, speaking within his own mind, his very powerful, enormous, multi-chambered mind. As president, one is struck by how solitary he was. He didn't have boon companions. More importantly, he didn't form alliances. He didn't do anything . . . to persuade people who otherwise might not go along with his agenda to do so. His four years in the White House were pain, just pain. Everything was hard. He achieved almost nothing. He probably wouldn't have succeeded very well, anyway, because he was very much the last of the line—a new world was coming into being, which Andrew Jackson would inherit.

There are other reasons that have to do with the contested election that made people think he was illegitimate, but a conventional politician would have found a way of saying, "OK, I won't propose this or that because they'll never get through. I'm just going to focus on this policy, and then I'm going to really work it hard to get it through." Adams never did that. He said, "I'm going to say what's right. I'm going to put it out there. Maybe nobody will vote for it, but it's the right thing, and eventually people will see that I'm right." Eventually, [nearly forty years later] Abraham Lincoln enacted a certain amount of Adams's very activist domestic agenda, but his was self-defeating behavior for any politician.

President Adams would wake up at dawn. He would take himself on a solitary walk. When he went out of the White House, he would either turn right towards Congress or turn left towards Georgetown and walk through the darkened streets. Nobody would ever see him. . . . He would walk and think and think; think his thoughts. He would come back and see the dawn rise from the White House, and then he would get to work. Normally, he would read the Bible for an hour in the morning. . . . He'd have breakfast later, and then he would get to work. Getting to work for him, a lot of it was writing. He was writing letters to other officeholders. He was responding to letters. . . . He would meet with his cabinet in the afternoon, and then he would go back and write some more. He would have a late supper, then he would usually write his journal late at night. He would spend an hour a day, I'm guessing, writing his journal because they were long entries. This is a guy who was unbelievably overworked, whose cabinet got worked into the ground, and he still wrote his journal.

Louisa Catherine [his wife] was a gregarious person, and when Adams had been secretary of state, she threw these parties that were the only way that Adams could connect with the larger world. She was very important to him politically in that regard. But once he got into the White House, he felt [socializing] was just a burden. He didn't want to do anything that would be seen as partial—he didn't want to invite this person and not that one. It was a completely unnecessary restriction.

John Quincy Adams, who had a critical eye for art, was said to have approved of this portrait by George Caleb Bingham. *Courtesy National Portrait Gallery, Smithsonian Institution, c. 1850, from an 1844 original*

When he first came to Washington as a senator, Thomas Jefferson would invite every interesting person in Washington [to the White House], and he and Adams had been great friends. . . . Adams and Louisa would go all the time, and it was great fun. Adams loved it. And so, he was quite accustomed to the idea of the White House as a social center, but he was like a bear in a cave as president.

He was consumed with these battles he was fighting, and Louisa Catherine absented herself. She went up to her White House bedroom and ate bonbons. . . . She was profoundly depressed. We would say now she was having a breakdown. During those times, she was so miserable and angry at him. She wrote a lot of poetry, and she wrote little fragments of a play. She would create these little mise-en-scènes. The most painful one to read, by far, begins as a processional. In it there was Lord Sharply and Lady Sharply. Lord Sharply is self-evidently Adams. He is seen as a man of absolutely irreproachable morals and perfect demeanor who is utterly devoid of human warmth and is dauntingly ambitious at the same time. You can't believe that a first lady would write this about her husband. There was one time in the course of writing my book when I was reading that play she wrote, and I [wondered], "Why am I writing about this man?" It was just awful.

[He and Louisa Catherine had three children.] John Quincy was a terrible father. The thing that strikes you is that this guy did not have an easy time as the son of parents who had high expectations. His mother [Abigail Adams] would write him these letters that would chill your blood. When he goes to Europe as a boy, she writes him a letter that warns him against the pleasures of Europe. She says, "I would sooner you perish beneath the sea than that you become . . ."—she doesn't say "a libertine," but you know that's what she means, and she means it. You would think that if you had grown up under this excruciating burden, and you were aware of the chill that had entered your own soul as a result, you would say, "I'm not going to make that mistake with my own children." . . . But Adams didn't think that way at all. He revered Abigail, and he wept when he learned that she had died. . . . He never dissented a jot or a tittle from either one of his parents. He worshiped them both. So, there was no part of him that said when he finally had children of his own, "I better not do to them what they did to me." Quite the contrary. He was worse. He had a terrible fear of failing, and so he drove his children unmercifully. He had a deep horror of improper or unacceptable behavior.

There were three boys, one of whom, Charles Francis, became the John Quincy Adams of the next generation. He always lived loosely, but he kept that from his father; his father didn't know. [Son] John was a real problem drinker, dissolute and irresponsible, and the cause of tremendous heart sickness to both parents. The other, George, was a deeply troubled person. There was something that just didn't grasp reality in George. He was a lovely person; people liked him, but he lived in a dream world. Adams, instead of recognizing what George was, laid into him for his unrealism. Even Adams finally realized at a certain point he wasn't getting anywhere. You could see in their later letters where he says, "I love you," and whatever else he can say to make him come around. But ultimately, George committed suicide. Now, do I think Adams is responsible for George's suicide? It's a terribly heavy judgment to make. I think George was a very strange young man from the time he was born, so who knows?

Louisa worried that her husband would think that she blamed him for George's suicide. I can only think . . . that secretly she did [blame him]. . . . Again, that's a mystery, but there was no question that he was a harsh and unforgiving father.

The part [of John Quincy Adams's life] that was the most riveting for me is his final phase when he is the former president of the United States and he is in the US House. What you would imagine in a case like that is a man full of years and honors speaking grandly. No, he was furious. He was a harpy. He would taunt and enrage the South. He was unreasonable. He was bitter. He was vindictive. All of his righteousness and his vile were provoked by slavery and by Southern smug opposition to the antislavery forces. This is really magnificent. At times Adams is like a hissing snake or a spitting dog, but, above all, he is the most formidable opponent.

He was so enraged by what he called the "slavocracy," the Southern slaveholders in Congress, that they twice moved to have him censured—the former president of the United States subjected to a censure proceeding. The first time, he defended himself alone. Nobody would come to his aid, and he beat the South alone. The second time—we're now into 1842, and there was more of an abolitionist movement—he had a whole community of people around him. He had a researcher in the Library of Congress. But, in the end, it was still his own floor speech for days that forced the South to cry "uncle." It's so magnificent. . . . This is the moment when this cantankerous old New Englander became a spitfire.

Here's the form in which he took on the slaveholders: the Constitution guarantees the right of petition. We don't think about that anymore because today if you want to influence your congressman you can join a lobby or a special interest group or write them a letter or give them money. In those days, the only way you had a voice besides voting was to submit a petition. . . . Starting in 1835, when the abolitionist movement in America really began—it was initially more an antislavery movement—they began to send petitions to Congress. . . . No one in Congress wanted to submit these petitions because the South dominated Congress. . . . So, Adams would present them.

At the beginning, Adams said, "I'm not even sympathizing with these petitions, but the fact is people have a right to petition, so I'm going to present them." This was a big threat because slaveholders said that slavery was a states' rights issue, and it could not be discussed or debated in Congress. . . . The slaveholders responded by doing something unprecedented. They proposed and then passed laws which stipulated that on the issue of slavery, and only on the issue of slavery, Congress would not receive petitions. . . . This was a congressional rule which expired with each new Congress; that meant at each Congress there would be this huge fight, . . . and every time the South would win. But the debates got closer and more ferocious, and Adams, after standing alone the first couple times, got more and more [compatriots]. He became a mentor to a whole generation of antislavery congressmen. The censure motions, in both cases, were consequences of Adams doing things preposterously to flout the rules. . . . Generally, congressional opposition to the Gag Rule built up. Finally, after ten years of nonstop battle, the Gag Rule was ended; Congress would no longer vote to sustain it.

Was slavery going to be ended by a debate in the House or the Senate? No. And so, one cannot say that Adams's heroism led to the end of slavery. [However,] it led to the free debate over slavery, which the South feared. That free debate over slavery is what ultimately led to the election in 1860 of an explicitly antislavery candidate, Abraham Lincoln. This convinced the South that it had no future in the Republican Party other than to secede, which led to the Civil War. In that indirect sense, Adams laid the foundation.

. . . Adams was not a good president. He was not a successful president, and if his career had ended at the end of his presidency, as his father's career ended at the end of his presidency, I don't think I would have written a book about him. But it didn't. He then had sixteen years when he goes back to Congress and becomes the great champion of the antislavery forces. To me, that trajectory of a man [cinched my interest in him as a biographer]. He leaves the presidency scorned and mocked and thought of as a fossil; even then he was thought of as an old fuddy-duddy and as the last link to a New England patriarchal past that an increasingly westernized America was moving [away from]. That was the judgment on him. Adams lived not just to reverse, to alter that judgment, but the same qualities that had made him a bad president, the same kind of moral intransigence, made him a great man.

ULYSSES S. GRANT

18th President, 1869–1877

Overall Rank: 22

— ★ —

Total Score: 557

Grant's 22nd-place ranking in 2017 is up from 33rd in C-SPAN's 2000 survey, which is the largest rise in the rankings of any president. Historians have given Grant increasingly high marks in several categories, including international relations (from 33rd to 19th) and moral authority (31st to 19th). One of the only categories where Grant has failed to improve is administrative skills (37th in 2017).

Party: Republican
b. April 27, 1822, Point Pleasant, Ohio
d. July 23, 1885, Mount McGregor, New York
First Lady: Julia Dent Grant
Age entering office: 46

Historian: **Ronald C. White**

Ronald White, historian and Huntington Library fellow, talked about his biography of the eighteenth president, American Ulysses: A Life of Ulysses S. Grant. *He was interviewed for C-SPAN's* Q & A *on October 6, 2016.*

[March 8, 1864, was] the first day Ulysses Grant met [Abraham] Lincoln. Lincoln had a habit of meeting his generals either at the White House or by going to where they served, but Grant was out in the West, so he had never met him before. They met that evening.

The troops were in their winter quarters, but Lincoln brought Grant east, preparing for what he expected to be the great spring campaign, which would start in May, the so-called Overland Campaign. Grant would march into Virginia, remembering that four times before, federal armies had marched into Virginia, and four times before they had withdrawn in humiliating retreats.

When Grant walked into the White House that March evening, nobody knew who he was. I tell the story of a tall Abraham Lincoln looking over the crowd and saying, "General Grant, what a pleasure to meet you," and he just grasped Grant's hands. They were in many ways a marriage of opposites. Grant was not a good public speaker; he was frightened by public speaking. Of course, we know that Lincoln was a tremendous public speaker. . . . Grant was not tall, five feet, seven inches, or so. He put on weight later on, but he mostly was 135 pounds. Not a man that you would particularly take notice of.

. . . Grant's lack of pomposity, the self-effacement—that's a part of who he is. He often wore a private's uniform; the only designation would be the stars on his shoulder. It's such a contrast to today's leaders of all kinds. It just says so much about who this man is and why America didn't simply admire him, but they really loved him.

[He was born in 1822 in] Point Pleasant, Ohio. [His parents] had migrated west. Although Grant is often lifted up as this great individual hero, he saw himself as part of a family story. He looked back through the prism of eight generations of Grants who would come in the 1630s to New England and gradually migrated west. His father had come west into Ohio as a boy and then settled finally in Georgetown, Ohio, and was a tanner.

[Grant] grew up in Georgetown and lived there until he was seventeen; it's fifty-five miles east of Cincinnati, close to the Ohio River. His father told him that he wanted him to go West Point. It says something about the relationship of parents to children. Ulysses didn't really want to go, but he said to his father, "If you think I should, I will." His father saw West Point as a free education and one of the only two or three engineering schools. . . . So, Grant headed to West Point. At age seventeen and just five feet, one inch tall, he barely made the cut.

When Grant arrived [at West Point], his name was actually Hiram Ulysses, but the congressman who nominated him got it all mixed up, and so when he registered, they said, "We don't have any Hiram Ulysses." Grant said, "That's my name." They said, "Unless you are U. S. Grant, Ulysses Simpson Grant,"—the congressman had remembered his mother's maiden name—"you won't be registering." So, he became U. S. Grant, and the other boys teased him, especially William Tecumseh Sherman, who called him Sam, "Uncle Sam has arrived." He was known as Sam Grant at West Point.

. . . He was there until he graduated in 1843. He was then posted to the Jefferson Barracks, which was the largest [army] posting; it was in St. Louis. This was where people were posted who were heading west to protect the settlers. [In St. Louis,] he met his roommate's sister, Julia Dent, about nine months after he arrived, and they formed a marvelous marriage.

He didn't get married right away because her father protested. He didn't want her marrying some vagabond soldier; he'd rather have her marry a businessperson.

So, Grant then participated in the war with Mexico, and did well, but he was a young man. He was assigned the duties of quartermaster, which he didn't really want. He wanted to be in the fight, and he was on a few occasions. He then came back and married Julia in 1848.

He was taken, not with Julia's beauty—she was afflicted by what people call strabismus, and it created a kind of a cross-eyed situation—but she was a woman of spirit, and he was drawn to her. She was much more vocal than he was. She was four years younger. They both loved horses and would ride together at White Haven, her family's country home. They just found this incredible match.

Grant's family was totally antislavery, strongly antislavery Republicans. Her family was strongly pro-slavery. Her father owned thirty slaves. Grant's family refused to come to the wedding. Her father gave her four slaves, which he called "servants." I think these two young people didn't quite understand really the dynamic of the family situation they were marrying into. They [eventually] had four children; three boys and Nellie, the single girl.

He was posted after the war with Mexico in both Michigan and New York, and then in 1852 he was sent to the Pacific Coast. He couldn't take Julia because she was pregnant. He was posted first in Oregon, near Portland, and then at Fort Humboldt, in northern California, near Eureka. Missing Julia, terribly missing her, he fell into despair, and probably drinking, and was threatened with court martial. And, literally, the day he received the letter appointing him to be captain, he wrote a letter back to the secretary of war, who was Jefferson Davis, and offered his resignation. He returned to Julia at their place beside her father in St. Louis.

Drinking was a part of his life. It was a part of military life. You had people who swore that he did a lot of drinking, people who swore he didn't do a lot of drinking. Probably, he drank when he was away from Julia. . . . I don't believe he was a drunkard. I don't think he was an alcoholic, and I think that the drinking disappeared when he became president. This was part of a younger person's life. But drinking was an issue he had to deal with.

The next seven years were very, very difficult for him—not always his fault. I don't want to say he necessarily failed, but the circumstances— the markets around them, farming, the weather—it didn't go well for him. They moved to Galena, which is in far northwest Illinois. They moved there in kind of a humiliating situation. His father said, "All right, I'll give you a place in the family leather business now. It's also in Galena. You will serve underneath your younger brother."

In the Grant story, there's almost been no mention of a faith story, but when Grant did move to Galena, a young twenty-seven-year-old pastor arrived fairly at the same time, whose name was John Heyl Vincent. He would become, thirty years later, founder of the famous Chautauqua that we know in New York State. He became a spiritual mentor to Grant. He visited him at City Point; he spoke for him at Galena; they corresponded; and so, there's a Methodist faith story here. Grant's parents were Methodist. Julia's grandfather was a Methodist minister. The first national church in Washington was not the National Cathedral. The Methodists were the largest Protestant denomination by 1850. They built the first national church, and they dedicated it four days before Grant was inaugurated as president, and Grant was a trustee. That's a story that hasn't been told.

Grant was [in the army the first time] from graduation in 1843 until 1854. He then re-entered in '61 [when the Civil War began].

I think the most fascinating [of Grant's early successful Civil War battles] is Vicksburg [in 1862]. The topography, the geography of it is just amazing. . . . There were no trees at that time; they'd cut them all down so they could have this free-fire zone. This was the most complicated battle; it took the longest to win. It was very important because it would secure the freedom of access in the Mississippi River for the Union forces. And so, with all the difficulties, this was a master stroke.

[Lincoln] writes Grant a letter after he learns that Grant has won the battle at Vicksburg. He says, "Dear Mr. Grant, I know we've not had the privilege of meeting. I merely wish to say, when you decided to do this, I thought that was wrong. When you thought of doing that, I could not agree less. When you did that, I didn't understand that." And Lincoln ends his letter by saying, "General Grant, I merely wish to say, I was wrong, and you were right."

[During the Vicksburg campaign] . . . Grant was very, very excited—angry—about the fact that Salmon Chase as secretary of the Treasury was allowing trading to take place in the very same area that the Union forces were trying to shut down the Confederacy. This trading, Grant believed, was really aiding the Confederacy because it was giving them supplies that he was trying to interdict. Grant, along with many others, believed that Jews were the leading traders. So, he issued what Julia later called "that obnoxious order," Order Number 11, in December of 1862, which was an order expelling Jews from his lines. When this order came forward and Abraham Lincoln saw this order, it was immediately rescinded.

Historian Jonathan Sarna tells us that Grant learned from this [mistake]. Grant became incredibly repentant for what he did. . . . Grant, more than any person up to that time, appointed Jews to significant positions in his administration; he attended the installation of the first Jewish synagogue in Washington; he reached out, and Jews became very appreciative of Grant's efforts on their behalf as president of the United States. So, yes, what he did [in 1862] was terrible, but he learned from it and changed his future dealings with Jews.

[Lincoln appointed Grant commander of all US forces in March of 1864, and several factors led to his success as commander.] If you think about it, no one had ever led an army of more than 14,000, which Winfield Scott led in the war with Mexico. So, you might have graduated first in your class at West Point, but that didn't mean you could manage an army of 150,000, 200,000, 250,000 men. Grant had the ability of what Lincoln called "pertinacity" to keep fighting. . . . He gave his chief generals the ability to manage their own theater of operation. He was not a micromanager. He trusted them, and this gave them the confidence to move forward. The difficult relationship was with George Meade, who had been the commander at Gettysburg in charge of the Army of the Potomac. Meade was sure that Grant would remove him when he came east. Grant said, "I'm not removing you. I'm placing my confidence in you." That allowed Meade to move forward and to play his role in the final months of the campaign.

[After the war, Grant] continued to be general in chief, in fact, quite remarkably, during Reconstruction. Even while he was running for president in 1868, he was both general in chief and candidate of the Republican Party. He retired from the military when he became president.

[As] . . . general in chief, he was very deferential to civilian leadership, so he wanted and tried to work with [Democratic president] Andrew Johnson, but pretty quickly discovered he could not. Andrew Johnson quickly [assessed] that Grant was very probably going to be the candidate of the Republican Party hoping to replace him in 1868. . . . Grant did become much more conversant with Congress. For a time, he even served as secretary of war; he was in Johnson's cabinet. So, he continued an active life during those three years of Reconstruction.

[Johnson and Grant's relationship became] more and more fraught with difficulty. Johnson tried to figure out a way to displace Grant, but he also understood the popularity of Grant. He tried to order him to Mexico. . . . [For his part] Grant was very reticent to criticize a political leader, but he finally just broke with Johnson. They literally stopped speaking. Not that Grant spoke out loud publicly, he just wouldn't speak anymore. He would attend the cabinet meetings, and he would give his particular military report from the War Department, and then he would excuse himself. He said, "I'm not going to participate in the rest of it."

[Their differences were over] the fact that the Congress, led by Republicans, was putting in place the Fourteenth Amendment and the Fifteenth Amendment [the Reconstruction amendments extending new protections to African Americans], and Johnson did not recognize this. Johnson wanted to re-seat all of the former Confederate states [in Congress], and often the delegates would have been Confederate generals. Grant saw that this was a way of destroying everything that had been fought for [for] four years, the whole meaning of the Union. . . . Johnson was a Southerner, and so he led from that point of view. He felt that the South had been unfairly maligned, and he wanted to bring

them back into the story. And . . . Johnson was not for the voting rights
for African Americans.

[In 1868, Andrew Johnson was impeached by the House and barely survived the Senate vote. Democrats sought a new presidential candidate
and chose New York governor Horatio Seymour; Republicans did nominate General Grant, who won with 52 percent of the vote.]

[During Reconstruction, Grant began accepting gifts from the public.]
This was not unusual. In other words, people stepped forward to give
homes to war heroes; they did this for Sherman. But in faulting Grant,
he should have been far more aware that there's no free lunch. Once he
begins to take money from these people, is he, therefore, in any sense
beholden to them? Grant received a home in Philadelphia; he received
money to buy a home in Washington; he received a home in Galena. . . .
Did Grant, therefore, hanker after something that had never been a
part of his life before—some money to support himself, perhaps in a
style that he could never quite imagine? He also became cozy with business leaders.

Mark Twain wrote his book, *The Gilded Age*, . . . and Grant and the
scandals of his second administration are often a part of that story. . . .
Grant brought people into his administration who had been loyal, able
people in the Civil War and then could not quite believe or understand
how power began to corrupt them. And so, when other people began to
make charges against him, Grant would be defending them when they
shouldn't have been defended. They became part of his Gilded Age,
part of his rushed, earned money. Grant was never implicated in any of
these scandals. . . . Nobody ever accused him [of corruption]; what they
accused him of was not being awake and aware, not being astute enough
to understand that this is happening around him, and then failing to
recognize when it did take place to say, "All right, I see what you're
doing, and I can no longer support you."

I'd give Grant a high mark [on racial justice]. At the end of his presidency, he convened a meeting of African American leaders in the White
House. He said to them, ". . . I look forward to the day when you can
ride on a railroad car, when you can eat in a restaurant, when you can
do so along with every other person, regardless of their race. That day

must come." It took ninety years for that day to come. Grant was the last American president to hold those kind of views [for many decades].

We think of Barack Obama as the first president elected with a nonwhite majority, but Ulysses S. Grant was actually the first president elected with a nonwhite majority. He only won the popular vote in 1868 because four hundred thousand African Americans voted for him. By 1890, only a few thousand were still able to vote in the South. This is a story of Ulysses S. Grant that needs to be told, that has not really been told, of a person who stood up against the voter suppression of his day. That was really the goal of the Ku Klux Klan, to suppress the vote. . . . He wanted to stop [voter suppression] and give these African Americans— freed people—their right to vote.

Grant retired from the presidency in March of 1877. Rutherford B. Hayes was elected, Reconstruction came to an end, and Grant set off for Europe on what he thought was going to be a private tour. . . . He arrived in Liverpool, England, and to his great surprise, he was treated as an American hero. He set off on what he thought would only be England, Scotland, and western Europe; then, money was provided through a good investment of his son, and he spent twenty-six, twenty-eight months traveling the entire world. He came back and did a variety of business ventures. His son, Ulysses Jr., went into a business venture on Wall Street, not realizing that the partner, Ferdinand Ward, was a crook. Ulysses Sr. put all of his money into this Wall Street firm, and in one day, everything collapsed. He walked home to Julia, and between them they had $130.

At that point, *The Century* magazine approached him to write his memoirs. He didn't want to write memoirs. Grant did not like memoirs because they were about settling scores, they were about lifting one's self up. But now, he needed money, so he agreed. *The Century* magazine . . . offered him $10,000. He was about to sign on the dotted line when Mark Twain heard this. Mark Twain rushed over to Grant's home. . . . He said, "I'll publish your memoirs." He persuaded Grant, which was very difficult, to step away from the contract. Twain said, "I'll sell three hundred thousand copies of your memoirs."

Almost at that moment, Grant was diagnosed with throat cancer. So, what I call "The Final Campaign" is his race against death as he writes these memoirs to earn money for Julia. There was no presidential

President Ulysses Grant was tasked with rebuilding the monetary system during Reconstruction. He has appeared on the fifty-dollar bill since 1913. *Photo credit: Leslie Rhodes and Ellen Vest, C-SPAN*

pension until the years of Harry S. Truman. Grant completes the memoirs three days before he dies. It's an amazing story. Twain publishes them, offers Grant 70 percent of the proceeds—not the standard 10 percent royalty—and the memoirs are still never out of print. It would earn for Julia $450,000 in nineteenth-century money. They are the classic American memoirs. Just remarkable.

There is no egocentrism in these memoirs. There is a wonderful power of writing, there's immediacy. Grant puts us right into the story, as if maybe Lee could win, maybe he would win. He masters the idea of writing with action verbs, and he eschews adjectives and adverbs. John Russell Young, who was traveling with him as a correspondent for a New York newspaper, elicits from Grant all kinds of personal reminiscences about the key figures of the era—Abraham Lincoln, George McClellan, Robert E. Lee. These become then part of the memoirs where Grant gives his own thumbnail sketches of why Abraham Lincoln, in his words, is the greatest figure of this whole era. It's just memorable to read this. It's in very clear, fair English language.

It took him probably about thirteen, fourteen months [to finish]. At one moment, the word was out that he would die before the morning came. Twain is living in Hartford, Connecticut, and he wrote in his journal, "The whole nation waits to hear whether Grant is alive or dead, and if Grant is to die, in every community across this nation, there will be bells that will be rung every thirty seconds. Sixty-three bells, that is the stature of Grant that is held by the entire country." Grant soldiered on, and he went to Mount McGregor near Saratoga Springs in the summer to try to get away from the heat and humidity of New York, and he was able to finish the memoirs. It's an amazing story. The doctors believed that Grant only lived as long as he did because he knew he had to complete the memoirs.

In a speech [in Grant's hometown of Galena, Illinois,] in the year 1900, the first year of the twentieth century, Theodore Roosevelt said, "Mightiest among the mighty dead loom the three great figures of Washington, Lincoln, Grant." This is the way TR understood it. But, Grant fell [in public esteem as time went on] . . . because of what we call "The Lost Cause," the idea first propagated by Confederate generals that the better side lost, . . . and they only lost because they were overwhelmed by greater numbers of military troops and by a greater industrial might. And, [they posited that the South lost the war because] "that butcher Grant" was willing to sacrifice his men. Our best Civil War historian, James McPherson, and others, have shown us that the casualties under Grant were actually less than the casualties under [Confederate general Robert E.] Lee.

The story that I want to tell is that Ulysses Grant defended the rights of African Americans, and surely he did. . . . The surprise is that when we get to the civil rights era of the 1960s and the whole abolitionist story is recast in a positive way, Grant doesn't seem to be a part of that story. He deserves to be. . . . I think Grant deserves a much higher ranking in terms of American leaders.

GROVER CLEVELAND

Overall Rank: 23

— ★ —

Total Score: 540

In 2017, historians assigned Grover Cleveland the 23rd spot overall, placing him in the bottom half of all presidents for the first time. This was a decline of six spots since the 2000 survey. Since 2000, his category ranks have declined in every category, with the most precipitous fall in administrative skills (from 12th to 22nd). In 2017, Cleveland's best category was public persuasion (20th); his worst was pursued equal justice for all (31st).

Party: Democrat
b. March 18, 1837, Caldwell, New Jersey
d. June 24, 1908, Princeton, New Jersey
First Lady: Frances Folsom Cleveland
Age entering office: 47 (first term), 55 (second term)

Historian: **H. Paul Jeffers**

> Military historian Paul Jeffers authored seventy books, including. An
> Honest President: The Life and Presidencies of Grover Cleveland. He was
> interviewed for C-SPAN's Booknotes on June 26, 2000.

[My book is titled *An Honest President*] because that's what he was. When he was running for president in 1884, Joseph Pulitzer wrote an editorial endorsing him, and he gave four reasons for wanting Cleveland to be elected. He said, "One, he's an honest man; two, he's an honest man; three, he's an honest man; four, he's an honest man."

He was born in Caldwell, New Jersey. His father was a Presbyterian minister assigned there, and Grover spent about four years there, and then his father, Richard Cleveland, was transferred to New York State, and that's how Grover wound up as a New York politician. His first political job was as an alderman. He ran for alderman, and then he was appointed assistant district attorney in Erie County. Served for two years; ran for district attorney and lost; and then some years later, by default because no one else would run for the office, he ran for mayor of Buffalo and was elected—a Democrat elected in a Republican city. He made such an impact there—his nickname was "The Veto Mayor" because he vetoed any bill that he thought was a blatant raid on the public treasury. And in 1882, the Democrats in New York were looking for someone to run for governor, and they said, "Why not this mayor of Buffalo?" And he got nominated and won in a landslide.

. . . When you were in school, there were certain things you knew about Grover Cleveland: he was fat; he was the twenty-second and twenty-fourth president of the United States; he got married in the White House; he had a daughter named baby Ruth; he had a child born in the White House, and that was about it. I just fell in love with the guy as I started getting into this [project]. If you look at his pictures, he's just this huge man, and he's got this walrus mustache. He looks very stern and off-putting. But he was quite a warm and even funny guy when you got to know him. He had quite a wry sense of humor.

What most people don't know is that Grover was his middle name. Growing up, until he was in his twenties, he was known as Stephen Cleveland, or Steve. His nickname was "Big Steve," and all his Buffalo friends called him that. But, for some reason, maybe because he was getting more serious in terms of his political life, he decided he wanted to be called Grover, and that's what it was thereafter.

What kind of a person he would have been depends on when you were around him. If you were with him in Buffalo, when he was a young man and an attorney, prior to him becoming mayor, and even when he was mayor, you would have spent a lot of nights in saloons and in German beer halls. You would have eaten a lot of sausage and sauer-kraut, and you would have played cards throughout most of the night. There would have been a lot of bawdy jokes, and there would have been hunting and fishing expeditions in the Buffalo area. When he became mayor, there was less of that because he was busy; he spent long nights working as mayor, so he wasn't out carousing quite as much. When he got to be governor of New York, he suddenly had a whole new cadre of friends. The politicians he met in Albany were a lot different than the ones he met in Buffalo. In Buffalo, you worried about water treatment and whether the sidewalks were broken and that sort of thing. In Albany, suddenly you're talking about taxes and the place of New York State as the primary state in the Union. There was a lot less carousing.

The relationship [between Theodore Roosevelt and Grover Cleveland] began when Grover became governor of New York and Theodore, TR, was a member of the [New York State] Assembly. They formed an alliance on a bill called the Five Cent Fare bill, which was a bill pending in the New York legislature to force the transit companies in New York City to reduce their fare from ten cents to five cents. TR was all for it because he regarded the guys like Jay Gould, the people that ran the transit companies, as thieves, and he just wanted to stick it to them. Grover read the bill and decided that if it became law, it was a violation of the US Constitution and that it was no business of the state of New York to get involved in private contracts. So, he vetoed it. That stunned everybody, including Roosevelt, who rethought his own position and said, "The governor's right about this. I was acting out of spite and not from the best interests of government." TR threw his weight behind upholding Cleveland's veto, and Roosevelt delivered enough votes for the veto to be upheld. Cleveland almost immediately called TR in for a meeting to talk about other things that might be of interest, particularly civil service reform, and they formed this amazing alliance. The prologue of my book is called "The Big One and the Dude." "The Big One" was a nickname for Grover Cleveland, and "The Dude" was the nickname applied to a young Theodore Roosevelt when he landed in Albany.

The famous campaign of 1884 when Grover ran for president [was a hard-fought contest against Republican James G. Blaine. During the campaign,] a political enemy of Cleveland's in Buffalo, who happened to be a minister, Reverend [George] Ball, wrote a piece for one of the Buffalo newspapers revealing the fact—and it was a fact—that ten years earlier, in 1874, a woman named Maria Halpin gave birth to a son, whom she named Oscar Folsom Cleveland. She claimed that Grover Cleveland was the boy's father. Oscar Folsom was Grover's best friend. Now, Maria Halpin was a widow, had come to Buffalo from New Jersey, and to put it delicately, she was a very friendly lady. She knew a lot of the gentlemen of Buffalo, including Grover, who was a bachelor, Oscar

Folsom, who was married, and a number of other of Cleveland's friends. There was a lot of speculation that, in fact, the child was Oscar Folsom's child and that Grover, being a bachelor, . . . basically stepped up to the plate and said, "The child is mine." The other story is that Maria Halpin really wanted to marry Grover and hoped to use the child as a way of coercing him into marrying her. All that happened in 1874, and . . . the issue was never raised at any time when Grover was mayor of Buffalo or when he was governor of New York. But when he ran for president, the story broke, and it was a big scandal. [His opponents taunted him with the slogan, "Ma, Ma, where's my Pa?"]

The question was whether or not it would keep him from being elected president of the United States. When his political advisers came to him and said, "What's this all about? What's going on here?" he said, "Yes, it's true, and whatever you do, tell the truth." There was no attempt at cover-up, no evading it. He said, "Yes, I was the father of the child. But in all these ten years, I've been paying for its upkeep." Some Cleveland supporters went to Buffalo, sort of an investigating committee, self-appointed, to look into this story and to prove that certain aspects of the allegations were not true, namely that Grover had promised to marry her and then reneged on it. They dug all that information up, and they got the Reverend Ball, who first broke this story, to retract almost all of it. In the end, while it caused quite a sensation, it really had no effect on Grover being elected president of the United States.

[His service in the Civil War] was also raised in the campaign of 1884. What happened was he was subject to conscription when the law was passed in 1863. His name was pulled on the very first day to be called up for service. But he had two brothers serving in the Civil War, and he was directly responsible and was financially supporting his mother and two younger sisters. So, he took advantage of an aspect of the law that allowed you to pay a bounty of up to $300 for someone to go into the Army instead of you. He found a guy who did it for 150 bucks, and so he didn't serve. But it was perfectly legal. There was nothing wrong with it. . . . This was raised in the campaign of 1884, but with very little effect because people understood that's what happened. And, the Civil War had been twenty years earlier.

The tradition then was pretty much that presidential candidates stayed home. They might make a speech now and then and grant

In 1886, bachelor president Grover Cleveland married Frances Folsom in the White House, a historic event depicted in this engraving by Thure de Thulstrup. *Courtesy Library of Congress*

interviews, but most of the campaigning was done by surrogates, and Grover made very few campaign speeches. . . . [In November 1884, Cleveland and Republican James G. Blaine were nearly tied in the popular vote; the electoral vote was 219–182 for Cleveland.]

[When Grover Cleveland arrived in Washington as president, it was the first time he'd ever been there.] Longest train ride he ever took was when he'd been to New York City when he was a young man. He worked for a year there with his brother at an institution for the blind. He was not a well-traveled man.

Cleveland got married in 1886, his first term in the White House. He was born in 1837, so he would have been forty-nine. He married Frances Folsom. Her nickname was Frank. Frances Folsom was born to Grover's friend and law partner, Oscar Folsom, in Buffalo in 1864, so Grover was considerably older than she. Oscar Folsom was thrown from a wagon and killed. Grover became the executor of his estate and the [de facto guardian] to Frances Folsom. He bought her first baby doll carriage, let her help write out some of the papers that he was working on when he was in his political offices, and, basically, raised her.

Everybody thought when Cleveland finally came to Washington as president of the United States that, ultimately, he would marry Emma Folsom, Oscar's widow. Grover said to his sister one day, "Why does everyone keep trying to marry me off to an old woman? Why don't they think that I might be interested in marrying the daughter?" And, in fact, that's what he did. She was twenty-one when they married; she had just gotten out of college. He had proposed to her in a letter the year before [when] she was visiting friends in Scranton. But very early on, when he was still in Buffalo and people were asking him, "When are you going to get married," his usual answer was, "I don't think I'll get married at all." But somebody asked him one day [when] . . . Frances was in the room. He looked at her and said, "Well, maybe I'm just waiting for my bride to grow up." So, he fell in love with her at some point and stayed in love with her, and they got married. They had a very, very successful marriage, had five children, and she turned out to be a really dazzling first lady, although he didn't like the idea of her being called first lady of the nation. He just wanted her to be Mrs. Cleveland. But she took Washington by storm, pretty much the way Jacqueline Kennedy did in the 1960s. . . . She just charmed everybody. There were a lot of rumors that went around that he was a brute to women—mostly circulated by his political enemies—that he beat her regularly. But Frances wrote letters excoriating people who spread those stories. He was very tender and loving towards her. In fact, when they were married, he changed her marriage vow and took out the word "obey" and put in ["keep"]. So, all this stuff about Cleveland having been not very nice to women just wasn't true. He certainly loved her.

He was very concerned about the publicity Frances was getting. He was furious whenever her picture would appear in a newspaper. So, he bought a property far north in Washington in what is now Cleveland Park, up near the National Cathedral. They bought an old house and had it renovated and turned it into a farm called Oak View. It had a red roof, and the newspapermen called it Red Top. And whenever they could get out of the White House, that's where they went.

Then later, he was invited to visit a friend in Buzzards Bay, Massachusetts. Cleveland was a great fisherman, and there's great fishing up there. He fell in love with that, and he bought some land to build a house, and that became his summer White House, mostly in the second term. They spent as little time in the White House as possible. The White House then was not like it is today. Cleveland's office was on the second floor, which is where the living quarters were. And when he decided to marry, he took one of the rooms that had belonged to his steward and had it made into a sitting room for Frances so that she would have something to do during the daytime. Once they got Oak View, they spent a lot of time there, largely because he wanted to get away from the press, which he hated.

Grover Cleveland ran for president in 1884, '88, and '92. Basically, he won all three elections in the popular vote. He lost to Benjamin Harrison [in '88] because he lost the state of New York, his own state, which threw it in the Electoral College to Harrison. He was never a party machine man and, in fact, had been greatly opposed throughout his career as governor to Tammany Hall, the New York City political machine. They never liked him, and they wanted him defeated. And another reason why he lost New York when he was first running for re-election had to do with positions he'd taken as president on the gold standard and particularly on tariff questions, which were important to New York, and they voted against him. He lost narrowly, but he lost.

Cleveland loved the Democratic Party, and he considered himself a Democrat, . . . but what he stood for as president of the United States is 180 degrees from what we think of the Democratic Party today, particularly on social welfare programs. In his first term, he was asked to sign a bill called the Texas Seed Bill. There'd been a drought in Texas, and a lot of the farmers down there got wiped out, and Congress enacted what we today would call a bailout, legislation to buy seed for them so they could get back in business. Grover vetoed it. He said, "The people support the government. The government does not support the people." He vetoed it also because he said it was not the responsibility of the federal government to aid individuals when those individuals had nothing to do with the welfare or future of the US government. He was not a welfare man, so it would make it very hard today to be a Democrat, and maybe even a Republican in some instances. He might be a libertarian. I don't know.

[Grover Cleveland did not accept blacks as equal to whites,] but very few white people in the 1890s did. It's in his own letters and the written public record. He was against slavery . . . but he thought that once blacks were emancipated and given citizenship, that act in itself gave them all that the federal government was entitled to give to them, namely citizenship. How they got on in their lives was up to them. He . . . viewed blacks as lazy and shiftless and not motivated and unambitious. He was very unwilling to admit that blacks could ever find equal footing with whites because [he thought], (a) blacks were incapable of it, and (b) whites didn't want it. He had the same view on the Chinese. There was a bill on Chinese immigration. A lot of Chinese had come to this country, particularly in the West, to build railroads. He was certainly woefully wrong on the black issue and woefully wrong on the Chinese. He said he didn't see at any time when the Chinese could ever assimilate into American society. . . . He believed whites would never accept them. But he was a man of his time; most white men in the 1890s felt that way.

This is going to sound funny in view of the [deficits] they're talking about today, but I think [his federal budget] was something like a $94 million surplus. Grover immediately wanted taxes cut, namely the tariffs, so that this surplus would diminish. . . . He wanted it returned to the taxpayers, in some form or other, because he was afraid that if it stayed there, Congress—this is going to sound familiar—would squander it. Well, he lost the election, and Harrison came in and, in fact, Congress squandered it. The next Congress got the nickname the "Billion Dollar Congress" because of their rush to spend the surplus.

His first term was [all] peace and prosperity in the 1880s, the Gilded Age. Things were fine. Congress, most of the time when he was president, was either totally controlled, or one house was controlled, by Republicans. There was one brief period where he was fortunate enough to have Democrats in control of both houses. He was the first Democrat elected president since [James] Buchanan; the first one since before the Civil War, twenty-four years. And even then, it was not sure that a Democrat could be elected because the country blamed the Civil War on the Democrats, on Buchanan, and the policies that led up to it. But he got elected in 1884, and the first term was pretty good. No problems. Second term, shortly after he took office in 1893, the stock market crashed, took a nosedive, the Panic of 1893 [ensued], and that led to what they called the Cleveland Depression. His second term was bad. A lot of the blame was placed on him because of his position on maintaining the gold standard and on reducing tariffs.

The Congress in this period had enacted laws that required the federal government to buy and coin all the silver mined in the United States and that the silver could then be redeemed for gold. There was another law that required the Treasury Department—this is going to sound really crazy considering the trillion-dollar budgets we have today—to maintain $100 million in gold as the underpinning of the American economy.

It was the big deal in the 1880s and '90s whether or not to have strictly gold or silver. There were the gold standard people, and there were people in the silver rights. The problem was if you had silver, you could turn it in for gold, and a lot of people started doing that, particularly from overseas. There was an outflow of gold, and the amount of gold in the US Treasury slipped below $100 million. At the same time, a major manufacturer of rope and twines, the National Cordage Company near Philadelphia, went bankrupt, and that caused a panic on Wall Street, and the bottom dropped out of the economy in 1893.

[Cleveland's] cancer was detected and the operation was performed at the very time that the Panic of 1893 was going on. What happened was that Grover woke up one morning, and he felt a sore spot on the roof of his mouth; he thought maybe it was a bad tooth or something like that. It persisted, and finally a doctor looked at it and said, "It's cancerous. If I were you, I'd have it out right away." Well, the country's in a state of panic. No one in the White House wanted to put on top of an economic panic the fact that the president had cancer. So, they arranged for an operation aboard the yacht *Oneida* as it sailed from New York City on the East River. . . . He was on his way to Buzzards Bay for his summer vacation. The operation was performed; the cancer was removed. In a portion of his jaw, a rubber prosthesis was put in. And except for the fact that, shortly after that, he lost a little weight and he looked a little wan every now and then, no one knew what was going on. The fact that he'd had this cancer operation was not revealed for another twenty-four years. It was finally revealed after he died by one of the doctors.

[The cancer] was in the roof of the mouth, the palate, and there were no visible outward signs of it. He boarded the yacht *Oneida* and spent the night on the yacht. The next morning people could see him from Pier A sitting out there on the boat, having his breakfast, smoking his cigar. A cigar's the last thing you would want to think of [with oral cancer]. And he continued to smoke after that, so far as I know.

By 1896, Cleveland was burnt out. He was fed up with being president. He thought he was the most unpopular man in the country because of the Cleveland Depression, and he thought, "Two terms it is for a president." At first, he just retired, and then he was made a trustee of Princeton University and was quite popular. He would have been in his mid-sixties, . . . and Frances was thirty-seven.

He thought he was the most reviled and hated president in American history. People kept asking him to write his memoirs, his autobiography, and he would say, "Who would read it? No one cares," until the Louisiana Purchase Exposition in St. Louis, the St. Louis World's Fair, [the origin of the song] "Meet Me in St. Louis." He was invited to attend, and he went. Theodore Roosevelt was president at the time, and Grover thought he would get a smattering of applause due to being an ex-president of the United States, more for the office than for him. When he was introduced, there was this unbelievable ovation. It dwarfed what Roosevelt got, and it told him that he wasn't the unpopular man he thought he was.

Baby Ruth was born between his two terms in New York City and was very popular. When she was twelve years old, when Cleveland was retired, she came down with diphtheria and died. He was devastated. Some of his letters are very, very touching. He writes about trying very hard to envision Ruth in the arms of her savior in heaven, and all he could think of is her body in the ground. He ultimately recovered from it, but he didn't live that much beyond her death. He died in 1908. . . . He'd been in Atlantic City on business, but he was ill. He'd had heart troubles, and he finally died of gastrointestinal problems and kidney disease and a series of heart attacks.

Grover Cleveland's racism was not very appetizing in retrospect, with 20/20 vision and hindsight. That's probably the only thing [I disliked about him]. I found him a very likable guy. I'm not a fisherman or a hunter, but I think it would have been fun to be up in the Adirondacks with him fishing and hunting. He has tended to be a largely forgotten, overlooked, underappreciated president. "Oh, yeah, that's the guy that had the two terms with another president in between them," and that's why I think my book was long overdue.

His political phrase, the one that sticks to him, although it was put together for him by a journalist, is "Public office is a public trust." He believed that an executive, whether it was governor or president of the United States, was exactly that, an executive officer. His job was to see that the organization was run efficiently and that the stockholders' money, namely the taxpayers', was not squandered or wasted. And he also believed, as he said, "The people support the government. The government does not support the people."

WILLIAM HOWARD TAFT

Overall Rank: 24

— ★ —

Total Score: 528

Taft has ranked 24th in all three C-SPAN surveys, and his category ratings have been similarly consistent. Historians have improved his ranking in administrative skills to 12th, making it his best category. However, his ranking in public persuasion has inched lower to 31st, and it now stands as his worst category.

Party: Republican
b. September 15, 1857, Cincinnati, Ohio
d. March 8, 1930, Washington, DC
First Lady: Helen Herron Taft
Age entering office: 51

Historian: **Jeffrey Rosen**

Jeffrey Rosen is the president and CEO of the National Constitution Center, a professor at the George Washington University Law School, and contributing editor of The Atlantic. *He has written six books, including* William Howard Taft, *part of The American Presidents biography book series. He discussed his book on C-SPAN's Q & A on July 31, 2018.*

If Americans think of [William Howard] Taft today, they generally think of him as our largest president.

There are all these cruel jokes about Taft in bathtubs, a kid's book about Taft in a bath, and this canard that he was stuck in a bath as president, a story by the White House usher Ike Hoover that's been confirmed by no other source. But he was large when he was president; he was 340 pounds, largely because he ate his feelings. He hated being president.

What's so remarkable about Taft's weight is that he lost it. After he was president, he went on a paleo diet of essentially fruits and vegetables and lean fish, and he lost seventy-six pounds in six months. It was an incredible example of self-discipline. And he kept it off for most of the rest of his happy career, so that when he was chief justice . . . he was basically at his college weight of around 280. What's so remarkable about this story of personal discipline is that Taft connected his own struggles with his weight to the struggles of citizens in a democracy to restrain their own passions. He gave a speech . . . quoting the Bible that says, "Citizens in a democracy, like those who struggle with weight or a taste for strong drink, have a responsibility to restrain their passions so they can discipline themselves for the rigors of citizenship."

[For William Howard Taft, it all started in] Cincinnati, Ohio, the cradle of presidents. He was born in 1857, on September 15, two days before the seventieth anniversary of the US Constitution, and he was born to a family that imbibed the Constitution. His father was Alphonso Taft, who wrote the Republican platform in 1856 that founded the Republican Party on the principles of defending the Union and the Constitution and resisting the extension of slavery into the free territories. His father went on to be secretary of war and ambassador to Russia and told Will when he was young that to be chief justice was more [significant] than to be president, in his estimation. And young Will imbibed from his revered father a reverence for the Constitution and a yearning to be chief justice that was finally fulfilled after a detour into the presidency years later.

Taft said that "everything I knew about the law, I learned at the expense of Hamilton County," where he was an assistant prosecutor, but he then fell upward into this series of golden sinecures that imbibed in him this reverence for the law. He went to Yale, where he excelled. He started as a young lawyer, as assistant prosecutor, where he watched a jury acquit an accused murderer and a mob burn down the courthouse. This created a fear of mob violence that defined his outlook for the rest of his life. He went on to be a judge at the young age of thirty and then a solicitor general of the United States, where he introduced the practice of confessing error, basically saying that when the government has made a constitutional mistake, it shouldn't profit by its error. Then he became a judge on the Sixth Circuit, a federal judge at the age of thirty-five, which he found a kind of heaven. He said, "I love judges. And I love courts. They're my idea of heaven on earth."

He then was summoned to a transformative career, governor general of the Philippines. President William McKinley asked him to [take this post], and he thrived there. He was a kind of Solon, a lawgiver, creating a constitution for a grateful people; extending some, but not all, of the protections of the Bill of Rights to the Filipino people because he thought you had to be educated in order to be ready for the duties of citizenship.

And then, what he really wanted to do is be on the Supreme Court. So, Theodore Roosevelt offered him a Supreme Court justiceship, and his wife, Nellie Herron Taft, made him refuse because she wanted him to be president. [As a young woman,] she had gone to the White House under President Hayes and said, "I hope to marry a man someday who will be president." Hayes said, "I hope you will, and make sure he's an Ohio man." So, Nellie is pining for him to join Washington and what she called the bigwigs, and she thinks the Supreme Court will sideline him. So, he turns down the offer of a Supreme Court seat with the greatest reluctance. He distinguishes himself in the Philippines, then he becomes secretary of war, where he is an administrative marvel.

Henry Stimson, who served as undersecretary of war under Presidents Taft and Roosevelt and Hoover and Truman, said that Taft was the greatest administrator of them all. He was extremely good at creating efficient procedures that would mass the government into an efficient whole. He was so effective as secretary of war that Theodore Roosevelt anoints him as his hand-picked successor, and Taft runs for president in 1908 and wins a resounding victory.

TR and Taft were extremely close, almost brothers, when they were working together in the government. Roosevelt relied on Taft to provide the administrative apparatus that would carry out his extraordinarily brilliant ideas. Roosevelt was this igneous force of nature who wanted to do everything by executive order. He was impatient and wanted to circumvent Congress. Even during the Roosevelt administration, Taft disapproved of Roosevelt's circumventing constitutional procedures. As president, Taft insisted on putting Roosevelt's activist executive orders on firm constitutional grounds by persuading Congress to enact them. But, the two were so close that Roosevelt predicted that Taft would be our greatest president since maybe even Washington or Lincoln; he was effusive in his praise. Although, after Taft's election he confessed to a journalist, "Taft means well to try to do his best, but he's weak." So, TR is beginning to have second thoughts right at the beginning.

Archie Butt served Roosevelt and Taft [as a military aide and close adviser], and [he later writes] a very intimate memoir. He's at Taft's side while Taft is dancing alone on the White House veranda to a gramophone, just for the joy of it, and while he is reading poetry. What's so interesting about Butt is that he admires both Roosevelt and Taft, so he watches the disintegration of their relationship with consternation and then sympathy for both men, whom he considers great. As for Taft, Butt says, it's almost as if he's too good for politics; the people can't appreciate him. Butt also noticed Taft's Achilles' heel, which is that he was "a great hater," as Butt called it, the greatest hater that he ever knew in politics. If Taft considered someone disloyal, he would take an instant dislike to him in a way that wasn't normal for politicians and then would lash out against them.

Similarly, as president, Butt observed Taft would engage in these self-defeating spasms of anger against people he considered disloyal, not only Gifford Pinchot, the environmentalist, whom he fired, but also Pinchot's deputy, [Louis] Glavis. These just had catastrophic political consequences. So, Butt has a clear-eyed but sympathetic view of Taft. He then has the most tragic ending: Butt went down on the *Titanic*, and Taft was just heartbroken; he loved Butt.

[Among Taft's accomplishments as president:] he lowered the tariff, which was an achievement that eluded every Republican president that preceded him. It turns out that tariffs, which we're still talking about today, were the biggest constitutional battle of the early republic, the question of how to fund the government in an age before an income tax. In the age of Alexander Hamilton, the government was funded mostly by excise taxes, that is, taxes on things like whiskey or carriages or particular goods. The income tax was only introduced during the Civil War by Lincoln, and it was temporary. Then there is a brief one again in the Cleveland administration, but it's very unpopular, and it's allowed to expire. There's the Supreme Court decision in the 1890s called the *Pollock* case, which rules the income tax is unconstitutional because the Constitution says that direct taxes have to be apportioned among the states. . . . It was a five-to-four decision. Taft thought it was wrong because Alexander Hamilton had thought that income tax didn't have to be apportioned, but Taft so respected the Supreme Court that he didn't want to embarrass them by trying to overturn the decision. He thought a constitutional amendment was necessary, and eventually the Sixteenth Amendment was introduced during his presidency and passed [codifying the income tax system]. So, tariffs are bubbling as a political issue during his presidency, and it splits the Republican Party.

The Republican Party had traditionally been devoted to protective tariffs for income but not protection—in other words, imposing moderate tariffs in order to fund the government but not to protect certain industries over the others. But tariffs naturally favored some people over others—Eastern manufacturers, like glove manufacturers, liked it, and Western farmers didn't because it raised the cost of raw material of goods. So, within the Republican Party there were three camps: they are the Stand-Pat Republicans, led by Speaker Joe Cannon, who want to keep the tariff as it is, or even raise it to pander to their constituencies; the insurgent Progressive Republicans; and the independents, like Robert La Follette, who want to really lower the tariff, although not eliminate it, like the Free Trade Democrats under Bryan. Taft is caught in the middle. The Republican platform pledges the party to revise the tariff, and like a lawyer, Taft takes that so seriously that he . . . calls Congress into special session days after his inauguration. They are all waiting for what he's going to propose, and the clerk reads the 320-word message that Taft scribbled that morning at the White House, [essentially saying]: "As I said in the Republican platform, we should revise the tariff. If you have any other questions, you can read what I said during the campaign. That's all I have to say." Everyone was stunned. They expected a state address, and he writes it like a lawyer writing a judicial dispatch; he was viewing it as a contract with America that he has to dispose. Then all craziness breaks because the politics are all [in play], and Taft refuses to intervene. Basically, he gets rolled, in that the initial bill proposed by Representative [Sereno Payne] does lower the tariff substantially, but then the Standpatters raise a lot of the tariffs. The final bill that emerges lowers some tariffs but not others. Still, it's the only tariff revision that was actually achieved since the 1890s, where the Democrats tried it and then lost the election.

Then Taft goes on the campaign trail . . . and said, "This is the best tariff bill the Republican Party has ever passed." Actually it was because they never passed another tariff bill, and it did lower tariffs a bit. But this goes viral on the wireless, on the telegraphs, and people are outraged. He's defending it, and it's flawed. So, it's an example of his being an anti-politician. . . . It was a better tariff revision than anyone else had achieved, and it sets the United States on a path toward the downward revision that Woodrow Wilson continued as a free-trade Democrat. Then, with a notable exception of the Smoot-Hawley Tariff in the '30s, it basically represents a bipartisan consensus until the election of 2016. So, Taft gets credit for trying, but not for being a very good politician.

Taft's other significant achievements are his constitutionalist vision of foreign policy. He sends troops to the Mexican border, where there's an insurrection, but not over it, because he thinks the Constitution gives Congress the power to declare war. He invokes as his model a young Congressman Lincoln who criticized President Polk for sending troops over the Mexican border. Lincoln demanded that Polk identify the spot where Mexican troops supposedly crossed over into the United States justifying an invasion, earning him the nickname "Spotty Lincoln." Taft, like Lincoln, the great constitutionalist, maintains the peace, resists the cries of his own party for war, and starts the United States toward this path. He has a vision of the legalization of foreign policy, culminating in an international court, which he thinks should adjudicate all questions including questions of national honor. That is later proposed by Woodrow Wilson in the League of Nations. It doesn't entirely succeed, but it's a vision of Taft's very judicial approach to foreign policy.

Taft brings more antitrust suits in one term than Roosevelt does in nearly two, and we think of Roosevelt as the great trustbuster. But TR was the guy who refused to prosecute US Steel because some said he was too close to J. P. Morgan. Whereas Taft, the constitutionalist, thinks that the machinery of law has to be allowed to see its course. So, we don't think of Taft as a progressive, but he was. He thought of himself . . . as a "progressive conservative." . . . He withdrew more lands for federal conservation in one term than Roosevelt did, including very significant national parks, but Taft did this according to proper procedures; he persuaded Congress to pass laws withdrawing the land, rather than doing it by executive order. Now, when we're having this big debate in America about whether the president should act unilaterally by executive order or should follow proper constitutional procedures, Taft's constitutionalism and environmentalism seem especially appealing.

[His appointment of six justices to the Supreme Court] created a conservative court. He served with many of those justices when he himself became chief justice. . . . It was a court that protected property rights and also, under his leadership, became a cohesive body. . . . The most dramatic appointment is when it comes time for him to appoint a chief justice. He's about to [elevate Justice] Charles Evans Hughes, the former governor of New York, who's a dynamo. . . . Hughes is dressing for the appointment on the way to the White House, and Taft can't bring himself to appoint Hughes. Taft wants to be chief justice, and Hughes is so young that Taft knows that he'll outlive him. So, he cancels the appointment as Hughes was on the way over and appoints instead [Justice] Edward Douglass White. He's a sixty-five-year-old overweight Southern Democrat whose only qualification is the hope that he'll expire in time for Taft to succeed him. So, Taft is laying the groundwork for his own appointment as chief justice. Taft loses the presidential election, and he's pining for White to shuffle off the mortal coil, basically to die.

Taft never learned politics [during his term in office]. He said he told his aide, Archie Butt, . . . "I will not play a part for popularity. If the people want to reject me, that's their prerogative." He has this Madisonian view. His heroes are James Madison and Alexander Hamilton, the authors of the Federalist Papers, and [Chief Justice] John Marshall, whom he considers the greatest American ever. Madison and Hamilton believed that majority should rule, but only slowly and thoughtfully over time so that reason rather than passion could prevail. Taft believes that the entire system is set up to slow the direct expression of popular passion, so that the people can be governed in the public interest rather than through factions, that is mobs, that favor self-interest rather than the public good. In the Philippines and as secretary of war and then as president, he's viewing everything through legal and constitutional terms. I say in my book that he was our most judicial president and presidential chief justice. So, as president he refuses to consider the political implications of his actions with disastrous political consequences.

It was his decision to fire Roosevelt's close aide, Gifford Pinchot, the environmentalist, that led to a scandal that ultimately led to a breach with Roosevelt. This led Roosevelt to challenge Taft for the Republican nomination and split the Republican Party. And, it was Taft's decision to bring an antitrust suit against US Steel, which Roosevelt had refused to bring, that so embarrassed and inflamed Roosevelt that it was the final straw that led TR to run for president [again against Taft in 1912]. So, he's really a remarkable example of the anti-politician as president, the judge as president, who instead of considering the popular implications of his actions, considers its constitutional implications—and the political consequences are pretty dire.

The reason Taft ran again in 1912, even though he didn't like being president and viewed his liberation from the White House with relief, was because he felt that the election of 1912 was a crusade to defend the Constitution against the demagogic populism of both Roosevelt and Woodrow Wilson. It's the most fascinating story, the election of 1912. [Columnist] George Will said that . . . all of [modern] American politics can be traced to the election of 1912, that you can tell who's a conservative today based on who they would have voted for in the election of 1912. He says conservatives would have voted for the constitutionalist Taft, who's trying to defend judicial independence and the rule of law against the demagogic attacks of Roosevelt, who says that the people should be able to overturn judicial decisions by popular vote.

It was that claim that most alarmed the great constitutionalist Taft and made him run for re-election. . . . Roosevelt, for the first time, insists that the president is a steward of the people who can directly channel the people's will. TR endorses instruments of direct democracy, like the initiative and referendum, that he believes empower the president to be a channel of populism. Woodrow Wilson, too, is a progressive populist who insists . . . that the president in Congress is like a prime minister who represents the people's will directly. This just appalls Taft, who says, "No, the president derives his authority not directly from the people but from the Constitution." The framers designed an Electoral College to filter popular will so that people elect wise delegates who will choose a president. This populist presidency, which became the imperial presidency in the twentieth century, appalled Taft's constitutionalist heart. So that's why he ran. It was a noble, but doomed, crusade. He came in last. He won only two electoral votes. But he felt it was necessary to defend the Constitution.

Taft thought that Roosevelt was acting like a populist demagogue. But here's what's really important, too—the tender-hearted Taft was wracked by this breach. After he unburdened himself of one of these attacks on Roosevelt, he went back to his railroad car, and a journalist found him with his head in his hands, weeping, saying, "Roosevelt was my closest friend." And, of course, Roosevelt is reciprocating his insults, calling Taft a "flubdub with a streak of the second rate." The aristocratic Roosevelt is no man of the people when it comes to those kinds of insults. But the story does have a happy ending of sorts. After the election was over and after both men have gone into the political wilderness, they ran into each other by accident in a hotel. They are in the hotel dining room, and they approach each other. At first they are wary, but then they start talking animatedly, and they're clapping each other on the back, and the whole dining room erupts in applause. So, they were reconciled in the end. That meant a lot to Taft that they made up before Roosevelt's death.

You couldn't imagine Taft remotely surviving in the age of cable news and Twitter. His entire premise as president is that it's the greatest sin to directly address the people; Madison in Federalist 78 says direct communication between the president and the people will foment popular passion and prevent the slow growth of reason. Roosevelt would be the precursor to our first tweeting president. . . . So, if we were to refight the election of 1912 today, Taft would maybe do even worse than he did at that time. Then you'd have a fight between Roosevelt and Wilson, both of whom were populists. Roosevelt was probably more charismatic than Wilson, a former Princeton professor. So, thinking aloud, maybe Roosevelt might have won.

President Warren Harding meets with Taft after his election in 1920 and says, "If there's a seat in the Supreme Court, I'm going to appoint you." Taft says it's got to be chief justice. Taft goes to see [Chief Justice] White, and White is fine. Then, miraculously, White drops dead a few weeks later. . . . So, Taft is appointed and confirmed almost unanimously, and it's the fulfillment of his lifelong dream. How many stories in American politics [are like this]? Taft is the only president who went on to serve on the Supreme Court. But here is someone who, ever since he was a child at his father's knee, had pined to be chief justice, and just waited meticulously, and finally achieves his dream. Then it's the most beautiful story of someone who has found his true calling, excelling in the most miraculous way.

Taft achieves three things as chief justice that make him, according to [contemporary federal] judge Douglas Ginsburg and others, arguably

William Howard Taft (center, seated), shown here with the 1925 Supreme Court, is the only president to later also serve as chief justice. *Courtesy Library of Congress*

the greatest chief since John Marshall, who was Taft's hero. First, Taft passes the Judiciary Act of 1922, which creates a conference of federal circuit judges. It creates the modern administrative apparatus of the federal judiciary and gives the judges the bandwidth to challenge the president and to engage in a modern administrative state. Second, he passes the Judiciary Act of 1925, which gives the court control over its own jurisdiction. Before that passed, the court had to hear almost any case that it was presented with; so, the justices are wasting their time with all these very obscure private disputes. By allowing the court to focus on great constitutional battles, Taft increases the prestige and significance of the court. And third, he builds the Supreme Court building, the gorgeous temple of justice designed by Cass Gilbert. It was a product of his lobbying Congress for the money and helping choose the site, and when it was finally opened after his death, Chief Justice Hughes gives him credit for it. And if that's not enough, "Dayenu" as we say in Passover, he also masses the court; he makes unanimity and consensus a primary goal. He persuades justices like Brandeis and [Oliver Wendell] Holmes to suppress their dissents in the interest of creating a single opinion of the court as John Marshall did. There are more unanimous opinions, especially early in his chief justiceship, than in any time since Marshall.

Taft and Justice Louis Brandeis had clashed dramatically during Brandeis's confirmation hearings. Taft opposed Brandeis, probably because he had the completely unrealistic hope that Wilson would have appointed him for the seat. Imagine that, having been defeated in the presidential election by Wilson, Taft hoped he'd get on the Supreme Court. So, Taft attacked Brandeis in 1916 in terms today that have an almost anti-Semitic tinge. Taft himself was no anti-Semite and gave a noble speech to a synagogue denouncing anti-Semitism in any form. After Taft and Brandeis get on the court, they bury the hatchet. Taft is so devoted to the institutional legitimacy of the court that he persuades Brandeis to join him in unanimous opinions. Brandeis embraces this vision and marvels to his friend Justice Felix Frankfurter, "Felix, how is it possible that we thought he was such a bad president, but he's such a good chief justice in his administrative role?" Frankfurter says, "The answer is easy. He hated being president, and being chief is all happiness for him." It's an example of these two great figures of the Supreme Court putting aside their personal differences because of their devotion to the institutional legitimacy of the Supreme Court.

[If I were able to sit down with William Howard Taft,] I would be eager to ask what he thought about American democracy in the age of Facebook and Twitter because I think it would represent his constitutionalist nightmare, his dystopia. His speeches are so eloquent, more eloquent even than Madison; he was clearer around this question about how the whole mechanism of the American republic was designed to slow down deliberation so people could have sober second thoughts. Rather than enacting their direct passions into law, they should be required to allow hasty, impetuous passion to cool so they can be guided by reason. What he would make of our current media landscape, I can imagine, but I would love to hear his own thoughts. I would also love to ask his wise counsel about how to resurrect Madisonian reason in an age of Twitter and Facebook and how to slow down deliberation in order to create the thoughtful second thoughts that he and the founders thought were necessary.

GERALD R. FORD

38th President, 1974–1977

Overall Rank: 25

— ★ —

Total Score: 509

Like many recent presidents, Gerald Ford earns widely varying category ranks from historians. Assigned an overall rank of 25th in 2017, Ford's category ranks ranged from highs in pursued equal justice for all (14th) and relations with Congress (19th) to lows in public persuasion (34th) and vision/setting an agenda (35th).

Party: Republican
b. July 14, 1913, Omaha, Nebraska
d. December 26, 2006, Rancho Mirage, California
First Lady: Elizabeth "Betty" Anne Bloomer Ford
Age entering office: 61

Historian: **James Cannon**

Author, journalist, and former domestic policy adviser to President Ford, Jim Cannon joined C-SPAN on March 23, 1994, for Booknotes. *He discussed his book,* Time and Chance: Gerald Ford's Appointment with History, *Ford's official biography.*

Gerald Ford said very little about his growing up. But I realized, after about a year and a half of research into my book, that the significance of Ford's growing up is that he was taught, trained, and educated in an environment of all the old-fashioned virtues that families in America seemed to have in the 1920s and '30s more significantly than they do today. For example, they were trained to be honest, to tell the truth, to work hard, to study hard. Their report cards were examined. Their parents were very assiduous about what they did in school and after. Ford grew up in a time, and grew up in a family and in a place, Grand Rapids, Michigan, where honesty and integrity were highly prized. So, I felt it was essential to understanding the presidency of Ford, indeed to understand how it was that he got to be president. I had to show how this boy grew up into the person he was, so that when the time came to find someone to replace Richard Nixon, they turned to a man who had the degree of integrity and credibility that Ford did. Nobody disliked him. Everybody trusted him.

The fact is that Gerald Ford does have a very interesting early life, an interesting growing up, being the biological son of a very wealthy, dissolute man who would never help him through all the perils of his life. [His name at birth was] Leslie King. Leslie King Sr. was an abusive husband. His mother, who was then all of nineteen, twenty years old, realized from the honeymoon on that she had a problem. Then she found that she was pregnant. She stayed with her husband through the pregnancy, but then he threatened to kill her and the baby—literally threatened her with a butcher knife. She talked to a lawyer, who advised her to get out of the house as quickly as possible. When the baby was sixteen days old, she took him, with the help of a nurse, found a carriage, and went across the river from Omaha to meet her parents, and they took her back to Chicago and then back to Michigan.

[Gerald Ford's story is about] how an honest politician from middle America took over from a lying crook of a president. I think that's the essence of the story. This is a story, a classical story of good versus evil. And what this story is about is what Richard Nixon did to put this country in such a state of constitutional peril and how this rather stolid, but honest, man came to the rescue and ended, a little raggedly, but ended, the national nightmare that Watergate had been.

I've felt that [Nixon was a lying crook of a president] since I read the tape [transcripts] and listened to the tapes and listened to what Nixon said subsequently to the public. One of the most fascinating things about my research into this book was the degree to which Nixon himself consciously and deliberately lied. He made a conscious decision to lie up at Camp David the day he fired [his aides Bob] Haldeman and [John] Ehrlichman. And as he'd written this in his book, "I either had the choice to tell the truth and risk being taken out of the presidency or to lie, and I decided to do the latter."

[June 1972 was the Watergate break-in. The election followed in November, and President Nixon was re-elected along with his vice president,

Spiro Agnew.] Watergate was such a powerful story, in and of itself, that the Spiro Agnew story seemed almost a sidebar. . . .

Spiro Agnew was a perfectly good governor of Maryland who was chosen in 1968 to be Nixon's running mate because Nixon couldn't have who he wanted. His first choice was [California lieutenant governor] Bob Finch, and his second choice was [Maryland representative] Rog Morton. For various reasons, they didn't think it was the best idea, and running late, so to speak, on making his choice at the convention in '68, Nixon turned to Agnew, who was about as surprised as everybody else.

. . . In 1972, Nixon wanted to dump Agnew from the ticket and replace him with [Texas governor John] Connally. But that was politically unfeasible, as John Mitchell, his campaign manager, and others argued. So, Nixon came to the conclusion, "OK, we'll make sure that Agnew is not the party's nominee in '76. We'll make sure that John Connally is." And immediately after the election of '72, Nixon made the first moves to make certain that Agnew was not going to be his political successor. The notes of their conversations are in the Nixon papers in the Nixon archives. There were Haldeman's notes from his conversation with Nixon on what they were going to do to make sure that Agnew would not be nominated in '76. Nixon with his skill in politics, the theme of what he was saying is that, "Look, we've got to cut him down. We've got to make sure he understands he's not our choice. But we can't go too far with this or be too abrupt about it, or it may be that he will react, and he has some support, too." So, at this point, the only true evidence is that it was more or less a coincidence—put it that way— that Nixon wanted to get rid of Agnew, and that weeks later that Agnew was first investigated for income tax problems.

Gerald Ford first found out that Mr. Agnew was in trouble on a trip to Connecticut with [outgoing defense secretary] Mel Laird, who was a close friend of his. Mel Laird always knew a lot about what was going on in the White House, and Mel Laird mentioned to Ford that he thought Agnew had a serious problem. And that's about all he said. Ford accepted that, said nothing to anybody, and had the impression that Mel might be testing him to see if he knew it and was ready to exchange a little information. But it was news to Ford, and so he simply accepted it. . . .

There was a lot happening behind the scenes. A lot. A new attorney general, Elliot Richardson, found out about Agnew's problem from the then US attorney in Baltimore and was almost literally sickened by the realization that we had Watergate already building up to a problem that may mean the impeachment of Nixon, and now we have charges that the vice president of the United States took bribes, including one physically in the White House. They found this out by pursuing a series of reports in Maryland that it had been common practice in Maryland for payments to be made by contractors who received public contracts, public works awards, highway contracts, and so on. They had gone back over time and found that some of these contractors had indeed paid cash payments. In pursuing them, they found out that Agnew, as county executive of Baltimore County and as governor of Maryland, had in their evidence, in their testimony, taken bribes and that these bribes had continued even after Agnew became vice president.

[A contractor named Les Matz apparently delivered one payment of $10,000, one of $5,000, and one of $2,500 to the vice president's office in the Old Executive Office Building near the White House.] This is the evidence that the attorney general and US attorney collected from the contractors who testified to this, who had each given detailed testimony about the payments he had made to Agnew. This collective testimony was put on the record deliberately by Elliot Richardson so that the public would know, permanently, that these were the charges against Agnew, and this was why he was being forced to resign.

. . . Agnew resigned because of the abundance of evidence against him and because, very frankly, as he wrote in his book and as his former national security adviser confirmed, Agnew was scared that Al Haig, then White House chief of staff, would have him killed if he didn't resign. Physically. This was the import of Agnew's concern, and . . . he decided he had no choice; that he knew what might happen to someone who resisted the president. He felt that the only course he had was to resign, and he did. He pleaded nolo contendere to one tax charge, but Agnew never admitted that he took a bribe. [In researching my book, I asked Mr. Haig whether he did intend to have Spiro Agnew killed.] He scoffed at the idea. He said that this simply was not true.

. . . When President Kennedy was assassinated, Johnson became president, and for a period of more than a year, the Speaker of the House, who was the next in line of succession, was John McCormack. John was quite old. There was considerable concern about whether he could function as president if, indeed, something should happen to Lyndon Johnson. Indiana senator Birch Bayh and a number of others thought it was a good idea to have a process created where if there was no vice president, then the president would nominate a candidate for vice president, and the House and the Senate would separately confirm him. Usually it's only the Senate that confirms a nominee, but they deliberately included the House because they wanted all the members of the House to have a chance to weigh in on so important a matter. So, the Twenty-fifth Amendment, which was passed in the late '60s, was fortuitously in operation when Agnew left office.

[House Minority Leader Jerry Ford was the choice of congressional leaders and ultimately Nixon's choice to replace Spiro Agnew as vice president.] In 1968, Jerry Ford chaired the Republican Convention as House Republican leader. In 1968, he had been House leader for four years and was hoping that in '68 or '70 or '72, or at some time in his life, the Republicans would elect enough House members so that he could be Speaker. His ambition was to be Speaker. He became leader of the minority party in the House . . . after the debacle of 1964, when, because of the Goldwater campaign and other reasons, the Republicans lost a massive number of House seats. Several leaders, including Bob Griffin and Don Rumsfeld and Charles Goodell from New York, felt that there had to be a change from Charlie Halleck, who was an old-fashioned, hard-driving, hard-talking, bibulous member of the House. The Young Turks in the House felt it was time for a change, and they turned to Jerry Ford, persuaded him to challenge Halleck. He did, and won by, I believe, three votes.

[Gerald Ford was nominated on October 12, 1973. The Senate voted 92 to 3 to confirm him on November 27. On December 6, the House confirmed Ford by a vote of 387 to 35. One hour later, Gerald Ford took the oath of office as vice president of the United States.]

It's interesting there was never any animosity between Agnew and Ford. In fact, on the day that Agnew resigned and Ford was chosen later that evening, when Ford got home that night he had a message that Agnew had called. He called him back, and they talked for a few

minutes, and Agnew congratulated Ford. And, then-nominee Ford told
Agnew that he was sorry it turned out that way.

[Seven months later, Gerald Ford found out that Nixon had lied to
him about Watergate]—on July 31, 1974. That afternoon Al Haig [then
serving as Nixon's chief of staff] came in, having insisted that the meeting be one-on-one, and he told then-Vice President Ford that he had
seen the transcript of the smoking gun tape, and there was no question
there was evidence against Nixon that would force him from office. It
was at that point, . . . and for the first time, that Ford understood it. It
had been a long course for him. He had been friends with Nixon for
twenty-five years, and he had been told by Nixon more than once that
he had nothing to do with Watergate. Ford was not only a man who
can be trusted, but he trusted, and he trusted Nixon. He believed what
Nixon told him, that he had had nothing to do with Watergate, until
that afternoon when Haig revealed the truth to him.

The Nixon pardon is . . . what is most often remembered about Ford.
I felt that I would have the best opportunity anyone would ever have to
collect and report all the details of the pardon. I knew all the principals
and was able to talk to all the principals except Richard Nixon. The
principals in the pardon are President Ford himself, Phil Buchen, Jack
Marsh, Bob Hartman, and Al Haig. They were the people that Ford
. . . called in to advise him on this.
    The story of the pardon is really in two parts. The first part of the
story must begin with Al Haig coming over to tell Vice President Ford
that there's evidence against Nixon that may force him out of office. At
the same time, he presents six options, he calls them. The sixth option—
which is in writing, which is very important—suggests that Nixon will
resign if Ford will agree to pardon him. The first five options are slightly
curious because they are all options that are open to President Nixon,
and Ford would have nothing to do with those. He couldn't do anything
about those anyway, but the sixth option was key because that is the
option in which Haig suggests that Nixon may be ready to resign if you,
Mr. Vice President, will agree to pardon him.
    The six options are in Ford's subsequent testimony that he presented
when he went up to [Capitol Hill] to testify after the pardon. Ford did
not turn down that sixth option right away. He was cautious. He was

On October 17, 1974, President Gerald Ford took the unusual step of testifying before a House Judiciary Subcommittee about his controversial pardon of Richard Nixon. *Courtesy Library of Congress*

careful. He told Haig he wanted to think about it and get back to him. He did talk later that afternoon with Bob Hartman, his speechwriter and senior political counselor. Hartman was outraged—and said so— that this was a terrible thing for Haig to have presented; that it was unthinkable that this should be done. But Ford did not yet agree. He talked that night with his wife, Betty Ford, who was concerned also, but she said finally, "I'll go along with whatever you think is the best thing to do." The next morning, he talked to Jack Marsh, who was then his national security adviser, and a longtime friend and a sage if there ever was one. Marsh told him also, "Mr. Vice President, Bob Hartman is right. You can't do this."

But Ford was still unconvinced, and Marsh said, "Well, who will you believe? You don't believe us. Who will you believe?" Either Marsh or Hartman suggested Bryce Harlow. Harlow was invited to come in and talk to Vice President Ford about it. Harlow had advised Eisenhower and Nixon, and any number of other public officials, and was widely respected by Jerry Ford.

Day one is the day the proposal is made for the pardon, and Ford learns he is going to be president. It may be six months; it may be six days, but he knows he's going to be president. And then Friday, August the first, is the day when Ford is finally convinced by Bryce Harlow that [a pardon is] unthinkable. The net message is that "Mr. Vice President, your own presidency will be tainted if you do this. You cannot do this." Ford says, "Well, what do you want me to do?" Harlow says, "Right now, don't call Nixon." He said, "That would be the worst possible thing you could do. But call Haig and tell him that none of this is to be regarded as a deal." And Ford, in effect, calls Haig on the telephone and says, "Al, no deal."

Mr. Haig expressed to me some shock that anyone would think that he was trying to make a deal. Nothing was wrong with a deal, frankly. What the deal was, was that Nixon would resign, Ford would become president and pardon Nixon right away. It was quite legal. There's nothing at all illegal about it. What happened next is that once Nixon found out that there was no deal, he told his staff and his speechwriter that he was going to stick it out, that he was going to force the impeachment and force a trial in the Senate. And he did plan to do that. We're now on Saturday and Sunday. He planned over the weekend to stick it out. Then, on Monday, August 5, the smoking gun tape is revealed.

What [the smoking gun] comes down to is that this tape on June 23 of 1972, six days after Watergate, in three instances, three times that day, Nixon tells his then chief of staff, Bob Haldeman, to have the CIA stop the FBI investigation of Watergate. That was obstruction of justice, a clear-cut case of it. Once it was revealed, Nixon lost all of his final support in the House Judiciary Committee.

Jerry Ford has a speech scheduled in New Orleans. He has a series of trips for three House members in Mississippi, and he's then going on down to New Orleans over the weekend. He and Hartman and Marsh agreed that the best possible thing for him to do is go ahead and carry out the schedule; that if he cancels it, it will raise more questions than they want to deal with.

Ford was not absolutely sure [that Nixon was going to resign], and, in fact, Haig told him not to be absolutely sure of it until he heard it from Nixon himself. He heard it from Nixon himself on Thursday, August 8, the day before Nixon actually resigned. Ford learned it at about noon, and Nixon made his [nationwide resignation] speech that night.

Ford had not promised the pardon. He had never discussed it with Nixon, by his account—and I believe his account. He never discussed the pardon personally with Richard Nixon.

[Gerald Ford is sworn in as president on the ninth of August.] The pardon is granted about five weeks later. The pardon is granted because Ford went in [to office] wanting to solve every problem and put this behind him. Indeed, he thought and said in his inaugural address, "The long national nightmare is ended." He thought it was over. Ford thought [that language] was too critical of Nixon and wanted to take it out, but Hartman, to his great credit, insisted, insisted, insisted, until Ford said, "Well, OK." Later, Ford, to his credit, said, "Bob, you were right. It was right to leave it in. It was the right thing to say."

Ford, at his first press conference, was asked, to his dismay, four or five serious questions about what he was going to do about former president Nixon. Unfortunately, Ford gave as many answers as there were questions, and he realized the confusion he had caused, that he'd simply made his problem worse. He realized also that there was no way to put this behind him unless something drastic happened. [The pardon] was a result of his thinking over the problem and what ought to be done about it. Essentially, Ford was convinced that the most important thing to the country was to get on with governing, to address the serious economic problems we were having, to address serious foreign policy problems we would have—to get on with that and get off the subject of Watergate. The only way, he felt, that we could get off the subject of Watergate was for him to pardon Richard Nixon. He decided to do it, and then he called his staff in and asked them to tell him how he could do it. President Ford told the whole group [of his senior staff]. Then, he said, "I don't want anybody to talk to anybody about this. This is within this room because I'm not sure that I'm going to do this or when I'm going to do it or how we ought to do it, but I want you to know it is my plan to pardon Richard Nixon." And he sent Phil Buchen out to research the question of how he could pardon him. The issue was: Could he issue a pre-emptive pardon? Could he pardon someone for a crime for which he had not yet been indicted? Al Haig [went ahead and] informed Richard Nixon of this discussion. When asked about this for my book, Haig said, "Well, there were certain communications going back and forth which were necessary." . . . There was no violation of the law [in communicating with Nixon], but it was a breach of the confidence of the new president for Haig to be communicating the new president's intentions to the old president.

. . . I think that Al Haig performed a great service to this country [during Watergate]. In effect, he was the acting president for almost a year [during Nixon's decline], and we owe him a great debt. But I think that he made a mistake in that after President Ford came in office, Al Haig, then still chief of staff, felt that he would continue with the same power that he had had under Nixon. Ford had no intention of letting Al Haig continue to run the White House and told him so.

We now get to the second stage. Two or three days after Ford granted the pardon, Nixon called him up and apologized for all the problems that the pardon had caused. And he said that maybe he ought to just decline to accept the pardon. Ford, who took very careful notes on this telephone conversation, said, "No. No. The damage is done. We'll let it stand as it is." Ford felt, correctly, for Nixon to then say he wouldn't accept the pardon wouldn't help anything; it would just make the whole problem worse.

[The Nixon pardon is the reason why Jerry Ford didn't win in 1976.] In the first place, Richard Nixon had left such an appalling impression on the country as a consequence of Watergate and his long delay in telling anything like the truth about Watergate, that people wanted a change. They found a change. They had a change in Ford, and they liked that change. But politically, the pardon damaged Ford and reminded voters and others in the country that we'd had a very bad time in the second term of Richard Nixon.

I did [ask Gerald Ford whether he would have granted the pardon again], and the answer is yes. He would because he felt it was the most important thing for the country. He did not believe this country should be put through the agony and the international humiliation of putting a former president in the dock. There was no question about Nixon's guilt; people understood his guilt. Not only had the special prosecutor found the evidence—and that evidence is in the National Archives—there was enough evidence there to put Nixon in prison for thirty years. The evidence turned up by the House Judiciary Committee, under [Chairman] Peter Rodino, was exhaustive, extensive, and is a matter of record.

[As president, and after leaving the White House, Gerald Ford rarely met or even talked to Richard Nixon.] President Ford did attend the opening of President Nixon's library, but their conversations were brief, small talk while the photographer was taking their picture—and never in a personal, revealing conversation such as they might have had when Ford was in the House and Nixon was president. . . . Ford was a forgiving man, but he could not forgive Nixon for deceiving him and deceiving the American people about what had actually happened in Watergate.

JIMMY CARTER

39th President, 1977–1981

Overall Rank: 26

— ★ —

Total Score: 506

Jimmy Carter's overall score is three points below that of Gerald Ford, the man he defeated for the presidency in 1976. Comparing the two, Carter ranks significantly higher in pursued equal justice for all (5th in 2017) and moral authority (14th) but trails Ford in relations with Congress (33rd) and crisis leadership (37th). Their scores are equivalent in public persuasion, tying for 34th place.

Party: Democrat
b. October 1, 1924, Plains, Georgia
First Lady: Rosalynn Smith Carter
Age entering office: 52

Historian: **Michael J. Gerhardt**

Michael Gerhardt is a professor at the University of North Carolina School of Law and the scholar in residence and director of content at the National Constitution Center. As a leading constitutional scholar, he has advised congressional leaders and White House officials on constitutional issues. He joined C-SPAN's Q & A on August 3, 2018, to discuss his book, The Forgotten Presidents: Their Untold Constitutional Legacy.

Jimmy Carter as a [president was], to some extent, what you still see today. Even though he's an ex-president, he is somebody who clearly almost leads with his heart. He is somebody who's got a lot of intense feelings and commitment to certain issues, and he was somebody who had a core of integrity, which was very important to his election and, really, to his life. And he was somebody who could be very demanding. He could be demanding of himself, and he could even be very demanding of the people around him. You can see that throughout his life.

[Before he ran for the White House in 1976,] he was governor of Georgia and had been a local politician in Georgia before that. As governor of Georgia, he developed an ambition, which I think surprised a lot of people, that he was going to consider running for the presidency. This was in the wake of Richard Nixon's resignation and Gerald Ford's elevation to the presidency, so it was at a time when the nation was in some turbulence, and there was some instability nationally. And there was a [growing] concern, as Carter himself would later encapsulate it—why not [have] the best? Why not look for somebody who's got integrity? Why not look for somebody [who] was going to try and raise our ideals? Why not look for somebody not from Washington but from, even, the Deep South? [Why not] be the first president in a long time to be elected from the Deep South, who might try to raise us all up, to some extent, to be a better country?

[His hometown of Plains, Georgia, and site of his peanut farm, brought to national prominence his brother Billy Carter's gas station and his mother, Miss Lillian, who would sit at the railroad station and greet people while rocking in her rocking chair.] I have a feeling, and there's certainly data to support this, that it probably all helped [Carter get elected] because it did show he was an outsider, but it also showed he was, to a large extent, a self-made person. And it showed further that he was coming from a very unpretentious background, which could have a great deal of appeal for a lot of voters. The idea that this person wasn't going to necessarily be full of himself and could at least appreciate what it means to have to work for a living, getting up early, and . . . working in the country, which can be physically more demanding—I think a lot of that had appeal for a lot of people. It also generated some skepticism from other people who perhaps were less familiar with him or who had preconceptions about what it would mean for somebody to be coming from the Deep South. One might want to remember that Jimmy Carter was educated at the Naval Academy, obviously one of our most prestigious and demanding institutions. He was . . . a well-educated person; was a very smart guy. People sometimes don't expect that combination of things to happen for somebody who's coming from the Deep South.

[In 1976, he unseated Gerald Ford, the Republican incumbent.] I think Carter had a couple of advantages: one was being the outsider, not being the incumbent. Ford, also a man of tremendous integrity, had unfortunately inherited the mantle of the Nixon administration. That probably weighed him down more than anything else. Ford also pardoned Nixon in an attempt to put the whole Watergate episode behind us, but the pardoning of Nixon might have actually connected Ford more closely with Nixon in a way that wasn't necessarily good for Gerald Ford. Ford also might have made a mistake or two in the presidential debates. He was a tremendously good man, but also perhaps one might go so far as to say a little bit bland in terms of his demeanor, at least as it came across on television; and television was beginning to capture people's imagination at this time period. So, Ford may have had some things working against him, on the one hand, and Carter had the idea of freshness, newness, on the other—and also a commitment to ethics, which was a very important element of his campaign and later in his administration.

Carter wanted to restore ethics in Washington, and he particularly wanted to restore ethics in the White House. . . . And he, as president, would later put into effect the Ethics in Government Act [1978], which would be a very important cornerstone in modern ethics law as it pertains to federal officials. Carter could make those promises, and perhaps they had some appeal and some believability for a lot of people. In the wake of Watergate, a lot of the country, or at least half, thought, OK, perhaps it is time to turn the page and see if we can do things better.

There are a number of [Carter-era ethics reforms] that still remain in effect that apply to judges and to other federal officials—disclosure requirements and other things. . . . A lot of that is still what we'll call good law, still around in one form or another today. [This created] what some people may perceive as an obsession [with ethics reporting], to some extent, on the government's part. If you look at Congress, for example, . . . there's an ethics committee, and there are a lot of different forms that people who work there have to fill out and [rules to] comply with. If you look at the executive branch and elsewhere, there are a lot of disclosure laws, a lot of requirements about what people can do and not do in terms of the interactions they can have with certain other people—all of that gets its genesis from the Carter days.

[Carter's Southern roots] had a great deal of impact on Washington, and maybe even beyond the town, perhaps on much of the country.

The South had a good deal of pride in Carter when he came into the White House. Because Carter wasn't a Washington creature, because Carter had not developed as a politician in Washington at all, hadn't really spent his formative years there, had not been an administrator there—he was a genuine outsider coming into Washington. [And] he was an outsider coming into Washington from a place that many people in Washington may not have a lot of respect for. That made Carter's job harder. People had expectations about what a Southern governor would be like, particularly one that had a Southern accent like Carter and came from a place called Plains, Georgia, which most people couldn't pick out on a map. So, Carter had to not just come into Washington in an effort to change it, but he was coming into Washington and facing people, even in his own party, who were skeptical about him and maybe even had disdain for him. That all made his job harder.

. . . President Carter [also] had the idea, early on, that he was going to be his own chief of staff. The idea behind that was he was going to not have an intermediary between himself and the people that had to interact with the presidency. Another idea behind it was he didn't want anybody else to determine his agenda. If he could be his own chief of staff, he could determine who had access. He could also determine the agenda. In the abstract, those are good ideas, but the unfortunate thing is that the presidency at the time Jimmy Carter came into it was a lot more complex institution than it had been in the nineteenth century. At the time Carter came into it, being your own chief of staff and somehow trying to be president was much more than he could handle, so there was a sense of chaos and a sense of disorganization that marked his administration from the beginning.

There were a lot of things that [negatively] impacted Carter's presidency, and [granting amnesty to Vietnam War draft dodgers on his first day in office, January 21, 1977] was probably one of them. Carter was, even to some extent like Gerald Ford, trying to think of how we heal the country, how we bring people together, people that have been divided by one means or another. The people that had left the country and avoided the draft because they didn't like the Vietnam War or didn't believe in it, those people were viewed by some Americans as unpatriotic and bad. Carter looked at it rather differently; Carter wanted to find a way to bring these people back again, to heal some divisions. So, the pardon, from his perspective, made sense; it also signaled to people on the other side, particularly in the Republican Party, that Carter was going to be too sympathetic to people that didn't follow the rule of law and to people that were viewed as hippies and far-to-the-left liberals, the draft dodgers. Carter's pardoning of those people may have aligned him with a group that wasn't popular with the people who were going to become Carter's critics.

Until Carter came into office, there was some difference of opinion about the importance of the vice president. For many presidents up until Carter, their vice presidents were just simply something to be ignored or something to be cast aside, or, in the case of Richard Nixon, his vice president Spiro Agnew, to be thrust aside and pushed out. Presidents oftentimes didn't think about their vice presidents as partners or people that they could turn over some administrative responsibilities to. Carter thought instead, no, my vice president, Walter Mondale, could actually be somebody who could be important; he's not just important to my election, but he could be important in my administration. Mondale became involved with all the important national security matters early on in the Carter administration. . . . . That set a modern precedent, which has been followed since.

Mondale was, to some extent, an outsider within the Carter clique. He wasn't somebody that had known Carter before; he wasn't somebody that had grown up with Carter. He was probably viewed as an outsider from those people closest to Carter. On the other hand, Mondale, in an attempt to be a good team player, was trying to help Carter realize his initiatives. They wouldn't necessarily agree on a lot of different things, and sometimes Mondale wasn't part of a smaller network that was interacting with Carter on some issues. So, while Mondale was involved more [than prior vice presidents], he probably wasn't involved as much as Mondale would have liked.

The economy was not strong [in 1976], and it was one of the challenges Carter was going to have to face. Carter had a lot of challenges coming at him very fast that he had to address and hopefully, from his point of view, successfully. The international situation was becoming more precarious; there was the disorganization throughout the executive branch.

All of this was on his desk, so to speak. . . . Who does the president need to talk to figure out all this stuff? Exactly what would the initiatives be that the Carter administration was going to address on the home front and in foreign affairs?

President Carter brought in a number of advisers to try and help him figure out how to deal with [major economic drivers, such as the price of oil, gasoline, and inflation]. He was also beginning to think about deregulation in some ways that was rather innovative and different at the time. Carter was thinking about [the economy] in a way that may have marked not just him, but perhaps marked his party, to some extent. He was thinking about it from the federal government's perspective: What should the federal government be doing to try and fix the economy? And that might have meant more federal intervention rather than less, and so, that was Carter's mindset. And Carter was thinking about reorganization at the time. Part of that was an attempt to not just balance the budget, but to make the government perhaps a little more efficient. There were several departments that had to be reorganized at the time, including the Department of Health, Education, and Welfare, which later would get transformed to Health and Human Services.

Carter [also] wanted to reduce the amount of federal management over the airlines. That became a very big hallmark of his administration, to deregulate the airline industry.

He eliminated the Civil Aeronautics Board, which was part of the regulatory scheme over the airlines, to try and turn over the management to the private sector. That was one of the areas in which, in fact, the federal government was going to be less intrusive, or less assertive, than it had been. Carter's deregulation was not nearly as radical [as Ronald Reagan's would later be]. . . . To the extent that Carter had a well-developed political philosophy, less government wasn't necessarily part of it. Making government smaller was obviously something that was very central to Ronald Reagan's approach. Carter's ideas, roughly speaking, were to make government better, maybe a little more efficient, make it more ethical. The effort toward airline deregulation . . . turned out to be more controversial than he might have expected. As often turned out to be the case with Carter, there would be things he would do that he didn't expect to be trouble; and then there was trouble, and he'd have to somehow figure out how to deal with that.

There was a lot happening [during the Carter administration], and not just domestically. We've got the hostage situation arising in Iran, which is going to become a real big problem for Carter, and he's also developing some interpersonal friction between himself and some other key officials, including Cyrus Vance, secretary of state. Vance was a very eminent, very well-respected civil servant, a secretary of state of great prominence. But he didn't feel fully appreciated, and he didn't have Carter listening to him all the time, so this did come to a head. Carter, who had already tried to remove a number of other cabinet officials, was happy to get rid of Vance as well. That created a rift, which was not just in the cabinet, but it is going to create a rift in the party.

[His nomination of former John Kennedy aide] Ted Sorensen for the CIA [failed]. What we're seeing there is something that's going to become important, not just to Carter, but to other presidents throughout American history. As presidents try to fill certain positions, it turns out that for the Senate, which has the power to confirm, some of those positions will be in areas that are more heated, or raise more important issues politically, for presidents. Among those positions would be secretary of state, but also the head of CIA, secretary of defense, attorney general. Those are the officials that get a lot more attention, and the nominees for those positions get more attention. Sorensen was one of them, and the rejection of Sorensen became a signal from the Senate to Carter that they weren't going to just accept his people because they were his people. What we are seeing is a rift with Cyrus Vance and now a rift with the Senate, and these things are going to become more expansive problems for Carter.

[On September 17, 1978, the historic Camp David Accords between Israel and Egypt were signed in Washington. Here] Carter became, to some extent, his own worst enemy. This is part of the legacy that's going to haunt Carter. In taking not just the responsibility, but also in trying to give himself credit [for Camp David's outcome], Carter was stumbling to some extent because he wasn't leaving the praise to others. That made Carter appear, as some critics would suggest, more arrogant. Carter's moral arrogance, which he may have had in common with another Southerner, Woodrow Wilson, became a liability for him as a politician. Carter was . . . trying to shape his own legacy. The Camp David Accords, by all accounts, was a historic moment in foreign affairs. But Carter also

In September 1978, Jimmy Carter addresses a joint session of Congress about the Camp David Accords. Seated behind are Vice President Walter Mondale and House Speaker Thomas P. O'Neill. *Courtesy Library of Congress*

signaled that it was his moment. There wasn't a team of people he was going to bring in to help do it; he did it. And that arrogance came back to haunt Carter.

. . . Jimmy Carter is the only president to have served a full term without a Supreme Court appointment, which is remarkable. That was a tremendous disappointment to his administration, and probably to him, personally. Nonetheless, federal judgeships became important to Carter in a way that they hadn't been important before. They were important for the purposes of increasing the diversity of the federal bench, to bring more minorities, more women on to the federal bench, in a way that was historic and expansive and inclusive. Carter tried to find ways to implement those objectives, one of which was to develop judicial commissions. He tried to use those commissions to advise him and to maybe, in some respects, diminish the role of the Senate. . . . [Of course his appointees] will later have to get confirmed in the Senate, so Carter's approach began to tear apart his relationship with the Senate. It became a very controversial matter; it was one of the things that created differences between Carter and Senator Ted Kennedy, something that would later become a bigger problem. But Carter's approach also set the Democratic Party on the path that it still tries to follow to this day: in trying to pick judges, we're not going to just pick white males. We're going to think about what other qualified people are out there—people that "look like America," as Bill Clinton would later put it—people that we could put on the bench and they could become judges and important officials in government. Carter was very much a trailblazer in that regard.

FISA, the Foreign Intelligence Surveillance Act, that's an important development as well with Carter. We don't think about these things when we look back in history and think about the impact of certain presidents and what their legacies may be. That's because we're thinking in such big terms; we're thinking of big dramatic stuff, like wars or Nixon's resignation. But with Carter, some of the details matter a great deal. Carter was putting into place institutions that continue to this day. With FISA, for example, he was trying to respond to a problem that had occurred in the Nixon administration. [At issue] were the boundaries between the CIA and the FBI and who could look at what [intelligence information] and on what grounds could they [surveil], particularly with respect to spies that may be present in a US territory. How do we deal with that? Carter tried to put together institutions to address that.

[My book covers thirteen lesser-known presidencies. Among them] Carter may be a little harder to grasp just because he's a little more recent and because it was such an active four years. [We are still] trying to get a handle on all the things that happened during that time period, both in terms of what worked and what didn't work, and what remains important lessons, and what can we glean from that period, and what may have been his legacy then and as it's evolving. . . . One of the themes of my book is that people come into the office, and the office shapes them; but the [presidents] themselves also help shape the office.

CALVIN COOLIDGE

30th President, 1923–1929

Overall Rank: 27

— ★ —

Total Score: 506

"Silent Cal" entered the C-SPAN rankings rated 27th overall in 2000 and hasn't made much noise since, as his category rankings have stayed in a narrow range. His highest ranks are in relations with Congress (18th) and moral authority (21st). His most significant improvement has been in pursued equal justice for all, where he has improved from 34th in 2000 to 29th in 2017.

Party: Republican
b. July 4, 1872, Plymouth Notch, Vermont
d. January 5, 1933, Northampton, Massachusetts
First Lady: Grace Anna Goodhue Coolidge
Age entering office: 51

Historian: **Amity Shlaes**

Amity Shlaes is a historian, professor, columnist, and chair of the board of the Calvin Coolidge Presidential Foundation. She joined C-SPAN's Q & A on January 24, 2013, to discuss her biography of the thirtieth president, Coolidge.

I think [Calvin Coolidge could still be elected president today]. That's really the challenge of my book, whether we can choose someone who's as principled as he is as president. Coolidge, who was president from 1923 to 1929, did not believe that perception is reality. He thought principle was reality. Reality is reality. Often, the challenge for us is, do we just have to have someone who's good-looking or speaks well, or is a good salesman, or can we have someone who's got principles? I think we can. We deceive ourselves, generally, that we need looks alone, perception alone.

[Calvin Coolidge] was born in Plymouth Notch, Vermont. It's a simple place. It will change your life if you see it. You can see the room upstairs where he worked. You can see the church where one of his ancestors bought a pew. [In my research,] I got very involved in the town records because the Coolidges were allergic to debt. They were terrified of debt. This is a story of how you overcome debt as a country or as an individual. . . . Their economics, their businesses, their small farms were so important in their lives. You have a feel for how hard it was in Vermont in that time.

Coolidge happened to go to Amherst College, a very interesting college. It had a motto, "Let them illuminate the earth." Basically, it was a college for future ministers, generally Congregationalists, although, there were other denominations there in Massachusetts. At the time he went there, it was a Greek school; . . . it had a lot of fraternities. Fraternities were all over, and most kids were in them. What's interesting about Calvin, and this is true all the way through his life, he didn't seem like he was going to make it, [but in the end] he got there. He wrote his father before he arrived saying that [he wanted to be in a fraternity], and then he wasn't chosen. Imagine being in a very Greek school with boys richer than you and being kind of shy. . . . [While] he wasn't sure he wanted to give up that much of himself to a group, it's always nice to be asked, and he was quite disappointed when he wasn't asked.

There was another boy at Amherst called Dwight, who was actually poorer than Calvin, maybe shorter and had a little physical disability. Dwight was a happy boy and much-loved and went into a fraternity. Coolidge knew him, and they ate lunch together once in a while. Apparently, Dwight black-balled Coolidge at one point for a fraternity. . . . Well, Dwight was one of those friends you have who thinks it over, changes his mind, and has great regret. Dwight decided he had underrated Calvin. That Dwight was Dwight Morrow, who then went to law school and became a big partner at J. P. Morgan. . . . Eventually, Calvin, as president, sent Dwight to patch things up with Mexico in a terrible time; Dwight was our ambassador there. He had a daughter called Anne Morrow. Coolidge sent down Charles Lindbergh to cheer up the Mexicans, to bring some comedy to the place, and that is how Anne Morrow became Anne Morrow Lindbergh. So, a lot of history came out of that understated, and a little bit sad, beginning of undergraduate life at Amherst for Calvin Coolidge.

[Coolidge graduated from Amherst in 1895 and was admitted to the Massachusetts bar in '97. In 1898, he was a city counselor in Northampton; in 1901, a city solicitor in Northampton; in 1906, a state representative for Massachusetts; in 1909, the mayor of the city of Northampton; in 1911, a state senator for Massachusetts; in 1913, president of Massachusetts Senate; from 1915 to '17, lieutenant governor; and then he was governor of the state of Massachusetts in '18. He went on to be vice president in 1921 and president in '23.] He almost never lost.

He told someone, "You have a hobby. My hobby is politics. Running for office is my hobby." One thing was the Republican Party and the Democratic Party were different, and there was a path, so if you helped the others, they helped you. He was in the party. It was [like] a club. . . . Back then, the Progressives said, "Coolidge climbed the greasy pole of Massachusetts politics," but it wasn't just that. There was some good in the party. The party trains you. It helps you work efficiently. But it's also [illustrative of] his incredible personal perseverance. . . . Northampton, Massachusetts, was the county seat. So, after college, he looked around. He couldn't really afford law school. . . . So, he went to read the law. In the way they did then, you could clerk and pass the bar that way. He went with a firm of two men who liked Amherst [alumni] and were important lawyers in the town, running for office themselves. And he looked around and learned about his county seat. "Why don't I just try this?"

He was good to the Republican Party, and the party was good to him. He learned pragmatism. He practiced law on and off the whole time [he held office]. He was very careful not to be corrupt. . . . Remember, his youth is the [time of the] Progressive Republican Party, so you can see a Progressive record in Coolidge when he was a state lawmaker. He worked on busting trusts in theaters, if you can imagine. They saw trusts everywhere in the Progressive Era, and the hero of that era was Theodore Roosevelt. . . . So, he's thinking, "Is this a good policy or not?" What Progressives do is fight the big fight, reform government, and clean it up. Well, he liked that part, and he certainly had to work at it because he was often assigned to clean up government, to prune, to shut down offices. But he's evaluating [his beliefs] the whole time.

. . . Coolidge had a . . . [challenging] situation as governor of Massachusetts. Because of certain anomalies in their law, the governor had a say in the police department in Boston. The policemen in Boston went on strike after World War I. They were nice guys. They were underpaid. There was terrible inflation nobody was acknowledging. Their station houses had rats; rodents chewed on their helmets—[there were] eighteen ways they deserved a raise. They deserved better treatment; they were overworked. . . . So, they walked off [their jobs], and this was during a very rough time in American history. . . . There was chaos and violence and rioting and looting in Boston. Coolidge was the leader of the team that fired these policemen. They went into a union with Samuel Gompers, not even a very radical union, and the union that was the favorite of President Wilson. Coolidge said, "No right to strike against the public safety by anybody, anywhere, at any time." Those were his three phrases. . . . "I'm drawing a line." What's incredibly scary about this from a political point of view is that he had an election a few months away. He liked Irishmen; he was famous for getting the Irish vote. The policemen were Irish. He's firing them, and they're nice—what a bold, controversial move. Why was it at all good? Nobody knew at first. The reason that it was good is there's a limit to what a public-sector union should do, and jeopardizing the city's safety is going too far.

This would be 1918, 1919, 1920. We had unemployment in the United States. Our budget had gone up; it was $1 billion and went to $18 billion, eighteen times. We wondered whether we were bankrupt from World War I. All this was going on, so you needed to keep the peace. . . . The police of Boston affiliated with Gompers, thinking they'd be safe because they were on President Wilson's side. They were all fired except the ones who stayed, the ones we would call "scabs." They hired new [policemen], and that was to make a point. That is rough, deterrent justice of a very old-fashioned variety that we find incredible today. Wilson waffled. . . . He was kind of on the side of the public-sector unions. . . . Wilson didn't know how to deal with it, and he just kind of puts it off, and the governor of Massachusetts deals with it instead; that was Coolidge. And then Wilson says, "OK, I accept this because the unions can't go too far." Even Gompers was ambivalent [about the police going on strike].

After that move, the unions in the cities didn't [strike] anymore, and the cities felt safer and commerce was easier. . . . He received national recognition for his bravery, including from Wilson. Coolidge did win his election again, even though he had turned his back on these

Irishmen, . . . and that gave him national stature. And it's why he was chosen [for vice president in 1920, on the ticket with Ohio senator Warren Harding].

But, he had a problem [getting the nomination]: Henry Cabot Lodge, the senior senator from Massachusetts, was a great snob, an institution in the Senate, the leader of the Senate. Lodge wasn't sure he liked Coolidge. Lodge was vain; it was all about Lodge. There are Coolidges all over Massachusetts; it's a big Massachusetts name. Calvin Coolidge was from some kind of swamp, [Lodge thought]; he was not the kind of Coolidge that Lodge knew from Harvard. They considered Amherst backwoods, and he didn't really take Calvin Coolidge seriously. [Lodge] also toyed with him. At times, he told him he thought he might be a good candidate. Other times, not.

If your own state is not [voting] for you at the convention in Chicago, surely you're not going to be nominated to be the vice president. So, Coolidge didn't even go to the GOP convention in Chicago. We've heard about the Blackstone Hotel and the smoke-filled rooms where Harding was chosen to be president. But, there was a bit of a rebellion [among the delegates] that the Senate was running the whole thing, . . . [and] out of that rebellion, someone said, "I'm going to nominate a governor." . . . It was a Westerner who stood up and said, "Coolidge for vice president. He's a governor. Let's have him." There was a lot of applause all of a sudden at the convention, and that's how Coolidge got [the vice-presidential nomination] unexpectedly. And, I would estimate, to Lodge's displeasure.

[Warren Harding and Calvin Coolidge were sworn in on March 4, 1921, and they served together for two years and 151 days. Warren Harding died suddenly in California on August 2, 1923. Vice President Calvin Coolidge was awakened at his family farm in Vermont and sworn into office by his father, John, a justice of the peace, at 2:47 a.m.]

[Who Coolidge surrounded himself with as a new president is a] very important question. Coolidge came into office from being vice president, . . . so there was a cabinet already there and some of them were compromised. Remember, the Harding administration was a period of scandal. So, do you keep them? The modern position might be that our political advisers would say, "Clean sweep. Brooms out and get them out," so you would have the appearance of integrity. But Coolidge also prized a respect for Harding. Those people weren't condemned

President Calvin Coolidge, August 4, 1923, wears a black armband to mourn President Warren Harding, who died two days earlier. *Courtesy Library of Congress*

yet. They were innocent until proven guilty and he wanted continuity for the sake of the people and the markets. So, he kept the Harding cabinet for a while. Eventually, some people left. Harry Daugherty, the secretary of the interior, left. The figures who were compromised in the Harding administration eventually left, and Coolidge did have an investigation. He named a bipartisan team—that's very modern—to look into corruption in the Harding administration. But, he thought first of continuity when he became president at that moment in August 1923.

Andrew Mellon was his [secretary of the Treasury], and Harding's before him and Hoover's after. Mellon was a great figure like [former Federal Reserve chairman] Alan Greenspan today, or Ben Bernanke. It was said of Mellon that three presidents served under him. Who was Mellon? Mellon was a very wealthy man. He made much of his own money. He created an empire in Pittsburgh of steel and aluminum. Mellon was also what we might call a venture capitalist. He would give a man money if a man had a good idea, see what happened, maybe in the end sell his shares when the man succeeded. Sometimes he butted in, sometimes he didn't. He loved new ideas. He created a whole institute to generate patents. . . . [He was] very production-oriented, . . . a creator of wealth. So, Mellon came to the job of Treasury secretary, with a wealth of experience from the private sector and a few convictions. His best partner among the three presidents . . . was Coolidge, who understood Mellon. One thing we have to admire about Coolidge is he knew how to work with other men. It wasn't all about Calvin.

[The federal budget under Coolidge] depends how you count it, but the way he counted, it was about $3 billion, which would be less than 5 percent of the US economy. He was [determined] to get it down to $3 billion; that was his Holy Grail. . . . The Coolidge administration didn't just cut the tax rates, they cut the budget, and this is different from our modern supply-siders who tend to put the tax rates first. Coolidge always twinned them. He said, "You can't just cut taxes, you have to cut the budget." You'll see a photo somewhere of two lions someone gave him, and those lion cubs were named "Budget Bureau" and "Tax Reduction."

[The Coolidges' son, Calvin Jr., died during his first term.] This is like a Lincoln story; it's an amazing tragedy. Calvin Jr. was about sixteen, and he got a blister [playing] on the tennis court of the White House. The blister went septic, and he died within about a week. If you can imagine, from a blister to death—this was just before antibiotics came in—what a story. And there was nothing that they could do about it. Coolidge had lost his sister, he'd lost his mother, and now he was losing Calvin, who was the lucky child of the family, . . . and he didn't know what to do. Other historians have told this story, the death of Calvin Jr., which came at the end of the initial Coolidge presidency. This was in 1924. He was elected that year on his own for four more years, and they say he was depressed for the next four years . . . but I don't see that. It's not a story of "yes, but," the death of Calvin; it's "but, yes"—he persevered, notwithstanding a blow almost no one, he nor Grace, could understand.

The president himself said, "The joy of the presidency went out for me." But, I see him pursuing in a grand campaign his "civil war," the tax campaign. He poured his energy into that instead, and he did prevail in the tax campaign in 1926. He won the presidency outstandingly. Can you imagine, your son dies and then you win in 1924 as president, beating a third party, the Progressive Party, and the Democrats combined? The Republicans had the absolute majority in 1924 even though a lot of the Progressives were former Republicans, so he was tremendously popular, in part because of his perseverance.

[His vice president was Charles Dawes.] . . . He was the rogue deputy from hell. Dawes was a wonderful man. He was in charge of procurement and distribution in World War I, getting stuff for the generals to the front line. He gave a famous speech called the "The Hell and Maria" speech, where someone was picking at how he spent money to get stuff to the front lines to win the war. And he said, "Hell and Maria, we would do anything to win that war." Then he went the other way and was in charge of cutting the budget after the war, a crucial job. . . . Dawes cut the budget. He did the Dawes Plan, helping Germany. We loaned them money, the Germans, and they paid everyone else back. What a statesman. Banking family, Chicago land family, but he was a maverick. He'd go his own way. What infuriated Coolidge was that Coolidge had some close confirmation hearings planned, and Dawes used his inauguration speech to get up and berate the senators for their poor behavior and abuse of the filibuster. He antagonized the Senate rather than following orders from Calvin, his president, to appease, make friends with, grease the wheels, for the nominations to come.

[Coolidge was given the nickname "Silent Cal."] He was very silent. We have many stories [about this]. There's a famous story where a lady said, "I bet I could get you to say more than two words at this dinner." And, as Grace Coolidge, his wife, told the story, Coolidge responded, "You lose."

He left office in March of '29. The stock market was at 100 for a long time then; it went up to 200, very high. It doubled. That's sort of like our 1990s, for example. . . . If you look in the past, you see some incredible doublings. Then it went to 381—that would be in September of 1929. Coolidge didn't approve of that; he'd seen a lot of recessions. He'd spent a lot of his life with the stock market at 100 or below. He knew, every sinew in him knew, that was wrong. He just didn't believe it was the job of the chief executive to intervene. It was the state of New York's [responsibility]—where the New York Stock Exchange was, where the Dow Jones Industrial would be. He knew the owner of the *Wall Street Journal* and Dow Jones, Clarence Barron, but he didn't think the president or the Treasury secretary was really in charge of that. Remember, the Federal Reserve was also young. There is a record of him looking into it. Another Amherst man was Charles Merrill, who founded what we call Merrill Lynch. Merrill went to see him, and they talked about it. Coolidge was terrified because he was so conservative, and he knew what a crash was, but he didn't see it as the president's role and neither did Merrill. . . . Another factor in that period was what Fed policy was, and Benjamin Strong, the great Fed leader, died and another Fed head came in. Maybe the Fed was too loose, and that's an important discussion.

I do not blame [the 1929 stock market crash] on Coolidge in the least. One of the important factors you always want to look at is, was the growth in the '20s real, or was it all champagne and a lie? The '20s growth was real; or, most of it was real. The stock market went too high, and people shouldn't have bought on margin, but it was not a lie of a decade. That view must be revised—and my book is an effort to do that revision, to expose the true 1920s.

. . . The government came in starting with Herbert Hoover and messed up something good. Beyond all the things Hoover did, bigger government was Hoover. Then Roosevelt followed with even bigger and more arbitrary government. . . . The economics of the 1920s—which we don't discuss that much—historians tend to depict them as a lie, *The Great Gatsby*, Prohibition. . . . The markets of the '20s were really interesting, looking at it from the point of view of the people. The single thing that Coolidge did that we want to remember is that when he left office, the budget was lower than when he came in. That's the story for us now. How did he do that? The economy grew a lot, maybe more than

3 percent sometimes. Unemployment was below 5 percent. The budget was balanced due to his own parsimony. How did he manage, though, to make the budget go lower, and how did that help the economy? A lot of it was because he got the government out of the way of the economy.

[After the White House,] he had another career as a successful journalist: Calvin Coolidge, columnist. Coolidge wrote a column every day. Can you imagine? He stopped after a year, just like he decided not to run again in 1928. He stopped, said that's enough, I've done them. A lot of papers took the column. He made $75,000 as US president. He made more as a columnist. It was an embarrassing amount of money; remember how many papers we had then. I believe he made $200,000 alone from the column, and in hard times, that was a lot, but it was honest work. He wrote the columns [himself and] he was exceedingly popular.

Someone paid him to write ten columns for $2,000 each. He sends them in, he gets the money, and they publish only six. He summons the editor and says just what the editor expects him to say, "I wrote ten and you published only six." What does the editor say in response? "But, we paid you," which is the standard answer. Coolidge said, "Well, maybe those columns weren't good enough. Here's a check for the columns you didn't print, $8,000 back." Then we ask, why would he give back the money if the contract said $20,000? He was entitled to keep it. That was Coolidge's business lesson, his philosophy lesson, because he wanted to do business with the other party again. He wanted to be a good citizen. Very rare behavior now, and I admire that.

[Calvin Coolidge died of a heart attack at his home in Northampton, Massachusetts, at the age of sixty, shortly after his presidency.] A lot of the presidents died [soon after their terms]. We're blessed today with the angiogram. We're blessed with statins, with Crestor. Men now know exactly how well their hearts are doing. It was pretty clear that he had something cardiac going on. You see men dying all the time in politics, and especially in the presidency. Harding died [of a heart attack while in office]. Coolidge said Harding was tired out, wore himself out. His predecessor, Wilson, had that terrible stroke and never really recovered. So, the two preceding presidents had been killed. Coolidge was proud that he made it [all the way through his presidency]. I don't think he was aware of the extent to which his heart was bad until the end, that something was really wrong.

It was reported that [the famous columnist] Dorothy Parker said when he died, "Who could tell?" That's a very mean comment. If you go back and look at Coolidge, he was a conservative hero. His tax rate was a gold standard tax rate: 25 percent was what he got the top rate down to, and he fought like crazy [for it. The rate] started, remember, with Wilson in the 70 percent range, so that was an epic battle. When you look at what all the Washington socialites said about Coolidge, how cold he was, you want to remember that they were probably from families that endorsed different policies, especially Alice Roosevelt Longworth, whose father had a different model of president. TR was a "Let's get 'em," be active, bully pulpit presidency, and here was Coolidge, prissy and cold and not giving out favors. Alice Roosevelt said he looked as though he'd been weaned on a pickle. Coolidge's silence was cultural. He was from New England. Farmers don't talk a lot or wave their arms about, . . . and he was of that temperament. He was a shy person, but it also had a political purpose. He knew that if he didn't talk a lot, other people would stop talking. A president is constantly bombarded with requests, and his silence was his way of not giving in to special interests; he articulated that quite explicitly.

[Calvin Coolidge should be remembered today for this:] that he struggled with [our national] debt and found a solution, as we do today, and we look for our own solutions.

RICHARD M. NIXON

37th President, 1969–1974

Overall Rank: 28

— ★ —

Total Score: 486

Despite being the only president to resign from office, historians do not place Nixon in the bottom 25 percent of all presidents. He benefits from a very high rank in international relations (10th), along with several other rankings in the mid-twenties. However, historians rank him 37th in relations with Congress and second to last (42nd) in moral authority, ranking above only James Buchanan.

Party: Republican
b. January 9, 1913, Yorba Linda, California
d. April 22, 1994, New York City, New York
First Lady: Thelma "Pat" Catherine Ryan Nixon
Age entering office: 56

Historian: Evan Thomas

Journalist and historian Evan Thomas spent thirty-three years as a writer and editor at Time *and* Newsweek, *including ten years as the Washington bureau chief. He has also spent time teaching writing and journalism at Harvard and Princeton. He joined C-SPAN to discuss his book,* Being Nixon: A Man Divided, *on June 19, 2015, on* Q & A.

I don't think you can do a Richard Nixon [biography] without doing the personal [side]. You watch Nixon, and you wonder, what is driving this guy? What's behind him? What's it like to be Nixon? I called my book *Being Nixon* because I was really curious: What is it like to actually be Richard Nixon? He seems so possessed at times, haunted at times, troubled at times, enthusiastic at times, proud at times. His chief of staff, H. R. Haldeman, called him "the weirdest man I ever met." That's from his loyal chief of staff. He was, for better or for worse, a weird man.

[I wanted to understand] how one of the most introverted politicians ever became one of the most successful politicians in the twentieth century. He was on five national tickets. He won the presidency twice, the last time by one of the largest landslides in history. His record is equaled only by FDR, and yet, he could barely make conversation. If he was here talking to you, there's a chance that he wouldn't be able to speak at all. Sometimes he would just spin his hands. . . .

He would just blurt things out. There's a scene where he runs into Jacqueline Kennedy Onassis at Martin Luther King [Jr.]'s funeral. He doesn't know what to say, so he says to Mrs. Kennedy, "Mrs. Kennedy, this must bring back many memories." Well, that's just cringe-making. Nixon would do that kind of thing all the time. We all do this. I do this at cocktail parties. You just blurt things out because you're uncomfortable. But Nixon would do this all the time. He was terrible at small talk. He liked to be alone. He was always writing on yellow pads, and people used to say his best friend was his yellow pad because he didn't really have any best friends.

Nixon was in a Latin play when he was a high schooler. He was doing *Dido and Aeneas*. He was Aeneas, and he had to kiss Dido. He'd never kissed anybody before, so he lumbers over the stage to kiss her, and the high school students erupt in laughter, derision, mocking him. It was an early case of Nixon having to deal with real adversity. He was humiliated. The girl hated him for it, and yet, interestingly, afterwards he tries to make up with the girl, who becomes his girlfriend. He learns to deal with adversity, to be mocked and to be jeered, but come back and show people.

[That first girlfriend was Ola Florence Welch.] There are hundreds of oral histories about his high school and college years at Whittier College and at Cal State Fullerton, . . . because when he became president, they went around and interviewed all of the old friends. Ola gave a lot of interviews. She was quite touching about Nixon. She thought he was kind of an odd duck, but she also found him to be impressive, not your normal high school kid. And although she first wrote in her diary, "I hate Richard Nixon"—that was her first thought about him—she was his girlfriend for four years. He tried to marry her, and she finally dumped him. He was sad about that, but he found Pat [Ryan, married her in June 1940,] and was pretty happy.

His father, Francis, was a bully and his mom, Hannah, was a saint, he said. [She was] kind of a passive-aggressive saint. There's some oral history that suggests that she was very withholding, and it was hard to win her love—and he desperately tried. His older brother was quite charming. Died of TB. And one of his younger brothers, who was a very sweet boy, also died. The mom said that Richard tried to be both of those boys, and he couldn't be. It just was something he could never do. So, he was never comfortable; he was a very forlorn little boy. He was very clean. He always had a clean white shirt. . . . He walked barefoot but carried his shoes around in a bag. One of his cousins said he never wanted to be picked up and hugged. He was kind of a lonely, forlorn boy trying to please his parents in a way that I don't think ever succeeded, even unto becoming president.

Nixon actually was accepted to Harvard out of high school because he was such a smart kid but couldn't go because the money had all been used to take care of the older brother. And, in fact, his mom had gone out into the desert in Arizona and rented a place to take care of [his brother]. In those days, TB sufferers would go to dry places because this was pre-antibiotics. And so, Nixon loses his mother to go take care of his dying older brother as a teenager. I think that was tough for him.

He was a poor boy. His father made some money running a gas station, so it got better, and I guess relative to the other poor boys at Whittier College, he was probably OK. But Nixon used that poorness. He understood outsiders. He used his shyness to understand outsiders. When he was at Whittier College, there was a cool guys' fraternity called The Franklins. Nixon started a fraternity for uncool guys, knowing that there were more uncool guys than there are cool guys. This is the beginning of the "Silent Majority," [a term he would use as president]. Nixon was elected president of his class by getting all the outs to run against the ins. He was doing that thirty, forty years later as a politician. He understood what it was like to be on the outside. He empathized with those people. He shared their hopes and their resentments, and he knew how to exploit them.

[After serving in the navy in World War II, Richard Nixon returned to California and entered politics. He was elected in 1946 as representative for California's twelfth congressional district. In 1950, he mounted a bruising campaign for the Senate against Democratic congresswoman Helen Gahagan Douglas and won.]

[Bebe Rebozo was one of Nixon's lifelong friends. Senator] Nixon was down in the dumps in 1951 or so, depressed—he was subject to depression. George Smathers—who was this high-living senator, a friend of Jack Kennedy's from Florida, a Democrat—to cheer him up, brought him down to Florida. [He planned to] have a guys' weekend, drinking and girl chasing out on [Rebozo's] boat. Nixon really was not good at either of those things, and at first Rebozo thought, "Who is this guy? He's no fun." But a kinship was established because Rebozo saw something real in Nixon, that there was a vulnerability and a sincerity there that the public never saw. But Rebozo did see it, and Rebozo understood that what Nixon needed was companionship without talking. And that was the basis of a friendship that went on for years and years.

[Nixon served as Dwight Eisenhower's vice president for eight years, from 1953 to 1961. Then, the 1960s were his] . . . wilderness years. Nixon had lost [his own presidential bid] in '60. He runs in '62 for [California] governor, loses, and holds his famous press conference, saying, "You won't have Dick Nixon to kick around anymore." People figure he's finished, but he's thinking about coming back right away. He said to . . . others that if he didn't go back into public life, he would be mentally dead in two years and physically dead in four. He'd read this book by Dr. [Arnold] Hutschnecker, his psychiatrist, called *The Will to Live*, and Hutschnecker suggests that people who are destined for greatness have got to be in public life or they're going to die. And Nixon believed he was destined.

This is one of the positive things [about Richard Nixon]. We think of Nixon as being a pol and a bit of a hack, [yet] as a young congressman, Nixon, when everybody else is an isolationist—and remember he's a Republican—he's an internationalist. He realizes the United States has got to be out confronting communism, saving Europe. He was pro-Marshall Plan, even though his constituents back home thought foreign aid was an operational rat hole, that it was just wasting money. Nixon goes against his own constituency because he believes in American power for good, to save Europe in that case, and stand up against the communists.

So, he always has this grand vision of himself as helping the United States fulfill its destiny as a great power, with Nixon front and center.

Nixon . . . actually admired Lyndon Johnson and felt a kinship. Both men were destroyed by Vietnam; both were politicians with a capital P, and both understood power with a capital P. . . . In 1968, when Nixon fiddled a little bit at the 1968 campaign and kept the North Vietnamese government from going to Paris, he arguably disrupted these peace negotiations [in order] to win the presidency. It's a murky and not good chapter in Nixon's history, and Johnson called Nixon a traitor for having done that. And yet, there's still this kind of an affinity [between them]. You could see that he admires what a man LBJ was. He was a man, [and] poor Nixon wanted to be a man. He got himself in more trouble on those [White House] tapes by trying to appear macho—all that swearing and profanity. Nixon wasn't even good at it. He was bad at it. It wasn't natural to him. It was natural to LBJ. If you listen to LBJ swear on his tapes—he's good at it. Nixon was trying to be something he wasn't. He wasn't an LBJ, crude, macho guy. Nixon was an intellect—a shy, intellectual, thoughtful man. But he couldn't let himself be that. He had to be something that he wasn't. I think that's one of the reasons why he destroyed himself.

[Nixon won the White House on his second try in 1968. For his family it was] not that joyful the night of the election. Nixon, typically, was in one room [at a hotel], and the family was on a different floor. Nixon with his yellow pad, all alone. They heard that the votes were being held back in Chicago. Now, this brings back terrible memories because in 1960, Chicago mayor [Richard] Daley allegedly stole the election for Jack Kennedy, and they held back the votes in Chicago. Nixon always believed that election had been stolen from him. And so, in 1968, they hear that the Chicago votes are slow coming in, and it's a razor's edge race. Mrs. Nixon hears this, and her daughters can hear her vomiting in the bathroom; she was so upset about this. Finally, at about seven o'clock in the morning, they get Chicago to deliver their votes, and they find out they have won. Nixon is happy. . . . He goes home to his apartment on Fifth Avenue and puts *Victory at Sea* on the record player and opens up all the windows and conducts *Victory at Sea* as it blasts out the windows. All alone. No family there; it's just Dick.

Since I was writing a book called *Being Nixon*, I needed to find people who were around him, physically close to him. They all were young men. [There was] Dwight Chapin, his body guy; Jack Brennan, his military aide; Ray Price, his speechwriter; [and] Larry Higby, who worked for H. R. Haldeman. . . . Years later, they were still a little defensive around the press, and they were a little defensive around me. I'm East Coast establishment—I worked for The Washington Post Company. But what the heck—a lot of years have passed, so they were pretty generous with me. . . . And they were sympathetic. Yes, Nixon was a weird guy, no doubt about it. But he was a considerate boss, a thoughtful boss. He tried to buck up his troops, and I think they wanted to get that side across.

. . . He was a good talent scout for young talent. Brent Scowcroft, later the famous national security adviser, was a young Nixon military aide. He talked to me, and he was very interesting. Henry Kissinger talked to me, of course, because he's interested in his version of history, but also he's a very thoughtful, perceptive critic of Nixon. Don Rumsfeld [later George W. Bush's defense secretary] was a young aide who worked for Nixon, and he talked to me. George Shultz [Ronald Reagan's secretary of state] was a young cabinet secretary. He talked to me. A lot of these names who became more famous later got their start with Richard Nixon because he had a good eye for talent. Somebody I didn't talk to, but I wished I had, was Roger Ailes, [the now deceased founding] head of Fox News. Roger Ailes was a fairly obscure daytime TV producer when Richard Nixon discovered him in 1968 and put him as part of his media team. . . . Nixon plucked him out of the crowd and gave him this kind of responsibility. He did that kind of thing all the time. For all the craziness of Watergate, Nixon had a really talented staff.

The Georgetown set, today, doesn't really exist, but back then, . . . it was really powerful. This was a group of CIA, State Department [officials], mostly going to Harvard and Yale, very charming, pleased with themselves. . . . This is a world I know because I worked for The Washington Post Company, and [its chairwoman] Katharine Graham was at the center of this world, as was Joe Alsop, the famous columnist. . . . I came in at the end of this world as the bureau chief of *Newsweek*, and so I used to go to Mrs. Graham's for dinner and I saw this. They hated Nixon. . . . They made no bones about it. Mrs. Helms, who was the wife of the CIA director under Nixon, Richard Helms, said there was no mercy for Nixon at these dinner parties. No mercy. Henry Kissinger was often the honored guest. Kissinger, who could be shamelessly flattering of Nixon in the White House, would go out to dinner with the Georgetown set and make fun, gently, but make fun of his boss. Nixon knew this, and he rationalized it. He said, "Well, Henry has to do this. Henry needs this. He needs to be popular." But it hurt him, and he would say, as Kissinger went off, "Well, there goes Henry to talk to those awful people in Georgetown." And the Georgetown people, particularly the *Washington Post*, which was at the center of the Georgetown set, was out to get Nixon. And you know what? They got him.

[The Watergate scandal began with a plan for Nixon campaign operatives to break into the headquarters of the Democratic National Committee at Washington's Watergate complex and wiretap their phones. On June 17, 1972, the "burglars" were discovered, and the scandal leading to Richard Nixon's resignation ensued.]

. . . Nixon was hardly the first president to wiretap and bug. One of the things that afflicted Nixon was that he was envious of the Kennedys and Johnson. He thought the Kennedys were better at dirty tricks than he was, and he was trying to catch up to the Kennedys. He wasn't totally wrong about that. I wrote a biography of Bobby Kennedy. The Kennedy machine was tough, and Bobby Kennedy [as attorney general] did more wiretapping than Richard Nixon ever did, including wiretapping Martin Luther King [Jr.]. So, it's not like the presidency was innocent and along came evil Richard Nixon. Executive power was concentrated in the '50s and '60s in the White House. The rules about wiretapping and bugging were blurry at best. The FBI [under J. Edgar Hoover] was only too happy to be an instrument of the White House and spy on the president's enemies.

There are endless ironies about Nixon, but one of [the] things that destroyed him was that the FBI got out of the business of working for the president, doing this kind of bugging. Hoover said, "We're not doing this anymore." Hoover, smart guy knowing about his legacy, could feel the lawsuits coming on in the Warren Supreme Court—this is a more liberal era in American government, and the rules are about to change. So, Hoover says the FBI's not doing this. What does that mean? Nixon goes in-house. He creates the "plumbers," [giving him] an in-house capability to spy. Unfortunately, the people his aides hired—Hunt and

Liddy, names that resonate in history—were not that competent. They may have once been competent, but I'm not even sure of that. E. Howard Hunt's reputation in the CIA was pretty bad. He was one of [Nixon's] chief plumbers. G. Gordon Liddy was a very colorful figure and brave in some ways, but kind of a screw-up as far as I can tell. Those guys made a lot of mistakes. They were not competent in what they did, and they got caught. And Nixon got caught with them.

[H. R. Haldeman was one of many Nixon aides who got caught up in the Watergate scandal. On April 30, 1973,] he's just fired Haldeman on national TV, and after [the broadcast, Nixon phones him]. . . . He's upset that nobody's calling; in the old days, Haldeman would arrange to have people call. So, he says to Haldeman, "Bob, do you think you could get people to call me, like in the old days?" Haldeman goes, "I don't think I can do that, Mr. President." Nixon hears himself, and he says, "All right. I love you, Bob. I love you." It's poignant. It's heartfelt. He actually does love the guy he just fired on national TV. His heart breaks [as you're] listening to this; you can tell Nixon is going down. He's going to be in office for another fifteen months, so it's going to take a while, but he's finished as of April 30, 1973, and you can hear it in his voice.

. . . There is, of course, a huge debate about how much Nixon drank. I can't resolve it. He had a low capacity. [But] towards the end, even Julie, in her memoir, says in that last year [of Watergate] both her mother and her father drank more than they should have. I don't think he was the crazy drunk that emerges in some of the literature. Although, I've got to say there's a conversation between Kissinger and Brent Scowcroft where Kissinger casually says that they couldn't put the president on the phone to the prime minister of Britain because he was "loaded." That's October 1973, and Nixon is in the throes of Watergate—it is really getting ugly. Scowcroft told me that he would go to Nixon with Kissinger's cables, and, after a couple of drinks, sometimes Nixon would say, "Bomb 'em." Scowcroft knew enough to ignore the order because Nixon really wasn't capable of giving an order. I was a little shocked that Scowcroft told me that story.

[Nixon resigned from office on August 9, 1974, as impeachment threats loomed—the only president ever to resign.] One of the many tragedies

Richard Nixon departing the White House on August 9, 1974, after resigning as president. New president Gerald Ford, his wife Betty Ford, and Pat Nixon walk with him to a waiting helicopter. *Courtesy Richard Nixon Presidential Library and Museum*

of Richard Nixon was that although he was very self-conscious, he was not very self-aware. . . . And he was afraid, in a way, of looking at himself in a realistic way. He would say, "I don't carry grudges." Hello? Richard Nixon was one of the great grudge-carriers of all time. He could be very un-self-reflective, and this hurt him because his lashing out at enemies is what destroyed him. If he'd only realized that about himself. As he leaves the White House, almost his last words are to the effect of, "Don't hate your enemies, because if you do, that will destroy you." It's self-awareness, but it's way too late. He's about to get in the [Marine One] helicopter and fly away.

Poor Nixon. After he left office in disgrace, he almost died. He had phlebitis. He was passing out. The nurse was slapping him, "Richard, wake up, Richard." He was near death. . . . Very much to his credit, he crawled back; he started playing golf with Jack Brennan. Not very good golf, but every day. He built himself back up. He talks to his friends; I guess he [still] had a few. Walter Annenberg invited him to his estate. . . . [There was] Bebe Rebozo, Bob Abplanalp, but not a lot of friends. Nixon was so broke that [his daughter and son-in-law] Tricia and Ed Cox had to give their bank account to him. It was a loan, but he was that broke. . . . There was literally a question of whether the Nixons were going to be able to pay for their groceries, he was so broke when he got out.

[Pat Nixon died in 1993, a year before the former president passed away.] Henry Kissinger told me a very affecting story that Nixon asked him to come for dinner at the [White House] residence with Mrs. Nixon. As they were walking over, Nixon said, "Would you tell Mrs. Nixon about some of my foreign policy accomplishments?" Then Nixon goes off to the bathroom because he's too shy to do this himself. Kissinger dutifully starts in and starts telling Mrs. Nixon about Nixon's foreign policy achievements, and Mrs. Nixon says, "Henry, you don't have to." She understood her husband and how awkward he was, even with his own wife. I actually think the marriage was much closer than we think. We've seen all these photographs of her looking pained and unhappy, and late in Watergate it was pretty bad. Nixon says in his memoir that he doesn't tell his own wife that he's resigning. He tells his secretary, Rosemary Woods, to tell Mrs. Nixon. So, you wonder how close they were in August 1974 [when Nixon resigned]. But before that, in the early years, there are very touching love letters between them. Nixon is like one of these guys that can't believe his good luck that he married the prettiest girl. And she was the prettiest girl. If you look at the old photographs of her, she was gorgeous. She became gaunt later, but when she was twenty pounds heavier, she was a knockout.

Patricia helped him a lot in the early years. She stood by him, and when he felt weak or felt like quitting, she would say, "Richard, you can't. You can't, you just can't quit." She did that four or five times at key moments, the [1952] "Checkers" speech, and other times. So, it was a good marriage in some ways, but in the White House his natural aloneness and the terrible pressure he was under stressed it. Although,

I've got to say, the marriage resumed after he left the White House, and when she dies in 1993, he is undone. The photographs are amazing. He is just bawling. He's not just crying, he is convulsed with tears; he misses her so much.

Nixon was poignant. He has become, in the cartoon version, sort of a monster, and he did some monstrous things. You listen to [his White House] tapes, his anti-Semitism and all that. It is terrible. But Nixon was often somebody who wanted to be a better person. Late at night he would take those yellow pads, and he would write on them what he wanted to be. He would use words like "joyful" and "inspired" and "confident" and "serene." These are adjectives that really didn't describe Nixon. It's not really who he was, but who he wanted to be. Those yellow pads are preserved in the Nixon library. When I started doing this book, I was really struck by that because it was so in contrast to this idea we have of Nixon, scheming and rubbing his hands and swearing and saying anti-Semitic things. . . . Both Nixons are true. There's evidence for both, but you have to see the whole man to understand him—the good with the bad.

[Richard Nixon is] so endlessly fascinating. I didn't really expect that when I started. He's the great American novel. It's not fiction; it's nonfiction. But you cannot top his American story: this poor, shy kid who climbs to the very top, and then, overcoming all obstacles, defeated many times, gets to the top, and then destroys himself.

JAMES A. GARFIELD

20th President, 1881

Overall Rank: 29

— ★ —

Total Score: 481

The second of four presidents to be assassinated, Garfield's presidency lasted barely six months. Historians have given him relatively high rankings in pursued equal justice for all (20th), public persuasion (21st), and moral authority (22nd). These rankings support an overall ranking that keeps him out of the bottom 25 percent of all presidents.

Party: Republican
b. November 19, 1831, Orange (now Chagrin Falls), Ohio
d. September 19, 1881, Elberon, New Jersey
First Lady: Lucretia Rudolph Garfield
Age entering office: 49

Historian: **Kenneth D. Ackerman**

In addition to being an author, Ken Ackerman practices law in Washington, DC, and has served as legal counsel to two committees of the US Senate. He spoke to C-SPAN on June 19, 2003, for Booknotes *about his book,* The Dark Horse: The Surprise Election and Political Murder of President James A. Garfield.

I thought, . . . wouldn't it be good to write a book about a political convention when they really mattered, when they were passionate, exciting, bare-knuckled contests, unpredictable fights? I started looking for a good one to write about, and I came up with 1880, which was James Garfield. You put that together with the Garfield assassination, one of the more misunderstood events in American history, and the fact that there was a line of causation between the convention and the shooting of the president—to me, it made a compelling story for a book.

[When he was elected in 1880, James Garfield] was forty-eight years old. He was kind of a career congressman. He had been in Washington for

Ohio native James Garfield served only six months as president before being assassinated. This statue of him sits in Piatt Park in Cincinnati, Ohio. *Courtesy Library of Congress*

sixteen years serving in the House of Representatives. He had been the Republican leader. He had been chairman of several committees. He was one of the up-and-coming members of the Republican Party. He was also a Civil War veteran, and that made him a very popular figure. He had a house on I Street in Washington. He was from Ohio and had a farm that he had bought a few years earlier in Mentor, Ohio, just outside of Cleveland.

Garfield was very lucky in life in a lot of ways. He had a very good marriage. Early on, it was a very shaky marriage. During his first five years of marriage to Lucretia Rudolph, he was off fighting the Civil War, and then he was off on the political stump. In their first five years of marriage, I believe they lived together about twenty weeks. The rest of the time he was off being James Garfield.

The politics at that time, the Gilded Age, after the Civil War, was very much dominated by factional contests, raw power struggles, very similar to what was going on in the business world, very similar to what was going on in the Western frontier. At that time, the big fight was between two groups in the Republican Party called the Stalwarts and the Half-Breeds. Garfield got stuck in the middle of that fight. His nomination came after a thirty-six-ballot deadlock because the two sides were having a very strenuous tug-of-war that year, and he got caught in the middle. That's what eventually got him killed.

Charles Guiteau is the man who pulled the trigger of the gun that killed Garfield. He, at the time in 1880, was about thirty-nine years old. He was living in Boston, Massachusetts, selling insurance. What I tried to do that was a little different than other Garfield books was to show that the assassination of the president was not simply the result of a disappointed office seeker who took out his anger on the president. Charles Guiteau, while he may have, in fact, been insane, was someone who was very caught up in the political process. He was identified with one of the major factions. He worked with the Stalwarts. He considered himself a Stalwart. He went to New York at the beginning of the campaign and became chummy with their people. He hung out at their headquarters. He gave a couple of speeches. Even though the leaders of the Stalwart branch, people like General Grant and Roscoe Conkling, considered him very minor, he considered himself very major. And what happened to him was very much wrapped up with the larger politics of the era.

What Charles Guiteau tried to do was different than what any other presidential assassin had tried to do. What he tried to perform was a regime change. It wasn't simply to kill a person. It wasn't simply to destroy the president. He wanted to replace one ruling group, the Republican Half-Breeds led by Garfield and [Maine senator James] Blaine, with a different ruling group, the Republican Stalwarts, led by [New York politician Chester A.] Arthur, [New York senator Roscoe]

Conkling, and [ex-president Ulysses S.] Grant. That's what he was try-ing to do. He was able to do it because at the convention a compromise had been reached. Garfield won the presidential nomination, but as a payback to the Stalwarts, to give them something because they lost, they made Chester Alan Arthur, the Stalwart, vice president. So what Guiteau was trying to do was to put Arthur, who had befriended him personally during the campaign, into the White House. That's very different from any other presidential assassination. It's a very frightening thing, and it's very different than the way the assassination is remembered in most history books.

. . . The Stalwarts were the Republicans most loyal to Grant, and that's how they defined themselves; they were the hard-line true believ-ers in General Grant. In a way, the Radical Republicans of the Recon-struction era evolved into the Stalwarts of the post-Reconstruction era. They were the true believers. They were the hard core. There was very little ideology here; the differences between them became very much factional and personality-driven.

The Half-Breeds—that word came from the same era—it started out as an insult. The people who weren't very strong toward Grant were considered Half-Breeds. It was the way you would refer to someone almost as a traitor, that they weren't strong enough in their support of the team. After a while, though, when the Grant administration became tarnished with scandal and Grant's reputation fell, the Half-Breeds started to view that name as a compliment. They included a number of reformers at first, but over time, they simply became the opposite side of the Stalwarts.

[The two groups] were led by two very strong personalities: the Stal-warts by General Grant and increasingly by a group of Senate bosses, primarily Roscoe Conkling; the Half-Breed side was taken over by James G. Blaine, who was their leader in 1880.

[The two men's enmity began one] day in 1866. . . . James Blaine and Roscoe Conkling had a real dust-up [while they were both serving] in the House of Representatives, which caused a bitter lifelong feud between the two men. It started over an argument about whether to take away the job of an obscure military bureaucrat. In the course of it, Conkling used language which Blaine perceived as calling him a liar and possibly threatening him to a duel. This took place over two or three days, but in the end of the final day of it, Blaine took the [House] floor, read a long letter that accused Conkling virtually of fraud, of taking double payments from the government. Conkling responded with a very arrogant, dismissive gesture towards Blaine. Blaine came back and gave a two-paragraph speech, spontaneously, extemporaneously, where he referred to Conkling and his "grandiloquent turkey gobbler's strut," referring to his arrogance. He used classical allusion. He referred to Hercules and Thucydides. And at the end of it, the two men would never talk to each other for virtually the rest of their lives. This was all intramural within the Republican Party, and . . . it occurred to me that if an elder Republican had sat the two of them down—this is when the two of them were still young; they were in their thirties—and said, "Cool it. You're on the same side. Bury the hatchet," they probably would have done it. But instead, this got out of control and went on from there.

Ulysses Grant plays a very interesting role in this period. General Grant was not on good terms with Garfield. He very much wanted to win a third term in 1880, more than he let on. Grant was known for not sharing his feelings, for having immovable features. Those words are used with him a lot, his not being very expressive. But in 1880, he wanted to be president. People close to him noticed how anxious he got around the time of the convention, how he was counting the delegates, how he was following the news coming in on the telegraph.

After the Republican convention was over, and his backers failed to win it for him, after this thirty-sixth-ballot tug of war, Grant was very bitter. And he let some friends know it. He was disappointed in James Garfield because Garfield didn't pay attention to him when he went to see him and asked for patronage for friends of his, or made recommendations, or said, "You should support this person over that person." Grant was very close to Roscoe Conkling. Conkling had been very loyal to Grant over the years. So, when Garfield and Conkling had their falling out, Grant took Conkling's side. After that, the feelings between [Grant and Garfield] were very tense.

[Their falling out was over the position of] collector of the port of New York, . . . the most important political appointive post in the country and, clearly, in New York State. The reason was because it controlled the patronage. It controlled about two thousand jobs, plus a payroll of $2 million at a time when the political parties collected money by making federal employees pay a part of their salary to the party. So, the collector of the port of New York was an extremely powerful political position, and it was very heavily fought over. Roscoe Conkling, as the New York senator representing the Stalwart wing of the party, insisted that he have control of that position. Garfield, when he became president, after some hesitation, after being pulled back and forth on this, ultimately decided that he, as the president, needed to control the position, and so Garfield appointed a man who was a political enemy of Conkling.

Guiteau made the decision he wanted to kill James Garfield in mid-May. It was two days after Roscoe Conkling resigned from the US Senate because of the outcome of his battle with President Garfield over the control of the port of New York. Guiteau very much recognized his fate as being tied up in the fate of these larger political players. Guiteau at the time was lobbying very hard to become the consul to Paris for the US government. He came to Washington after the election and decided he wanted a political appointment. He felt he had worked in the campaign. He gave a couple of speeches. He was close to the Stalwart leaders. He had met Chester Alan Arthur several times during the campaign. He got a few recommendations, and he decided he wanted a job.

Guiteau was short; he had short dark hair, a beard. He had a strange walk. If he walked up to you, you wouldn't hear him. You would notice him standing next to you, but you wouldn't have heard him walk up to you. He talked in what's described as a confidential nature. He would talk standing right next to you in kind of a whisper. When you looked at his face, his eyes are a little bit uneven. In fact, when he was on trial for murder, the psychiatrists who claimed that he was insane pointed to the way his eyes lined up as a piece of evidence for his insanity. He dressed shabbily in the sense that he couldn't afford new clothes. He didn't have a job in Washington. He didn't have a bankroll. So, after a while, his clothes had rips that were never fixed. Several people pointed out that he wore rubbers instead of shoes, like you wear in the rainstorm to keep your feet dry, but very thin. He came to Washington, and many of his meetings were in March, in a year when there was snow on the ground. He wore very thin clothes. He didn't keep up his wardrobe very well, and that was very much noticed.

He actually got as far as meeting with President Garfield. They had a face-to-face job interview, but it was a very strange one. Guiteau had written a speech for the campaign. He got in to see the president. He gave the president a copy of his speech to look at. Garfield started reading it, and as he was reading it, Guiteau stood up and walked out of the room. He felt it was enough that Garfield was reading his speech, and he didn't want to press the point. It was three pages long. It was not especially striking in the sense of being terribly good or terribly bad, it was a typical speech of the time repeating the campaign slogans of the Republicans.

Guiteau also went to a reception at the White House; receptions were open to everyone. You could just go and get in line and shake hands with the president and the first lady. You didn't have to go through security; that was not a problem. And at this point, most of the ushers at the White House, who acted as guards to the extent that they needed guards, all knew who Guiteau was. He had been around several times waiting to see if there was any news on his job. He was always trying to get in, to push his application. When you think about it, it's a very logical thing to do if you're a job hunter, to go to the White House, to go to a reception, to make a point to meet the first lady, to try to put in a good word about yourself, and this is what he did. He walked right up to her, shook her hand, and said, "I'm one of the men who made your husband the president." They had a nice talk. She didn't think twice about it, and then she went on to talk to the next person in line.

Guiteau got in several times to the White House [but] he got to see the president just once. Then he walked over to the State Department, and he got in to see James Blaine [whom Garfield had appointed as his secretary of state]. Blaine would hold an open meeting several days a week that people could come in and simply see him; you didn't need an appointment, and Guiteau went repeatedly to those meetings. Most of the time, Blaine would put him off. He would say, "We're waiting." At the time, this was when the battle on Capitol Hill was going on between Garfield and Conkling over the collectorship in New York. Blaine would keep saying, "We're not going to make a decision about Paris, France, until the deadlock in the Senate is cleared up." And once that did clear up, once there was an outcome, Guiteau went back to

Blaine, and Blaine snapped at him: "Never talk to me about the Paris consulship again."

Guiteau [then] decided he wanted to "remove" the president. He was a very methodical person. He would sit in Lafayette Park [across from the White House], and he would track the president's comings and goings. There was no Secret Service protection at the time; that would not start until about fifteen, sixteen years later. President Garfield felt no compunctions at all about walking the streets of Washington himself alone at night. [And this was only sixteen years after Lincoln had been assassinated.]

[Guiteau] had never owned a gun before and did not quite know what to do with it. He would walk down Seventeenth Street to the Potomac River. At the time there was nothing at the river; it was just a deserted stretch of waterfront. He would take out his gun and practice shooting . . . either at a twig or at a bird or at just the water, just to see what it felt like to have a gun in his hand, to get used to the feeling of the discharge, the smell of the gunpowder, the way the gun would jolt back at him—so that he would get used to having it; so that he would be comfortable with it. For the two or three weeks that he was stalking the president, which is a frightening thing to think about in itself, he was walking around with a gun in his pocket most of the time.

One of the odd things about Guiteau was that he never had anything personal against the president. He said he liked Garfield as a man; he liked his wife when he met her. There was one of the early times when he followed them with a gun, thinking about shooting them, and Mrs. Garfield had a very bad case of typhoid or pneumonia. No one was quite sure what it was, but she had a very bad fever during the spring when Garfield was president. She really came within an inch of losing her life. Afterwards, Garfield took her to the ocean to help her recuperate. Guiteau followed them to the train station that morning with the thought of maybe shooting the president that day. But when he saw them getting on the train, and he saw how Mrs. Garfield was clinging to his arm, and how she looked very frail and very sick, he felt sorry for her and didn't want to shoot the president that day.

The Garfields went to Elberon, New Jersey, which is on the Jersey shore; it's the northernmost point. That was a very stylish resort at the time because it was just an hour-long boat ride from New York City. [Ironically] at the time, General Grant was there as well . . . in the cottage just across the street.

[The first lady stayed behind at the Jersey shore, and the president would travel back and forth.] Guiteau went to the train station a couple of times. When Garfield came back from the Jersey shore, he was there at the train station with his gun. . . . He was there, watching. All of this [logistical] information was in the newspapers. All you had to do was to read the *New York Herald* or the *Washington Star*, and you would know where the president was going.

Guiteau shot President Garfield on July 2, [1881]. Garfield had been president for just about four months when he was shot. He shot him in the . . . Baltimore and Potomac train station, which is on the site of where the National Gallery of Art is today. It was about 9:30 in the morning. . . . He chose the weapon that he shot him with for a reason. Guiteau, in a way, had delusions of grandeur about himself, and in a way, they weren't unrealistic. . . . He recognized his gun would probably end up in a museum. So, when he went to buy a gun, there were two that he saw in the shelf. One had an ivory handle and the other had a wooden handle. The calculation in his mind was that the one with the ivory handle would look better in a museum if he used that one to shoot the president. It cost an extra buck, but that's what he bought. I understand the gun is in the Smithsonian museum, but I have not seen it.

President Garfield was shot twice. One bullet hit him in the arm and grazed him. The other one hit him flat in the back.

Garfield lived for seventy-nine days. For most of the time, he was in the White House. They turned an upstairs room in the White House into a sick room for him, where the doctors took care of him, or arguably where the doctors killed him. . . . And then for the last few days, he was in Elberon, at the ocean. It was felt, both by the doctors and by Garfield and his family, that the atmosphere in Washington during the summer was very unhealthy. It was very hot; it was very uncomfortable. Washington at the time was a very swampy city. It was prone to epidemics during the summer, of malaria and other diseases. There were very bad smells and odors coming off the Potomac River. They felt it was very unhealthy, so the doctors agreed to let Garfield go to the ocean. The feeling at the time was that the salt air, the bracing ocean wind would maybe restore his health, or at least let him enjoy perhaps the last few days of his life.

One of the bullets was never found, the one that grazed him in the arm. The one that hit the president in the back, this was a question of some debate. They did ultimately find the bullet. The body had formed a cyst around the bullet, which ultimately formed an aneurysm. During the time, those seventy-nine days when Garfield was being treated by the doctors, they had no idea where the bullet was. They kept trying to figure it out. At one point they even brought in Alexander Graham Bell, the man who invented the telephone. He had invented a very crude form of metal detector, and they tried to use it to find the bullet. But the doctors were so far off, it turned out, in where they thought the bullet was, that the machine never worked.

Once he was arrested, Guiteau felt no embarrassment, no shame at any of it. He felt that he would be a hero, and so he very outwardly talked about everything he did. He dictated a long autobiography of himself to the *New York Herald* that was published. He wrote several long letters, and then he testified for several days. . . . What I tried to do with Guiteau, which I think is a little bit different than what other historians have done, is to take him at his word—to not start with the assumption that he was insane, but just take him at his word and see how he fit into context. Because it struck me that when you take him and put him into context, he oddly makes sense. I say oddly because where his logic led him is a very scary place. He decided in the end that . . . God was telling him to remove the president of the United States.

However, even given his personal insanity—whether it's medical or not—it very much fit in the context of the largest public debate going on in the country at the time. It was a time when the level of partisanship, of bad feelings, of personal attacks had reached such a level that Guiteau simply took it one step further.

They waited until Garfield had died [to charge Guiteau] because, for one thing, they needed to know whether it would be a murder charge or an attempted murder charge. The trial started about a month after the president died. [He was convicted and hanged early the next year in Washington.]

Part of Guiteau's defense was—and he had very good evidence behind him—that it was really the doctors who killed President Garfield. Guiteau shot him, but then the doctors examined him without washing their hands. And in the end, James Garfield directly died from a combination of infections and blood poisoning.

BENJAMIN HARRISON

23rd President, 1889–1893

Overall Rank: 30 — ★ — **Total Score:** **462**	In 2017, historians again ranked Benjamin Harrison 30th overall, at the head of a closely bunched group who are separated by only sixteen points in their total scores. Harrison's category rankings in 2017 ranged from 24th (pursued equal justice for all) to 33rd (crisis leadership).

Party: Republican
b. August 20, 1833, North Bend, Ohio
d. March 13, 1901, Indianapolis, Indiana
First Lady: Caroline Lavinia Scott Harrison
Age entering office: 55

Historian: **Charles W. Calhoun**

> *Specializing in late-nineteenth-century America, Charles Calhoun spent most of his career as a professor at East Carolina University and served as president of the Society for Historians of the Gilded Age and Progressive Era. He was interviewed for Q & A on August 9, 2018, for his book,* Benjamin Harrison, *a title in The American Presidents biography book series.*

Benjamin Harrison . . . is the scion of a family that goes way back in American history, back to colonial Virginia. In colonial Virginia, there were five Benjamin Harrisons in succession. Benjamin Harrison V was a signer of the Declaration of Independence, and he was governor of Virginia, the first state of Virginia, and his son was William Henry Harrison of Tippecanoe fame in Indiana. William Henry was president in 1841 just for a month. His son was John Scott Harrison, who was a congressman, a Whig congressman from Ohio for two terms. And his son was Benjamin Harrison, the president.

[Benjamin Harrison grew up in a Whig household.] The Whig Party was around roughly from the early 1830s. They began to call themselves

Whigs in the mid-1830s. They lasted until the early 1850s. They grew up in opposition to Andrew Jackson, but they also had a program. Henry Clay was the great philosopher of the Whig Party, the great intellectual leader and policy leader, a very strong believer in the protective tariff, internal improvements, and . . . the US bank. Henry Clay was one of Benjamin Harrison's heroes.

The Whigs in 1852 had a disastrous election year. Their candidate Winfield Scott lost [to Democrat Franklin Pierce], and the party basically fell apart in large part because of the slavery issue, which was moving toward center stage. . . . The Northern Whigs believed that the Whig Party was no longer an efficient vehicle for opposing slavery; Southern Whigs didn't want to continue to affiliate with people who felt that way, and so the party fell apart. There were other elements—the temperance movement had looked to the Whigs as being the party of temperance, and they weren't being very successful at pleasing those folks. Anti-immigration sentiment was rising in the 1850s. The Whigs had more or less fallen in with that kind of attitude; some people who were anti-immigrant felt that they weren't doing an effective job of keeping immigrants out. And so, all the constituent elements of the Whig Party fell apart. . . .

In the North, the Whig Party was replaced by the Republican Party. The precipitating event for the . . . birth of the Republican Party was the passage of the Kansas-Nebraska Act. It did open up new territory . . . into which slavery would now be possible to go, and that sent folks in the North, many of them, wild, who opposed this repeal of the Missouri Compromise. [Benjamin Harrison was among those who joined the fledgling Republican Party in 1856, and he supported the party's first candidate for president, John C. Fremont, that year.]

[Benjamin Harrison grew up around Cincinnati and began college nearby.] Caroline Scott was the daughter of one of his professors at a place called Farmer's College, where he went to college for the first two years, which was closer to Cincinnati. Harrison had a habit of visiting his professor more and more once he had met his daughter, and they did develop a ripe friendship that became a love affair. He fell for her. Harrison was very quiet, almost an introverted person with new people, and she brought him out of himself a bit. She was a much livelier kind of person and had a good sense of humor.

[He transferred to Miami University in Oxford.] Miami was a Presbyterian-dominated school. It was not unusual for them to have revival meetings; itinerant preachers were coming in and saving souls. Harrison attended one of those meetings and essentially was "born again" as a result of that. He remained committed to the faith throughout his life.

[The Harrisons eventually moved to Indianapolis.] He didn't want to be under the umbrella of his family; he wanted to strike out on his own and prove himself. He had a cousin who was living in Indianapolis already, and he had written to Harrison and said, "If you're looking for a place to land, this is a good spot. There are lots of good people here, good Presbyterians." Harrison had just passed the bar, [and his cousin said] " . . . You'll find the bar is full of men who are like-minded, and I think you'll flourish here." And so, Harrison and Carrie, his wife, did move.

Harrison's career evolved over time. . . . He was elected to be a reporter of the state Supreme Court and held that job until he [volunteered for] the army, and then held it after he came back from the [Civil] War. [Harrison rose to the rank of brigadier general by the war's end.] He was a very well-known lawyer. In 1872, he had been giving speeches for the party, and he thought he was in a good position to perhaps run for governor, but he was not particularly well-liked by the boss of the Republican Party in Indiana, a man named Oliver P. Morton, who was a senator. Although Harrison had lots of support for the nomination in 1872, it circulated through the hallways at the convention that Morton wasn't really too keen on this guy, so Harrison didn't get the nomination. In 1876, he was tempted to run for the nomination again but then decided not to. They nominated someone else for governor who had to resign from the ticket because of conflict of interest charges. In the early fall, the Republican State Committee said to Harrison, "We need you. Can you step in? Can you take over?" He made a valiant effort. He fought very hard, gave lots of speeches, but it was basically a Democratic year in Indiana. He came fairly close to winning, and after that he went out and campaigned in other states for the presidential candidate Rutherford B. Hayes. This is really what began to get him a national reputation.

Oliver P. Morton died in 1877, and that opened the way for Harrison to move into the position as leader of the [Indiana] Republican Party. . . . After the 1880 campaign when the legislature was elected, the

Republicans won it. . . . James Garfield, the president-elect said, "You want to come into the cabinet?" And Harrison said, "No, I'd rather be in the Senate." He did win a Senate seat fairly easily. He held the Senate seat for six years. Then in 1885, a Democratic legislature in Indiana gerrymandered the districts. . . . Harrison made a very vigorous effort on behalf of the legislative candidates. . . . [He] spoke all over the state, and he even bought a mimeograph machine to multiply his letters and get them out to as many people as he could. He really got a lot of national attention for that campaign. When the votes were counted, all the people running for the Indiana legislature on the Republican ticket get ten thousand more votes in total than the Democrats, but because of the gerrymander, the Democrats had more seats. . . . Harrison lost his Senate seat but had gained lots of reputation and notice nationally for the campaign that he had waged. Why was that important when he was running for president? We have to keep in mind that Indiana was one of those swing states. Here's a guy who can really work very hard in Indiana, who can perhaps win Indiana in 1888, and he might be someone that we will take seriously in looking at the candidates for 1888.

We often think of this era, the late nineteenth century, as a Republican era, . . . but in fact, the two major parties were very evenly balanced—just about as many Republicans and Democrats in the country equally, but they were spread out over two sections. The South was solid for the Democrats, and in any given presidential election, they could count on a body of electoral votes pretty darn certainly, and after 1876, certainly. The Republicans could count almost as reliably on a body of electoral votes coming from the Northeast, the upper Midwest, and most of the West as well. Neither one of those blocs of votes was large enough to win the presidency, and so what you had between them in those days were called "doubtful states"—New York and Indiana. Most of the campaigning was done in those two doubtful states.

. . . In Grover Cleveland's victory over James G. Blaine in 1884, there are only two states separating them—Indiana and New York—and both of them are quite close. In fact, Cleveland's victory in New York was something like one thousand popular votes out of a million cast, so just 550 votes the other way would have made a President James G. Blaine. Then you come down to the next election, Benjamin Harrison versus Grover Cleveland, and those two states were the only ones that flipped.

Benjamin Harrison was a transplant from Ohio to Indiana. This 1892 photograph shows a large painting of the one-term president displayed on the side of a barn with the artist standing in front. *Courtesy Library of Congress*

You have 233 to 168, and Harrison defeated Cleveland. Again, both of those states—New York and Indiana—very, very close. In 1892, [a Harrison-Cleveland rematch,] you had basically the same blocs taking place again in the South and the North, but there were some changes— the rise of the populists, disenchantment in the West, and other reasons.

Harrison didn't do as well as he had done in 1888. He lost Illinois and Wisconsin, which he had won in 1888, but he also lost New York and Indiana, so you see a wider spread of Cleveland's victory in 1892, and the populist James Weaver won twenty-two electoral votes.

[The country's reaction to the White House flipping back and forth during those elections] was as split as those votes would indicate. The Democrats were very happy to win the White House back. The Republicans were sorry that it didn't turn out well for them. There is an old story that . . . Frank Cleveland, Grover Cleveland's wife, on March 4, 1889, when the Clevelands relinquished the White House to the Harrisons, supposedly said to the servants, "Take care of the furniture. We'll be back in four years. . . ." [And they were.]

Harrison did not actively run [for the '88 Republican nomination] in the sense of going around and personally hunting for delegates. He had a good team headed by a fellow named Louis T. Michener, who headed up a committee that managed his pre-convention campaign. Michener, and Harrison himself, cultivated good relations as best they could with the supporters of James G. Blaine. Blaine had withdrawn from the '88 race, but there was some thought that he might accept a draft. . . . He was "Mr. Republican" in many people's eyes, and so the Harrison people realized, we've got to cultivate these Blaine people because they're going to have so much to say about who wins this nomination. The Harrison strategy, under Louis Michener and the others, . . . was to say, "Look, it's a wide-open convention," which it was. There were many, perhaps fourteen, people who were voted for on the first ballot. The idea the Harrison people had was, "Let's line up the second-choice people and see what we can do to get them after several ballots to come over to us." The key to that [successful] strategy was, of course, the Blaine contingent.

Benjamin Harrison did not travel around the country after he was nominated. Blaine had done that in 1884. He had made many speeches on about a six-week tour. At the very end of the tour, in New York, there were a couple of very, very serious gaffes that some people say cost Blaine the election. . . . So, Harrison said, "I'm not going to travel. What I will do is stay in Indianapolis." When he was nominated, he was in Indianapolis at his house; people thronged, and he gave four speeches that day. His campaign people said, "This is the thing to do. Let people come to you."

Over the next four or five months until the election, that's what happened. Harrison stayed home. He slept in his own bed. He would meet these visiting delegations from around the state, from around the country. Often, there would be special interest groups—the coal miners, the wheat farmers, cotton farmers, whatever—and Harrison would give them a short speech, mostly attuned to their own interests, but something that would resonate with people generally. He had his own stenographer take down what he said, and then he would go over it and make sure it was what he wanted people to read. They'd give it to the Associated Press, and the next morning it was in the newspapers all over the country. So, it was not a relaxing campaign, but at least it didn't have a lot of travel and the worries and headaches and fatigue of that.

[Harrison did not win the popular vote in 1888, but he won the Electoral College vote.] This is another thing we have to remember about the politics of that time: in most of the South, blacks were pretty much eliminated from voting after the collapse of Reconstruction. . . . What that meant was that the Democrats could rack up huge margins in the South. When you counted all the states together, President Cleveland did, in fact, have a plurality, ninety thousand votes more than Harrison in the national popular vote. In the states that Harrison won in the North and the West, the margins were closer, but he did win them.

[During Harrison's four years in office] . . . he had the opportunity to appoint four [justices to the Supreme Court]. The one that . . . we don't remember well, is the name that's on *Plessy v. Ferguson,* and that's Henry B. Brown. He was from Massachusetts. All of them were conservative jurists and pretty much were not in the business of widening the areas in which government could take action; [they were] more in favor of limiting government action of their time.

[Of Harrison's accomplishments,] the thing that we feel to this day may not have been most important at the time, . . . [is] the Sherman Antitrust Act. This is a period when the trusts are emerging. "Trust" is a generic term for these large consolidated businesses, Standard Oil and the others—cottonseed oil and the whiskey trust and the sugar trust. There's a growing sense in the country that they're dominating the economy more and more, and both parties in 1888 said, "We need to do something about these consolidations." . . . Harrison certainly believed that, and in his first State of the Union message, delivered on paper and not in person in those days, in December of 1889 said, "We ought to do something," and he was behind legislation. The spearhead, although he had other help, too, in framing the legislation, was John Sherman, a senator from Ohio.

Harrison was also very instrumental in pushing through the McKinley Tariff Act. Today, we hear a lot about tariffs, but it used to be that when we historians would talk about the tariff issues of the late nineteenth century, eyes would glaze over. . . . I think we have a greater appreciation why regulation of trade is so important, and Harrison was certainly in the forefront of pushing for a protective tariff. William McKinley . . . was [then] a representative from Ohio. . . . He was chair of the Ways and Means Committee in the first two years of Harrison's term. He was the real point man for developing this . . . very complicated piece of legislation.

The problem that lay behind this legislation, and that both parties were wrestling with at this time, was that the US government was running a surplus, . . . and it had grown quite large by the time you get to the 1880s. The feeling was [that] you shouldn't be taking all that money out of the economy. The Republicans, who agreed with that, also felt that we needed to have a tariff to protect industry from foreign competition, mainly from British manufacturers. [Their challenge was] how can you adjust the tariff so you're not collecting as much revenue and, therefore, reducing that surplus which people find damaging? They came up with a clever kind of way of doing this. One was to raise some rates so high that it cut off the imports. People said, "We're not going to pay that," and so that reduced revenue. They put sugar—a very important commodity in the revenue stream of the country—on the free list: don't charge any tariff at all on that, and that will reduce the revenue. . . . Blaine and Harrison worked out a scheme that said, "What can we give the farmers [whose crops are impacted by the tariffs]? Let's give them reciprocity." That is, let's give the president the power to negotiate agreements with other countries to open up their markets, especially for our farm products. So, it was a very complicated law, much more complicated than people tend to realize. It was industrial policy, writ large, if you will, . . . actively trying to frame legislation to further benefit the economy.

Harrison also was a very strong advocate of black rights, particularly voting rights. In the South, various mechanisms were developing, mostly intimidation, to prevent blacks from voting. Keep in mind that at that time, if blacks in the South were permitted to vote, they would have voted overwhelmingly Republican. So, there was a political motive here as well, but Harrison definitely believed that something should be done to protect their right to vote.

. . . Reconstruction had ended in 1877. Part of the reason nothing was done in the period since 1875 was that the Democrats usually had control of the House of Representatives, and with Grover Cleveland they also had the presidency—and they were against black voting rights in the South. When Harrison became president with a Republican House and a Republican Senate, they said, "We now are in a position to do something." The drafting of the legislation fell to a committee headed by Henry Cabot Lodge, a young representative from Massachusetts, scion of an illustrious family there. He put together . . . some legislation that [said] federal supervisors could be called in, in some situations in Southern states, to watch over elections.

Lodge essentially expanded that legislation in such a way that . . . it took the final certification of congressional elections out of the hands of state officials in the South, who were overwhelmingly Democratic and who were overwhelmingly against black voting. It would put it in the hands of federal supervisory canvassing boards and, if need be, federal judges. That's why the Democrats opposed it so vehemently and were willing to do just about anything to stop it. They were able eventually to prevent its passage, largely through the alliance of Southern Democrats with some Western groups.

[When Harrison was president, six states were added to the union—North Dakota, South Dakota, Montana, and Washington in 1889, and Idaho and Wyoming in 1890.] Harrison certainly endorsed the idea. Harrison, when he was in the Senate, had been on the Territories Committee. He had tried to get the Dakotas in earlier, but politics always played into the admission of states. The Dakota territories had a very small population, but nonetheless they would have a few electoral votes, and a few electoral votes could mean a lot in that era. But . . . they were largely Republican, and so, the Democratic House of Representatives wouldn't go along with the legislation to admit those states. . . . When Harrison was elected president in 1888, he did carry with him both houses of Congress; they were both Republican. This is the first time you had that since 1875, and one of the things they wanted to do was follow through admitting those states that the Democrats had been blocking. They did come into the Union—not that they voted reliably Republican. Some of them did give some votes to [the populist candidate James] Weaver in '92.

Caroline Harrison is interesting as first lady. . . . She did all the hostess duties, . . . [but] she was not a terribly comfortable person in the public role of first lady. She liked to paint china; she was something of an artist. They had lots of family living in the White House, and it was quite cramped, and so, Caroline Harrison conceived this idea that what we needed to do was to expand the White House. She worked with committees in Congress to develop an elaborate program that would have changed the White House into a quadrangle. As an architectural historian, I would say it was a monstrosity. It's one of the great things that it didn't happen, but [in the end] she did get some money to refurbish the White House.

Assisting Caroline in her social duties was a niece, her sister's daughter, a woman named Mary "Mame" Dimmick, who was a widow. . . . She spent a lot of time at the White House, and in fact, there was a short period where she lived there. . . . Harrison actually enjoyed her company quite a bit. He liked to take walks with her. She knew enough to not say much when he was ruminating during their walks, and she played billiards with him [and] became quite close with the president.

Caroline Harrison, in 1892, developed tuberculosis. . . . She was the person who, by the way, put together the origins of the White House china exhibits, and she had done a lot of rummaging around in the basement and the attic of the White House; some people said that she had gotten tuberculosis this way. . . . She went downhill through 1892, and she was moved to the Adirondacks for the cool fresh air. This was during the '92 campaign for re-election. In October, she said, "I'd like to go back to the White House," and she did die in the White House on October 25, 1892, a couple of weeks before the election.

. . . Harrison was devastated by the death of his wife. This is two weeks before the election, and then he lost the election, so it was a very, very bleak time in his life. After he left office, he went back to Indianapolis and tried to put things back together, and his daughter Mary moved with him and helped him refurbish the house and redecorate.

Then Harrison began to ask Mame to come out to visit because he enjoyed her company so well. She was living in New York at this time. They exchanged visits back and forth, '93, '94, '95, and then they did get married in '96. [He was sixty-two, and she was thirty-seven. The two Harrison children] opposed the second marriage vehemently. In fact, when it was apparent that it was coming on, Mary McKee, his daughter, left the Harrison house in Indianapolis and moved out her possessions. Russell, the son, whatever he had, he moved out, and they did not attend the wedding in New York. There was quite a strain. It was really tragic, in a sense. Harrison wrote to Mame, "I can't let them get in the way of my love for you."

Harrison went back to work in the law. He worked very, very hard. It was not usual at that time. He did not particularly take terrific care of himself, and the diets in those days were not particularly wholesome. He got pneumonia in the winter of 1901, . . . and he did die. His second wife was with him, and the children were not.

Benjamin Harrison is a man you can really learn a lot from. He was an intellectual. He was a good student of history. He knew his country very well. He was a good conversationalist in small groups that he knew well. He wasn't so good at meeting people cold. It's one of the things about his personality, and some people have pointed out it didn't work that well in politics. He didn't come across as a particularly warm person, and that hurt him sometimes with his interrelations with political leaders in his party. But once you got to know Harrison, you could benefit from his friendship and from his understanding of his country.

ZACHARY TAYLOR

12th President, 1849–1850

Overall Rank: 31

— ★ —

Total Score: 458

Historians have consistently placed Taylor just above the bottom ten presidents. His highest rank in 2017 was in public persuasion (27th), but he ranks in the bottom ten in pursued equal justice for all (34th), administrative skills (35th), and relations with Congress (35th).

Party: Whig
b. November 24, 1784, Orange County, Virginia
d. July 9, 1850, Washington, DC
First Lady: Margaret "Peggy" Smith Taylor
Age entering office: 64

Historian: Elbert B. Smith

Elbert Smith was a professor at several universities before joining the faculty at the University of Maryland. A former Fulbright Scholar of American History and International Relations, he later became president of the Fulbright Association. He joined C-SPAN on May 31, 1999, during the network's yearlong American Presidents *television series to discuss his book,* The Presidencies of Zachary Taylor and Millard Fillmore.

Zachary Taylor was born in Virginia, but he grew up in northern Kentucky near Louisville. His political opponents tried to make him out to be an ignorant, uneducated backwoods general who came from nowhere and didn't know anything. It's totally incorrect. I've always had trouble understanding why so many historians picked that up and got that myth going. Actually, he came from very distinguished parentage. He and President James Madison have the same great-grandfather, who was a very wealthy member of the Virginia elite. His mother came from a very prominent family, the Struthers family. Through her, he was descended from two leading people who came on the *Mayflower*. So, he had a very distinguished heritage.

His father was reasonably wealthy; he had a big plantation. Zachary Taylor had very little formal schooling. We can only speculate on this, but I have to believe that he probably had private tutors because he wrote very well and had a very strong vocabulary, and he had a very strong understanding of what was going on. He was criticized then and now because he never voted, but that's primarily because he was usually out on the wild frontier somewhere defending settlers against Indians, or in many cases, defending Indians against the settlers. That was [a] . . . reason I liked Taylor because he believed that the US government should honor its treaties. If the government said the Indians can keep this amount of land, he was ready to burn the houses of white settlers who got on it. So, he was never very popular with the white settlers. He believed that if the United States made a deal that we should stick by it, and he was furiously angry at his cousin President James Madison because Madison won't back him up on this. He wrote some very strong language to both Madison and the secretary of war on this.

Taylor had very little military training. What happened in the wars in those days, the lieutenants were usually selected from the educated, better-off families. So, he simply went into the army as a lieutenant, and by and large did get on-the-job training. From the beginning, he showed a tremendous ability to command. He went up the ladder; . . . he was almost always in command of something.

He had a strong voice. In battle, he was a great battlefield commander . . . and he was constantly exhorting his troops. He was a cheerleader-type general who exposed himself to great danger. It's a wonder he didn't get killed, or at least seriously wounded.

His wife [Margaret] went with him almost everywhere except when he was actually fighting battles. When he was commander of the different forts and bases out in the West, she was right there with him. And, if you can partly measure a man's enlightenment by his ambitions for his children, his daughters got the best education available; he sent them back East for a good education. His son spent a year in Paris in school, then spent a year in Edinburgh, and then came back and graduated from Yale. He didn't want his son to be a military man. He said, "Get a literary education," and he saw to it that his son got the best possible kind of literary education. His children adored him. Between commands, at one point where he had about six months off, he headed towards the North, and he took his family there. They went to New York. They went to Buffalo. They went to Boston. He traveled all over the North. He didn't . . . believe any of the Southern stereotypes about the North; he looked at the North for himself, and this is why he was ready to defend the North's right to oppose slavery.

One of the reasons why he didn't resent antislavery people was that he had no guilt feelings. Unlike Andrew Jackson who died broke and George Washington who died money broke [but land wealthy] and Thomas Jefferson who died money broke—all of these people who owned slaves and died broke—Taylor died a very rich man. He started with practically nothing. He inherited a very small plantation, which he sold, in Baltimore. Even though he spent all of his time in the army and got a very low salary, he kept accumulating plantations and slaves, and he kept making money. . . . So, Taylor never felt any guilt about slavery.

Perhaps one of his closest friends was [future Confederate president] Jefferson Davis. Taylor was serving out on the frontier, and Davis was a lieutenant under his command. Taylor's daughter fell in love with Jefferson Davis. Taylor did not like this. He tried to tell her, "Look at what a harsh, tough life your poor mother had to lead following me around out there on the frontier. You don't really want to marry an army officer." This made Davis so angry that at one point he threatened to challenge his commanding officer to a duel, but fortunately Davis's friends talked him out of this. . . . Taylor gave in; Davis ultimately left the army and married Taylor's daughter, but then [she] died shortly thereafter. Taylor and Davis were finally reconciled.

. . . In the War of 1812 and in the Indian wars, he performed very bravely and very skillfully, and he went up the [command] line. He was not popular on the frontier [because] he always spoke his mind. He thought the [1832] Black Hawk War, for example, was caused by the American government violating its pledges; but having spoken his mind, he obeyed his orders and fought them on the battlefield. He was against the Mexican War [1846–1848], and he had opposed the annexation of Texas; he didn't want to start this war, but once it started, he fought it and fought it extremely well. . . . He won battles. He treated the Mexicans with great respect. For example, after the [May 1846] Battle of Matamoros, he had his own doctors take care of the Mexican wounded and even, at one point, contributed several hundred dollars of his own money to help the people he had just defeated.

When he took Monterrey, Mexico, [in September 1846,] he incurred the wrath of President James K. Polk. Polk was, by this time, jealous of the possible presidential aspirations of Taylor. When he took Monterrey after several days of really fierce fighting and a lot of bloodshed, the Mexicans offered to surrender if Taylor would promise not to advance for a couple of months. General Taylor wasn't going anywhere for a couple of months anyhow because his army had just fought a terrible battle. So, he accepted this, and he always argued that he saved several hundreds of lives by so doing, and probably did. . . . He also put out proclamations, and did his best to enforce them, that there should never be any warfare against civilians and that, as much as possible, the daily life of people should go on just like it was. This was the way he handled himself with the Mexicans. . . . He was very honorable in this respect. He honored his opponents. He would win a battle, and he would make agreements, and he would keep the agreements.

When the Mexican War started, President Polk made Winfield Scott the commander in chief, but then Scott dilly-dallied around in Washington for three or four months getting ready, and Polk got impatient. He didn't exactly fire him, but he shifted the burden and made Taylor the commander in chief. When Taylor won these spectacular battles and people started talking about him, including Abraham Lincoln, . . . [as a potential candidate] for president, Polk then got jealous and reversed it. He made Scott the commanding general again and took most of Taylor's best troops and gave them to Scott for the invasion of Veracruz. He left Taylor with a bunch of raw recruits to withstand a much bigger army from Mexican general Santa Anna. Of course, Taylor won. Taylor got great satisfaction from the fact that he got elected president [in 1848] and Scott [who was also a contender for the Whig nomination that year] did not.

Taylor didn't find out he had been nominated for a month [after the Whig convention]. He often got what we today call fan letters, and they often came postage due. So, he simply sent a notice that he would no longer accept anything where postage was due. The official letter informing him that he had been nominated to run for president came postage due, and it got sent back to the dead letter office. [During the campaign,] he didn't make any speeches. He wrote a few public letters in which he expressed his principles, and one of those was that he would only veto bills that were unconstitutional.

He and [his running mate, former New York congressman] Millard Fillmore did not know each other before they were put on the same ticket. . . . The Whig Party had been waiting twenty years to get some of the federal jobs, the patronage. The Taylor administration had a terrible time passing out jobs; the cabinet was kept up night after night after night on this. It was a difficult situation. Patronage in New York was extremely important. Millard Fillmore was the leading Whig in western New York, from Buffalo. Senator William Seward was the leading Whig in eastern New York, from Albany. The most powerful newspaper in New York was run by Thurlow Weed, who dreamed of making his dear friend Seward president. There was a fierce rivalry between Fillmore and Seward. Seward ingratiated himself into Taylor's friendship and ended up getting the patronage and cut Fillmore loose. Fillmore's friends were very unhappy about this, and Fillmore was not happy about it either. It would have been difficult to be close to both Seward and Fillmore, and Seward got there first. So, Taylor and Fillmore's relationship was cool, but Fillmore always, in things he wrote and said, was very respectful. He admired Taylor. Fillmore was a good man in this respect, too. He did not build up resentments.

. . .William Henry Seward's . . . most noteworthy comment in the Senate was, "The Constitution recognizes slavery, but there's a higher law than the Constitution, God's law, which does not recognize slavery." Taylor loved to have Seward over [to the White House] for dinner and argue with him. Southerners were furious; . . . they believed that Seward was influencing him. Seward didn't influence him, but Taylor always remembered that he was a minority president. The other two candidates got 160,000 more votes than he did. He didn't have a majority in either house of Congress. He needed to unite North and South. So, I must say that Seward used Taylor, . . . but Taylor didn't use Seward, because he was trying to bring the two sections together behind some of the other policies that had nothing to do with slavery. And, as far as he was

This 1848 campaign banner labels Gen. Zachary Taylor as the "People's Candidate for President" and describes vice-presidential candidate Millard Fillmore simply as "Whig Candidate." *Courtesy Library of Congress*

concerned, the best way to do this was to keep the sections at peace, to deal fairly with each section, and to try to get them to look at the whole situation realistically, which a great many people did not.

Taylor's cabinet, particularly the secretary of the Treasury, William Meredith, got very close with him. In fact, if you read the letters that his cabinet wrote to their families, they had tremendous respect for him and affection for him. And while Taylor's enemies were saying that he was just the tool of his cabinet, they made it quite plain in their own writings that he was the boss, he was always the boss. Taylor made the decisions.

I'd done a book on the presidency of James Buchanan, so I knew this period very, very well, and I had more or less accepted a long-held view by a lot of historians. It's very dramatic and makes a good story, but it's not true at all, namely that Taylor opposed the Compromise of 1850 simply because he was jealous of Henry Clay and then he died just in time for Millard Fillmore to save the compromise. That's quite inaccurate. To begin with, Taylor did not oppose the Compromise of 1850.

As long as the compromise was in the form of separate bills dealing with each issue, Taylor was for it. But when they combined it into one bill, which could not possibly pass because there were too many people opposed to one or more parts of it—that he opposed. He considered, and I think quite correctly, that combining the compromise measures into one bill was a Southern ploy to get what they could get in return for a free California.

Taylor had sent a slaveholding Georgian out to California to help the Californians form a state. He believed that the best way to avoid a conflict between the North and South was to make California and New Mexico into states as soon as possible. Once they became states, there would be no arguments because state rights, after all, was a holy writ for the South. The argument always was whether or not they could have slavery while they were still territories because territories belong, in theory, to all the states. He instructed his envoy to California: don't take sides on the slavery issue.

The Southerners, by combining the measures into one, put in another part that Taylor was very strong on. When Texas won its independence from Mexico in 1836, it wrote a constitution, and it defined its boundaries to include large parts of four Mexican states that had never at any time been part of Texas. Texans always do things in a big way. This included two-thirds of present-day New Mexico. When the war started, and the United States invaded New Mexico, . . . the Mexican generals put out proclamations that they would fight to the death, and then they surrendered without firing a shot. . . . As part of the agreement by which Mexico surrendered, New Mexico was promised by the United States that it would maintain its integrity; it would be a territory and would eventually become a state.

Then, Texas starts claiming its rights in New Mexico. In 1848, the Texas legislature organized New Mexico and their six Texas counties and announced they were sending officials to take it over. . . . That was a very important sectional issue because as part of Mexico, both California and New Mexico had been free. . . . But if it belonged to Texas, it is slave because Texas is a slave state. Taylor was absolutely determined to enforce the promise that the US government had made. He sent extra troops to New Mexico to protect it. This is a very important issue; by tying the two together, the Southerners hoped . . . maybe they can make a swap. Taylor . . . knew if [the Compromise of 1850] ever passed, it would pass only with Southern support after they had amended [the bill] to give New Mexico to Texas—and he would not stand for this. Ultimately, Taylor had his way. After he died, they defeated the omnibus bill, and the compromise that passed was almost exactly what Taylor wanted: California came in as a free state; New Mexico kept its original boundaries and got a territorial constitution with no mention of slavery. . . . I've argued this [point] that I don't think he would have vetoed any part of [the compromise] bill at all.

If war had come, would Taylor have prosecuted it more vigorously than Abraham Lincoln? I think the answer is no. I do not believe that [President] Taylor would have ever drawn his sword, would have ever fought a war against the South. He owned 140 slaves. His son was later a Confederate general, and this is what he kept saying over and over: that he would defend the rights of the South, and he would also defend the rights of the North. His objective was to prevent a civil war in 1850. His approach to the South was, you can't get New Mexico, you can't get California, so why stir up the North about it? Why do you incur all of this enmity against yourself? Settle for what we've got. No one is threatening slavery at all in 1850. In fact, no one was threatening slavery where it existed in 1860. So, I don't think President Taylor would have ever gone to war against the South.

[On July 9, 1850, President Zachary Taylor died in office after a four-day bout with an intestinal disorder. Some conspiracy theorists suggested for years that he had been poisoned.] But if you're looking at Southerners wanting to get rid of Taylor, the vice president was Millard Fillmore, who was on record as an opponent of slavery. . . . Fillmore owned no slaves. He had no identification with the South whatsoever. Taylor did. Taylor said to Jefferson Davis, "So far as slavery is concerned, we, of the South, must throw ourselves on the Constitution and defend our rights to the last. And when arguments would no longer suffice, we will appeal to the sword, if necessary to do so. I will be the last to yield an inch." So, why would Southerners want to get rid of a man who talks that way in favor of one who has no connection [to the South]?

[In 1991, to try and get answers to the conspiracy theories,] they did exhume him, and tissue samples were examined by the Oak Ridge National Laboratory. They had a pretty good chance to examine him because his wife, Margaret, would not let them embalm him; she had trouble accepting the fact that he was dead. . . . People that I know in Kentucky thoroughly examined the remains and found no trace of poison whatsoever. I would not impugn either their ability or their integrity. So, I really do not think that he was assassinated or poisoned by anyone. His doctors did perform some horrendous medical steps, but they did that to everyone. They bled him; they blistered him; they dosed him up to here with calomel, which is part mercury. But these decisions really were raised by committee of doctors rather than just one. Taylor had several doctors watching over him.

I came to like Zachary Taylor very much. He was very straightforward. He was totally honest. He knew where he wanted to go. He had a better understanding of the [contemporary political] situation than most of his contemporaries. He never hesitated to stand up for what he thought was right. The fact is that he was a slaveholder, but he made it plain in letters to his former son-in-law Jefferson Davis that while he would fight for the South if necessary, he would also defend the right of Northerners to criticize slavery. He said, in effect, they have just as much right to criticize it as we do to defend it. And he [promised] he would be a president not of one section—that the North, East, South, and West would all have equal rights, and he would defend the rights of the entire nation, that he would be a president of the whole nation.

The last few lines of Zachary Taylor's inaugural address sum up his attitude towards what his job was. He said, "For more than half a century during which kingdoms and empires have fallen, this Union has stood unshaken. Upon its preservation must depend our own happiness and that of countless generations to come. Whatever dangers may threaten it, I shall stand by it and maintain it in its integrity to the full extent of the obligations imposed and the powers conferred upon me by the Constitution."

RUTHERFORD B. HAYES

19th President, 1877–1881

Overall Rank: 32

— ★ —

Total Score: 458

Although initially ranked 26th by historians in 2000, Hayes's rank had fallen six places by 2017. He scores well in economic management (25th), where he places two spots above his predecessor, U. S. Grant. However, his rankings in other categories range from 29th (administrative skills and public persuasion) to 33rd (international relations).

Party: Republican
b. October 4, 1822, Delaware, Ohio
d. January 17, 1893, Fremont, Ohio
First Lady: Lucy Ware Webb Hayes
Age entering office: 54

Historian: **Ari Hoogenboom**

Ari Hoogenboom was a scholar of the Gilded Age and a history professor, teaching for thirty years at Brooklyn College. He published two books on Rutherford B. Hayes, including Rutherford B. Hayes: Warrior and President, *which he discussed on April 28, 1995, on* Booknotes.

The Gilded Age presidents really are anonymous as far as most Americans are concerned. . . . Most Americans really don't know Rutherford Hayes from James Garfield or from Chester Arthur, and the questions frequently are, "Well, did he have the long beard?" And the answer is, "Yes, he did; he had a very full beard." But, most people really don't have a crisp, clear idea of Hayes unless it's in connection with the end of Reconstruction and in connection with the disputed election.

. . . The election of 1876 dragged on into 1877, and Hayes was not officially declared winner until a couple of days before his inauguration in March of 1877. This is the famous disputed election of 1876–1877. He did not have a majority of the votes that were cast. He was elected

The highly disputed election of 1876 was eventually settled by a congressionally created commission in favor of Ohioan Rutherford B. Hayes, shown here in a photo from the late 1800s. *Courtesy Library of Congress*

by one electoral vote, and that was only after a long dispute in Congress over whether the electoral votes of South Carolina, Florida, and Louisiana should be counted for either Hayes or his rival, Samuel J. Tilden of New York.

Hayes was from Ohio, lived in Cincinnati for several years, was born in Delaware, Ohio, but when he was elected president of the United States, he was living in the town of Fremont, Ohio. He was the solicitor of the city of Cincinnati, which means he was Cincinnati's lawyer, but it was an elected office. And then he went into the Civil War and became a congressman after the Civil War. He was elected twice to Congress, but he didn't serve two full terms, and then he became governor of Ohio and was elected governor three times. . . . All of his gubernatorial campaigns were extremely close.

His third term as governor was interrupted by the presidency. As governor, he was instrumental in the passage of the Fifteenth Amendment. He pushed that through the legislature of Ohio—that's the black voting rights amendment. Also, The Ohio State University—he was instrumental in establishing that.

Hayes first went [to the town of Fremont, Ohio,] because his Uncle Sardis, who was a successful businessman, had settled there, and Hayes went there, rather than to Columbus, after he graduated. [Hayes attended] Kenyon College, and he read law briefly at Columbus, and then he went to Harvard Law School. Hayes, after graduating from Harvard Law, had a choice of going to Columbus, where his mother and sister were, who would try to tell him how to live his life, or go to Fremont, where his uncle was, who would be a little more easygoing and could steer some business to him. Hayes went to Fremont and began practicing law.

. . . Ultimately, he went to Cincinnati to practice. He found Fremont was just simply too small a town for him to really make a name for himself in the law. Lucy Webb was in college there. They did get married fairly soon after he arrived in Cincinnati. She is the first first lady to have a college degree; all first ladies up to that point did not graduate from college. They had eight [children] altogether, and five survived into adulthood. They were very child-centered, the Hayeses, and they were very indulgent. When the Hayeses were young and Birch and Webb were little fellows, they would make an awful racket in beating drums, and the Hayeses seemed to be perfectly happy with all the commotion and turmoil. In fact, Hayes didn't particularly want his mother around at that time because he felt that she couldn't quite take all of the racket. . . . Hayes tried to tell her, "Take it easy on the children. They'll be OK. Don't have such high standards with them." He and Lucy were very easygoing with their kids.

Hayes was very much opposed to slavery and defended runaway slaves. Early in the Civil War, he was convinced that the war was a crusade to end slavery, and he felt that a good half of his life was spent in a crusade against slavery. [That passion came from] Lucy, to a large extent. In her family there were abolitionist sentiments; Hayes had always been antislavery, but never strong enough to really do much about it. After he married Lucy, he began defending runaway slaves.

Hayes had volunteered and served exactly four years in the Civil War. He was a colonel in the war, and he regarded himself as one of the good colonels. He did become a general ultimately, but as he said, "I never fought a battle with the title of general" because his promotion to general came after he fought his last battle and was wounded his fifth time. No president of the United States has seen as much frontline action as Hayes did. And no president was wounded as many times. One was very serious. He was shot in his left arm, and the bone was broken—fortunately, not shattered. If it was shattered, they would have hacked it off because they didn't try to set any bones that were shattered.

[He served in the] 23rd Ohio Regiment. He typified in many ways the value of these civilian officers because Hayes, as a colonel, was able to mediate between the West Point–trained higher officers and the volunteer soldiers and officers in the army. Hayes understood both sides. When the 23rd didn't get rifled muskets—they started out with smooth bore muskets, very inaccurate weapons—they didn't get them when they were promised, and the men were virtually mutinying. The West Point commander over Hayes didn't quite understand the men, but Hayes spoke to the men, calmed them down, told them the guns would be coming, to be patient, and to remember the goal that they had: to preserve the Union. He also got back to the immediate commander and calmed him down. That was rather typical of a lot of these volunteer officers in the Civil War army. . . . [Future president William] McKinley was in Hayes's outfit. McKinley volunteered as a private in that 23rd Ohio Volunteer Regiment. That one regiment gave the United States two presidents.

The year 1876 was the centennial year. Ulysses S. Grant had been president for eight years, two terms. His second term was really ending quite disastrously in a political sense: scandals broke, the Republican Party was in disarray, a great depression had begun following the Panic of 1873, the country was plunged into a depression. The Republican Party was in deep trouble because of accusations of corruption in the Grant administration, in deep trouble because of the economic collapse; in trouble also because many people were beginning to question the wisdom of continued military occupation in the South. . . .

Hayes was a Republican and was, as you would say in nineteenth-century terms, the "available man" in 1876. He had impeccable radical credentials; at the same time, as the governor of Ohio, he was a moderate. He was in favor of civil service reform. He was certainly an anti-corruptionist. He had a tremendous war record, and he came from Ohio, which was a state that the Republicans had to carry if they were going to win the election. . . .

[Hayes's opponent, Samuel Tilden, was from] New York. He was a railroad attorney, primarily, in private life, but he was governor of New York and a Democrat, and a very skilled politician, very skilled at organizing the Democratic Party.

[When the votes were counted in November 1876,] the most popular votes that were cast had Tilden by a long shot. There were probably 250,000 more votes. It's not a huge electorate because women weren't voting. [But there was] no question at all about Tilden winning the popular vote.

[In the Electoral College,] Tilden was certain of one vote less than he needed for election. Hayes was certain of considerably fewer votes. But if you added the votes of Florida, South Carolina, and Louisiana to Hayes's total, he would win the election by one vote. All Tilden had to do was pick up one electoral vote from any one of those three states—South Carolina, Florida, or Louisiana. Both the Republicans and the Democrats claimed to have carried those three states.

. . . Hayes thought he . . . had lost for several days after the election, and he would not have contested it at all. The decision to contest the election was made at the Republican National Headquarters in New York City—a rather bizarre affair with a man named Daniel Sickles making the key decision to send out telegrams. The Republican National chairman, Zach Chandler, had actually gone to bed [on election night] with a bottle of whiskey to console himself because of the loss of the election.

First, the parties sent representatives down to those states to try to convince the . . . official returning boards [vote-counting entities] in those states that [their party had actually won the state's tally]—Republicans that Republicans had won; Democrats that Democrats had won. In round one, the Republicans win. They controlled the returning boards in those [contested] states, and they threw out enough Democratic votes to give the Republicans the majorities. They had a perfect legal right to do this because in areas where there was intimidation of voters, these returning boards were empowered to throw out the entire vote of those precincts, those districts, those counties, even. And so, it was really a struggle between Democratic intimidation, on one hand, on Election Day, and Republican fraud [after the election], on the other hand, the throwing out of Democratic votes. And the question is, "Did the Republicans commit more fraud than the Democrats had intimidated voters?"

To solve this, the returns went back to Washington, where the Democrats had control of the House of Representatives. They were not about to stand idly by while Hayes was counted into the presidency by the president of the Senate, who counts the electoral votes in the presence of both houses of Congress. Only extreme supporters of Hayes said that the president of the Senate could count the votes, make the decision, and Congress would just watch. All Democrats and many, many Republicans thought that some kind of commission had to be created to give the winner of that election some kind of legitimacy, and not just simply being counted in an arbitrary manner.

[The commission they created was made up of fifteen members] evenly divided except for one Supreme Court justice who originally was supposed to be an Independent, David Davis from Illinois. Davis was elected senator from Illinois at the very moment of the passage of the Electoral Commission Act. . . . [The commission had five members of the House, five members of the Senate, and five members of the Supreme Court.] Three-two, three-two, and then two-two plus one, but the one ultimately turned out to be a Republican. It was really a monumental miscalculation on the part of Democrats in Illinois. Tilden's nephew was involved in influencing the Illinois state legislature to elect David Davis. They assumed that David Davis would be beholden to the Democratic Party for making him senator and that he would stay on the commission and that he would vote for Tilden as a result. David Davis was so thankful to get off the hook because, in effect, he would be individually deciding the election. He was perfectly happy to disqualify himself from the commission, which he did. And then, a Republican was selected.

The electors met in states around December first. The Congress began trying to count these votes, debating over this, throughout December. The commission bill passes, and in January the count begins. And the count goes smoothly, quickly, until they hit Florida, one of the disputed states; then both houses of Congress adjourned, and the Electoral Count Commission met. Then they heard arguments and finally settled the Florida case on the basis that they would not go behind the official returns, and they would not hear evidence about fraud in Florida or, for that matter, intimidation in Florida. They would simply accept the official returns as certified by the canvassing boards in those states.

[Future president James Garfield was appointed a member of the commission.] It's curious. He was one of the members for the House, and yet . . . was a so-called visiting statesman in the South, counseling the Republicans in Louisiana on throwing out Democratic votes. And then he was appointed to the commission and sat in judgment of the work that he did in Louisiana. That only points up the political nature of this whole compromise.

[During the time that the Election Commission was meeting, Hayes didn't say much] simply because he wasn't really expected to. He made it clear that his program—and he outlined this in his acceptance letter, which is his statement of what he thought the campaign should be based on—that he was willing to give home rule to the South, as long as the South would adhere to the Fourteenth and Fifteenth Amendments. He didn't really stray from that. There was not as much bargaining as people make out that there was. People negotiated, and people made agreements, but those agreements didn't have a great deal to do with the outcome of the Senate filibuster when the election was finally decided. [When it was all over, Rutherford B. Hayes was sworn in as president on March 4, 1877.]

[Reconstruction began] toward the end of the Civil War and lasted, technically, until 1877. Hayes is castigated for ending it, but that's kind of an exaggeration. The end of Reconstruction in 1877 meant the removal of the federal troops that were supporting Republican governments at the capitals of Louisiana, in New Orleans, and Columbia, South Carolina. These Republican governments supported by federal troops had control of a few square blocks, and that's about it, around those capitals. The rest of those states had already been taken over by rival Democratic white supremacy governments.

. . . Hayes was faced with the problem of what to do about these Republican regimes that were still existing by a thin thread in both of those states. What it really boiled down to is that Hayes did not really have a decision whether to withdraw those troops. His decision was, when would he withdraw those troops and what could he possibly extract from Southerners in exchange for withdrawing those troops?

I say that because he was elected with the poorest of mandates. The whole country was suffering from a great depression, and people were more concerned about getting a job rather than politics in the South. Northerners were no longer interested in maintaining a military presence in the South, in what its enemies called a "bayonet rule." The Democrats had control of the House of Representatives, and the Democrats had already refused to appropriate money to the US Army. The army was very small and very weak—about twenty-five thousand men, most of them out in the West and along the Mexican border as well.

It simply was an impossible situation for Hayes, . . . to sustain Reconstruction. Ulysses S. Grant had already ordered the withdrawal of troops from Louisiana at the end of the controversy over the disputed election. Hayes, in all probability, countermanded that order because it never really was carried out. What Hayes did was, he extracted from South Carolina Democrats and from Louisiana Democrats solemn promises that the civil rights of black and white Republicans would be carefully preserved, and also that equal educational opportunities [be made available], which Hayes felt were terribly important. This was pledged by [Governor Wade] Hampton's government in South Carolina and [Governor Francis] Nicholls's government in Louisiana—Democratic governments—and they reneged on their promises, certainly within a year.

Hayes traveled more than any [president] up to that date. In fact, they called him "Rutherford the Rover." He went on long trips after business was pretty much wrapped up in Washington—late summer, early fall. He wouldn't campaign for individual candidates, but he would preach the particular doctrines and policies that he was very much in favor of and would give these rather short speeches—sound bites—that would elaborate on one issue and wouldn't tire the audience, but would hammer home his point of view. He was the first president to travel to California to put across the policies that he was in favor of. In other words, . . . he anticipated the presidential politics of the twentieth century. In many ways he was the first modern president. He fought battles with Congress over the power of appointments, and he won. He defeated the notion of senatorial courtesy. He had a tremendous battle with the Democrats over vetoes—the Democrats were attaching riders to . . . needed appropriations bills to force Hayes to accept legislation because he needed money to run the government. Hayes vetoed them and went through a long battle. The legislation was to repeal enforcement acts to the Fourteenth and Fifteenth Amendments—the voting rights amendment and civil rights amendments. Hayes defeated the Democrats so that [he], at the end of his presidency, was making appointments that he wanted to make, and the veto, which he used very freely, enabled him to prevent the Democrats from pushing through legislation that Hayes did not want.

The Hayeses always had a lot of guests in the White House. They were very Western, with open hospitality, and Lucy always had a bevy of young women [visiting] from Ohio. Lucy Hayes was a very jolly, cheerful person and incredibly vivacious.

There was some alcohol served at the first state dinner for some visiting royalty from Russia, but Hayes decided not to have any more in the White House. This pleased his wife, who people now refer to as "Lemonade Lucy," which is quite unfair; nobody referred to her as "Lemonade Lucy" at the time. Hayes made that decision, not her. He didn't like to see congressmen in their cups, primarily, but he also made that decision for sound political reasons. Hayes was opposed to prohibition, but he was in favor of temperance. He himself was a temperate drinker until he went into the White House, then he became a total abstainer. He thought he would set a good example. He thought that that's the way the temperance movement should go, and he thought a good example would be set by him and Lucy not serving wine in the White House. By the way, there was a shrewd political argument by Hayes behind this whole issue. He figured that if he made this kind of public stand, that Republicans who were temperance-minded would not join the Prohibition Party, . . . [which] was an important third party. And, in fact, that party was quite weak by the election of 1880, at the end of the Hayes administration. . . . Hayes predicted this. He said, "Don't give up on this idea"—it was a shrewd political move because those who drank didn't really care whether Hayes had liquor in the White House or not, and those who didn't drink were very happy about it.

Rutherford B. Hayes was president for only four years [1877–1881]. He resolved to run only for one term, which I think was a mistake. He said that up front, and he consistently adhered to it. He's a curious combination of an ambitious man, and yet, a man that kept his ambitions in check.

[After his term as president,] he was in Ohio, back home. He was annoyed at [his successor, James] Garfield, because Garfield was backtracking on civil service reform, in which Hayes had scored some noticeable advances by instituting reform in the New York post office and custom house. It was the success of civil service reform in those two offices under Hayes's auspices that enabled the reformers to say, "The system works." And when the Pendleton Civil Service Reform Act came up in 1883, they could argue that it was not a figment of theoreticians' imaginations, but was a workable, practical system.

Hayes became involved in social causes after he was president. He was very much involved in movements to educate poor Southerners, mostly black children. . . . He was head of the Slater Fund, and money was used from the fund to help educate blacks in the South. He was also ardently in favor of a piece of legislation that never passed called the Blair Bill, which would have given federal funds to poor school districts throughout the nation, primarily in the South and in the West. He wanted that bill passed very badly in order to provide educational equality, which would provide, he thought, equality of economic opportunity—he tied the two together.

Lucy predeceased him. She died in 1889. He missed her dreadfully. He was very much devoted to her, and, as he said, "The life has just gone out of the house," and pretty much out of his life. But, on the other hand, then he'd get interested in these educational projects. He was always interested in young people and found himself refreshed.

He died in January of '93, twelve years [after the White House, at age] seventy-one—a heart attack. He hadn't been in bed [sick] since his very serious wound in the Civil War until he had this heart attack.

Today, I'd suspect Hayes would be a liberal Democrat. He was really a precursor of the Progressive movement. He was opposed to what he called plutocracy, a maldistribution of wealth. He was very much in favor of traditional republican—that's with a small R—values of political equality, equality of economic opportunities, and that's why he stressed education so much. . . . He favored confiscatory inheritance taxes. He just simply didn't think that large estates should be passed on to children. . . . Remember, it was the Republican Party that ended slavery and the Republican Party that backed Reconstruction. Republicans have become a good deal more conservative in the twentieth century.

GEORGE W. BUSH

43rd President, 2001–2009

Overall Rank: 33

— ★ —

Total Score: 456

George W. Bush entered the C-SPAN survey in 2009 as his second term ended. Historians initially rated him 36th overall, which improved to 33rd in 2017. His ranks improved in public persuasion (from 36th to 25th) and pursued equal justice for all (24th to 19th). These improvements were offset by continued low ratings in economic management (36th) and international relations (41st).

Party: Republican
b. July 6, 1946, New Haven, Connecticut
First Lady: Laura Welch Bush
Age entering office: 54

Historian: **James Mann**

Author James Mann spent thirty years as a journalist, including over twenty years at the Los Angeles Times *in Washington and overseas. Mann currently writes books as an author-in-residence at the Johns Hopkins University School of Advanced International Studies. He joined* Q & A *on September 4, 2018, to discuss his book,* George W. Bush, *a title in The American Presidents biography book series.*

George W. Bush was a guy who was the son of a president [George H. W. Bush] who had trouble dealing with that fact for the first forty years-plus of his life. And then [he] got his own personal life together enough to be a quite successful and shrewd politician to be elected governor of Texas and then become president of the United States. The first thing he would be known for at the time of his presidency, now and forever more, will certainly be the fact that he was president at the time of the September 11 attacks and chose to wage a war in Iraq that turned out to be a disaster.

George followed in his father's footsteps, and I say that quite literally, because he was forced, almost, to go to prep school at Andover. And, he also went to Yale. . . . He once said many years later there were differences between him and his father, starting with the fact that he went to Sam Houston Elementary School and his father went to Greenwich Country Day School in Connecticut. He grew up in Texas, where his father had not, and he identified with and took comfort in the idea, the image of himself, as a Texas good old boy, and he became very good at playing that role.

. . . George was the go-to guy for fun. That's at Andover, and then that very much continues at Yale, where he is the head of a fraternity, Delta Kappa Epsilon. He is the guy who organizes the toga parties. The first time George W. Bush's name ever appears in the *New York Times* was to defend his fraternity from something; it may have been its hazing practices. He was the spokesman for the old fraternity life at a time, and this is the context, when Yale itself was changing. There were certainly fraternities and parties there, and there were certainly lots of other students at Yale who were the sons of former Yale people. [However,] Yale was gradually becoming, in the early '60s, a meritocracy like many other schools. People were admitted on the basis of their test scores. It was becoming a more intense place. The faculty were more professional than the old genteel faculty in the past, and George didn't like it. He developed such an antipathy to Yale that he went three years into his presidency before he was even willing to come back to the campus. . . . He eventually, during his presidency, made a kind of peace with Yale, but it took a long time.

When Bush left Yale, he lived a single's life down in Texas. His parents left Texas in the early '70s. They went to the United Nations, and then they went to China, . . . and Bush went into the Texas [Air] National Guard. He, like the sons of other Texas politicians, went into a special Texas National Guard unit that was really for politicians' sons and members of the Dallas Cowboys. This is during the Vietnam War. It meant that he really didn't have to fight. There have been disputes going back decades about how much pull was used. I found in researching the book that no one has ever found his father, George H. W. Bush, intervening or making calls to get him into the Guard, but friends of his father and Texas political leaders did so.

George W. [received an MBA from Harvard in 1975, entered the oil business, and] married Laura Welch in the late '70s. Friends arranged to get them together at a barbecue. They were in Midland, and she was a local librarian. It's interesting to me that even his choice of a spouse reflected this kind of anti-elite [sensibility]. He chose someone from Texas, not someone from the social set of his parents. If you read Laura Bush's memoir closely, she says quite gently, "It took me about ten years to be comfortable with Barbara Bush." Barbara had an acid tongue, and Laura is quite the reverse.

George W. [first] ran for office . . . in 1978 for a seat in Congress, and he lost to a guy named Kent Hance. It's interesting, in light of what we later know and think of George W. Bush, that in that campaign his opponent, Hance, attacked him for being this East Coast preppy guy from out of town who couldn't possibly know Texas well. Hance portrayed George W. Bush almost like his father. Bush began to develop responses to this [line of attack]. One thing many people agree on is that George Bush has a good sense of humor. Hance at one point said, "We've got a candidate who was born in New Haven, Connecticut. He's an outsider." Bush said, "I was born in New Haven, Connecticut, because I wanted to be with my mother that day."

[Two words describe the change in George W. Bush's life: drinking and religion. . . . They] come together in the mid-1980s, in the period of 1985 and 1986. In 1986, he celebrates his fortieth birthday with friends. He's off in Colorado at the Broadmoor Hotel. He stays up late drinking with his friends, and he wakes up with a terrible hangover. He's had a drinking problem for a good while. He sometimes describes it that way, sometimes not. He's also been arrested for driving under the influence, so this has been a chronic problem. He wakes up the day after and says, "That's it, I'm not going to drink." And he doesn't. He gives up drinking.

The second thing that happens is that he becomes an evangelical Christian, and during this same period begins to turn to religion regularly. In my view, there's an interesting political component to this, which is that both of these things happened [in George W.'s life] within a couple of years after his father decides to run for president.

. . . In April of 1985, his father calls the entire Bush family together in a meeting at Camp David, and he brings out Lee Atwater, a now famous political consultant, scoundrel, and great political tactician. Lee Atwater addresses everybody and warns people, "Your father is going to be running for president; you've got to be careful. Anything any member of the family does could come back to hurt him." . . . This is only a year before George W. decides to give up drinking altogether. And so, that's the background on drinking. He's had these warnings. He doesn't want to get into trouble. As far as religion, I'm not going to say if someone's religion has a political component in its origins. But I will say that as soon as George W. Bush becomes an evangelical Christian, he becomes the liaison for his father's presidential campaign with the evangelical Christians. It's a role he plays throughout the 1988 campaign and up to and through the '92 campaign.

[When his father ran for president in 1988,] George W. Bush, at that point, was out of the oil business. He was relatively free. When he expressed some mistrust to Atwater about how his father's campaign would be run, Atwater said, "If you don't trust me, why don't one of you come to Washington and work alongside me, watch me every day." George W. Bush did. He went and worked alongside Lee Atwater for over a year. He actually moved to Washington and helped. His first role in the campaign, as he called it, was loyalty enforcer. With all these politicians and political figures running around, he was the guy watching out for his father's interests. . . .

I became convinced that George W. had his own [political] ambitions at that time. . . . Everybody says that he developed his ambitions after his father lost [in 1992]. No, I think he held his ambitions in check while his father was president. In fact, Barbara Bush at one point discouraged George W. from running for governor of Texas in 1990 because she thought it wasn't a good idea while George Bush Sr. was president. Anything that one of them did could reflect on the other.

[He made his first bid for governor of Texas in 1994.] The best line on that came from his father, George H. W. Bush. He wasn't always full of great quips, but he said that for George W. Bush to get elected president after he was governor of Texas was "like a six-inch putt." It was harder for him to first be elected governor. There was a very popular, now well-remembered Democratic governor, Ann Richards. She was the one who said of George H. W. Bush that he was "born with a silver [foot] in his mouth." Richards was quite popular, but George W. ran hard against her. He had a very good political adviser, Karl Rove, and together they worked out the strategy to beat her. One of the tactics that they had, which people saw again when he was president, was incredible message discipline. This was one of the characteristics of Bush as a politician. He would never have particularly penetrating or very long answers, but he would develop a handful of one sentence, two sentences, three sentences and deliver them over and over. Years later, Ann Richards said in frustration, and she meant this as a political compliment, "If you asked George Bush the time of day during that campaign, he would say, 'We must teach our children to read.'" He would give the same response to everything.

[George Bush won a landslide second term as Texas governor in 1998. So, how did George Bush get elected president?] . . . He learned from his father's loss in 1992. He developed what he felt were strategies to win where his father lost, and, too, he noticed his father's errors. He needed to bring together within the Republican Party three different constituencies. One of them is the traditional Republican conservative constituency, the old country club constituencies, the people who wanted their taxes cut. Lesson number two was, don't raise taxes; that's what his father did. He also needed to develop much better support from evangelical Christians than his father had, and he needed support from the hawks, or the neoconservatives, an important faction in the party.

People forget now, but the evangelicals were not always a solid constituency in the Republican Party. In fact, they had supported Democratic candidates for many decades. Richard Nixon made some inroads getting some evangelical support. They ran back to Jimmy Carter, a Southern Baptist Democrat. Reagan developed much more support from evangelicals, and then his father, George H. W., lost that support. Bush worked both for his father and then for himself to bring evangelicals into the Republican Party. That was one part of his political tasks that he succeeded in.

As for the hawks of foreign policy, the neoconservatives, it's hard for people to remember now, but in the 1992 campaign, they tended to support Bill Clinton. They were so unhappy with George W.'s father. This had to do with the fact that [George H. W.] Bush supported Gorbachev, that he supported the breakup of the Soviet Union, didn't support an independent Ukraine for a long time. . . . Bush Jr. goes to work and develops their support as well. He pulls together all the wings of the Republican Party, and then he has no trouble at all winning the Republican nomination. And when running against Al Gore, he runs against Bill Clinton and the Lewinsky scandal. George W. Bush says, "I'm going to bring honor and dignity to the White House."

. . . Bush gets attacked politically during the campaign for not knowing enough about foreign policy. Here is [his Democratic opponent] Al Gore who's been the vice president, and he was a foreign policy specialist before that. Bush had been governor of Texas, but still, the foreign policy he's done, as he would joke, was his experience with Mexico, and that's about it. He gets attacked for not knowing much and says, . . . "I've got the finest group of foreign policy advisers around." And by that, he's talking about this group who are basically people who had served with his father.

Secondly, during that 2000 campaign, he chooses Dick Cheney as his vice president. Karl Rove doesn't want Cheney. Karl Rove listed Cheney's disadvantages: he comes from a tiny state [Wyoming] that's already Republican; he's not going to bring votes the way, say, Lyndon Johnson would carry Texas for John Kennedy. And he's too conservative. Bush wants Cheney mostly because of his experience. He's choosing his father's advisers, and that goes all the way up to, and including, his own vice president. And once he takes office, he really does rely on them. He has the bridging figure of Condoleezza Rice, who was a friend of his, to be national security adviser.

After all these great political stratagems, it was not enough to win a majority of the country; it was enough only to produce a deadlock in the Electoral College and a long Supreme Court battle. So, it wasn't as though it was some overwhelming victory; it wasn't at all. I thought [the outcome was] a travesty. In my career I put in about eight years covering the Supreme Court, and one thing I thought I had learned was that the conservatives on the court of that era—people like Chief Justice William Rehnquist—were in favor of what they would have called federalism, or states' rights. I thought that when the Florida Supreme Court, based on the Florida Constitution, awarded the state of Florida to Al Gore, that based on its own principles, the Supreme Court would simply allow that to stand and say, we're not going to interfere. That's not what the court did; they developed their own theory. It never made any sense to me.

. . . Most people thought that having not won a majority of the popular vote and winning such a narrow victory in the Electoral College, that President Bush would start out very carefully, that he wouldn't take any bold initiatives and that most of what he did would be directed at winning over Democratic support. In fact, Bush started his presidency very boldly, asked for a tax cut in his first year, and succeeded in winning just enough Democratic support to get it passed. It was quite a radical move; . . . he'd actually been, by most accounts in Texas, a centrist, moderate governor, but he ran as a very strong conservative with bold initiatives [and] focused that first year mostly on tax cuts.

[On September 11, 2001, eight months into his administration, the country experiences the Al Qaeda terrorist attacks.] The legacy is about as profound as any president has ever faced. It's the first time the US homeland has been attacked since the War of 1812. It changes the country automatically, immediately, into one obsessed, in big ways and small, with protecting its security. To take the most obvious example, the way that 325 million Americans go through airports today started on September 12 and has never gone back to what it was on September 10. It affected American foreign policy. We can say that it had a profound effect on Bush's foreign policy team and played a role, certainly, in the decision two years later to invade Iraq.

. . . The September 11 attacks had caught the administration in its [early stages]. They're eight months into the administration; they haven't paid enough attention to the warnings they had gotten about Al Qaeda. This administration thought of themselves as—I'm talking about the foreign policy team, people like Cheney and [Defense Secretary Donald] Rumsfeld—they are the professionals. They've served in office before; they know how to run things. . . . They are also focused on old issues involving [nation] states. So, their issues of foreign policy before September 11 are getting out of an arms control treaty with the Soviet Union, maybe dealing with North Korea, they have a moment with China. They are dealing with the things that they have been familiar with in past administrations, country to country, the United States versus another country. September 11 hits, and here's the quote that meant the most to me from a memoir by [Bush's second defense secretary,] Bob Gates, who says that these guys were "traumatized" by September 11. They hadn't imagined this kind of problem coming from a nonstate actor, from a terrorist group that wasn't a state. And they spent much of the rest of their time [in office] trying to make sure that this could never happen again. Between the lines in Gates's description is a lot of guilt that they had for allowing September 11 to happen. . . .

The decision to go into Afghanistan followed immediately after September 11. The thinking of the administration within hours after September 11 was that we want to punish the people who did this—they knew right at the start this was Al Qaeda—and any countries that assisted them. In this case, since Al Qaeda had been based in Afghanistan, that meant Afghanistan. They gave Afghanistan a warning fairly quickly to turn over Osama bin Laden, and then proceeded to attack within weeks.

Bush gathers his war team together at Camp David the weekend after the September 11 attacks, and there are one or two proposals that they go beyond invading Afghanistan. In one particular case, there is a recommendation to attack Iraq at that very first weekend meeting. But that is generally put aside. I choose those words carefully. It's put aside, but it's not rejected; for the time being they decided to focus on Afghanistan. That takes a few months for them to bring in CIA teams and then eventually for the military to dislodge the Taliban from Kabul.

Now, how did we invade Iraq? That is a much longer story. So, there has been this recommendation at the very first meeting to attack Iraq. It came from [Deputy Secretary of Defense] Paul Wolfowitz, . . . and he does not get support from the others there. If you can envision this meeting, it's the members of the cabinet—it's Cheney, Rumsfeld, [Secretary of State] Colin Powell, Condoleezza Rice. Wolfowitz is at the back bench. . . . During those next two months, while the war in Afghanistan is being fought, a couple of noteworthy things happen. One is the anthrax scare. So, in what turns out to be something entirely unrelated to Al Qaeda as far as we know, people in Washington and on Capitol Hill, and so on, are opening their mail and finding this powder, which may or may not be anthrax. That further scares the top levels of the administration. . . .

... So, after September 11, they are not going to allow [terror strikes] to happen again, and they get the anthrax scare. They develop slowly the concern that Al Qaeda could somehow get weapons of mass destruction. Yes, they're concerned about a nuclear weapon, but they are concerned about chemical weapons, and they are particularly concerned about biological weapons, that somehow Al Qaeda could get those. So, that's the second thing that happens.

And then there's the political level: Karl Rove, Bush's political adviser, plays a part in some of this. They develop this language about the "war on terror," although no one can quite define what that is. And they develop the language that Afghanistan is merely phase one of [that] war.

By December of 2001, they've defeated Al Qaeda, or they've dislodged it from Kabul, and the question starts to arise, OK, what's phase two? . . . There are small [Al Qaeda] units in countries of lesser importance. Meanwhile, there's Iraq; it's still out there. And, the first sign you get of the administration thinking about going to war in Iraq is in Bush's State of the Union address at the beginning of 2002, when he talks about the "axis of evil." The axis of evil is Iraq, Iran, and North Korea.

George Bush made a huge mistake [in deciding to prosecute the Iraq War.] To the extent that Bush has admitted mistakes, he admits tactical mistakes that were central to the war without ever saying that the entire war in Iraq was a mistake. He's admitted that he made a mistake in the "mission accomplished" landing on an aircraft carrier. He has admitted, and others have admitted, that the way they handled the postwar was a mistake—by allowing the disbanding of the Iraqi army and their expulsion of the Ba'ath Party members from government positions. He's never said the war in Iraq itself was a mistake. . . .

Cheney, Powell, and Rumsfeld, who Cheney had brought in as defense secretary, . . . are supposed to know how all this works. And Bush relies on them. He relies on them before September 11. Then, he has this problem in the run-up to the war in Iraq that his advisers don't actually agree with each other. . . .

All the way through that first term, President Bush tends to support what Cheney wants. You get to the end of his first term, and the war is not going well. The war turns out to be a bigger and bigger problem, and his advisers are bickering with each other. He decides at the beginning of his second term that he is going to change the foreign policy team, and the first thing he is going to do is replace Powell. To Powell's surprise— he thought that Rumsfeld would also be replaced, but Bush doesn't replace Rumsfeld. So, you are left with Cheney and Rumsfeld, and Rice becomes secretary of state. Rice is closer to Bush than anyone else in the administration, including Cheney, and that changes the dynamic. This is followed two years later by replacing Rumsfeld [as Defense secretary]. Meanwhile, Bush is developing more confidence in his own judgments. It takes a good four years, but he sees how this works. And he sees how things can go wrong. And he gets to the point where he doesn't rely on Cheney, that's for sure. He is then the most important person on foreign policy in his own administration; he wasn't at the beginning.

[George Bush's legacy will also include two other major events: his administration's response to Hurricane Katrina, a category five storm that hit several Gulf states in late August 2005, and the 2008 financial crisis.] There are several interesting things about the financial crisis for Bush and his team. Several things that Bush did helped play into it, like his tax cuts. At the Fed, interest rates were kept so low that people kept buying more and more houses, and prices just kept going up and up. You get a classic bubble, [yet Federal Reserve chairman] Alan Greenspan insisted that it was not a bubble.

It hits in September of 2008 with the collapse of Lehman Brothers. When it hits, Bush decides that he needs to intervene and needs to intervene vigorously. . . . Bush refuses to go along with the party's libertarian right wing. He develops a massive program, TARP, Troubled Asset Relief Program, to try and buy up these assets that are collapsing as a result of the financial crisis. The right wing in Congress opposes him, and it was a very, very difficult fight to get congressional approval of this TARP program. He and Cheney, himself a fairly conservative Republican, are strongly in favor of this, and they succeed mostly with Democratic support.

The crisis happens in the middle of the 2008 campaign. . . . [Republican nominee Senator John] McCain had said, "I'm going to stop campaigning. We need to have a major Washington meeting to decide what to do about it." Bush allows this meeting. [Democratic nominee Senator Barack] Obama is also there. You get all the congressional leaders of

George W. Bush requested Yale classmate Robert Anderson to paint this portrait of him at Camp David. President Bush began painting as a hobby after leaving office. *Courtesy National Portrait Gallery, Smithsonian Institute; gift of several donors*

both parties and John McCain from Bush's own party. Cheney writes that Obama was more impressive than McCain, and some of that came through to the public . . . and it was a major help to Obama. It hurt John McCain [who lost the 2008 election to Barack Obama].

[George Bush left office in 2009. Sometime later, he admitted to being bored with his post-presidential life.] I think for a good while Bill Clinton was bored, too, because you're spending twenty-four-hour days [dealing with issues as president], whether you're sleeping, or playing golf, or not; it's always with you—until you're out of office. And then, there is a tremendous sense of decompression.

Bush began to paint [as a hobby], but without telling anybody outside his family. The only reason we know about this is that someone hacked into the emails of family members and found these paintings being sent back and forth. It interests me that he took up painting but really didn't want the public to know about it at first. [By the time I published my book, he'd also made 140 speeches, picking up $15 million for himself, personally. He also sold two million books of his own, *Decision Points*.] George W. and Bill Clinton have both had a lot of time [after leaving office] to do this. I can remember right after Reagan left office [in 2009] that he went to Japan to give a speech, and he was probably paid $2 million, and that was a big deal. . . . Just the idea of a former president speaking for money was unusual at that point.

It's true for any president that it takes many decades for historians to judge, and that may be true with parts of what Bush did. But it's not too soon to judge some aspects of his legacy. It's not too soon to judge the war in Iraq. Why? Because it didn't accomplish what he thought it was going to accomplish before he started the war. It cost four thousand-plus American lives. It cost $2 trillion. I write in my book, and I don't think this judgment will change, that it was one of the biggest strategic blunders in American history. So, those kinds of judgments can be made. There is the truism that people's judgments of presidents do change as time goes on, but I don't think that one is going to change much.

. . . AND ALL THE REST

MARTIN VAN BUREN
8th President, 1837–1841

Overall Rank: 34

— ★ —

Total Score: 450

In the 2017 survey, historians ranked Van Buren among the bottom ten presidents for the first time. Van Buren's declining overall rating has been fueled by drops in economic management (from 34th in 2000 to 40th in 2017) and vision/setting an agenda (from 27th to 33rd). Historians ranked Van Buren 30th in pursued equal justice for all—eight spots above the man he succeeded, Andrew Jackson.

Party: Democrat
b. December 5, 1782, Kinderhook, New York
d. July 24, 1862, Kinderhook, New York
First Lady: Angelica Singleton Van Buren (daughter-in-law)
Age entering office: 54

Historian: **Michael Douglas Henderson**

Historian Michael Henderson was the superintendent of the Martin Van Buren National Historic Site in Kinderhook, New York, when he joined C-SPAN on May 3, 1999, as part of the network's yearlong American Presidents *television series, to discuss President Van Buren.*

In the election of 1836, Martin Van Buren is the anointed, the chosen son [of Andrew Jackson], and the economy is still reasonably booming. There's still lots of turmoil, but Van Buren wins with a reasonable majority in 1836. Several weeks into his administration, the United States suffers its first major economic recession, or depression, depending I suppose on where it fell on you.

Martin Van Buren was about five feet six, so he was certainly one of the shortest of our presidents. He was a delicate-featured young man with red hair, and he balded quite early in his life. He got to be relatively rotund, about 170 pounds, so he was sort of plump and pleasant, and he was supposed to have the most intriguing, sparkling blue eyes, which were . . . quite captivating. He was a native Dutch speaker, although he certainly spoke English quite fluently. The Dutch language survived in the Hudson Valley a couple hundred years after the British conquest. So, he may have had a Hudson Valley accent to his English speaking, but he was also not a great orator. He didn't have a wonderful rolling voice that would gain him popularity in public speaking; he had a high voice.

Van Buren's wife Hannah Hoes died in 1819 after twelve years of marriage. One child died in infancy, Winfield Scott Van Buren, but he had five kids who grew to maturity, and they were a very close family.

Van Buren didn't own slaves in his house [in Kinderhook, New York]. After he had inherited slaves from his father's estate, he was rid of them quite quickly. But wage labor [which he employed] was also very hard, although certainly not the evil that slavery is. . . . It's important to talk about slavery in the North. We often go to Southern plantations, where we talk about slavery, or we talk about slavery in the South, or in Washington. It's important to talk about slavery [in the North, too]. Kinderhook was a large slaveholding community. When Martin Van Buren was a young man, Kinderhook was one of the largest slave-owning communities in New York State outside of New York City.

. . . Van Buren started out his career as a lawyer. It was something that his mother was interested in. He was . . . schooled formally to the age of fourteen. He then was apprenticed in a lawyer's shop and read for the law. Although he passed the bar by the time he was twenty-one years old, he always, in his career, felt a little uncomfortable about his [lack of] formal education. His interest in politics was pretty early on, and I don't know that it was necessarily a search for power as much as it was a search for power to do good and to continue this experiment in American democracy.

[He helped develop] the Albany Regency, . . . the first formal political machine in the country. New York State was split into four districts at that time, and what Van Buren did while he was in the state assembly and state senate was ensure that the party would be in Albany for votes, a critical thing when you're trying to keep an agenda, just making sure people show up. Also [he insisted] that there was a political orthodoxy. . . . For the first time, a party actually defined what they were; they had a platform, and they actually showed up for votes. So, that's the core of what the Albany Regency was. What it allowed him to do as a politician was to say, "I can deliver New York State." It gave him a lot of clout and a lot of power to bargain with.

[Martin Van Buren was Andrew Jackson's second-term vice president in 1832.] Andrew Jackson's first vice president was John C. Calhoun. Calhoun was certainly a man of many grudges and many strong feelings. Throughout the beginning of the Jackson administration, there were many disagreements between the cabinet members over the Margaret [Peggy] Eaton [scandal], and there were many opportunities to be downwardly mobile for Mr. Calhoun. Calhoun was in a position where he thought he could try to oust Martin Van Buren, who was secretary of state, from any further political career. After the resignation of the entire cabinet [over the Peggy Eaton affair], Jackson appoints Van Buren to be the ambassador to Great Britain. . . . Van Buren goes off to England and then is highly embarrassed by the fact that the Senate does not confirm his nomination.

His appointment was rejected by the Senate by one vote and very consciously—the one vote was the tie-breaking vote of the president of the Senate, who is the seated vice president, John C. Calhoun. Calhoun thought that this was his opportunity to finally get rid of Van Buren. Calhoun was much more extreme in his states' rights views. There had been lots of bad blood between Calhoun and Van Buren, and Calhoun thought that this was the way to just kill Van Buren once and for all. Van Buren had already traveled to Europe. He was already in England, the Minister Plenipotentiary to the Court of Saint James, . . . the most important ambassadorial position. Andrew Jackson doesn't take this well. He had nominated Martin Van Buren for this position, and he is quite upset, to say the least, about this vote in the Senate. And, in effect, what happens is Calhoun shoots his own career in the foot.

The Eaton affair is interesting [and it essentially set Martin Van Buren up to succeed Andrew Jackson as president in 1836]. Van Buren referred to it sometimes as "Eaton fever" or "Eaton malaria." John Eaton, who was one of Jackson's cabinet members, married a young woman who was from Washington, Margaret Eaton. She was very much [disdained] by other members of the Jackson cabinet. One of the reasons that Van Buren and Jackson engineered the whole resignation of the first cabinet during the first Jackson administration was to try to clear out Calhoun and clear this mess up.

Peggy Eaton . . . was a young woman who . . . was very much acting in a "masculine" fashion and was relating to the masculine world. As such, she was very much resented and detested by other cabinet members' wives, particularly Calhoun's wife. They implied that she was a slut. Peggy Eaton's problem was that she was in some ways liberated in an area and put in a social elevation where she couldn't [fit in]. The Eaton affair really backfired, again, on Calhoun. Calhoun keeps getting stuck in these terrible positions. Calhoun's wife detested Peggy Eaton, and the other cabinet members wouldn't . . . be seen with her. Van Buren is a bachelor, so it's very easy for Van Buren to be polite and cordial; it's his nature to begin with, and he sees no problem with entertaining both Mr. and Mrs. Eaton. Andrew Jackson is still bitter and hurt over his wife Rachel's death and feeling that Rachel's death was brought on prematurely by people who maligned her because of her not-quite divorce and then marriage to Jackson. . . . Jackson feels that Mrs. Eaton is being hard done to, and there is Van Buren taking up Mrs. Eaton's cause. Van Buren is in a position of looking like a gentleman and supporting this woman who is being much maligned by these bickering cabinet wives. Van Buren, known as the "Little Magician," manages to pull this one off well. It's a fascinating story about political intrigue.

[Martin Van Buren was fifty-four years old when he went into the White House in 1837.] His popularity went continually down. Needless to say, he had the problem of the United States having its first major recession weeks after he was in office. He said, and probably rightly so, it was due to the expansion of credit. But he also . . . really believed that it was not the role of the federal government to save individuals. That was the role of the states, or the communities, or the church, or somebody else. The Constitution didn't give that role to the federal government. [But] people were hurting, and they wanted the president to do something.

Van Buren was a strict constructionist in his interpretation of the Constitution. He very strongly felt the way the Jeffersonians did, that if it wasn't in the Constitution, these were powers that were either given to the federal government, denied to the federal government, or reserved for the states. And, spending federal moneys on improvements that didn't benefit the entire nation was something that shouldn't be

An economic recession and the fractious slavery debate plagued the presidency of Martin Van Buren, who is depicted in this c. 1840–1862 photo. *Courtesy Library of Congress*

done. You would see that occasionally federal moneys were spent on the improvement of harbors because a harbor is a point of entry for the entire country.

Van Buren used the White House for his charming little dinner parties, much along the lines of his political nature, on a one-on-one basis. There was an interesting episode in which he, again, lost some favor politically. First, he renovated the White House, which, at best, hadn't been done since the first Jackson administration. So, there was a request for several thousands of dollars to renovate the White House that got him in a little trouble with the Congress. And then Angelica Singleton Van Buren decided for her opening at the White House—her debut as the daughter-in-law of the president [and official hostess]—that they would do a stylized tableau in Grecian form. Guests entered the White House in their Grecian tableau, and it didn't go over well. It smacked of imperialism and of "King Martin." They . . . didn't do that again.

[On the slavery issue] Martin Van Buren runs a very difficult course throughout his entire career. He was born into a family that owned slaves;

he inherited two slaves from his father. He is putting together a political party, the Democrats, of which the primary concern is the maintenance of the Union, to keep the Union together. [They believed] that this very new experiment in American democracy had to be preserved. The founding fathers weren't able to deal with the issues of slavery; they even wrote it into the Constitution. So, by the time you get to Van Buren's generation, this second generation of Americans, it's a very testy issue. The country is becoming polarized, . . . and Van Buren's position shifts throughout his career.

Van Buren is a supporter of the Gag Rule [employed in the US House from 1835 to 1844]. He is the chief magistrate of a country that is perpetuating one of the greatest evils known to mankind, chattel slavery. But he is also trying to push the envelope against the tide of slavery. He's certainly always against the extension of slavery into free territories. You see in his losing the Democratic nomination in 1844 and again in 1848, when he's running on the Free Soil Liberty Party, that Van Buren's position on slavery is actually moving to the left, which is unusual in older politicians to become more liberal.

. . . [The *Amistad* case happened during his administration. In 1839,] Africans who are "cargo" on a Spanish ship mutiny. The ship is captured. It comes into Long Island, then the slaves are brought to Connecticut. The Van Buren administration realizes that this is going to be a lose-lose situation all the way around, and their initial effort is to keep it out of the courts. This is a very complicated issue. . . . So, the administration's initial response is to say that this is an issue of international affairs. This is cargo because Africans who are slaves are "cargo"—as difficult as that is to talk about—perhaps belonging to the Spanish crown. Spain, at this time, is a superpower and not a country to be ignored.

Later, once the issue of how the Africans are going to be handled comes into the courts, it becomes a different issue, and the Van Buren administration then says it's a judicial one; the executive branch is not going to go into it. It's a very difficult situation for him, politically, because this is opening up wounds which are just under the surface. We had just been through the nullification crisis with South Carolina. We already have Southern Democrats who are on the edge of deserting. And in hindsight, it's very easy to look back and say, "Well, the Civil War was a long way away." At the time, nobody quite knows what's going to happen. John Quincy Adams, who's also a fascinating character, the old man, [the seventy-four-year-old former president who has been elected to the House of Representatives, represents the *Amistad* slaves before the Supreme Court in 1840–1841]. He absolutely detests Martin Van Buren [because] Van Buren is supporting the Gag Rule, which means you can't mention the word "slavery," the S word, in the Congress, which is absolutely the most undemocratic and un-American thing you can imagine. The reason people are supporting the Gag Rule is they don't know what's going to happen. So, the *Amistad* event, which goes over the course of several years and several trials, is a very interesting blip in what's going to become this polarization in American politics. John Quincy Adams takes full advantage of this. In his famous 1841 [*Amistad* closing argument] speech, . . . Adams is talking about the evils of the Van Buren administration and Martin Van Buren. Adams is taking this opportunity to politicize this issue.

Indian removal [first] became a big issue during the Jackson administration. Jackson was wholeheartedly for the removal of Indians. . . . [Martin Van Buren, however,] grew up in the East. The Indians were already gone from the Northeast, so it was very easy to have a slightly softer position on Native Americans. From 1830, when the legislation is passed for Indian removal, through the actual removal, which is during the Van Buren administration, 1838, it's another one of those nasty things that's being done. The Indian removal and the Trail of Tears weren't intended to be as harsh as they were, but it was harsh. These people were basically exterminated. They were walked to death. It was a terrible thing. Van Buren speaks about Indian removal in many of his speeches in a kind of Jeffersonian way, that if we remove the Indians, it will help them be preserved. That's a lame argument. . . .

By 1840, the Whig opposition basically decided that they wanted to oust Van Buren at any price, and that the Whigs needed to be back in power. As the electorate is expanding through the Jacksonian period and more free white males are enfranchised to vote, the nature of politics changes, and the nature of campaigning changes. So, by 1840, you have the first real modern campaign with mudslinging, with campaign songs, slogans like "keep the ball rolling." There were all kinds of modern pieces of a political campaign that come by 1840. Martin Van Buren did not campaign in 1840; he stayed in the White House and did business. He felt that it was somehow unbecoming to campaign, much as some of the founding fathers thought that it was in bad taste to go out and pound the pavement for a job, that anybody who wanted it that much probably shouldn't get it. In many respects, he lost the election of 1840 rather than William Henry Harrison winning it. . . .

[Even though he had lost the election in 1840, Van Buren] . . . went into the 1844 Democratic committee meeting assuming that he had the nomination tied up. He was the heir apparent. He was the leader of the Democratic Party, but he got caught up in a question about the annexation of Texas. There were a lot of issues associated with Texas: the extension of slavery into a new territory, but there were also debts associated with Texas. Van Buren was concerned that if we annexed Texas too quickly, we might go to war with Mexico. He wrote a very long position paper, almost like a state paper, the Hammett letter, where he talks about how, legally, the US federal government is to treat territories. This letter got out before the convention. It was published, and although Van Buren was seen in the convention as not supporting the annexation of Texas, it was not exactly true. He was not supporting the immediate annexation of Texas.

He loses the floor fight in the Democratic convention, and James K. Polk, a much more hot-headed Westerner who is very supportive of the annexation of Texas, wins. Andrew Jackson supports Polk at this point as well. Van Buren feels a little hard done to because he really expected the blessings of his party. This is a party he worked years to create and to hold together and a party that he believed would hold the Union together. He really felt that this annexation of Texas was a hot-headed thing and might roll us into a war with Mexico, and indeed it did. He felt very cheated by this nomination, although he didn't give up the ship. Van Buren comes back again in 1848, but on a different tack.

By 1848, more has gone on: the Southern wing of the Democratic Party has really become beholden to slave power. The very delicate balance of power in the Democratic Party between the Northerners and the urban Irish immigrant populations and the Southern slaveholders is beginning to crumble. Each side is becoming more polarized, and the Southern slaveholders are becoming so strong within the Democratic Party that they make the question of the extension of slavery in the new territories a litmus test. . . . The Democratic Party accepts a plank for the annexation of Texas. When you create those types of political litmus tests, you polarize the issue and the party. So, by 1848, Van Buren has moved on. He's never willing to renege his party membership; it means too much to him personally. He spent his whole life creating the Democratic Party. But he is willing to put his name in the ring for something that his son, John Van Buren, is very interested in, which is this coalition of the Free Soil Party and the Liberty Party. They are the barn burners, the wing of the Democratic Party so interested in getting the slaveholders out of the party that they're willing to burn the barn down to get rid of the rats.

In Van Buren's case, he gives it a lot of thought. His son John Van Buren, who becomes attorney general of the state of New York, is really on the antislavery side. Van Buren has moved that way, and he's willing to accept the nomination in 1848 because he thinks that it's time to draw the line in the sand. He's been a compromiser his entire life. The issue becomes, how far can you compromise? If you're going to dance with the devil, how long are you going to do it? And in that respect, Van Buren, in 1848, that's his last chance to make a statement about his vision of keeping the Union together. [He received just 10 percent of the vote.]

[After the White House, Van Buren returned to Lindenwald, his home in Kinderhook.] Lindenwald was run as a working farm. While he was running for president up through the 1840s, he always had a farm manager. After that, he ran the farm himself. He was very interested in agriculture, and he had very political motivations for purchasing Lindenwald. This is an urban guy, always well dressed. He came from a rural background, but for most of his political career, he's a mover and a shaker in Washington. He realizes during his presidency that he's espousing all of these Jeffersonian agrarian values, but he hasn't engaged in them himself. So he buys the farm and . . . fixes it up and spends the next twenty-one years of his life here. In 1850, in the census, he lists his occupation as "farmer."

When he came back to Lindenwald, his son Abraham and his wife Angelica Singleton . . . came there. . . . He was very much a family man: like George H. W. Bush, his family referred to him as "Poppy." He had grandchildren he adored. He loved spending time with his

grandchildren, and all of the sons and their spouses had favorite bedrooms that were theirs to come and stay in.

Henry Clay was a guest; Thomas Hart Benton was a guest; many of
the political leaders of the day came to his house. . . . Van Buren, even
though he's no longer president, is still a driving force in American politics, and you see Van Buren as a major character in political cartoons
well into the 1850s. Long after he's left the presidency, he is an elder
statesman who people come to consult with.

He lived to be seventy-nine and a half years old. He died in July
[1862].

Martin Van Buren was chief magistrate at the time that the United
States was perpetuating the worst crime of humanity on a large group of
the population. I'm a black American myself; I feel this awful [legacy],
but I also feel that it's important to have this conversation [about slav-
ery]. Martin Van Buren, like all other humans, do the best that they can
at the time and make compromises. . . . The compromises Van Buren
made should not have been made. . . . He did many good things, but he
also did many terrible things, certainly Indian removal on the Trail of
Tears, the supporting of the Gag Rule. These were all calculated political measures [on his part] to keep the Union together.

If you look at Martin Van Buren's political career and focus the whole
thing through Union maintenance and how critically important that
they felt that this experiment in democracy was, it gives you a different
angle to look at. In no way do I want to say that Martin Van Buren was
a great hero or ignore the evils that were carried out under his administration or during the period. But if you look at Washington through
Lincoln, those sixteen presidents all are the chief magistrates charged
with upholding the laws of the nation, a nation which has slavery written
into the Constitution; it was constitutionally legitimized. . . .

Van Buren's leadership style was very much behind-the-scenes. He
was a coalition builder. He was a compromiser, like his quote, "Mutual
forbearance and reciprocal concessions." We all have to give a little bit
in a democracy that's based on a majority. In order to get a majority, a
lot of people have to give up a little bit. His legacy is that it's not through
wars, not through coups, but through parties and through discussions
that we can have this experiment in democracy continue.

CHESTER A. ARTHUR

21st President, 1881–1885

Overall Rank: 35

— ★ —

Total Score: 446

With thirty points separating his total score from Hoover's, the next lowest president in the rankings, Arthur can be said to have escaped being ranked among the worst presidents. In 2017, his category rankings ranged from 27th in pursued equal justice for all to 37th in public persuasion.

Party: Republican
b. October 5, 1829, Fairfield, Vermont
d. November 18, 1886, New York City, New York
First Lady: Mary Arthur McElroy (sister)
Age entering office: 51

Historian: **Scott S. Greenberger**

Scott Greenberger is the executive editor of Stateline *and former staff writer at the* Boston Globe *and* Austin American-Statesman. *He joined C-SPAN's* Q & A *on September 7, 2017, to discuss his book,* The Unexpected President: The Life and Times of Chester A. Arthur.

Every president has an interesting story. Chester Arthur may be, if he's not the most obscure president, he's certainly one of them. . . . The only thing that most people remember about him is his very distinctive facial hair, his muttonchop sideburns. But there are a few reasons why it's an interesting period to focus on. First, it's the Gilded Age—the era beginning with Reconstruction and leading up to Teddy Roosevelt and the Progressives. It's a period that a lot of people give short shrift to in American history in schools. . . . But this is a period where a lot of what we think of as the modern world, modern America, really starts to take shape. This is the era where Americans, for the first time, heard the term "millionaire," and the country really was transformed from a largely agrarian country to an industrial country with very large

Chester Arthur, referred to as an "accidental president," is better known for his mutton chops than for his significant civil service reform. He is seen in this 1881 oil on canvas by Ole Peter Hansen Balling. *Courtesy National Portrait Gallery, Smithsonian Institution; gift of Mrs. Harry Newton Blue*

corporations that were beginning to exert their power politically as well as economically.

Chester Arthur is . . . really a story of redemption. His father was a very rigid abolitionist preacher, and he was a guy who grew up in that very religious environment. Shortly after college, he was a teacher, became a lawyer, moved to New York, and was involved in a very important case that results in the desegregation of New York City streetcars. So, he was on this moral path. Then he also was a quartermaster in the Union Army during the Civil War, in New York City. It was a very important job with a lot of opportunities for lining his own pockets, which he did not do, but as many others did.

After the war, he became involved in the machine politics of that era, and he became very close to the New York Republican boss, a very flamboyant and interesting character named Roscoe Conkling. I would have to say that Chester Arthur is my favorite character [of the period], and Roscoe Conkling would be a very close second.

There was no income tax [in the 1870s]. Something like 70 percent of the [federal] revenues came through the [New York] Custom House. New York, then as now, was a major port, and importers paid duties on the goods that came in. There was a system, the moiety system, which was designed as an incentive for the officials to find malfeasance. If somebody was found to be shirking their responsibilities in terms of paying duties, then they had to pay a fine and the officers in the Custom House, including Chester Arthur, got a cut of that. So, it was a high-paying job, and Arthur also benefited from this moiety system.

Ulysses Grant was the president who appointed, at Conkling's behest, Arthur to the Custom House, so Grant really got Arthur started on his formal political career. During his second term while Grant person-ally wasn't tied to any corrupt activity, certainly, many members of his administration, up to the cabinet level, were. Grant was tainted by that second term, and that really cleared the way for Rutherford B. Hayes, who was a reformer. People wanted something different. They were tired of Grantism, as it was called.

Rutherford B. Hayes [who was Grant's successor] also was a Civil War hero. He also pledged to serve only one term, and the idea was that he was going to reform the civil service, which was the gigantic issue of the time. By agreeing to only serve one term, it would be easier for him to do that. Civil service reform was a huge issue because at the time the program was largely, if not entirely, populated by people who were pol-itical loyalists. There was no thought given to who might actually be able to do the job, who had the proper education or qualifications, et cetera. It really was a way for the party in power to perpetuate its power. They also required people who had gotten their jobs because of their party to contribute to the party. They had what were called assessments, which were basically mandatory contributions. . . . In fact, there was a street near the Custom House called Hanover Street, and the workers of the Custom House used to call it "Handover Street." That's where they had to go and sign over a portion of their checks to the Republican Party.

Civil service reform was important [in this era]. And in the sweep of history, it's also important because in later years, the Progressives and Teddy Roosevelt—as did later presidents—wanted to imbue the federal government with more powers and a more active role in everything from the safety of food and drugs to the national parks. All of this needed to be . . . overseen by people who knew what they were doing. So, civil service reform laid the groundwork for the more expansive role that the federal government played later on.

James Garfield [who became the Republican presidential candidate in 1880] was a fascinating figure. He had also served in the Civil War, was a self-made, Lincolnesque figure in that sense. [He] grew up poor but was very academically inclined—ended up graduating from Williams and rose pretty quickly through the ranks. While he was still serving in the Civil War, he was elected to Congress. Once he was in Congress, . . . he managed to straddle both sides on a lot of issues, which, of course, can be a formula for success. . . . He was very much a surprise choice for president in 1880, and there was this very dramatic convention in which he was the classic dark horse candidate. When the convention was deadlocked, and couldn't decide on a candidate, they chose Garfield as somebody who apparently would appeal to everybody.

The Republicans really needed [New York senator] Roscoe Conkling's help to win that election. New York at that time was the most populous state in the Union and had the most electoral votes.

. . . The whole reason that Chester Arthur ended up as vice president was an effort by the Republicans to placate Conkling and to make sure that New York would throw its support behind Garfield. So, Arthur was an accidental vice president, and he didn't have any relationship at all with Garfield. It was a time in history, frankly, when vice presidents didn't have close relationships with the presidents.

[James A. Garfield was elected president in November 1880 and was shot on July 2, 1881, less than four months into his term.] When Garfield was shot, Chester Arthur was up in Albany trying to help Conkling win back his Senate seat. Garfield was trying to institute reforms, fighting back against machine politicians like Conkling. He insulted Conkling by putting someone in the New York Custom House without consulting him. Conkling and the other senator from New York resigned in protest thinking that, certainly, the New York legislature would very quickly restore him to his seat . . . and that he would have made his point. But as it turned out, the legislature had enough of Conkling's antics, so getting his seat back was a tougher job than he had anticipated. Chester Arthur went to Albany to help Conkling and this was in direct opposition to what Garfield was trying to do.

It was widely noted that Arthur, even though he was Garfield's vice president, was in New York doing Conkling's bidding, and therefore opposing Garfield, at the time when Garfield was shot. In fact, the tensions between these two factions, Garfield's Reform wing of the Republican Party and what was known as the Stalwarts wing of the party, home to Conkling and Arthur, was so great that when Garfield was shot, there were many people who suspected that Arthur and Conkling had something to do with it.

The "Stalwarts" name referred to the fact that when Conkling and his wing of the party wanted President Grant to serve a third term, which would have been unprecedented, the Republicans who stood together at the [1880] convention and stuck with Grant vote after vote became known as the Stalwarts.

[Charles Guiteau was President Garfield's assassin.] He had a very troubled childhood and young adulthood, and probably was mentally ill. In fact, his life story bears a lot of resemblance to some of the other characters throughout American history who ended up doing the same kinds of things that he did. It's pretty fair to say that modern medicine would have judged him to be mentally ill. However, the direct instigation of his act was the fact that he thought that he was owed an office for the work he had done for the Garfield-Arthur campaign in 1880. When he was rejected, he decided that the problem was Garfield and that if he would remove Garfield, then the split in the Republican Party would be mended and the Republic would be saved. When the shooting took place, immediately a police officer on the scene seized Guiteau, who said, "I'm a Stalwart . . . and Arthur will be president." That statement only added to the suspicion that somehow Arthur and the Stalwarts had something to do with the assassination.

Chester Arthur served as president from 1881, when Garfield was shot and eventually died, until the end of [what would have been Garfield's full] term in 1885.

Julia Sand was a woman in her early thirties who was bedridden, or at least confined to her home, in New York City. She didn't know Chester

Arthur; Arthur didn't know her. During that long summer where Garfield was lingering on what would end up being his deathbed, Sand started writing letters to Arthur urging him to return to his better self, the person he had been as a younger man. Even though she had never met him, she really seemed to have a sense of where he was psychologically. He'd already been very deeply affected by the shooting of Garfield and the very intense criticism that he faced in the wake of that shooting and the suspicions that, somehow, he'd been involved in this assassination attempt. At this point, he began to think about his political career and the kind of politician he had been, and if he were to become president, what sort of responsibilities would be on his shoulders and what he had to do to meet those responsibilities.

Sand wrote twenty-three letters to Arthur, which are now archived at the Library of Congress. He saved the letters, which I think is interesting because before his death he ordered almost all his papers to be burned. He was ashamed of what he had done before his time in the White House. But he made very explicit instructions that those letters from Julia Sand were to be saved.

Sand called herself "a little dwarf" because in a royal court, the dwarf, or the court jester, traditionally was the one person who could speak truth to the king. She viewed herself as the one person who would speak plainly to Chester Arthur. Even though she didn't know him, even though she wasn't in his court or wasn't an official adviser, she spoke her mind and was very bold, considering he was the vice president and then president of the United States. She didn't pull any punches.

I quoted long passages of her letters in my book because they are so compelling and so interesting. Not only did she give him political advice, but she advised him on his health and teased him about his weight. He had gained a little weight, and she jokes that riding is very good exercise, but be conscious of the fact that it's not really fair to the horse if he has to carry too much weight. So, the letters are very entertaining. [Here is a passage from her first letter to him: "The hours of Garfield's life are numbered. Before this meets your eye, you may be president. The people are bowed in grief but do you realize it—not so much because he is dying, as because you are his successor. What president ever entered office under circumstances so sad?"]

It is just amazing because she really seems to have, even though she has never met him, some insight into his psychology at this point. We have other reports of how distraught he was during that summer, and these charges [regarding the assassination] in the newspapers . . . were deeply wounding to him. I think he recognized that he really wasn't qualified for the job. He had ended up on the ticket by accident. He was surprised to be there. He never imagined that he would be president of the United States, and then all of a sudden, he's on the threshold of the office. There are reports that right after he got the news that Garfield had finally succumbed to his wounds, his doorkeeper says to a reporter who comes to the door, "He can't come right now; he's in his office sobbing on the desk."

[Sand also wrote in that first letter: "Great emergencies awaken generous traits which have lain dormant half a life. If there is a spark of true nobility in you, now is the occasion to let it shine. Faith in your better nature forces me to write to you, but not to beg you to resign. Do what is more difficult and brave. Reform."]

Reforming the civil service is what she's talking about. This is the major issue at the top of the national agenda. It has divided the Republican Party. The civil service reformers are holding meetings in all the major American cities. They write songs about this cause. The amount of importance and emotion attached to this issue is really hard for us today to imagine.

She's asking him to return to the sort of person he once was—the idealistic lawyer who once helped desegregate the New York City street cars. As Arthur takes office and starts to do some of the things that she wanted him to do, and specifically to push civil service reform, she sends him subsequent letters encouraging him to carry on. She is saying, "Look, people say this is just window dressing, that you're just acting; you don't mean it. I know better. You are surprising people but I am not surprised. I know who you really are." These are really extraordinary letters.

During this period when she was writing to him, as she became more and more comfortable with him, she kept inviting him to visit her, noting that they both were New Yorkers. She said she lived close to Central Park, and "you could easily go for a ride in the park and just stop by and see me." Arthur finally did come by and pay her a surprise visit. . . . He was president, and he just showed up unannounced, which is pretty extraordinary. It's that visit, combined with the fact that many of the specific bits of political advice that she gave him in her letters that he ended up following, that have convinced many people that Julia Sand really did have an impact on Chester Arthur.

. . . You can't really understand the Julia Sand letters and put them in any context without knowing about Chester Arthur's father, William Arthur, who was this rigid preacher, abolitionist, and a moralist, and about Chester's career as a teacher and as a young lawyer and the Civil War. This all leads up to a guy who started down a certain path and then veered off onto a darker path in search of power and wealth and fame. That happens to a lot of people. Then, he got jerked back.

Arthur put civil service reform in his first annual message, which was what we now call the State of the Union address. It was written; presidents didn't go before Congress to deliver this address. But he delivered it in writing, and he did call for civil service reform, which surprised a lot of people, given his history. It didn't go anywhere. Basically, no one in Congress had an interest in pushing this; they all benefited from the system in one way or another; both parties did.

It was only after the elections in 1882 when the Republicans got beaten pretty badly that there was a general sense among the politicos of the day that this had been a reaction against machine politics and against the status quo. The momentum had now gotten to a point where it was time for Congress to do something, and they did pass what was called the Pendleton Act, a piece of legislation [mandating merit-based federal hiring] that had been lingering for some time.

Arthur signed it, which was nice, but people noted at that time that as the executive, he was going to have the ability to short circuit this if he wanted to stall—to not appoint the members of the new Civil Service Commission, et cetera. He surprised everybody and vigorously pursued these reforms and really laid the groundwork for future reforms and for a more expansive role for the federal government. He doesn't get much credit for that today, and isn't really remembered at all.

Chester Arthur started the rebuilding of the navy, which Teddy Roosevelt also accelerated as president, but civil service reform really is his lasting legacy. The irony, of course, is that he was a creature of [the] spoils system and Chester Arthur was the last person in the world that people would have imagined who would have done this.

HERBERT HOOVER

Overall Rank: 36	Although the historians have consistently placed Hoover in the bottom ten presidents, they have also assigned him a high ranking in administrative skills (14th in 2017). This is more than offset by extremely low ranks in crisis leadership (40th) and economic management, where he ranked last (43rd) among all presidents in 2017.
— ★ —	
Total Score: 416	

Party: Republican
b. August 10, 1874, West Branch, Iowa
d. October 20, 1964, New York City, New York
First Lady: Lou Henry Hoover
Age entering office: 54

Historian: Richard Norton Smith

Biographer and presidential historian Richard Norton Smith has served as the director of five presidential libraries, including the Herbert Hoover Presidential Library and Museum. He joined Q & A on August 28, 2018, to discuss his book, The Uncommon Man: The Triumph of Herbert Hoover. Mr. Smith is one of three advisers for C-SPAN's Historians Survey of Presidential Leadership.

[The title of my book, *The Uncommon Man,* is] taken from the title of a relatively famous Hoover speech about the uncommon man. Vice President Henry Wallace, who was the second of FDR's vice presidents, gave a famous speech in 1942 about the century of the common man. Wallace, from a left-of-center perspective, was projecting the goals and ambitions of the generation that was fighting World War II. It wasn't enough simply to defeat the Nazis, but to create at home a true democracy, a place where the common man would finally come into his own. Hoover approached this from a different place on the political spectrum. He was making the case for what we might call a meritocracy—when you get sick, you want an uncommonly skillful doctor; when we go to war, we want an uncommonly able general. . . . The advances in society were brought about not by common, but by uncommon individuals. It was Hoover wit. He said, "I've never met an American parent who is proud to have their son or daughter called common." It's an interesting outlook.

It seemed to me that this phrase applied to Hoover more than anyone else. Hoover said, "When all is said and done, accomplishment is all that matters." Which, when you stop to think about it, is rather unsentimental—the sort of thing you would expect an engineer to say. And that's one of the keys to understanding his life, his success in everything but the presidency.

Herbert Hoover's life began in August 1874. General Grant was in the White House. His father was a blacksmith, Jesse Hoover. His mother, Huldah Hoover—first of all, they're both Quakers, which meant that she was an equal presence in the church, in the community, in the home—she was a lay preacher, if you will. So, religion was a significant part of his early days. He remembered—again, it seems to me such a window on his later shortcomings as a politician in particular—as a boy sitting in the stark, cold, barren meetinghouse that the Quakers used in West Branch, Iowa. His feet didn't even touch the floor. Along with all the adults, women on one side, men on the other, [he was] waiting for the divine light to illuminate his life, to move him to speak as it moved others in the congregation. He also said something terribly poignant. He said he was ten years old before he realized that he could do something for the sheer joy of it without offending the Lord.

When people wrote about the adult Hoover being an enigma, an emotionally distant man who was nevertheless clearly very moved by the suffering, particularly of children, in Belgium and thereafter—they had trouble making the two Hoovers blend. And in some ways, it's a preview of his strengths with a mirror side of his weaknesses.

He was orphaned [young]. Jesse died first, and Huldah [died when Herbert] . . . may have been ten. He was put on a train with ten cents sewn into his underclothes and some homemade vittles and sent to Oregon to live with a Quaker uncle by the name of Minthorn in Newberg. . . . And there he was trained in business. His uncle was a businessman, and Bert, as he was known, went on to Stanford. He was in the original class. In fact, Stanford became probably the closest thing to a home away from home. He would be a trustee for over fifty years. He built his home there; today, it's the university's president's house.

Bert loved Stanford. He ran a laundry business. He ran other businesses, so he had this entrepreneurial streak in him. [He] studied geology and engineering; met and fell in love with Lou Henry, also from Iowa, a unique woman in many ways, the first [woman] at Stanford to earn a geology degree. They had this real respectful partnership from the beginning. They were intellectual equals. The best evidence of that is they were married in 1899, and the government of China had invited him to help develop that country's mines. They sailed, on their honeymoon, . . . to Tientsin, where they were promptly caught up in the Boxer Rebellion, which was the uprising of native forces against the Westerners, who for too long had subjugated and exploited a very weak China. They were in Tientsin during the siege, and there are these wonderful letters. Lou was the perfect wife [for Hoover] because she loved adventure, and to her the Boxer Rebellion was an adventure. She writes letters home saying, "You're missing one of the great sieges of the age." She also said later that she got up every morning and swept the bullets off her front porch.

They had two children, two sons. Lou designed—you can see it at the library in West Branch—a cradle exclusively for use on board ocean liners. By the time Herbert Junior was eight years old, he'd been around the world five times. Hoover, who began digging ore in Nevada, was then hired by a London mining firm at the age of twenty-three and sent to Australia. He found fabulous riches there for his employers. And then he went to London. By the time he is in his thirties, he's generally regarded as the world's foremost mining engineer. In fact, one of the things that would come back to haunt him throughout his political career, throughout his public life, were those among his own countrymen, nativists, who believed that he was not sufficiently American, that he was somehow really British. It's reminiscent of some of the allegations made against Barack Obama when he ran for president.

Hoover was forty years old in 1914, living in London, hugely successful and restless. . . . He had a Quaker conscience, and he was bored with just making money. He was a millionaire several times over, and he was not terribly impressed with wealth. And so, in 1914, at the outbreak of World War I, he was very receptive when he was approached by some fellow engineers. The first crisis of the war was something approaching

120,000 American travelers who were in Europe at the time the war broke out who managed to make their way to London, but then they had to get home. Hoover agreed to lead this group—that [he even funded] . . . at times, which managed to organize transportation to get all of these people out of the war zone—to get them home. The thing to remember about this is, for all the checks he wrote, and he wrote a lot of checks, he said later on only $500 wasn't repaid, which is a fraction. It taught him a lesson, for better or worse, which is the foundation on which everything that follows rests: he had an unlimited faith in the generosity, the basic goodness, and the trustworthiness of the American people. That's important because subsequently, within a matter of weeks, he was approached about taking on an enormous task, something never before attempted, something that no one could really put their arms around because it was unprecedented.

Belgium had been invaded early in the war by the Germans. It was out of the war, but there were seven and a half million people in Belgium who faced starvation. At one point, Hoover was told they were down to about five days' food supply. In addition, there was a corner of France [that was similarly impacted]. Between the two, there were ten million people who confronted the real specter of starving to death. In the face of that, Hoover was asked to abandon his career for however long the war lasted and undertake the organization of what I call an independent republic of relief. No one had any idea of the dimensions of the task. They learned that the hard way.

Eventually something called the Commission for the Relief of Belgium, or the CRB [evolved]. Remember, Britain was blockading Europe and Germany. The Germans didn't want to feed the Belgians. The British were shocked that anyone asked them to feed the Belgians, who, after all, had been invaded by the Germans. What Hoover was doing, or attempting to do, had never been done before. In the end, it was a four-year effort that cost over $1 billion, when $1 billion was real money. Much of it was voluntarily raised, some of it provided by warring governments, but he kept the Belgians alive.

. . . Lou said later on that he was never the same after Belgium, after what he saw, particularly the children. Remember, he was an orphan, and all his life there was something about Hoover. He was not naturally gifted in social interaction, but with children he was a different person. And Belgium stamped him, for better or worse. The other remarkable

Herbert Hoover, here in a 1929 photo with his wife Lou, became internationally famous for his humanitarian work during World War I. *Courtesy Library of Congress*

thing, . . . [the relief effort] was all voluntary. He appealed to the American people. He said of the American people, if you tell them what you need, they will give you the shirts off their backs.

At this point, the United States wasn't in the war. That reinforced Hoover's belief so that all his life he was looking for a third way between laissez-faire capitalism, which he abhorred, and socialism, which he dreaded. And he came up with this term—it's terribly clunky, very Hooveresque—"voluntary association." The idea was that without government coercion, without legislative edict, you could reach Americans at the grassroots through churches, through community chests, through the Red Cross, through a whole host of volunteer organizations. That was the backbone of America. That was the strength of America. That was what gave voice to American ideals. That was great, and it worked.

And then, Woodrow Wilson asked Hoover to come home. He had become a phenomenon, as you might imagine. Wilson entrusted him with something called the American Food Administration. It's all voluntary. There are no ration cards in World War I. He uses propaganda. He uses public relations, this new embryonic science, to reach people and touch people and motivate people to respond to his appeals. So, there were meatless Mondays, and there were wheatless Wednesdays. Not every campaign worked. . . . The idea was the American people would grow more, save more, and together they would feed their allies across the sea.

There were two problems with that. Again, it confirmed Hoover in his belief, which by now was a bedrock conviction, that whatever the problem, you didn't need a government solution, you just needed to organize. . . . Economically, the legacy was that farmers grew more and more [crops]. They became addicted to surplus purchases overseas. Of course, in the 1920s, no more war, no more European markets. There's a slump. So, there was an agricultural depression in America long before 1929, and that was one of the things that bedeviled presidents throughout the period.

Both parties in 1920 had flirted with the idea of nominating Hoover. Wilson told his brother-in-law that if it was left to him, he would choose as his successor Herbert Hoover. Hoover talked to some Democrats in 1920, but he decided he was a Bull Moose Republican; he was a Teddy Roosevelt Progressive Republican. He was not a Standpatter. In fact, his problem with the Republican Party throughout the '20s and throughout his presidency was from the right wing of the party. They never really trusted him. . . .

The Harding administration [was elected in] 1920. Warren Harding, rather touchingly aware of his own limitations, set out to recruit a cabinet of the best men. Charles Evans Hughes became secretary of state. Harding gave Hoover a choice, and Hoover picked the Commerce Department, which in those days was perhaps the least important department in the cabinet. Hoover being Hoover, soon there were cartoons portraying him as secretary of commerce and under-secretary of everything else. He did ruffle a lot of feathers. . . . He created something [larger] out of what was already there, the Federal Radio Commission. Radio is regulated because Hoover started it, a forerunner of the FCC. From the outset, he was certain that he did not want a BBC-type arrangement. He wanted government to regulate the [broadcasting] industry, but he didn't want government to run the industry, with enormous repercussions ever since. The first airfield in Washington was Hoover Field, where the Pentagon is now. He wrote zoning regulations that could be adapted all over the country. He promoted the construction of new housing with standardized products. Hoover was an engineer. He thought like an engineer. He ate like an engineer. In the Hoover White House, it was famous that no state dinner could last more than sixty minutes. He once ate five courses in thirteen minutes.

He was commerce secretary for . . . seven and a half years under Harding and Coolidge.

Hoover accompanied Harding on his cross-country voyage of understanding to Alaska, where Harding fell ill. And then they returned to San Francisco. . . . Harding was clearly impressed by something, and he couldn't get it off his chest. He couldn't sleep, and he played bridge endlessly, game after game of bridge. It's funny, Hoover, who loved cards, permanently lost his taste for bridge . . . because that trip had worn his tolerance for the game but also because of the tragic consequences of the trip. Harding asked him at one point, cryptically, "If you knew of some great scandal within the administration, what would you do?" Hoover's advice was to go public with it all, totally. He said, "You would at least get credit for exposing the wrongdoers." Harding didn't bring up the subject again, but it was very clear to Hoover that Teapot Dome and the other Harding scandals had broken through. Later on, he said, "People don't die of broken hearts. But people can get exhausted and be vulnerable to heart attacks because of profound disappointment." And clearly Warren Harding was disappointed.

The completion of that story: Harding died in August 1923. Coolidge becomes president, and he retains Hoover. They don't have the same chemistry that Harding did. Coolidge was as suspicious of activity as Hoover was unwilling to be inactive. Plus, I think Coolidge sensed Hoover's ambition. And yet [it was Hoover he turned to] when the Mississippi River overflowed—to this day, by some measurements, the greatest natural disaster in American history, 1927. The flood covered thousands and thousands of square miles in the South. There was no government agency; there was no expectation that government would respond in any way. There was only Herbert Hoover, who had this nickname, the "Master of Emergencies."

In 1928, Hoover ran [for president] against a very impressive governor of New York, Al Smith, a charismatic figure, in many ways seen as the father of modern liberalism before Franklin Roosevelt. No one writes about 1928 without emphasizing the anti-Catholic bigotry that Smith ran into, particularly in the South. It's not Barry Goldwater who broke the solid South, and it's not Dwight Eisenhower. It was Herbert Hoover who carried Texas and several other southern states. The assumption is that he only carried them as a measure of the anti-Catholic bias that existed in the Deep South, and that clearly was a factor. But there's another factor that tends to get overlooked, and that is the gratitude that people in the Deep South felt because Hoover was the face of relief at the time of the floods. He was the only person associated with government who had tried to address their needs.

He won big. He won by six and a half million—21.5 million votes to 15 million votes. However, beneath those numbers, there were portents for the future. . . . You had the makings of an early realignment. Had there not been the Great Depression, had Hoover's reputation not been destroyed during his single term of office, what is fascinating to speculate is, would that breakthrough in the South . . . have been a one-time event, attributable to Al Smith as an opponent? Or, might it have foreshadowed a two-party system?

I can't tell you [how the Great Depression came about]. I think there are a lot of economists who would, if they were honest, respond the same way. There are clearly a number of factors, some of which are easily identified: [with] the dislocations of the war; we had this crazy, crazy quilt [of issues]. As part of the Versailles agreement, crushing reparations were demanded by the victors of a defeated Germany, which was really in no position economically [to pay]—although it had been largely unscathed by the war. So, you had this crazy system where Germany is borrowing money from the United States. The United States came out of World War I as the new financial centerpiece of the world. New York supplanted London. The United States came out of World War I, for the first time in its history, as a creditor nation; the rest of the world owed it. But you had this system where American banks were loaning money to Germany, which then used the money to pay off the reparations.

In addition, domestically, you had a rotten banking system, totally unregulated. There were banks that were speculating on the stock market. There were banks that were doing things with depositors' money that would shock us today. You had Wall Street speculation, rank, overheated, baseless. Lots of people were buying stock on margin, which is to say, they were borrowing funds. And if the stock market ever went down, particularly if it went down sharply, then they would have to sell their stock to pay off what they'd bought. The whole system was jerry-built. Hoover believed that it was the cumulative impact of the war; the dislocations brought about by the war. And it's true that it was an international phenomenon; it was not limited to the United States. But I, for the life of me, can't give you a single reason [for the Great Depression]. One very important contributing factor was that glut of consumer goods in the 1920s. Ironically, it was Hoover who celebrated the abundance of modern industry. Cars were affordable, so were refrigerators, so were other appliances. [There were] all of those homes that he built, but lots of them were bought on credit. Radio. Aviation. You had these new industries that were taking off, but the market became literally glutted. One thing economists know is that wages failed to keep pace with prices, so you had this gap which grew. At the same time, you had millions of people who were overcommitted. They were living paycheck to paycheck. They were speculating in stocks. And, 40 percent of the American workforce in the 1920s was in agriculture. So . . . nearly half the country was depressed long before Wall Street collapsed.

When Herbert Hoover became president in 1929, the federal budget was less than $4 billion, and a substantial part of that was going to veterans. . . . Criticism of Hoover for not being sufficiently aggressive in exerting the potential of government to affect the economy overlooks how limited was the effect. In retrospect, we see all kinds of things that we didn't see at the time, [such as] Keynesian economics, the idea that government in bust times should bust the budget—in other words, that it should do everything it can to boost purchasing power. Depressions are all about deflation, so if you could inflate the economy, presumably, that's the necessary medicine. But nobody knew about Keynesian economics in the 1920s. . . .

This is not to excuse Hoover. . . . Hoover exists in the shadow of FDR who did so much more [to ameliorate the impact of the Depression]. But in the context of the time, what Hoover did was seen as so much more than his predecessors. We'd had great depressions before: Martin Van Buren and President James Monroe when they were president; Grover Cleveland in the 1890s. The notion that the federal government would step in and try to correct the economic cycle was heresy. Depressions were acts of God. There were booms, and there were busts, and there was nothing you could do about it. . . . But the other thing was, we tend to think that the stock market collapsed in October 1929 and the next day there were bread lines. In fact, this was a story that took time to evolve. Early in 1930, the *New York Times,* among other media outlets, praised Hoover for doing more than any president before under the circumstances.

. . . Hoover immediately [turned to] voluntary association. Hoover called to the White House for job [creation], dozens of the nation's leading business executives. He got them to agree to undertake an increase in their commitments. And on wages—he went and talked to Henry Ford, who initially agreed to increase workers' wages. He contacted all the governors of the forty-eight states and appealed to them to accelerate public works programs. He himself went to Congress and asked for $150 million, which was more than any president before him—in fact, it was more than most presidents combined, and that was just the first installment. So, the idea that he did nothing is pretty thoroughly disabused.

So why is Hoover, seventy to eighty years later, pilloried? Why is he indelibly, personally, associated with the Great Depression?

There are a number of reasons for that. One, the Democrats brilliantly hired a man named Charlie Michelson who, . . . you might say, invented negative politics in the way that you and I would understand it. Charlie Michelson's sole job every day, day in and day out, was to blacken the reputation of the president, to drive home in voters' minds the fact that this man was heartless; this man was responsible for the Great Depression, et cetera. Hoover unwittingly contributed to that. Hoover's great failure, you could say, was a failure of imagination. He should never have signed the Smoot-Hawley tariff in 1930, which, at the worst possible time, built walls around the American economy and encouraged other countries to do the same. That was a real error of judgment.

But Hoover's great failing was temperamental. He tried to make a virtue out of this. He would say, "You can't make a Teddy Roosevelt out of me." Go back to that ten-year-old boy who didn't know that he could do something for pleasure without offending God. I always thought there was a direct connection between that child and the adult Hoover, who was in many ways emotionally stunted. He was the most improbable politician. His story is unique; I suppose every president is unique in his way. One of the lessons that Hoover's story teaches us is, beware of successful businessmen. The qualities that drive business success, the ability to work with a board of directors, the knowledge that your order will be carried out—that's not the same as working with Congress. Hoover had poor relations with Congress, which was nominally Republican the first half of his term and then marginally Democratic the second half. He didn't have the political gift. He knew he didn't have the political gift. But that's the other lesson of the Hoover presidency. Hoover is one of those very rare presidents; William Howard Taft comes to mind, quasi James Madison comes to mind—people who are almost too rational, too cerebral, who don't have in their DNA whatever that political gene is that enables a Lyndon Johnson, in the most extreme example, to thrive.

He ran again in 1932. He was nominated by a listless Republican convention. One thing we haven't mentioned is Prohibition—another issue that complicated life, particularly for the Republicans because they had a lot of rural supporters. The Republican Party was split on the issue of Prohibition. Hoover was a cosmopolitan figure who didn't mind taking a drink, but who was sworn to enforce the law. And in 1932, he was on the unpopular side of the issue. By 1932, there were a lot of people, including original supporters of Prohibition, that concluded that this experiment had not worked, and that in many ways it has backfired. So, he was carrying that dead weight. He had the Depression. He had his own inability to inspire. . . .

The [veterans'] Bonus Army came to town [demanding payment of their World War I bonuses], and measures are still being debated [in Congress], still the subject of controversy. He dispatched Douglas MacArthur, of all people, [telling him] not to cross the bridge over into Anacostia and set fire to the veterans' camp, as MacArthur took it upon himself to do. Hoover sent explicit orders to MacArthur, and they were disobeyed. It was not the last time that Douglas MacArthur was to disobey executive authority.

FDR swept the country. Hoover had fifty-nine electoral votes. . . . I don't think anyone has ever gone from such an overwhelming mandate when he was elected to so powerful a consensus that he should leave office. Roosevelt carried all but six states, and with it, Congress.

And then, what put the seal on Hoover's reputation as a failed president was the next three months. The Hoover-Roosevelt interregnum was so bad that the Constitution was amended. Presidents used to be sworn in on March 4. It was decided that that was too long because it was too long in 1932–1933. The two men had virtually no communication. Hoover believed that FDR was deliberately avoiding having any responsibility in the hopes that if things did go to hell, that he would then receive the credit. And in many ways, that's exactly what happened.

The banks were crashing at the end; the roof was falling in. Hoover could have closed the banks, but there was that—some would say stubbornness, some would say principle—I would say lack of political finesse. He insisted that FDR had to agree with him, that it had to be a joint undertaking. And there's a difference: FDR is not only a born politician, but a natural pragmatist. It's FDR who says, "Try something. If it doesn't work, try something else, but above all, try something." That is exactly what the American people wanted to hear after four years in which it was felt that nothing had been tried. In fact, a lot had been tried, but it came very soon to be overshadowed by the scale and the scope of what FDR undertook.

[As for his legacy] you could look physically at Hoover Dam. It was no accident that his name was put on it because he, as secretary of commerce, negotiated a compact with seven Rocky Mountain states over the waters of the Colorado River that they were all fighting over. . . . That's the most obvious physical legacy. Much more important is the example of a businessman who walked away from his fortune—he said, literally, "Let the fortune go to hell"—first, to feed Belgium, and then to organize American relief, and ultimately to go on to save more lives than Hitler, Stalin, and Mao together could eliminate. Not a bad epitaph.

MILLARD FILLMORE

13th President, 1850–1853

Overall Rank: 37 — ★ — **Total Score: 394**	Assuming the presidency upon the death of Zachary Taylor, Fillmore is the first of three consecutive antebellum presidents that rank in the bottom seven of all presidents (the others are Franklin Pierce and James Buchanan). In 2017, he ranked among the bottom ten presidents in every leadership category. His highest ranking was 27th in crisis leadership in the 2000 survey, but this fell to 34th in 2017.

Party: Whig
b. January 7, 1800, Cayuga County, New York
d. March 8, 1874, Buffalo, New York
First Lady: Abigail Powers Fillmore
Age entering office: 50

Historian: Edna Greene Medford

Historian and Howard University professor Edna Medford is a specialist on America's Civil War and Reconstruction period. In 1999, she gave us this interview for C-SPAN's American Presidents *series about the Compromise of 1850, signed into law by Millard Fillmore in September of 1850, just months after he assumed office. Dr. Medford is one of three advisers for C-SPAN's Historians Survey of Presidential Leadership.*

When Millard Fillmore becomes president in July 1850 [following the sudden death of President Zachary Taylor], the country was undergoing sectional tension. There had always been that tension from the very beginning of the country, but by 1850, it was intensifying as a consequence of the Mexican War. . . . Fairly early in the war, David Wilmot, a congressman from Pennsylvania, had attempted to attach a provision to an appropriations bill for the war indicating that any territory that was acquired from Mexico as a consequence of the war, that slavery should not be allowed anywhere in that territory.

The Wilmot Proviso caused tremendous debate in Congress and throughout the nation. There were various positions held, with Southerners being enraged at the idea that they would not be able to take their [slaves, in other words their] property, anywhere they wanted. And so, by 1850, when Millard Fillmore becomes president, there is that issue of what's to happen with this territory that has been acquired from Mexico. There are also issues of the acceptance of California into the Union and whether or not California is going to enter the Union as a slave state or a free state. Before Taylor died, he had suggested that California might be admitted to the Union as a state, . . . just bypassing the territorial phase . . . attempting to bypass the whole issue of slavery. So, Fillmore certainly is burdened with that as well.

We tend to emphasize slavery and the whole idea of the expansion of slavery into the territories, but we do that because that really is the key factor dividing the society [in the mid-nineteenth century]. So much emphasis is placed then on what's going to happen in terms of the expansion of slavery. Then, there is the issue between the North and South over the slave trade continuing in the District of Columbia. Some people were concerned that in a free society there should not be this kind of thing happening in the nation's capital. There were slave markets in the District of Columbia; Northern abolitionists certainly were concerned about that. There were a series of issues that divided the North and the South during this period. It had become so bad that the South would talk about meeting in a convention and discussing the possibility of secession.

At that point, the great compromiser, [Kentucky senator] Henry Clay stepped in and attempted a compromise bill. It was not approved by both houses of Congress. What happened, though, is when Clay left to return home, because he was quite ill at that time, [Illinois senator] Stephen A. Douglas took up the whole issue and was able to push the measure through Congress by splitting it up into several different measures. As a result, California was admitted as a free state. The territory that was in dispute between New Mexico and Texas went to New Mexico, but Texas got a $10 million fee from the federal government that allowed it to settle its debt with Mexico as a consequence of its war with Mexico.

The Fugitive Slave Act was enacted [as part of the compromise] because Southerners had been concerned that the original fugitive slave clause in the Constitution was not very effective. Northerners were assisting runaways, fugitives from slavery, to get to Canada. Southerners were very much concerned about that, so there was a much more stringent Fugitive Slave Law passed. These kinds of measures, for the moment, appeased both sides but did not appease them all totally, and it simply forestalled the problems that came later. It was just a stopgap measure because within a year or two, there was yet another problem that the Fillmore administration faced.

[Millard Fillmore was a Whig.] The Whigs were beginning to be fragmented, so certainly this did not help. There were certain groups of the Whig Party, the Conscience Whigs, who were more in the abolitionist's vein, who certainly were devastated by the idea of this Fugitive Slave Law. What that law did was to make Northerners equally responsible for the apprehension of enslaved people. What the measure indicated was that Northerners, or citizens in general, had to assist the authorities [in apprehending fugitive slaves] if called upon to do so. The measure was so hated by certain Northern elements that some of the states passed personal liberty laws that said that their authorities and their institutions would not be used for the recapture of fugitives from slavery. This did not do any good for the Whig Party; it simply continued to fragment.

The Democratic Party was beginning to fracture as well. We have to remember that even though there was sectionalism in the country, these parties are national, but by the 1850s, what we see happening is that the parties become more and more sectional. People start voting based on their sections as opposed to their parties. The kinds of issues that would have held them together, the principles that would have held them together at an earlier time, . . . are dividing them. All of the parties are suffering as a consequence, some more so than others, and certainly the Whig Party is suffering more than any other.

Abolitionists were absolutely livid over this measure and saw it as yet another example of the slave power conspiracy. This was seen as an attempt to force slavery on everyone, and they thought there was even a possibility that eventually the Southerners would move their slaves into Northern states. Southerners were pleased with the Fugitive Slave Act. Of course, they were not so pleased with the compromise ending the slave trade in the District of Columbia. They would have preferred to have kept that, but it was a compromise measure, and so everyone got something and lost something. Northern moderates would have preferred, as well, that the Fugitive Slave Act had not been passed and were very much concerned with the slave power conspiracy that people were talking about.

. . . The Underground Railroad was this connection of people, of abolitionists, who are assisting fugitives from slavery to the North initially, and then eventually to Canada. Especially after the Fugitive Slave Act of 1850, they are assisting them all the way to Canada. Fugitives don't feel comfortable in the North anymore because there's that possibility that kidnappers, as they're called, can come into the North and re-enslave them. Even free blacks who had never been enslaved felt uncomfortable once that measure went into existence. . . . Before [the law] some Northerners, at least, felt quite comfortable with assisting escaping fugitives. Now there is this real concern that the law is requiring them to help in the apprehension of alleged fugitives.

[The publication of *Uncle Tom's Cabin* contributed to the issues facing the Fillmore presidency.] Harriet Beecher Stowe was from a very prominent family in New England. Her father, Lyman Beecher, was a minister; her brother Henry Ward Beecher was a minister as well; and her sister, Catharine, was an outspoken abolitionist. Harriet Beecher Stowe writes the story. It's a fictional account of an enslaved family and of the consequences of slavery—not just to enslaved blacks, but to whites as well. She paints a picture that is very unfavorable to the Southern position. Southerners are enraged at the idea that this Northern woman who knew nothing, they felt, about their "peculiar institution" would do something like this. They once again talked about how they were being mistreated by the North, and perhaps they would be better off if they were leaving the Union.

The book sold very well. It was serialized initially in newspapers and magazines, but in the first year of its publication, it sold over three hundred thousand copies. What was important about the book was that it exposed Northerners to the institution of slavery, people who had not given a great deal of thought to slavery before, who may have looked at slavery from the perspective of enslaved people competing with white labor but had not looked at the moral issue. Harriet Beecher Stowe was able to do something for the abolitionists' cause that the abolitionists themselves were not able to do because the abolitionists were, in general, seen as rather radical people. Here you have this woman who is able to capture the horror of slavery in a nutshell, and it really does take off in the North.

Certainly, this is a period of tremendous expansion, not just in terms of land, but in terms of industry as well. There is great railroad building that's going on in the early 1850s.

There are attempts to acquire even more land; although they have this land from Mexico, there is still that attempt to acquire additional land. For the most part, industry is growing in the North especially— not so much so in the South. The South remains very much an agrarian society, but you do have industries still growing in the North. You have that railroad expansion, and there is that concern that Northern interests, which are more industrial, are going to clash with Southern interests.

Millard Fillmore is someone who is concerned about making sure that the nation is not torn apart, so he is very much in favor of the Compromise of 1850. He is in favor of anything that's going to stabilize the situation because he understands that there are two very different economies here. Certainly, with the Compromise of 1850, people were happy that they were given a reprieve, but by the end of the Fillmore administration, you have *Uncle Tom's Cabin,* and people are concerned once more that this is going to be a problem—at least Southerners are very concerned. You got the Fugitive Slave Act that is beginning to divide people once more. By the end of the Fillmore administration, people are perhaps not as pessimistic as they were at the beginning of it, but it's about to hit them in the face again.

The 1850s is a decade of ongoing sectional tension. It never ends. There may be a moment or two when people can sit back and relax, but in an instant, they are right back where they were before. There is tremendous tension during this period throughout all of the presidential administrations. [During this time] you have some presidents who are able to distract the country a little bit more than others, in terms of looking beyond the whole slavery issue.

Famous Civil War photographer Mathew Brady took this photo of President Millard
Fillmore c. 1850–1874. *Courtesy Library of Congress*

C-SPAN's program on Millard Fillmore for our American
Presidents *television series offered this brief biographical overview of
our thirteenth president's life, produced by C-SPAN's Mark Farkas.
We include it here to round out our chapter on President Fillmore.*

On the night of July 9, 1850, Vice President Millard Fillmore received
a knock on the door of his Willard Hotel Room in Washington, DC. He
was informed of the death of President Zachary Taylor. The following
morning at 11:00 a.m., he entered the House chamber and, in front of
the gathered members of the House and Senate, was quietly sworn in as
the thirteenth president of the United States.

Millard Fillmore was born into poverty on January 7, 1800, in a log
cabin on a farm in Locke Township near Moravia in New York. The
second of eight children, he held odd jobs and taught himself how to
read with a Bible and a dictionary. At age nineteen, he entered school
and became the favorite student of twenty-year-old Abigail Powers. The
two eventually married in 1826, but not before Fillmore became established as a lawyer in East Aurora, New York. His son Millard Powers was

born in 1828, a year before Fillmore became a New York assemblyman. Daughter Mary arrived in 1832, the same year he was first elected to Congress. Fillmore was elected to three more terms in the House and served as chairman of the Ways and Means Committee, where his major achievement was passage of the Tariff of 1842, signed into law by President John Tyler.

During his time as president, Fillmore's critics complained that he lacked the ability to take a stand on issues. During the debate over the Compromise of 1850, he was quoted as saying, "I detest slavery, but it is an existing evil for which we are not responsible, and we must endure it and give it such protection as is guaranteed by the Constitution till we can get rid of it." Milestones during Fillmore's term [in addition to signing the compromise legislation] included the laying of the cornerstone for the current House chamber, plans for the layout of the National Mall and South Lawn of the White House, and the launching of the expedition to Japan by Commodore Matthew Perry.

[Denied his party's nomination in 1852, Fillmore left office in March of 1853 and the Whig Party continued its dissolution.] After the White House, Fillmore traveled extensively throughout Europe. In 1856, he was nominated for the presidency by the American Native Party, also referred to as the Know-Nothing Party, but he received less than 22 percent of the popular vote, coming in third behind James Buchanan [the Democratic candidate] and John Fremont, the first nominee of the new Republican Party.

WILLIAM HENRY HARRISON   9th President, 1841

Overall Rank: 38

— ★ —

Total Score: 383

"Tippecanoe's" term lasted only thirty-one days, giving historians a relatively small presidential legacy to assess. Known for giving the longest inaugural address of any president—nearly two hours—it is notable that historians assigned him his highest ranking in public persuasion (28th). His second highest ranking is in moral authority (31st).

Party: Whig
b. February 9, 1773, Charles City County, Virginia
d. April 4, 1841, Washington, DC
First Lady: Anna Symmes Harrison
Age entering office: 68

Historian: **Ronald G. Shafer**

Ron Shafer spent thirty-eight years at the Wall Street Journal *as an editor, reporter, and columnist. He joined C-SPAN's Q & A to discuss his book,* The Carnival Campaign: How the Rollicking 1840 Campaign of "Tippecanoe and Tyler Too" Changed Presidential Elections Forever, *on December 9, 2016.*

I live in Williamsburg, Virginia. It's right next door to where William Henry Harrison and John Tyler were born. [In 1840,] they ran the first modern presidential campaign with rallies and presidential speeches. Before this, when you campaigned for president, you didn't go out and give speeches. You didn't have rallies. You just sat at home and you wrote letters to people who wrote to you about the issues. In this election, for the first time, they had huge rallies, and Harrison became the first president to go out and give speeches.

This was very much like our election in 2016. It was politics, and it was entertainment. There was demagoguery. There were personal insults. And, it involved the oldest man ever to run for president. At that time, it was Harrison, who was sixty-seven years old.

Martin Van Buren was the [incumbent] president in 1840. He was known as the "Little Magician." He was a professional politician from New York and the protégé of Andrew Jackson. Jackson served two terms. Van Buren was his vice president, and so he anointed Van Buren as his successor, and Van Buren won. Unfortunately, he won in 1836 and then came the Great Panic of 1837, which was a depression and the economy fell apart. Jobs were lost, wages went down—so it was a terrible time to be running for election as president. . . . Eighteen thirty-seven was the worst depression until the [Great] Depression of 1929. It was awful. People couldn't get work. They couldn't get food; there were food riots in New York. The main theme, if there was one, of the Harrison campaign, which tried to avoid issues as much as possible, was to promise better times ahead. They were going to help you with the economy, . . . and that you could count on them to at least worry about you, where the Democrats, they said, did not care about you.

Van Buren was a Democrat. Back then, the Democrats were out of the Thomas Jefferson philosophy. They believed in no federal government at all, or at least the smallest federal government. So, when the Panic of 1837 hit, they did nothing. They believed the government should not do anything, that you are on your own. This, of course, alienated the voters. The Whigs [Harrison's party] believed that there should be some government help—mainly involved in building roads connecting the states, but they promised to offer some help. They, in effect, offered to make America great again, except their slogan was "Harrison and reform." Not quite as catchy, but it worked.

William Henry Harrison was born at Berkeley Plantation, which is near Williamsburg and Richmond. His father, Benjamin Harrison V, was a signer of the Declaration of Independence. . . . When Henry was young, they had dinner guests—people like George Washington, Thomas Jefferson, James Madison—so you can imagine the conversations that he heard. And then when he was fourteen, he was sent away to college. Most kids could not go to college then, but he was sent off to college and then to medical school and ended up in Philadelphia.

His father died, and suddenly he had no income. He inherited some land from Berkeley Plantation, but since he was the youngest of seven children, . . . the oldest son got the plantation, and Harrison had to find something to do.

He really didn't want to study medicine; he wanted to go fight Indians. So, he got a commission in the army, but instead of going in as a private, his father had an old friend who was now president of the United States, and his name was George Washington. Washington made him an officer. [Harrison] left Philadelphia and went to Fort Washington near . . . Cincinnati; he walked most of the three hundred miles. He was a big lover of Roman history, so the only thing he took with him were some volumes of the works of Cicero. He finally arrived in Cincinnati to fight for the general [who was] heading up the fight against the Indians in Ohio.

[In 1795, at age twenty-two] . . . he married Anna Symmes, daughter of a wealthy landowner there who sold him this little log cabin on the west bend of the Ohio about fourteen miles west of Cincinnati. [In 1798] he started looking for a better job, and again, with some help from an old friend of his father's, President John Adams, he got appointed as secretary and then governor of the Indiana Territory, which was a big job.

This is how Harrison became famous: [in 1811] he had a run-in with [the famous Indian leader] Tecumseh because Tecumseh was trying to get the Indians not to sell their land to Harrison. Tecumseh came to [Grouseland,] Harrison's home [near Vincennes], and during the discussion, he drew his tomahawk; Harrison drew his sword, and they parted ways. Tecumseh and his brothers set up a town near Lafayette, [Indiana,] called Prophetstown, and they were causing some trouble. So, Harrison decided to close down the town. He got a troop of men from the federal government and from the Indiana militia and went down and camped outside the town before entering the next day. During the night the Indians attacked. There were lots of casualties on both sides. . . . Nevertheless, Harrison prevailed and closed down the town the next day. Word spread across the country, and [Harrison] became known as "The Hero of Tippecanoe," which led to his [later] nickname, "Old Tippecanoe." [He resigned as territorial governor and returned to the military in 1812, attaining the rank of brigadier general and winning numerous battles in the War of 1812.]

Harrison's retirement [from the military in 1814] was very controversial because he had just won the Battle of the Thames. He went to Washington, and there were parades all the way as he went. He gets to Washington, and what happened was that the secretary of war didn't get along with him, and so now that that battle was over, he was going to assign him to some meaningless post. Harrison didn't want that. He resigned and sent a letter to President Madison. He figured that Madison, the old family friend, would not accept it, but Secretary of War [John Armstrong] intercepted it and said, "Okay." He replaced [Harrison] with a guy named Andrew Jackson. Harrison was assigned to do some peace talks with the Indians, which he did [resulting in two successful treaties].

William Henry Harrison was able, at that time, to use his fame to get into Congress. . . . He was in the US House [representing a district in Ohio, where he had moved], and he was in the Ohio Senate, but as the years went by, the fame faded, and he lost a couple of elections. He finally convinced the state legislature to appoint him to the US Senate . . . [and] was back in Washington. He was a senator, but he really wanted a higher-paying job than that. He wants to be the [envoy to Colombia]—a job had just opened up under John Quincy Adams. Adams said, "Oh, this Harrison, he is always begging for jobs. He is the worst guy. What am I going to do with this guy?" But his secretary of state, Henry Clay, said, "Why don't you give him this job?"

Harrison did take the job, which paid a lot of money, but it took him a year to get to Colombia. He was there just a few days when Andrew Jackson became president. He and Andrew Jackson did not get along, and the first thing Jackson did when he got in office was to say, "You're out of here." Harrison had to go all the way back home. [Jobless,] he ended up being the county clerk at Hamilton County near Cincinnati, which paid pretty well, but he was a lowly clerk. [He was still serving in this position when he ran for president.]

[In 1840, when Harrison sought his party's nomination] . . . this was the first Whig convention ever. It was in Harrisburg because they had just built a new train station so people could come in from Washington. Henry Clay, who had started the Whig Party, figured he would get the nomination. He was the leader on the first two votes, but he did not get enough to [win], so they had to keep voting. . . . Eventually, the support

swung to Harrison because he was known as a man who was not supporting the abolitionists. . . . Finally, on the fifth vote, Harrison won.

[None of the three Whig candidates were actually] there. That was
the other difference from now. Back in those days, you were supposed
to pretend that you weren't running for president, so all of these men
were at home. Harrison was back in Ohio. Clay was in Washington. General Winfield Scott was in New York. So, they didn't even know about
this [contentious voting] when it happened. Harrison found out about
it a week or two later. There was a little notice in the Cincinnati newspaper that he had won. Finally, he got an official letter from the Whigs
that he was the nominee, and so he answered. He said he was very happy
about this and [proclaimed] that he was very surprised, even though he
had been lobbying for this.

The log cabin became the symbol of his campaign. . . . The plan was
to portray him as the General Washington of the West, that he would
be this leader on a white horse leading the people. The week after the
convention ended, some reporter in an opposition newspaper wrote
this article that Harrison, who was sixty-seven years old, was really just
an old granny and that he'd be content to be given some hard cider
and a pension and stay home in his log cabin instead of running for
president.

Well, this just threw the plans in a fire. So, two people in Harrisburg,
an elderly banker and a young newspaper man, met at the banker's
mansion. Harrison knew nothing about this. They said, "What are we
going to do about this?" The banker said, "Well, why don't we just go
with it? The log cabin is the symbol of the common man. Hard cider
is what the common man drinks." The editor gets out a piece of paper
and draws this log cabin with raccoons on the top and he's got a barrel
of hard cider there, and he says, "Why don't we do something like this?"

Within a month, you had parades with log cabins on wheels—
something like fifty feet wide and carrying forty people, pulled by twenty
horses. This became a symbol in every parade they had, and he was portrayed as the champion of the common man living in a log cabin. In
fact, he lived in a mansion in Ohio. He had a big house on the river.
That little cabin they had bought from his wife's father, well, they had
ten kids, so they expanded it, and it was very modern. He had thousands
of acres and estates, so he was actually a very wealthy man, but he was

portrayed as the champion of the poor. Again, here was a parallel to the [2016 presidential election].

. . . He started out following the very same pattern [of past campaigns]— he would answer letters. One day, a fellow in New York said he had written Harrison asking him about some issues, and he got a letter back [that] wasn't from Harrison; it was from some committee. This was an outrage. The Democrats jumped on this and said, "He has a conscience committee. He is being kept, the poor man, in an iron cage. They don't even trust him to answer his own letters." Harrison was humiliated by this, and he decided he had to do something. He got an invitation to speak at a ceremony at Fort Meigs, where he once commanded, near Toledo. He accepted it.

He started on his way, and it's a long way. It's two hundred miles. But by this time, the log cabin theme had kicked in, so he kept his silk hat at home and took his farmer's hat and his plain clothes . . . to keep with the image. He stopped in Columbus, Ohio, overnight at the National Hotel right in the middle of town. He went to see the boys at the Tippecanoe Club the next morning. He was leaving, and there was a crowd gathered outside. He starts to say a few words, and pretty soon he is giving a speech. It is June 6, 1840—the first speech ever by a presidential candidate. Then he continued up to Fort Meigs and gave a speech for thousands of people, continued over to Cleveland, and then gave more than twenty speeches. . . . [Harrison was soon] going all around the state like an aging rock star—like the Mick Jagger of politics at the time.

[Their campaign slogan] "Tippecanoe and Tyler Too" refers to "Old Tippecanoe," William Henry Harrison and John Tyler as his running mate. Tyler was his cousin; he grew up right down the road from Berkeley Plantation at another plantation. His father was friends with Harrison's father. Tyler's father, his roommate at the College of William and Mary was Thomas Jefferson. They had a lot of these interconnections, although Harrison was seventeen years older. . . .

I can tell you how that Tippecanoe slogan came about. That first big rally in the campaign was in Columbus, Ohio. They had thirty thousand people in Columbus, a town of about three thousand people. They had a huge parade, and one of the things in the parade was this big rolling ball—it was about ten feet high—that came in from Cleveland and had

After a modern-style campaign, the first inaugural parade, and the longest inaugural address, William Henry Harrison, seen in this c. 1850 daguerreotype, only survived a month into his term. *Courtesy Metropolitan Museum of Art*

slogans all over it. There was a jeweler from nearby Zanesville in the audience, and he was so taken by this that he went home to his Tippecanoe glee club and wrote a song about this ball called "The Great Commotion." The chorus line was, "for Tippecanoe and Tyler, too," and the name just caught on—or in modern terms, it went viral.

Nobody had ever heard of anything like this and never seen anything like this, so Harrison started drawing more and more people. By the time he got to Dayton . . . people came from all over the area, and it was sixty thousand to one hundred thousand people just to see him. They probably could not hear him because they didn't have microphones at that time, but he gave a two-hour speech in Dayton, Ohio, with one hundred thousand people and another one in Cincinnati that also drew an estimated one hundred thousand people. The population of the United States was about [7] percent of what it is now, so it was quite amazing the kinds of crowds he drew. It probably has never been matched. I think Barack Obama drew one hundred thousand at a rally in Manassas, Virginia, in one of his elections, but very rarely matched.

They turned on poor President Van Buren. He had no idea why people were saying these things [calling him, among other things, a "weasel"].

It was a very, very nasty campaign. Even his friends turned on him. Washington Irving, the author, grew up in the same part of New York State where Van Buren had, and he was his friend until Van Buren would not appoint his brother to a federal job. He switched over to Harrison and supported him. If you were running for president in those days, you better be ready for a lot of insults.

In those days, there was a lot of bribing of voters. You are talking about voter fraud. There was no secret ballot. People would coop up—they called it cooping—people in houses and give them wine and food and tell them, "Okay, now you go out and vote for this person," and they would do it. They sent bullies to the polls to chase away somebody from the opposition, so a lot of voting was not exactly on the up and up, but that was really on both sides.

. . . This was the first campaign that women were involved with. They couldn't vote, of course, but the Whigs decided they would be great allies because they could persuade their husbands and boyfriends to vote for Harrison. It became a great movement where women wore sashes reading, "Whig husbands or none," and they refused to marry their boyfriends unless they said they would vote for the Whigs. Women came to the parades, and they waved handkerchiefs. Some gave speeches. Some wrote pamphlets. It was very shocking. They were criticized by the Democrats, who said that these women should be home making pudding. This was the beginning really . . . of the movement for the women's vote. One of my favorite anecdotes: at a rally in Springfield, Illinois, the horses stampeded, and this woman was heard saying, "If any are to be killed, let it be the ladies, for they can't vote."

An amazing total, 81 percent [of eligible voters voted in 1840, which] was the highest ever at that time. One reason they went to this log cabin campaign theme was that the voter rolls had expanded to include most of the white males in the country. Before this, you had to own property, or you had to be in the militia, but they expanded it that year so that the number increased. And then this entertaining campaign increased voter interest so much that the voter number increased by 60 percent for this election, . . . so it was really incredible.

[William Henry Harrison got 1,275,390 votes, 234 electoral votes, and President Van Buren got 1,128,854 votes and only 60 electoral votes.]

It was, again, somewhat like the 2016 campaign. Harrison won in states that got him the electoral votes while Van Buren picked up a lot of popular votes. There was some feeling that maybe this circus campaign started to backfire by the end because it really didn't have much substance. But . . . the vote total was fairly close. The funny thing about Van Buren, Andrew Jackson said, "Wait until you see the final returns. Don't give up yet." Van Buren had a messenger go to the polling place every day because people voted over several days at those times. Finally, he got word that he lost New York, which is when he knew he lost the election.

There were a lot of cartoons about Van Buren stomping down the stairs of the White House as Harrison moved in. In fact, when Harrison arrived in Washington, he stayed at a local hotel. Van Buren invited him over to the White House. He was very gracious. He invited him to move in ahead of the election to get away from the crowds. Of course, there was no Secret Service protection then, but Harrison stayed at the hotel. Van Buren brought his cabinet over to meet Harrison and then had him over for dinner. He did not attend the inauguration because that was not the custom at the time, but he turned out to be a very gracious loser.

[Harrison held the first inaugural parade in history] mainly because this was the hallmark of his campaign, these big rallies with the log cabins on wheels. They had the first official inaugural committee, and they arranged this parade, which would pretty much look like a rally with the log cabins and the marching bands; music was very important in this campaign. The Whigs in Baltimore got a brand-new wagon for Harrison to ride in, but he did not want to ride in it. He rode his horse, Old Whitey. He did not wear a coat. He did have a hat, but he kept doffing it as he went down Pennsylvania Avenue. They paraded down to the Capitol, and once he gave his speech, they paraded back to the White House.

Harrison gave the longest inaugural speech in history, and maybe the most boring inaugural speech in history—an hour and forty-five minutes. It was not raining, [but] it was very cold. The wind was blowing. He did not wear a coat or hat. He wanted to look very young. But he did not get sick; he went to three inaugural balls that night. He was fine.

Two weeks later he went on a walk—he walked every morning from the White House. There was no [security] in those days; you could just go out. He got caught in the rain, and he rushed back to the White

House, but didn't change his clothes. A couple of days later, he came down with a cold. It got worse and worse, became pneumonia, and he was dead a month after he was inaugurated as president.

[The nation was] totally surprised because everything you read going up to that time said, "Oh, he looked so young. He looked so vigorous." He may have been helped along by his doctors who treated him with all kinds of wild treatments like bloodletting, giving him laxatives, then giving something to make him vomit, and some Indian snake weed. Later they discovered—at least one study found—that though they claimed they were treating him for pneumonia, they were treating him for the common cold. If he had better treatment, he might have survived.

[Harrison died thirty days, plus twelve hours, into his presidency.] There was panic because the vice president was not [in Washington]. In those days the vice presidents had nothing to do, so Tyler had gone home to Williamsburg, Virginia, to his plantation. They sent two guys; they took a steamship and a train and then horses to ride to his house and got there in the middle of the night. . . . They rushed Tyler back. Now, he'd had some wind that Harrison wasn't doing well, but he didn't think it was proper to rush to Washington and hover over the body.

Tyler was sworn in, and then the problem was, what do you call him? This had never happened before. The Constitution didn't really say what to do; it just said the vice president takes the duties of the president. It didn't say he was president. But John Tyler said, "Call me President Tyler."

JOHN TYLER

10th President, 1841–1845

Overall Rank: 39 — ★ — Total Score: 372	In 2017, historians ranked Tyler one spot below William Henry Harrison, the man he succeeded as president. In earlier surveys, their relative positions were reversed. Tyler's decline in overall rank was due in part to a fall in economic management from 31st to 39th. Historians rank him third from last in relations with Congress, above only Andrew Johnson and James Buchanan.

Party: Whig
b. March 29, 1790, Charles City County, Virginia
d. January 18, 1862, Richmond, Virginia
First Ladies: Letitia Christian Tyler (1841–1842) and
Julia Gardiner Tyler (1844–1845)
Age entering office: 51

Historian: **Edward P. Crapol**

Edward Crapol is a professor emeritus of American history at the College of William and Mary. On May 17, 1999, he joined C-SPAN during our yearlong television series, American Presidents, *to discuss his book,* John Tyler, the Accidental President.

John Tyler was forewarned about President William Henry Harrison's serious illness [in the spring of 1841]. He had received letters from friends, and I think he knew that he might face the possibility of being a vice president who would succeed to the presidency. So, I think he planned ahead, and he planned ahead very decisively and successfully.

People did not expect the vice president to become the president, and at the time that Harrison died, the assumption was that Tyler would serve as acting president. Tyler went to Washington, once being notified of Harrison's death, with the intent of being president, not acting president. He took an oath of office to make sure that his legitimacy as president would be recognized. He gave a speech—some called it an inaugural address. Then he moved to have Congress—there was a special session of Congress that Harrison had called in late May, early June—successfully pass resolutions, and both houses recognized him as president. So, one of the big accomplishments of John Tyler is setting this precedent that the vice president will, in fact, become the president in all regards. He will occupy the office, and he will have all the duties and privileges that go with the presidency.

William Henry Harrison and John Tyler were both natives of Charles City County [Virginia]. They were both born within five miles of each other. . . . William Henry Harrison and John Tyler served in the Congress together. I wouldn't say they had a close relationship, but nonetheless they were friends. When they were placed on the ticket for the 1840 election, it was a political decision rather than a personal decision. John Tyler was placed on the ticket to secure the Southern vote and to make sure that the ticket was successful.

Tyler started out as a Jeffersonian Republican, and he always considered himself as a follower of Jefferson and Madison. He did support the Democrats, [but] he became disillusioned with Andrew Jackson. He felt Andrew Jackson was becoming much too strong an executive. He essentially broke with the Democrats and identified with the Whigs, but his relationship with the Whigs was always tenuous. He was placed on the Whig ticket in 1840 with William Henry Harrison, but I think from John Tyler's viewpoint, he never made any commitments about a Whig program or any commitment to Henry Clay's American System. And so, consequently, when Tyler does take over as president, he feels that he is independent of the Whigs and that he is a president without a party.

He was notified of Harrison's death when he was living in Williamsburg and before he left [for Washington]. He spoke to one of his friends, Nathaniel Beverley Tucker, about his predicament of not having a party. Tucker said, "Well, you should build a party or find a party." Tyler said, "I have no opportunity to do that."

It's instructive in Tyler's case, being a president without a party. He is never really able to mount a legislative program, and that's the reason he turns to foreign policy as an area in which he can at least have some accomplishments. I think he hoped, as a Madisonian, to use foreign policy to overcome sectionalism, to overcome domestic issues that stood in his way. . . . He had a very contentious relationship with

Congress, . . . and so, his areas of accomplishment are not in terms of legislation but rather in the realm of setting a precedent, becoming the first vice president to become president, and also his foreign policy accomplishments that would include Hawaii, Texas, and the treaty with China.

During his presidency, he and his secretary of state, Daniel Webster, were very interested in expanding American influence in the Pacific. They were, as a number of historians have noted, Pacific-minded. They were interested in gaining access to [territory] on the western coast of North America and California for the United States. In 1842, Tyler and Webster issued what's known as the Tyler Doctrine, which extended American influence into the Pacific and guaranteed the independence of Hawaii, or the Sandwich Islands, as they were known. As part of that, Tyler—this is Tyler the nationalist rather than simply a champion of the Old South—sought to appeal to Northern commercial interests. Webster was very influential as well. They sought the United States' first treaty with China. Caleb Cushing, a New Englander, was sent as the US representative to get the United States its first China treaty, which they did in 1844. Webster, by that time, had resigned as secretary of state, but he was instrumental in setting it up. In that particular treaty, . . . the United States gained access to ports in China, received the privileges of extraterritoriality, and established the principle of most-favored nation.

. . . Texas had established its independence, and the previous administration, Van Buren's, had not sought the annexation of Texas. Texans wanted to be annexed to the United States. The reason that it was controversial was because it would add a slave state to the Union. John Tyler, early on, was interested in annexing Texas to make his mark as a president. His first secretary of state, Daniel Webster, a Northerner and not a supporter of slavery, was not keen on annexing Texas. So, Tyler essentially waited on his move to annex Texas. After Webster resigned—they split over the Texas issue—his next secretary of state, Abel Upshur, secured a treaty of annexation. In January of 1844, it appeared that there was sufficient support in the Senate for the approval of this treaty. However, Upshur was killed in the explosion of the USS *Princeton* in late

February 1844, and his replacement as secretary of state was John C. Calhoun. John C. Calhoun also wanted the annexation of Texas, but he made it an issue of slavery and about the expansion of slavery [which he strongly favored]. Consequently, that treaty was then defeated in the Senate because it became identified with the expansion of slavery.

Tyler, nonetheless, remained interested in the annexation of Texas. After the election of Polk in 1844 and before he left office, one of the last things Tyler did was to secure the approval of an annexation treaty by [using the legislative tactic of] a joint resolution of Congress. That's another one of his precedents—essentially finessing the Senate's role in approving such a treaty by getting a joint resolution. That approach cast a long shadow over American expansion in the nineteenth century. Following presidents looked back at Tyler—for example, Grant, when he faced resistance to his efforts to annex Santo Domingo, brought up whether he should follow John Tyler's precedent. He did not. The other example is William McKinley, who as president in 1898 could not get a treaty of annexation through the Senate either, so he emulated Tyler and [successfully pursued a] joint resolution for the annexation of Hawaii.

Tyler, while president, settled an ongoing war with the Seminole Indians in Florida in 1842. . . . John Tyler was proud of that, that he had achieved a peace. In terms of the way he viewed Native Americans, he wanted them treated with justice, [but] he also had a very paternalistic viewpoint. He looked upon them as people that had to be guided and educated.

[John Tyler had two wives and fathered fifteen children. First lady Letitia Tyler died in the White House in September 1842. John Tyler soon married the vivacious and thirty-years-younger Julia Gardiner. The new first couple entertained at the White House regularly.] John Tyler, as a president and as a host, apparently, in the White House was very gracious and had very elegant manners. He was able to charm most people. There's an account of Charles Dickens visiting the White House in 1842. . . . Dickens thought Tyler was a very fitting head of state for the United States and is recorded as having said that it was a nice contrast to the members of the House of Representatives, many of whom were "tobacco-spitters." John Tyler would never have stooped to such ill manners as that.

Musicians and historians can dispute this, but [during] the various levies and celebrations that he hosted in the White House, he began the tradition of playing *Hail to the Chief* late in his presidency. This tradition was then taken over by Mrs. Polk. She, I think, gets most credit for it, but it began in Tyler's presidency.

... During his presidency, Tyler ... is ostracized, certainly, by the Whigs. They are very angry with him, ... openly hostile. John Tyler suffered great abuse; he was burned in effigy; he was censured once for his veto of a tariff. There were calls for his impeachment. So, he suffered mightily for not having a party. I think his standing in history is influenced by that. Most people look at it from the viewpoint of the Whigs rather than the viewpoint of Tyler.

Tyler, by 1843–1844, was trying to mount a third-party candidacy so that he could seek re-election in 1844. He was unsuccessful, and he really framed the campaign for [Democrat] James K. Polk and Polk's platform of expansionism. Tyler then became identified once again as a Democrat [and retreated from public life].

[In 1860] when Lincoln was elected, Tyler was quite upset. He saw Lincoln as someone who would stop the expansion of slavery, and for John Tyler, that was crucial—the ability for the slave states to continue to expand. He was part of a Washington, DC, peace conference in February of 1861; he attempted to forge a compromise that would prevent civil war, but he was unsuccessful [and ultimately opposed the resulting peace treaty]. Tyler then left the peace conference, came to Virginia, and participated in the state's convention that debated secession. He was appalled at the suggestion of some western Virginians, those that ultimately formed the state of West Virginia, when they spoke out against expansion and found no difficulty in accepting the limitations on the expansion of slavery. That angered John Tyler a great deal, and then he voted for secession.

As the secession movement grew, he was elected a member of the Confederate Congress, but he died [in a Richmond, Virginia, hotel] before the session began. As ... a member of the Confederate Congress, he was technically a traitor. [John Tyler was buried in Richmond in a casket draped in the Confederate flag.]

John Tyler became president after William Henry Harrison died a month into his term. Virginian Tyler, seen in this 1841 lithograph, was later elected to the Confederate congress but died before taking office. *Courtesy Library of Congress*

Tyler's citizenship [was later posthumously] restored in a general amnesty. His wife's, Julia's, citizenship was never challenged. She became an active American citizen after the defeat of the Confederacy.

In terms of slavery, John Tyler was opposed to the slave trade. He also spoke out against auctions of slaves in DC; he wanted to outlaw that. However, he never manumitted any of his own slaves, and he never sought any amelioration of slavery. And in the secession crisis, he ended up being a supporter of the "peculiar institution" of slavery.

In doing the research for my book, I'd become fascinated with this notion that this man, who was identified principally as a states-righter and a champion of the Old South, was in fact someone who had also enhanced the role of the presidency and played an important role in making the executive position what it is today. . . . Certainly, when he left office in 1845, he felt that he had improved the state of the nation, he felt that he enhanced the office of the presidency. He left the office feeling that he had helped restore prosperity from a depression, he had helped expand trade into Asia. He also felt that there had been growth in commerce and manufacturing, and he believed that he had helped in terms of urban growth. Historians are very critical of John Tyler, yet I, for one, would . . . say that his accomplishments were also fairly significant.

WARREN G. HARDING

29th President, 1921–1923

Overall Rank: 40
— ★ —
Total Score: 360

Historians have consistently ranked Harding in the bottom five of all presidents. His scandal-plagued presidency is reflected in low ranks for moral authority (40th), vison/setting an agenda (40th), and administrative skills (42nd—second from last). His highest ranking is in pursued equal justice for all (33rd).

Party: Republican
b. November 2, 1865, Corsica, Ohio
d. August 2, 1923, San Francisco, California
First Lady: Florence Mabel Kling Harding
Age entering office: 55

Historian: John W. Dean

As the White House counsel for President Nixon, John Dean was at the center of events surrounding the Watergate scandal. He is currently an author and political commentator. Dean joined Booknotes *on January 16, 2004, to discuss his book,* Warren G. Harding, *part of The American Presidents biography book series, about a presidency marked by scandal.*

I grew up in Marion, Ohio, which is Warren G. Harding's home base. He wasn't born there, but he came there very early in his life, and he was the big name in town when I was growing up. In fact, my paper route took me right by his house when I was about fourteen. . . . Most of my friends were much longer-time residents of Marion, and Harding was somebody who fascinated everybody in town because of his persona. The high school was named Warren G. Harding High School. There was this Harding memorial, and that Harding memorial, and so on. So, he's a major figure in the town and the first president I really had an awareness of.

Harding died in San Francisco. He had taken this western trip up to Alaska, the first president of the United States to go to Alaska, and he foresaw the potential of statehood for Alaska in 1923 when he went up there. He died [during his return trip to Washington] at the Palace Hotel in San Francisco. When the train brought [his body] back across the country, people lined up; they were in fields; they were at cross-ings; they were hanging off the rooftops of buildings. Apparently, a most moving thing was that the crowd would get clustered, and they would be singing some of Harding's favorite hymns. It was apparently quite a moving experience all across the country. It hadn't been since Lincoln had died, really, that anything had been quite as emotional. And then it wouldn't be until Roosevelt died, and, of course, in our lifetimes, the Kennedy assassination—we all recall how that impacted our lives. Harding had a big impact.

He was president in 1920, and he died in office in 1923. He was in office about 880-some-odd days. There are a number of presidents that haven't made a full term. I'm sure he would have been re-elected had he stood for re-election; he was a very popular president at the time he died, and he was very beloved in office. . . . [Yet] when presidents are ranked, he's considered the worst president of the United States. [Editor's note: In C-SPAN's survey, Harding ranks 40th.] He really got bashed by history after he died in office. Initially, there were a lot of very popular works that were overboard in their praise—and then it all started to turn.

Warren went to college at fourteen years of age, to a college [Ohio Central] that no longer exists. He taught for one year after he got out of college and was looking for a career. When he came to Marion, he realized that there was a newspaper for sale called the *Marion Star*. It had been not a very successful paper. It had been in existence for seven years and was up in the sheriff's office for repossession. Warren Harding had loved the newspaper business. As about a thirteen-year-old, his father, who was a doctor, had apprenticed him as a "printer's devil," which is a printer's handyman that does the dirty work—a "gofer" today. Warren had a facility with words, and he set type very quickly for such a young person. . . . In college he started, while he was a senior, a paper in Iberia, Ohio, where the college was located, and it was a relatively successful lit-tle six-page paper. . . . [At nineteen] he finds the [*Marion*] *Star* and says, "Let's make a go of it." He gets a couple of friends together, and they raise the three hundred bucks. Dr. Harding, his father, co-signs a note, and they get the paper, which really launches his career.

. . . Harding [had gone] to his first [political] convention as a nineteen-year-old kid. Because he's bought this newspaper, its most valuable asset was a free pass for all the railroads. So, he goes off to Chicago in 1884 to his first Republican convention. That's one of the defining events of his life, this country boy goes to Chicago and sees [James G.] Blaine as the Republican nominee. He sees Theodore Roosevelt putting people into nomination and a lot of the great speakers, and it obviously catches his fancy.

. . . His first really important [political] job was when he ran for the Ohio Senate and was in the Senate for several terms [1899–1903]. He retires from the Senate, and he ran a gubernatorial race once [in 1910] and was defeated. He didn't want to run; the party wanted him to run. He thought it a bad idea, and it was a bad idea. It was a very divisive time in Ohio politics. . . . While he was in the Senate—and this is one of the things that history has overlooked with Warren Harding—the Ohio Senate really had a fair amount of corruption in those days, and Warren Harding was not corrupted. He made a good living. He was a successful businessman long before he went into politics. He lived comfortably. . . . He became very respected in Ohio for that reason alone because everyone knew he was clean and that he was the go-to guy, somebody who could solve problems.

. . . He [concentrated on his newspaper business for the next several years and] really gets back into politics when there's an opening for the US Senate. Those who know him say, "Why don't you take a run at it?" He is, at this point, matured. He's in his early fifties, and he decides to take a go at it and very successfully runs. He is an interesting politician in the sense that, particularly in primaries, he refuses to speak ill of other Republicans. He followed Ronald Reagan's "11th commandment" long before Reagan: . . . he won't campaign hard against other Republicans for the nomination. This works. People like the fact that he's not a divisive politician, and he was elected to the US Senate on the first bid. That year was the first direct election [for US senators], 1914.

Florence Harding [was his wife and partner in the newspaper business. She] had been married once before she married Warren Harding.

She was married to the town rake, a fellow by the name of Pete DeWolf who was her next-door neighbor. She was a Kling, that was her family name. Her father was a very tough cookie, might be the best way to describe it. She was a disappointment to her father. . . . He'd always hoped to have a boy, and when Flossie came along, he raised her like he might his son rather than a daughter. [Her father] was actually the richest man in town of that era. He had a hardware store, and he took Flossie to the store, and she grew up around men. She was five years older than Warren Harding. At one point, she got into an affair, and the consensus is she did it because she was trying to escape from her very domineering father. It was a common-law marriage, and they had a child by this marriage. They left town. Old Man Kling, as he was known in Marion at the time, wouldn't help support the child or his daughter; she'd made her situation, and he wanted her to work it out, and she did. Later, she was teaching piano lessons and taught Warren Harding's sister the piano, and that's where it's believed she first met Warren. . . . Warren Harding would have been in his mid-twenties when they got married.

Harding was a person who collects people all the way through his life who become lifetime friends. Jim Phillips is one of them. Phillips married a lady who was supposed to be the most beautiful woman in Marion at the time. . . . Carrie Phillips was about ten years Florence Harding's junior. . . . There must have been a long-burning relationship because what happens is, Warren goes off and he's elected to the Ohio Senate. He gets active in Ohio politics. The newspaper and the supplement that the Hardings have get successful, and he becomes successful. Florence Harding falls very ill. . . . One of these times when she became ill, Carrie Phillips had just lost a child, and Jim Phillips had had a nervous breakdown. Warren arranges for his friend Jim to go to Battle Creek, to a sanitarium there. . . . Meanwhile, Carrie reaches out, and she's this attractive woman, and they start an affair that will go on for fifteen years. . . . It was well known [in Marion] long before it became public knowledge. It was known when I was growing up, for example, but it really didn't become widespread knowledge until 1968, when a fellow by the name of Francis Russell wrote a book called *The Shadow of Blooming Grove*. He discovered Harding's love letters from Carrie Phillips.

The best I can tell, his affair with Carrie Phillips lasts while he's in the US Senate. It's handled discreetly. They fell in love, and Carrie Phillips wanted Harding to divorce his wife. He refused to do so, and that's what breaks up the affair; Phillips then goes off to Europe.

[Harding was elected president in 1920, one of only three sitting senators ever to be elected president.] Harding has always been considered a dark-horse candidate who was put there by a cabal of senators. Not so. And the famous "smoke-filled room" story developed around Harding, but it didn't happen that way.

. . . Harding was a poker player and played his cards very close. He loved poker, played seriously. Every game he played was a good poker game. In the Senate, he was a favored player because he was a good player and won more than he lost. He played his nomination very much the same way. He held his cards very close, knew what he had and how to play his hand. And he and [longtime campaign aide] Harry Doherty came up with a very interesting scheme—running in the back of the pack. Everybody else would destroy themselves during the convention, and then there would be an opportunity for somebody to be the peacemaker. And that's how Harding would get the nomination. They would go through several ballots where he would not even be in play, and then slowly Doherty released the ballots that he had at the convention. . . . We had just gone into direct elections in the primaries, and the bosses were having less and less influence, so you really had a very legitimate nominating convention in those days. [Harding won the nomination on the tenth ballot. Massachusetts governor Calvin Coolidge was his running mate.]

He ran against [Democrat James] Cox who had Franklin Roosevelt as his running mate. Cox was the Ohio governor and a good governor. Harding ran one of these campaigns where he understates his case. He doesn't get nasty. He runs, in a sense, against Woodrow Wilson's policies rather than against Cox. Cox and Roosevelt had gone back to Wilson after they had gotten the nomination and said, "We will run on the League of Nations. We will make that the issue." The league had been something that Harding had been on the fence about in the Senate, and he decided that was a good campaign issue.

There were sixteen million votes for Harding, nine million votes for Cox. It was the largest landslide at that time in history with good coattails—[he ended up with both a Republican Senate and House].

Harding put together a very remarkable cabinet. He had Charles Evans Hughes [as his secretary of state], who was on the Supreme Court and then left the Supreme Court when he ran for president [against Wilson in 1916] and later went back on the Supreme Court—one of the finest minds on the court. [Herbert Hoover was his Commerce secretary, Andrew Mellon his Treasury secretary, John Davis at Labor, Albert Fall at Interior, and Harry Daugherty at Justice.]

I'd say his largest accomplishment was his 1921 disarmament conference. It was a major event. There had been some effort in the Senate to have such a conference take place. Harding, who was purportedly from the cabal of the Senate, told the Senate, "We'll do this on my terms when I'm ready," and he and Charles Evans Hughes worked this out. . . . It was a remarkably successful disarmament conference at the time. They got a substantial reduction of capital ships and a fair balance between the Brits and the US and the Japanese, who were the other major power at the time. He really pegged his foreign policy on [disarmament] because the nation was weary from war. It had been an unpleasant war, so it was very timely. That was his major foreign policy accomplishment.

In domestic [policy], his most lasting accomplishment was that he created the Bureau of the Budget in 1921, when he first got there. There had been talk of it by prior presidents. Wilson had rejected it, . . . but Harding believed in it. He'd been in the Senate, so he knew that there was a need for a good operation for the budget.

[He wanted a billion dollars cut from the federal budget.] That's huge; that's trillions by today's standards. So, he did a major cutback in spending. He brought in a fellow by the name of Charles Dawes, who would later become vice president [under Calvin Coolidge]; Dawes was the first director of the Bureau of the Budget. Dawes had a series of conferences over at the Department of Commerce's auditorium. They brought in all the senior civil servant people, supervisor level and above, as well as the cabinet. Harding put out an order that he wanted everybody to come, and Harding went to the first one. Dawes got up and did a show-and-tell at one point. He had two brooms in his hand, and he said, "This broom cost X dollars, and this broom cost Y dollars," which was much more expensive. He explained how the navy had purchased [one style of broom] and the army had purchased the other. And while the navy ran a surplus, the army purchased all these other brooms at excess cost because they didn't like the binding around the top of the straw. He said, "This is never going to happen again. We're now going to be a much more efficient government." It made a point. Dawes, when he later left office, took his broom and took the sign on his door, which was cardboard and handwritten, "Bureau of the Budget." He refused to even have a printed sign made for his office.

[Harding appointed four Supreme Court justices in his eight hundred days.] It had a very large impact. He would put William Howard Taft on as chief justice. Taft was a former president at that point. He would put other justices [George Sutherland, Pierce Butler, and Edward T. Sanford,] who have stood the test of time well, but I think that the Taft appointment is probably the most important.

[The Harding administration has become associated with scandal, but] the only one that came up at all while Harding was alive was the Veterans Affairs scandal, where the man he'd appointed [Charles Forbes] was there bilking the place; he was selling off surplus supplies. When Harding learned of it, he called Forbes over to the White House and wanted to know about it, and he was lied to. Harding finally fired him for insubordination as soon as he had heard there was a problem.

. . . There were two people that went to jail in the Harding administration [Interior Secretary Albert Fall and VA Chief Charles Forbes], and you also had Jess Smith at the Justice Department, who was probably up to his eyeballs in misbehavior, but he committed suicide.

[Interior Secretary Albert Fall and the Teapot Dome scandal] happens after Harding's death. . . . Fall went to prison for bribery. He was reportedly bribed by a fellow by the name of Edward Doheny, an oil man, and Harry Sinclair. [However,] both Sinclair and Doheny were acquitted of bribing. Fall was also part of a conspiracy case, but he was not indicted in that. As the case goes along and he gets older and he's very ill, he's finally convicted of bribery [and ultimately served one year in jail].

Doheny was actually a friend of Albert Fall's. They had both once panned for gold in New Mexico, and then Fall had become a very successful businessman in New Mexico. He had been very instrumental in bringing New Mexico into statehood. Fall came back to DC and represented New Mexico in the Senate, and that's where he met Warren Harding. Doheny had . . . continued looking for oil and struck it in California and became one of the wealthiest men in the nation at that time. He did a deal with Fall. Fall always said that he had borrowed $100,000 from Doheny because they were old friends, and he was short. Fall had told Harding when he went into the cabinet, "This [government service] is really a stretch for me; I need to get back to work." Fall was a very successful corporate lawyer and had big clients, and it just doesn't seem right to me that he would be so stupid to take a bribe so conspicuously.

[The president and first lady both died before Harding's term would have been completed.] Florence Harding was very ill, but the president

Warren Harding's scandal-filled presidency was cut short by his sudden death in 1923. This c. 1921–1923 photo shows him outside the White House. *Courtesy Library of Congress*

was not physically in any way debilitated while he was in the White House. We now know he had a bad heart; he'd had a bad heart all of his life. He had a White House doctor who at one point, after he came back from a very bad bout with the flu, sent him to Florida. In fact, one of the things that Harding has been accused of is being lackadaisical—he would go out and play golf three days a week. This was actually prescribed by his doctor, and the way Harding played golf, he almost made it an aerobic sport. . . . No one wanted to play with him because while he was president, . . . he'd take no mulligans. He played exactly by the rules, and he played very quickly. He would shoot, and then he would walk very quickly to the next shot, so, he would get his heart rate up because he knew he had to take exercise.

Because Charles Evans Hughes was secretary of state for Harding, he was the senior member of the cabinet, and he would give Harding's eulogy. At the time, there was still thought that Hughes was presidential timbre and would run for president, and so [it was suggested] he should back off a little bit because of some of the corruption that occurred during the Harding years in the Veterans Administration. . . . Hughes's aides are telling him, "Don't be too good to Harding in this eulogy." Hughes says, "What I have to say about Warren Harding, I know firsthand." It is a wonderful eulogy. It's a very honest eulogy. Florence Harding would write him and say, "I couldn't change a sentence in what you said." Hughes said that he had based this on the man he knew, the man he'd worked with.

After Harding dies, a story comes out that he has an illegitimate daughter. In fact, it really becomes one of the turning points of his reputation. In 1927, a woman by the name of Nan Britton publishes a book called *The President's Daughter*. The girl's name is Elizabeth Ann, and in the book, Britton says the father had never met the child and that the affair had started in 1919, while he's still in the Senate, and continued while he was in the White House. During the Bill Clinton years, this story came up a couple of times. I had the gravest doubts about this happening. When you really start getting into some of the people who had knowledge [of the time period], it seemed to me much more myth. [Britton says in the book that the Secret Service interrupted the two of them in a closet somewhere in the White House.] The chief agent of the Secret

Service, a fellow by the name of Edmund Starling, denied all this. It just didn't seem possible to me, even though the White House wasn't anything like it is today, as far as security.

I'd actually been talking to Warren Harding III about this [story]. I know where there is DNA, but I didn't want to do a DNA test to resolve it until I had the permission of both Elizabeth Ann or her family and the existing Warren Harding or his brother George. . . . I think this would be a great mystery to resolve, but Elizabeth Ann may well not want to know her paternity issue.

[Editor's note: After Elizabeth Ann Blaesing's death in 2005, her family and some of the Harding relatives did consent to a DNA test, which proved that she was, indeed, the daughter of Warren Harding, settling once and for all the decades-old controversy.]

The reason history got so astray on Harding is that it was long believed that his presidential papers had been burned by Florence Harding. She did burn some, but what actually had happened is his longtime secretary . . . had all of his Senate papers and then took all of his presidential papers and put them in the basement of the White House. They were there until 1929 when they were discovered during the Hoover administration. They were all sent off to Marion, Ohio, and they stayed in the basement of his house. Finally, in 1964, they were approaching the hundredth anniversary of his birth, and the Ohio Historical Society convinced those who had control of the papers for the Harding Association to make them available. . . . I used those extensively because I'd never had a chance to look at them all these years.

[After reviewing the documents, here's my conclusion:] none of [this administration's scandals] really involved Harding himself. He died before all of this happened. Harding is tagged with Teapot Dome, which occurs after he's dead. He's not involved in any corruption that there's any sign of—in my estimation and that of other historians who've looked closely at it.

Because of my own background and experience [in the Watergate scandal], I wanted to make sure this man had a fair shake. I think that's true with any president. I was very interested in how the myth of misbehavior had grown up around Harding. I didn't want to pick a fight with historians, but I would track down [some of] their sources and would find it was third-hand hearsay, at best, that was being relied on. I didn't think this was a fair way to treat a president. . . .

I think if historians really start mining this area . . . we would have another "hidden-hand" presidency, like Eisenhower, who was later discovered to be much more involved. Warren Harding was thought to be lazy and lackadaisical. Not true. Here is a man who has had tremendous self-confidence his entire life. He is a man who has succeeded by not trying to get himself out in front. He is a man who does not toot his own horn. He really becomes president by under-running rather than over-running. I think that Charles Evans Hughes saw this quality in Harding and realized, this is a fine mind. This is a good man. He had done a nice job. After Wilson, it was a very turbulent time. We were in the aftermath of World War I. Wilson had a stroke at the end of his presidency, so the nation really was adrift when Harding comes in. The economy was in trouble. And Harding is also—by Wilson's standards—a very progressive president.

[My book is part of historian Arthur Schlesinger's biography series on the presidents]. . . . When I finished, Arthur said, "John, you have made me rethink Harding, and I think you'll make a lot of other historians rethink him too."

FRANKLIN PIERCE

Overall Rank: 41

— ★ —

Total Score: 315

Historians have placed Franklin Pierce third from the bottom in all three C-SPAN presidential surveys, ranking him above only Andrew Johnson and James Buchanan. Moreover, in 2017, he ranked among the bottom five presidents in every leadership category, including a next-to-last ranking in pursued equal justice for all (42nd).

Party: Democrat
b. November 23, 1804, Hillsborough (now Hillsboro), New Hampshire
d. October 8, 1869, Concord, New Hampshire
First Lady: Jane Means Appleton Pierce
Age entering office: 48

Historian: Peter A. Wallner

Peter Wallner is a retired history teacher, adjunct instructor at Franklin Pierce University, and most recently the library director at the New Hampshire Historical Society. He was interviewed on Q & A on October 25, 2004, about his book, Franklin Pierce: New Hampshire's Favorite Son, *the first in his two-volume biography of the president.*

Franklin Pierce is probably the least known and least studied president. . . . He had a twenty-five-year career in public life before he ever became president, and I felt it was worth studying that . . . separately as a way of establishing who he was and what he stood for before his very controversial presidency.

[He's frequently near the bottom of historians' rankings.] It's not entirely fair, but I certainly understand why he's there. The Kansas-Nebraska bill and the resulting violence [between pro- and anti-slavery forces] in Kansas was seen as the turning point; from there on, it was a downward slide right to the Civil War. Pierce is often blamed for the Kansas-Nebraska Act and for the coming of the Civil War as a result. That's the reason why he's ranked so low. But there are other factors in his presidency that should give him a slightly higher rating, mainly the fact that it was a very honest administration. One historian called the period of time that Pierce lived in "the plundering generation." All the presidencies from Taylor up through Grant were known for their corruption. Pierce's administration is a beacon of honesty and integrity. There were no scandals in his administration.

He was president from 1853 to 1857. He was not renominated. He's the only [elected] president to be denied nomination by his party for a second term who wanted it.

Franklin Pierce grew up in Hillsborough, New Hampshire, about twenty miles west of the state capital, Concord, in what was known as the hill country of southwest New Hampshire. He lived thirty years in Hillsborough and the rest of his life in Concord.

Pierce's father, Benjamin Pierce, was a Revolutionary War officer who settled on cheap land in southwest New Hampshire and eventually built up a very successful life for himself as a farmer and a tavern keeper. It was a tavern on the stagecoach lines. He was a businessman and a politician. Benjamin Pierce became governor of New Hampshire. Franklin was the seventh of nine [children], the fourth of five boys. . . . He went to several schools. He went to a little schoolhouse in Hillsborough for his early years. Then he went to several boarding schools in nearby towns. Eventually he went off to Bowdoin College, which was his father's choice, apparently, because his father knew the president of the college.

He was . . . elected to the US Congress when he was only twenty-seven years old. He served two terms in Congress, and then the state legislature chose him [in 1836] for a term in the Senate. . . . He lasted about five years, and then he left in 1842. The reason he said he was leaving was because his wife didn't like politics. He had, at that point, two young children at home in Concord, and he wanted to concentrate on his family. However, I contend that he really left because the Democrat Party in New Hampshire was divided, and he came back to New Hampshire to take over the leadership of the party. He did an effective job of that in the next ten years. He was basically the boss of the Democratic Party in New Hampshire.

Pierce did have a drinking problem. . . . There were several instances in his life where drinking was a factor. One time in Congress, he had been involved in an incident at a theater in which he was clearly drunk with several other congressmen, and that was used against him later on. But he joined the temperance movement for a number of years; he was actually president of the New Hampshire State Temperance Society for a while. He did battle with his alcohol problem throughout his life; . . . but it was only at the very end of his life that it was totally out of control.

As soon as the [Mexican] War was declared [in 1846], Pierce went down to the local office in Concord and volunteered as a private. At the time, there were no regiments being organized in New England. About six months later, when the Congress finally got around to creating some new regiments, Pierce was immediately promoted to colonel. He was told to raise a regiment in New England. Then, within a few weeks, they made him brigadier general and told him to organize a whole brigade of three regiments and take them to Mexico to join Winfield Scott on the march to Mexico City. Scott was a brilliant general, one of the best generals in our entire history, but he was also a very difficult person to deal with. His nickname was "Old Fuss and Feathers," which demonstrates his personality. Every picture you see of him, he's wearing every ribbon and braid you could possibly wear, and he had literally created his own uniforms. He was also quite a prickly character, someone who tended to argue and fight with all of his leading officers. But his strategy was terrific, and he was a real professional soldier who wanted to professionalize the American military. He made a tremendous contribution to the professionalism of the American Army. [And, in 1852, the Whig Party nominated him as their presidential candidate, running against Pierce.]

After the Mexican War, there was all kinds of new territory that we had to decide how to organize and put on the move towards statehood. California's Gold Rush occurred very soon after the Mexican War, and California suddenly had enough people to become a state. California was applying for statehood as a free state. That would have been the thirty-first state—there were fifteen slave and fifteen free states at the time. If you took in a thirty-first state and it was a free state and there were no other Southern states coming in, this would offset the South's equal balance in the Senate. The South had a veto in the Senate because they had an equal number of senators, so they insisted, if we're going to take in California, then let's try to solve some of the slavery problems that we're having; [we need] some assurance that if we're going to be outvoted in the Senate, it is not going to impact our slave system.

They insisted on a stronger fugitive slave law, which the North was opposed to. And there were a whole other series of compromises. The slave trade was finally banned in the District of Columbia. Utah and New Mexico territories were organized and set on the road to state-hood with the issue of slavery not being mentioned, apparently, there-fore leaving it up to the settlers of those two states. The Texas debt was resolved; Texas had a debt owed to foreign countries from when it was an independent nation. . . . So, there was a whole series of compromises which eventually were passed in 1850 and which many politicians at the time claimed were a final settlement of all the issues existing with regard to slavery. Of course, that wasn't to be the case.

Franklin Pierce won [the 1852 Democratic nomination] on the forty-ninth ballot. That was one of [the] things that I found in my research that was most interesting. It's always been assumed that he was chosen because the party couldn't agree on anybody else and they just picked Pierce, who according to the history books was sort of an amia-ble nonentity, out of the blue. . . . But, in reality, Pierce had a very small but determined group of politicians that he had mentored in Concord. They were known as the "Concord clique." Several of them had gov-ernment jobs in Washington, DC, and they had begun to consider him a presidential candidate a year in advance of the convention, and they devised a strategy. . . . He knew he was a candidate, but they kept it a secret. At a time when the leading candidates were knocking each other off by criticizing each other, he stayed under the radar screen. At the convention they waited for the right moment, and they got the Virginia delegation to nominate him, more as a test, to see how it would fly with the other delegates. But it was well planned, well crafted in advance, and it worked exactly as they planned.

. . . [During the 1852 campaign, his opponents] were claiming that Pierce's military record had been exaggerated, that he had not been a successful general, that he had actually been a coward. Pierce had been injured in the very first major battle that his brigade engaged in. . . . This was at the Battle of Contreras on the outskirts of Mexico City in 1847. . . . Pierce's brigade was ordered to charge an entrenched Mexican force that was on top of a hill; the artillery barrage apparently startled his horse, and his horse threw him and landed on him, and he was injured and knocked out of that battle.

[The criticism of Franklin Pierce's military performance wasn't warranted.] He was knocked out and had a very severe knee injury, which made it impossible for him to walk for a couple of days. [The criticism that] was made of him was, how could you claim to be a courageous officer when you were out of the battle without shedding a drop of blood? . . . But, what's interesting about the 1852 Pierce versus Scott presidential campaign is that almost all of the Mexican War officers preferred Pierce to Scott. . . .

. . . He was forty-seven when was elected, forty-eight when he was inaugurated, the youngest president up to that time. . . . It was quite a landslide, at least in the Electoral College. It was the largest Electoral College victory since 1820. He only lost four states out of the thirty-one states in the Union. On the popular vote, it was closer, but he still had 50 percent and about a 250,000-vote lead over his Whig opponent. . . . Three million, one hundred thousand [votes were cast]; about 70 percent of the electorate voted in those days, and even then, it was one of the lower turnouts of the nineteenth century. Only white adult males [could vote then].

Benny Pierce, his son, was killed on January 6, 1853, after Pierce had been elected president and before he was inaugurated. He was killed in a train wreck in Andover, Massachusetts. Franklin Pierce, his wife, and son were on the way back to Concord after visiting relatives over the holidays. . . . Just outside of Andover, the car in which they were riding, the rear axle broke. The car started bouncing violently along the tracks. Pierce grabbed his wife. He was sitting in the front bench of the car with Jane. He tried to reach behind him for Benny. He missed. The car tumbled down the embankment, and Benny's head was crushed, and he was killed instantly. He was eleven and a half at the time.

This was covered greatly [by the press] throughout the nation. There was a tremendous amount of sympathy for Franklin Pierce. Many of his friends read about it in the newspapers, and they were all very shocked.

Benny was their youngest of three sons and the last surviving child. Their first child died a few days after he was born in 1836. And their second son, Frankie, died in 1843 of typhus at age four and a half. For the next two weeks, Pierce was going through the ceremony of the funeral. His wife didn't even attend the funeral. It took place in Andover where the accident occurred. Then, Franklin Pierce accompanied the body back to Concord by himself. . . . There was a burial ceremony at the Old North Cemetery, where Franklin Pierce is buried. Then he stayed in Concord for a while and received visitors and also began to deal again with his cabinet. He made frequent trips back and forth to Andover, where Jane remained with relatives. Jane was in such a bad state mentally as a result of the accident that [Franklin] spent a lot of his time in Andover trying to comfort her and then running back to Boston or Concord to meet with key political leaders as he began to choose his cabinet.

Franklin Pierce was certainly devastated by the death, and it came at a very crucial time politically. . . . By the time he got back to the position of making selections, he was under a lot of pressure from different groups and wasn't able to choose the cabinet that he wanted.

[When Franklin Pierce was putting his cabinet together,] he went to James Buchanan for ideas. . . . He and Buchanan were very similar in their political views, in their views of the Constitution, Jacksonian Democratic views. But in their methods, they were somewhat different. Pierce really wanted a coalition cabinet. He was elected by all branches of the Democratic Party . . . in 1852. He believed that, therefore, he had a responsibility to try to keep that coalition together and to appoint people from various wings of the party into his cabinet. Buchanan had a different view. He believed that you only appoint your close friends, those totally loyal to you personally. [Buchanan agreed to serve as US ambassador to the United Kingdom and was out of the country while the Kansas-Nebraska debate roiled.]

Pierce was called a "doughface"—a term that referred to Northern politicians with Southern sympathies, . . . more pro-slavery. The term came from John Randolph, a senator from Virginia, and it was first used to refer to Northerners who voted for the Missouri Compromise back in 1820. Randolph referred to them as "doughfaces," meaning that they were easily manipulated.

I don't think Pierce was [a Southern sympathizer]. I think he had a strong set of political principles, which tended to be the same as those in the South. He believed in the strict construction of the Constitution. He believed in limited power of the federal government. He believed in states' rights. This was his political philosophy. It was also the political philosophy of the Jacksonian Democratic Party, of which he was a member. So, when people say that Franklin Pierce was pro-Southern or pro-slavery, that's not actually true. He was simply a strict constructionist and a Jacksonian Democrat, and that was their stand at the time.

In Franklin Pierce's cabinet was Jefferson Davis [future president of the Confederacy]. Davis and Franklin Pierce were very good friends, which would cause Franklin Pierce enormous difficulty when the Civil War began. . . . Pierce first met Jefferson Davis when Pierce was a young senator. Jefferson Davis had come to Washington to spend a few months to lobby for a commission in the army. He was a West Point graduate but had left the army a few years earlier because he saw no future in it for himself. Then Congress passed a bill to create some new regiments, and they thought that maybe he could return to the army as commander of one of these regiments. So, he came to Washington and met Pierce. They became good friends. Pierce, in fact, took Davis to meet President Martin Van Buren.

In 1852, we always think of slavery as the big concern, and it was a major concern. At the time Pierce was elected, it was somewhat muted because of the Compromise of 1850. But the Fugitive Slave Law was causing a lot of anguish in the North, as Northern federal marshals and Northern officials were expected to return runaway slaves. Other issues, though, were emerging. There was a lot of immigration. . . . Over half a million immigrants were coming into the United States every year. There were many who believed that this was a danger to the nation and that it should be slowed down. There was a strong anti-Catholic sentiment at the time, which later would blow up into what was known as the Know-Nothing Party. There was a concern about a transcontinental railroad. California was a new state. There was a definite need for a transcontinental railroad. The problem, of course, was, where do you build it? The South wanted it to go through Texas. The North wanted it to go farther north. And, in foreign policy—we still had a lot of problems with Great Britain over Central America. There was a desire to take Cuba, which becomes one of the big issues in the Pierce administration. Spain had control of Cuba, as it did until the late nineteenth century, and the South saw Cuba as a natural growth of its territory.

There's a lot about Pierce's presidency that is not usually studied because of the Kansas-Nebraska bill. That got all the attention. But in reality, there was a lot going on with regard to foreign affairs that is quite fascinating. . . . He definitely had an aggressive foreign policy. He believed in the expansion of the nation, believed in nationalism, and his goal was to acquire more territory.

[James Buchanan long had his eyes on the White House. In 1856, Franklin Pierce didn't find out that he wasn't going to be his party's nominee] until the Democratic convention in June at Cincinnati. He thought he had a chance. He had support. He knew James Buchanan was a leading candidate, but Franklin had a coalition with Stephen A. Douglas that he thought would possibly get him the nomination. Douglas supporters agreed they would vote for Pierce in the early ballots if the Pierce people would switch to Douglas in later ballots if Pierce's candidacy was not going to succeed. After the second or third ballot, the Douglas people deserted Pierce and went to Buchanan, and Buchanan got the nomination.

. . . Pierce was very gracious about it. He was very kind to Buchanan, was very helpful in the transition. He seemed to take some measure of gratification in the fact that the Democratic Party won the election, that it was the same platform that he had run on. I think Pierce understood that he was personally too unpopular.

Pierce was only fifty-two years old, and he never worked again. He spent the rest of his life trying to take care of his wife, and she finally died in 1863. But he never held a job after he left the White House.

He remained involved in politics. He was very upset about the move towards the Civil War. He spent two and a half years in Europe after

President Franklin Pierce, seen in this c. 1855–1865 photo, was denied renomination by his own Democratic Party. Although only fifty-two when he left office, he never worked again. *Courtesy Library of Congress*

he left the White House; he and his wife went on an extended tour. He returned just before John Brown's raid at Harpers Ferry. He was very upset about that and spent a lot of time writing letters to people and sending letters to the papers, talking about the need for what he would consider the silent majority to speak out against this fanaticism that he saw happening on both sides, North and South. When Lincoln was elected, and the Southern states began to secede, Pierce proposed that all the former presidents gather in Washington and issue some kind of statement. It didn't happen. None of the others would join him. So, he worked very hard to try to prevent the war from occurring.

He spoke out many times saying that he thought slavery was a moral evil, that he wished it didn't exist, that he thought it was a moral stain on the nation. But he believed that it was up to the individual states to decide what to do about slavery. He also thought—and he sincerely believed this—that if the North hadn't attacked the South so much for this moral sin of slavery, that the South eventually, over time, would have ended slavery on its own. He felt that the Civil War was unnecessary. He always said that, and he never took it back, even at the height of the war itself. He always believed . . . that it was brought upon the nation by fanatics on both sides.

He died before his sixty-fifth birthday . . . in 1869. . . . When he died, he was very unpopular. Not only was he an unpopular president, but his actions during the Civil War made him extremely unpopular. He spoke out continuously and loudly against the Lincoln administration, particularly because of the suspension of the Writ of Habeas Corpus, the imposition of martial law, the restrictions on freedom of the press and freedom of speech, which the Lincoln administration imposed on the North. Pierce believed that was unnecessary and was not justified. He spoke out very loudly about that, so much so that he was considered a traitor by many people in the North.

Franklin Pierce was a more significant figure as a political leader in the mid-nineteenth century than he's generally considered to have been. If you read his views, if you read what he believed in at the time, it wasn't so far removed from the mainstream of political thinking, even today.

Pierce's political career spans a very interesting time. He was involved with the rise of the common man in politics; with westward expansion; with the rise of corporations, banking, and railroads in this country; with immigration; with religious intolerance and anti-Catholic sentiment; and with the rise of manufacturing. Pierce engaged in all these things. He was involved in all these issues in his twenty-five-year career before he even got to the presidency. When you study someone like Franklin Pierce, whether or not he was a great man, you're dealing with all the big issues of the time.

ANDREW JOHNSON

Overall Rank: 42

— ★ —

Total Score: 275

Historians have ranked Andrew Johnson, the first president to be impeached, next to last in all three surveys, above only James Buchanan. He ranks last in administrative skills and relations with Congress. His highest rank is 37th in economic management.

Party: Democrat
b. December 29, 1808, Raleigh, North Carolina
d. July 31, 1875, Carter County, Tennessee
First Lady: Eliza McCardle Johnson
Age entering office: 56

Historian: **David O. Stewart**

David Stewart spent many years as a trial and appellate lawyer arguing before juries, the US Senate, and the US Supreme Court before becoming an author and serving as president of the Washington Independent Review of Books. *On July 19, 2018, he joined Q & A to discuss his book,* Impeached: The Trial of President Andrew Johnson and the Fight for Lincoln's Legacy.

Andrew Johnson was a hard man. He was intelligent. He pulled himself up from nothing; never attended school, even for a day, a totally self-made man. . . . He had a rather bad disposition. He was an angry man, and he was rigid, and those were qualities that served him terribly as president. He was smart, although self-educated. He knew the Constitution and understood laws. He had a lot of political experience, had held most positions you could hold in this country, and had been elected to most of them. So, there's a good deal to admire in him. As president, his qualities probably would have been unfortunate any time, but at that moment in history, they were a terrible mismatch.

[He got his political start] in Greeneville in eastern Tennessee. He had opened a tailor shop and made a success of it, ran for local office—alderman, mayor, state senator—moved up the ladder, became a congressman and a senator. His moment of public attention was at the beginning of the Civil War when almost all of the congressmen and senators from the South left—they all went back to their home states. Tennessee did secede, although by a fairly close vote; they had a referendum, and it was reasonably close, but Johnson refused to leave the Senate, which did get attention: here was a Southerner who was remaining loyal to the Union.

His father died when he was very young; he was only three or four. He didn't really grow up in the family much. He was apprenticed out at a very early age—nine or ten. He ran away from his master. He didn't like being an apprentice. . . . His own family that he made with his wife was a little bit sad. His wife Eliza, while in the White House, never left her room. She came downstairs once for a grandchild's birthday party. He would see her every day; he always would go visit her a couple of times during the day. He had a couple of sons who ended up badly. They became alcoholics and didn't end well. His daughters were quite admirable, had families of their own, and one served as his [official] hostess in the White House, and they were admired even by people who didn't like Johnson.

Johnson had been military governor of Tennessee, appointed by President Lincoln. . . . In the 1864 election, Lincoln feared that he would lose. The war had dragged on a long time. Lincoln was being opposed by a war hero, General [George] McClellan. So, Lincoln did what we would call today a move to the middle. He figured that all the good abolitionists and Republicans had to vote for him; they certainly couldn't vote for the Democrats. So, he wanted somebody to appeal to Democrats. At that time, Republicans were the liberal figures and Democrats were the conservative ones. So, he reached out to Johnson, whom he didn't know particularly well, as a Southern Democrat who was pro-Union and would broaden his appeal. And it [either] worked, or else Lincoln would have won anyway, but he did win. It wasn't a smashing win. He got 55 percent of the vote, and that's only in the loyal states. The Southern states, of course, weren't voting for him, and he wouldn't have gotten any votes there. So, I think Lincoln had been right as a politician to be concerned. And then, Lincoln was assassinated just six

Democrat Andrew Johnson, shown here in an 1860 photo, was chosen by Republican Abraham Lincoln to be his 1864 running mate as a conciliatory move; he became president upon Lincoln's assassination in April 1865. *Courtesy Library of Congress*

weeks into his second term as president, and Johnson, who was not especially well prepared for the job, was president.

Johnson did start on the wrong foot. He wasn't feeling well in the morning of Lincoln's inauguration. He got to the Capitol; he had an attack of nerves, which was odd. He'd been in the Senate . . . for years, and he'd done an immense amount of public speaking. And so, he asked for some whiskey. The account we have is that he downed three tumblers full of whiskey, which even for a heavy drinker would have an impact in a short period of time. So, he went out to take his oath of office, and everybody in the Senate chamber could tell he was drunk. He spoke erratically. He said things that didn't make a lot of sense. It was a humiliating experience, so humiliating, frankly, that he left town for at least a week thereafter and stayed in Silver Spring, Maryland. When he came back into town, he was very invisible until the time of the assassination just because it had been such a mortifying experience.

When the assassination occurred in April of 1865, Johnson was in his hotel room. The assassination was a larger plot than just killing Lincoln.

They sent someone to kill Secretary of State William Seward, and they sent someone to kill Johnson. Johnson was fortunate that the man who went to kill him, George Atzerodt, lost his nerve and didn't even knock on the door; he had a couple of drinks in the hotel and then vamoosed up to Gaithersburg, Maryland. So, Johnson slept through it until he was awakened in the middle of the night with the terrible news. He was sworn in as president the next morning when official word came that Lincoln was dead.

Johnson initially struggled to find his feet. Seward was terribly wounded in the attempt on his life and was not available to him. Johnson started out being very vengeful in his public statements. He made it clear he wanted to hang a lot of Confederate leaders.

When Seward recovered and came back, it appears he persuaded Johnson that this was not the right public stance to take. At that point, Johnson did a 180 and came around to the view that we should be very charitable towards the South. Of course, that was what Lincoln had said, but it translated into actions that surprised and upset many Northerners and Lincoln would have found very odious.

Johnson had no problem with slavery. He owned slaves. In his first year in office, . . . former Confederates would come to him for pardons—something he spent several months doing was meeting with rich former Southerners who could pay for their pardons—and he often told them, "If you'd only listened to me and stayed in the Union, we'd still have slavery." And he thought that would be great. Underlying it, to be honest, he had very racist attitudes, which came out several times in public statements and also in his policies. He really did think that the freed slaves were a lesser form of human, and it shaped everything, and it was tragic.

Johnson's White House anteroom would be described as filled with Southerners there to pay court. He had been a poor boy, and he always had a great class resentment towards the aristocracy of the South. And here, all of these people he pretty much hated all his life were crawling to him, came to him on their knees [seeking pardons], and the accounts are he enjoyed that tremendously.

[As he takes office,] we're still winding up the war. There's a significant Confederate Army. Joe Johnston's army is still in the field, and [General Robert E.] Lee has surrendered just days before, so Johnson has to make some peace. There's another group in Texas, which takes a little longer to get to surrender and give up their arms. Johnson has a lot of struggles with Ulysses Grant over the treatment of the former Confederates. Grant gave his word to the soldiers that they would be treated benevolently, wouldn't be punished for their role in the war, if they surrendered. Johnson didn't want to do that. He did want to hang some of them, but Grant succeeded with [changing Johnson's mind].

Then the first order of business was what to do with the [former Confederate] states. We had no state governments down there. The South was an occupied hostile territory. Congress was not in session. This is an era when Congress only sat four or five months a year through the winter and into the spring. Johnson went ahead and began reconstituting state governments on his own. Lincoln had done that with . . . Louisiana during the war, but Lincoln had war powers then. . . . It wasn't clear at all that Johnson had the power to do this. It was very controversial because what happened was that former Confederates were elected and took control of the new governments. They were the natural leadership of the area, so you had lots of former generals and former Confederate congressmen and cabinet members who were now leading their states, and they managed to get elected as US congressmen and senators.

Reconstruction, in concept, was rebuilding the Union. . . . Over half a million people were killed [in the war]. Comparable numbers today would be thirty million, in terms of the proportion of the population. It was an immense period of bloodletting, and the result was a tremendous amount of hate between people. Something had to be done to fix that and also to create a government structure that didn't allow for slavery. The Thirteenth Amendment had been adopted. Slavery had been abolished. And that's all Johnson wanted to do. He wanted to have state governments established, . . . beyond that, his view was they were on their own; that was what the Constitution intended from 1787, and that was what was right. If they wished to discriminate against black people, if they wish to disadvantage the freedmen in any way they chose, it was their business, and they were answerable to their own voters.

[The Thirteenth Amendment had been adopted December 6, 1865, the end of his first year as president.] He didn't oppose it. The Fourteenth Amendment, [the due process and equal protection amendment, was adopted July of 1868, in his last year]. He opposed that. He thought it was dangerous. Most of the provisions of the Fourteenth Amendment—we know about equal protection and due process of law, which is section one—but there were a couple of provisions that dealt with the former Confederates and how we were going to structure our politics now that we were reunited. Johnson disliked those provisions. He thought they were too restrictive and not good for the South.

Johnson's friends [in the capital] were Democrats and Southerners. [William] Seward had been a prominent Republican leader but threw in with Johnson very early. It's a complicated story about Secretary of State Seward because he had been seen as a great abolitionist leader, and then he turns out to be essentially the helpmate of this very anti-freedmen president.

[Of] his adversaries, the most significant one, and the one I found most compelling, was Thaddeus Stevens from Pennsylvania. He was a congressman, a fascinating guy. He had been born with a club foot and had to overcome that at a time when being disabled was a real mark. You were thought to have the mark of the devil on you. He was incredibly smart, tough, and totally devoted to the causes of underdogs. . . . People were afraid of Thaddeus Stevens. They were afraid to debate with him in Congress because he was so quick, he was so incisive, and he'd just leave them gasping on the House floor with a quick repartee, which would make everybody else laugh. So, Stevens was a powerful guy within Congress simply by force of personality and talent. He was devoted to the abolitionist cause. He was an inveterate hater of slavery, and he believed in equality in all things. He was, in many ways, the heart and soul of the Reconstruction effort built in Congress and, ultimately, the impeachment effort.

Edwin Stanton was another tough guy, very talented, smart lawyer; Lincoln had called Stanton his "Mars," for the god of war, as his secretary of war. He was incredibly productive and efficient and effective as the senior military bureaucrat, a civilian bureaucrat in the military world. I think that was part of [his troubles with Johnson], that Stanton was just good at his job. I also think Stanton was probably just flat out rude much of the time. He was a difficult man. He didn't put up with fools at all, and he probably managed to intimidate Johnson a little bit, which wasn't easy. . . . By the time Johnson wanted to get rid of Stanton, he was at war with Congress, and it became the political flashpoint that led ultimately to the impeachment effort.

Ulysses Grant was general in chief of the army. A real crisis developed because the army was in the South trying to enforce all of these laws that Congress had adopted over Johnson's vetoes. [Their mission was] to protect the freedmen, to take care of the ex-slaves, make sure they weren't shot down in the street, to give them the vote, to give them a voice in their governments. The generals who were in charge often would intervene to enforce the law, and as soon as they did, Johnson would toss them out. He ended up removing four of the five who had initially been appointed. This upset Grant tremendously, both because he thought they were good officers doing what they should do, but he also had become a believer in ending slavery. . . . Stanton was also infuriated by [Johnson's removal of the generals]. So, both Stanton and Grant developed a program of resisting Johnson from within. They were, at some level, profoundly disloyal to their president.

The Tenure of Office Act was enacted to be in Johnson's way. It was the brainchild of Thaddeus Stevens. They knew in Congress, the Republicans who were opposing Johnson, that he was scheming against them and that he was firing lots of patronage employees. This was an era of tremendous patronage. The Republicans had won the 1864 elections, so all of the officeholders were theirs, and he was replacing them with Democrats, which was driving them nuts; the whole point of winning was to get the jobs. So, they adopted the Tenure of Office Act to make it hard for Johnson to [fire appointees]. It focused on this ellipsis in the Constitution. The Constitution is very clear how you appoint these senior officials, a cabinet official—the president appoints, and the Senate confirms—but it doesn't say anything about how you get rid of them. . . . Stevens is smart enough to know that there was a respectable argument that it was constitutional to have Senate approval required for removing a senior officer. That was what the Tenure of Office Act required. It also created a criminal penalty for violations of it and then added, just because Stevens was a good lawyer, that it was a high crime and misdemeanor. This is the language from the impeachment clause of the Constitution. So, it was a trap that was set for Johnson. Johnson was way too smart not to know that. He knew that if he fired Stanton, which he ultimately did, [he'd be caught]. So, he first tried to remove him under the procedures of the act, and then he suspended Stanton. He sent the notice to the Senate and asked them to confirm his removal.

The Senate didn't. Johnson stewed about that for a time and then just removed him.

There had been efforts to impeach Johnson before. . . . The second time was a more serious one in the fall of 1867. It was led by Republicans, of course, who thought his policies and his performance in office was a disaster, and so, they wrote that up as impeachment articles. It was reported out by the committee that heard it, the Judiciary Committee. Then on the floor, the minority member of the committee made a very powerful argument that if we remove Johnson because we disagree with him, we're never going to stop having to argue about whether we should remove the president. There has to be some substance. There has to be something specific. There has to be a crime. . . . It was a persuasive argument for the congressmen, and so that effort failed by a pretty wide margin. So, they'd been to the well twice, but then when he fired Stanton, Stevens and others think, "OK, we've got him now. He violated the statute. We've got a crime. It says it's a high crime and misdemeanor. Now we can move against him."

. . . The House votes to impeach him and remove him from office without having specific articles in front of them. Everybody knows what they're going to charge, but they haven't written them up yet; they move so fast; they're so angry. And a couple of days later, Stevens presents the articles of impeachment. They are amended, and then he adds another one at the end. The House proceedings lasted no more than four days. It was very fast.

There were no hearings. It went right to the Senate. This is Thaddeus Stevens; he did stuff; they got it done. In the Senate everything slowed down, and it should have. They gave both sides: you have the House managers, and then Johnson appoints a number of defense lawyers starting with his attorney general, Henry Stanbery. The Senate gives them time to prepare their case. Through this whole period, you have a tremendous amount of publicity, as you can only imagine. It takes about six weeks before the trial begins.

Thaddeus Stevens was an old fellow at that time, in his seventies and sick. People watched him decline. The newspapers were on a death watch describing how bad he looked every day [of the trial], and he really couldn't perform in the courtroom. He was just too weak. The man who took control of the case was a first-term congressman from Massachusetts named Ben Butler, who was a colorful, but not a great, character. He had had a checkered career as a political general during the war; he was known as "Beast" Butler for the way he treated the occupation of New Orleans. His military achievements were modest at best. He was a clever lawyer, but he was not a judicious lawyer, and I think he tried the case badly, speaking as a trial lawyer.

They addressed the Eleventh Article [of impeachment] first. . . . I think the House managers decided that their best chance was on the Eleventh Article, which was what I call a catch-all article; it included a bunch of allegations. Very tough sort of thing to defend against, including the Tenure of Office claim concerning Stanton. But it also contained some of the more generic accusations that Johnson really was tearing up the country and disregarding Congress. Johnson had called this Congress illegitimate because the Southern states were not represented. They felt that because it had multiple accusations in it, they might pick up the most support with it, and they fell one vote short.

[Benjamin Curtis, a former Supreme Court justice, defended Andrew Johnson.] That was powerful. He'd left the court, but he had been a justice and was from Massachusetts. Everybody knows what that means during Civil War times; it's the abolitionist stronghold. But even more powerfully, he had been a dissenter in the *Dred Scott* case, which was one of the causes of the Civil War, when the Supreme Court upheld slavery in [that] decision in 1857. Simply having him stand up on behalf of Johnson was a powerful statement that Johnson had adherents who were not crazy pro-slavery people. He also made a very strong legal argument on the Tenure of Office Act. He said, "I don't think it's constitutional. The president didn't either. But you don't have to decide that. All you have to decide is, did he have good reason to think it was unconstitutional. Even if you think that's the wrong position, is it rational? Is it possible? And if it's just possible, then his actions were justified."

It was a party-line vote. The Republicans voted to impeach, and the Democrats did not. In the Senate . . . they needed a two-thirds majority to convict him and remove him from office, so he needed nineteen Senate votes to be acquitted. [The effort fell short by one vote.]

[The Senate voted on two more of the eleven articles, Article 2 and then Article 3, which had the same outcomes.] Johnson was pleased.

He wasn't ecstatic; it wasn't his makeup, really. He didn't go into public and trumpet it. He had to pull in his horns a bit. One of the things that people at the time noted was during the three months or so of the impeachment process, he was not anywhere near as aggressive or controversial as he had been. He was reassuring people, "I'm not going to do terrible things." He had appointed a very inappropriate guy to succeed Stanton as secretary of war, so he overruled himself and appointed a Union general, John Schofield, who was acceptable and pretty presentable. So, Johnson was calibrating his behavior in a way that made him less threatening and less disturbing. The rest of his presidency, he became a lame duck very fast. He didn't behave great for the rest of it, but his powers were pretty limited by then. The impeachment proceeding had clipped his wings.

Johnson hoped to run [again in 1868] as the Democrat candidate. He knows the Republicans will not nominate him. He thinks he's done what Democratic voters wanted him to do, and if you have the Southern states back in the Union, he thinks he's got a shot. [He lost on the first ballot.] Republicans wanted to have Grant. Grant is not a wildly politically ambitious guy. He'd never been in politics, and he'd had a humble career until the Civil War started. But Grant is frankly appalled by Johnson as president and has come to terms with the fact that he is going to be a candidate for the office [and ultimately wins the election that year].

John Kennedy's *Profiles in Courage*, . . . it's terrible, the chapter on Johnson. The chapter on Johnson should be expunged from every library in the country. It focuses on a fellow named Edmund Ross, who was credited with casting the single vote that saved Johnson's tail. It calls Ross's vote the most heroic moment in American history. I actually thought . . . that Ross's vote was purchased. Saving Johnson was not a heroic moment. . . . [In all, seven radical Republicans voted to acquit.] One, Ross went back to Kansas. He ended up as territorial governor of New Mexico for the Democrats, which was where he probably belonged. A number of the other [acquitting Republican] senators ended up resigning because they decided not to pursue their careers. They were not broken men in any way. This melodramatic story was good theater, but not accurate.

I wanted to write a book about [the Johnson impeachment] case because . . . this case made no sense. I couldn't figure out who was arguing about what. You read the legal arguments, and they're clear on their own, but they don't tend to fit the facts of what's going on. I finally concluded that it was sufficiently confusing that it wasn't going to help either side in my case, so I went past it and just moved on to things that mattered to me. But it always bothered me. Here was this huge moment in our history, this presidential impeachment, that I figured if I didn't understand it, most people didn't understand it very well.

JAMES BUCHANAN

Overall Rank: 43

— ★ —

Total Score: 245

Historians have ranked James Buchanan last in all three C-SPAN surveys, consistent with most other presidential rankings. The gap between Buchanan and next-to-last Andrew Johnson is significant: thirty points. Buchanan ranks last or next to last in every leadership category except administrative skills, where he bested Andrew Johnson and Warren Harding to rank third from last.

Party: Democrat
b. April 23, 1791, Cove Gap, Pennsylvania
d. June 1, 1868, Lancaster, Pennsylvania
First Lady: Harriet Lane (niece)
Age entering office: 65

Historian: **Robert Strauss**

Journalist and historian Robert Strauss has been a reporter and feature writer for a variety of news outlets, including the Philadelphia Daily News, NBC, *the* New York Times, *and the* Washington Post. *He joined C-SPAN's* Q & A *on October 25, 2016, to discuss his book,* Worst. President. Ever: James Buchanan, the POTUS Rating Game, and the Legacy of the Least of the Lesser Presidents.

I do think you can learn from failure. I think that if the next president wants to aspire to be like somebody, they would probably want to aspire to be Washington or Lincoln. Well, you can't recreate the country, and you can't have the Civil War. So, what do you do next? Do you aspire to be James Monroe? I don't know. But what you can do, is you can aspire not to be James Buchanan.

Buchanan was a good lawyer. Early on, he was a star student at Dickinson College in Pennsylvania. He got thrown out for a while, but they let him back in. But he was always a top student, and he was always very sure of himself. He goes to Lancaster because it was then the capital of Pennsylvania, the largest inland city in America with six thousand people. America was pretty small then. He becomes the best lawyer there. Even though the capital moves to Harrisburg, he decides to stay in Lancaster. He defends a lot of people of note, and he makes a good buck.

He never married. There was always the speculation of whether he was gay or not. But early on . . . he gets engaged to Ann Coleman. Her father was one of the richest men in America; he was an iron maker. He was an older man; this was his next-to-youngest daughter. He looked after her very well. He didn't approve of this relationship that she was having with Buchanan, but he let it go.

At some point, Buchanan comes home from Philadelphia, where he'd done some business, stops off at his friend's house. His friend's wife's cousin is there, apparently a beautiful woman; he's there for an hour or two. Of course, gossip goes around Lancaster, and Ann Coleman . . . breaks off the engagement.

Buchanan doesn't know quite what to do. He stands back and says, "Well, if I let it go for a couple of weeks, it will all blow over." In that interim time, Ann Coleman goes off with her younger sister to see their older sister. They get to Philadelphia, she doesn't feel well; the other two go out to the theater. By the time they come back, she's in convulsions and she dies—presumably suicide, at least that's the speculation, that she killed herself over this relationship not working out. So, whether she killed herself or not, the idea that a guy who eventually runs for president has his fiancée dying when he's young has to be a big story somewhere.

In a certain sense, Buchanan is the most qualified man by virtue of a government résumé to ever run for president. He was a state legislator in Pennsylvania, then he was in the US House. He was in the US Senate. He was ambassador to Britain under Franklin Pierce. Prior to that, he was ambassador to Russia under Andrew Jackson, and he was secretary of state under James K. Polk. I don't know if we'd call it distinguished, but he had a long career in government service—pretty unusual. He was ambassador to Britain at not a particularly crucial time, but he was that. [He was also, at one time, being considered for the Supreme Court, but] he always waffled. That was his big problem, that he waffled about everything, and he was waffling about this Supreme Court decision. But he was known as the best partier in Washington. So, he has a great big party with a celebrity chef, and he keeps giving little parties to supplement it. But then in the end, he decides he doesn't want to be on the Supreme Court, so, in a certain sense, he's done all this for nothing. So, if you go by the number of years at a major post, he definitely is [the most qualified man to be president]. But here's something about him: he has never proposed any significant legislation, or he never got any significant legislation passed. He was a conciliatory man.

He was a serious candidate for president three times prior to becoming the actual candidate in 1856. He was always at the top echelons, but you know the cliché about the bridesmaid who's never the bride. There was always somebody else who had the ear of the bureaucracy . . . that ran the party. But eventually, in 1856, he's the last man left standing. And on the seventeenth ballot in Cincinnati, he becomes the Democratic nominee. . . . [And in November, Buchanan was elected in a three-way race between Republican nominee John C. Fremont and American Party nominee and former president Millard Fillmore.]

Buchanan comes to office with his long résumé, [but] he was sort of boring to people; he was sixty-five when he was elected. After him, nobody until Reagan [and now President Trump] was that old. Two things about him are, one, in all of his papers, he never says anything bad about anybody. I don't know what he said in verbal terms. Even people he didn't like politically, he never said anything bad about them personally. And, [second, we know that] he loved giving parties. The inaugural ball of 1857 was the greatest party in nineteenth-century America.

He gives a fantastic inaugural ball. They put up a huge tent on Lafayette Square. Six thousand people come. Now, six thousand people is a lot in a country that only has twenty-three million people, and it's star-spangled: a big orchestra, food that you can't imagine, saddles of meat and oysters. Harriet Lane, his niece, is the first lady. She is the Jackie Kennedy of her time. Everything she wears, all the young women want to wear. They have trading cards that are Harriet Lane trading cards. They name a Coast Guard cutter after her, the USS *Harriet Lane*. It eventually fires the first shot of the Civil War from the Union side. It gets captured by the Confederates and they don't rename it; she's too popular. It was still called the CSS *Harriet Lane*.

So . . . Buchanan starts out in such a favorable way. All the digni-taries come. The recounting of his inaugural in the *New York Times* and other papers are just wonderfully written stories about the pomp and everything that had been gone from Washington, DC [under the preceding presidents]. And, then the *Dred Scott* decision comes down.

Buchanan comes to office at a crucial time, but it doesn't seem any more crucial than Pierce's term or Fillmore's term. Slavery is the overhanging problem. He becomes president in March, as they did then, instead of January, . . . 1857, and he sees as his mandate to solve the slavery ques-tion. It's not to get rid of slavery; it's to solve the slavery question.

Buchanan was called a "doughface," which was a Southern-leaning Northerner; they said you could massage their faces like dough. [As a politician,] he lived in Washington, and Washington was a Southern city. He was a bachelor. He went back to Pennsylvania, but most of the time he was in Washington. His friends were Southerners because more Southerners than Northerners took up residence in Washington. The railroads got the Northerners back [home] a lot easier. And, he was predisposed to think like his friends.

He wants to solve this slavery problem to keep the Union together, and he sees this court case going around. It's called the *Dred Scott* case: Dred Scott was a slave to a military man in Missouri, who for a time went to what is now Minnesota, free territory, and then came back to Missouri. [The slave owner] dies. Dred Scott sues, saying, "I was free in Minnesota; I should be free."

It comes up that the case could be on the Supreme Court's docket. Roger Taney was the Supreme Court chief justice, who like Buchanan went to Dickinson College, so they had some sort of bond.

Taney had slaves his whole life. He was from Maryland, and he was Francis Scott Key's brother-in-law—to show that everybody was connected [at this point in the nation's history]. They have this discussion before Buchanan takes office, and he says you can't just have a decision that's Southern versus Northern. The court was split five Southerners and four Northerners. It was not going to amount to much. So, Buchanan takes it upon himself to find a Northern justice that will go along with this [rul-ing]. He finds a guy named Robert Grier, who, coincidentally enough, also went to Dickinson College, so, they have this bond. Grier says, "OK, I'll go along with whatever Taney does." And another Northerner from New York says, "I'll write a concurring opinion." So, it's essentially seven to two; now, you can have a decision that might mean something—Northerners going along with Southerners.

The decision comes out two days after the inauguration. It's said that on the inaugural platform, before Taney gives him the oath, they discuss something. Buchanan had distributed souvenir transcripts of his inaugural address, and there were a few lines written into it that in it allude to this decision that's going to come out, and that we're going to all be happy about it. But the *Dred Scott* decision is generally thought of as the worst decision that the Supreme Court has ever made. . . . It essentially says that every state is a slave state. It says that Dred Scott can't sue in court. He's not a free man; he therefore can't sue. In fact, he's still a slave, and in fact, slavery can't be outlawed by individual states. It reinstitutes the most heinous parts of the Fugitive Slave Law. It negates all the compromises from before, all the ones we remember from high school, the Missouri Compromise, the Compromise of 1850, and it essentially makes the United States a slave country.

We'd had a twenty-year expansion; things have been going great. The country's opening up: the Louisiana Purchase, Oregon Territory, Texas, all these other lands that we're getting. People have the American dream going on. If you don't make it in Pennsylvania, go off to Ohio, go off to Illinois, go off to Missouri, wherever. You can make it. The railroads finance this, essentially; people speculate on different railroads. Suddenly this decision comes out. Let's say I've got a tin cup factory in Cincinnati that's going pretty well, so maybe I'll open one in Dayton. Uh-oh, maybe this guy's going to come up from Kentucky with his slaves [as labor] and be my competitor. So, I don't do anything; I stop expanding. The country immediately stops expanding. People who have speculated on railroads aren't doing so well, immediately. They go bankrupt. . . . Other businesses fail. So, within months, we're in this tremendous economic panic; a greater precipitous depression than the Great Depression.

All the banks in New York close for a day. They decide not to take scrip, so you don't have gold scraping off of that to pay your employees at the tin cup factory. But in the South, it doesn't affect them as much because they're an agricultural society. You can feed and clothe your

Pennsylvania's James Buchanan, here in a c. 1850–1870 portrait, consistently ranks last in most presidential leadership polls. *Courtesy Library of Congress*

family, at the very least. You can probably sell your cotton and your lima beans. But in the North, where manufacturing has gotten sway, it's really precipitous. So, that divides the country even more.

Because the monied class was so much smaller, they were affected so greatly, so quickly. Our most recent [2008] recession—I'm not belittling it—was not like this, was not a dive off a cliff. Things happened in a matter of course, as opposed to just precipitously.

. . . As people who look at coins know, coins were big [in size] in the nineteenth century. . . . Then suddenly in 1857, coins are sized like a dime. I asked [a coin dealer why]. He said, "Oh, the Panic of 1857." That was Buchanan's great idea: "We'll make the coins smaller. . . ." The rest of his ideas were like "to heck with you; you speculated, you deserve it. Why don't you be like the people in the South who work hard with their hands?" So, he does nothing to ameliorate [the depression]. He just figures it's going to play itself out. And sure enough, it does because eventually we had a lot of munitions to make in 1861 [once war broke out].

The next upcoming state is going to be Kansas. Kansas has a problem; is it going to come in free or slave? A slave contingent comes over from Missouri, makes the capital in Lecompton, a small town, and gins up a constitution that allows slavery. Non-slave people come to Topeka; they have a similar constitutional convention, just the opposite, of course. There were six slaves in all of Kansas at the time; it wasn't like it was going to be slave territory. But the South needed another slave state, . . . so, of course, they were supporting it, especially people in [the slave state of] Missouri.

Something's got to happen. Buchanan's got to say something; he's got to choose one side or the other. He's got to say there's going to be an election; or, there's got to be something that's going to resolve this before it becomes a big problem. But, of course, he doesn't; he makes no decision. He sends several people out to be governor of Kansas, but he doesn't listen to any of them, [as they were] saying this very thing. . . . One of the things that happens in this maelstrom is that people start firing at each other. . . . [Abolitionist] John Brown, who becomes much more famous later, is said to have murdered several slave owners and their families—now it's called "Bloody Kansas." Still, Buchanan makes no decision.

Brown gets away. It's not like he was doing things in secret; he meets with Harriet Tubman and Frederick Douglass and other antislavery people. Eventually, he comes to Harpers Ferry in 1859. Harpers Ferry, if you go to it now, it's a bucolic setting. . . . But back then, it was a big munitions maker, with other industries. And, it was just forty miles down the road from Washington. Brown comes there; it's not so foolish. If he can get some of these munitions and gather some more people to his cause, maybe he can have this slave rebellion that he wants. For two days, Buchanan does nothing—nothing! He says, "Oh, let them handle it in Virginia." Harpers Ferry was part of Virginia then.

[He takes no action] until this prominent scion, Robert E. Lee, comes home from his post in Texas to Arlington, Virginia. He goes to Buchanan and says, "I think we ought to do something." Buchanan says, "All right, take some troops out there and see what you can do." Well, Lee does capture Brown, and they have sort of a show trial. Brown eventually gets hanged, but by this time, he is a martyr. Victor Hugo is writing about him, Ralph Waldo Emerson is writing about him, Walt Whitman is writing about him. And, of course, that angers both sides [North and

South, slavery and antislavery leading into the 1860 election], exacerbating any problem there is because of Buchanan's inaction.

I think the differentiation of good presidents and bad presidents—Washington, Lincoln, and FDR are always at the top of the surveys that historians take—they were decisive men. You can't come to the top of the ladder and not be decisive. Buchanan was a waffler; James Polk hated him for being a waffler as his secretary of state. He always went back and forth on decisions, . . . and that's how he was as president. I could go on with the list of things that make Buchanan the worst president, and all of them have to do with not making a decision when he had to make a decision. So, that's what the next president, whether it's this president, or succeeding presidents, should learn: at some point, you've got to say, "This is the way it's going to be."

HISTORIANS' PERSPECTIVES ON PRESIDENT DONALD J. TRUMP

DONALD J. TRUMP

45th President, 2017–

The 45th president, Donald J. Trump, won the White House in 2016 with an Electoral College majority, but without the popular vote. Sitting presidents are not included in our leadership surveys until they leave office.

Party: Republican
b. June 14, 1946, New York City, New York
First Lady: Melania Knauss Trump
Age entering office: 70

Historians: Douglas Brinkley, Edna Greene Medford, and Richard Norton Smith

Although President Trump is not yet part of our leadership survey, we felt our book must include him in order to be complete. So, on August 31, 2018, we assembled our team of historian advisers, Douglas Brinkley, Edna Greene Medford, and Richard Norton Smith, and asked them for some historical context to President Trump's path to victory and his first years in office.

DOUGLAS BRINKLEY: [John Quincy Adams, Benjamin Harrison, Rutherford B. Hayes, George W. Bush, and Donald Trump all were elected without popular vote majorities.] That makes it harder for a president to establish his credibility right out of the gate. When George W. Bush was elected—but it had to go to the Supreme Court due to the problems in Florida—Bush had a tough time trying to convince a lot of Al Gore supporters that he was the real president. We see that now with Hillary Clinton's supporters. I can't tell you how many times I've heard people say, "Hillary Clinton won by three million votes; she should be president; Trump is not the real president." It presents huge challenges for a president out of the gate because there is some residual anger that somehow there's an asterisk next to their name, that they didn't win the popular vote. Some of it comes to the fact that we may not be teaching civics properly. A lot of people are confused about the Electoral College. They really believe democracy is about one person, one vote, and our system perplexes them through a lack of studying political science.

EDNA GREENE MEDFORD: Despite that fact that there were challenges that these presidents faced, there haven't been so many that we have been willing to move forward to discard the Electoral College. I think we would all agree that the country was very different when that first occurred, when you had John Quincy Adams winning over Jackson, a very different era. We know why the Electoral College existed initially, but we still are not willing to move forward and simply embrace the idea of the use of the popular vote.

[Donald Trump was able to win the 2016 election because] there was a perfect storm of sorts. You had a situation where you had the first black president who had served two terms, and you had people who were still reeling from that change in American politics. You had, at the same time, a concern that demographically the country was changing, and that people who had been accustomed to power might soon lose that power. Trump gave them the hope that perhaps they would regain what they felt that they had lost. There was also a segment of the population that did not benefit initially from the changes that were being made economically. As the country was getting better economically, their lives had not changed very much, so they felt that they have been left behind. And then you had that whole political tribalism. There was tremendous partisanship during that period, which continues into the . . . Trump presidency, but certainly it was there long before he arrived. And so, those things together helped to pave the way for him to become president.

RICHARD NORTON SMITH: Edna's comments are well taken in terms of the profound and sometimes hard to quantify changes that are taking place in the culture. You go back to people talking about Trump as populist; I think that's highly questionable. But, nevertheless, there's an element of populist appeal, of us against them—them being the so-called elites. You could go back one-hundred-plus years to the late nineteenth century when authentic populism came to life, particularly in the Midwest, the dissatisfied farmers, miners, the people who made William Jennings Bryan, for example, possible not once, but three times.

More recently, I'd say fifty years ago . . . you had a country that had been and was going through tumultuous times—the assassination of a president, an increasingly unpopular war, increasing doubts about the truthfulness of the government regarding that war, the civil rights revolution, the women's movement—a whole host of almost subterranean seismic changes that were going on, and that bred insecurity on the part of those who, as Edna says, were accustomed to holding power. And then, there was increasing economic insecurity; but clearly, racial factors are involved. George Wallace, in 1968, was avowedly running on what we would recognize as a racist platform. But to be perfectly blunt, there were many who believed that the Republican campaign that year, Richard Nixon's campaign, through code words like "law and order" was sending out early versions of what we today call "dog whistles." In other words, there was a sense that the times were out of joint, something was broken, and we were headed in a direction that made many people uncomfortable, even as it offered some degree of encouragement to millions of people who until that time had, in many ways, been left out of the political and economic equation.

[There have been other times in history where there have been major changes from one presidential administration to the next:] 1933, going from the Hoover depression, as it was popularly thought of. Ironically, historians taking the long view have actually seen elements of continuity between much of what Hoover was doing and many of the programs that FDR instituted. But clearly it was in Roosevelt's interest and a measure of his political skill that he emphasized just how different he and his approach to governing would be.

MEDFORD: I was going to say from Lincoln to Andrew Johnson, which is a tremendous difference in terms of ability and in terms of how the two looked at what the country should be.

And, certainly, the Andrew Jackson–John Quincy Adams comparison is extraordinary because you have two people with very different personalities: John Quincy Adams, who would be seen very much as an elitist, who came from a blueblood family in New England, versus Andrew Jackson, who was considered rather brash and from the frontier, who was educated but certainly not in the same way that John Quincy Adams was. You have someone like John Quincy Adams who's calling for a national university, while Andrew Jackson what he's remembered for is reaching out to the common man, but at the same time he's also promoting Indian removal. . . .

BRINKLEY: I really look at things from a post–Civil War perspective: How does Donald Trump fit in after the Civil War? Once the original sin of slavery is abolished, how do presidents behave? Race has been a big part of Trump's presidency from the time he [announced] and started on "build the wall" and saying that Barack Obama wasn't born in the United States. I see him as an Andrew Johnson–like president, meaning somebody who has impeachment swirling around him and somebody who's not able to heal the racial divide in the country. I don't see him like other presidents. Some people will say that he's a business person and Herbert Hoover was a business person. Well, no, Herbert Hoover was a Stanford engineer who happened to make some money. We've never had a president that's a business person like Donald Trump. CEOs have a board to report to, and President Trump has never had a board in his life. He was his own boss, kind of like a family kingpin. He got used to just barking orders, and people would jump. And, obviously, being president, that's tough because we have a Justice Department, FBI, a State Department; there's protocol. If he's had a deficit as president, it's constantly trying not to abide by the rules. We often call it an "unprecedented" presidency, but it's really just that he's somebody who has never in his life had to take orders, or follow protocol, from anybody else.

SMITH: [Donald Trump has declared the mainstream media an enemy.] Certainly, Richard Nixon shared Trump's general attitude toward the press, that is to say, he looked upon the press as an enemy. Nixon thought of the media as a conglomerate. There were individuals here and there who might, on occasion, give him and like-minded people a fair shake, but overwhelmingly it was an "us against them" approach that he took to the office. Look at the number of journalists who showed up on his enemies list. . . . This was something that went back a long way, certainly to the 1940s, at least a generation, just as

Nixon was emerging and in some quarters was a hero for his pursuit of Alger Hiss. . . . The irony is—and this completes the circle—we get back to television. . . . We all think of JFK as the first television president, but actually it was Richard Nixon, with his "Checkers" speech in one half hour in September 1952, who not only saved his place on the ticket, but overnight established a bond with millions of people whom he later would call the "Silent Majority." . . . Trump has inherited a very different kind of media climate, but it is still possible for him, like Nixon, to portray the media as somehow out to get him, and indeed, ironically, a danger to democracy, as he defines it.

MEDFORD: There was a real animosity between the press and presidents as early as John Adams because he was the person who was pushing for the Sedition Act of 1798. What that act does is to try to prevent criticism of the government and of the president; anybody who is criticizing, it's criminalized. We think that we have always been in favor of a free press, but in actuality we have not always behaved that way—at least our leaders have not, especially when they're being criticized. You have someone like Woodrow Wilson who was tampering with the freedom of the press by censorship and by propaganda because of World War I. You have a Committee on Public Information that is established during this period. Truman certainly didn't like newspaper publishers. Johnson had problems with the press because of the response to the Vietnam War. So, what we see in President Trump may be alarming to some people, but it's not new in American politics. . . .

BRINKLEY: . . . Even Jack Kennedy tried to get the great David Halberstam banned from the *New York Times* because he didn't like his coverage. But in Donald Trump, we're dealing with a demagogue who is most like [Louisiana's] Huey Long. . . . You can see exact parallels of Donald Trump in the way that Huey Long tried to punish individual reporters [in the 1930s], get his backers to heckle and try to attack the personal lives of reporters. It's a page straight out of what demagogues do. Fortunately, in American history we haven't had many demagogues. Richard Nixon had a problem with the press and warred with the press, as Richard spoke to, but nothing to the extent of what Donald Trump is trying to do, where he's trying to almost incite violence against individual reporters. . . . We haven't had a president going after reporters [to this extreme].

I have had no trouble with Donald Trump's appearances on Fox News; he's welcome to go on there as often as he likes. The problem becomes when Donald Trump repeats that the press is the enemy of the people. He has [former Fox News executive] Bill Shine now working in the White House. He talks to Fox's Sean Hannity all the time. So be it. Politicians, presidents are going to have favorite reporters and favored news outlets. It's only [troubling] when you start trying to incite the American people to go after individual reporters by name or to try to demonize a particular media executive in a reckless fashion.

SMITH: I have to say there's a huge difference between [going on] a program like *60 Minutes* [which invited President Obama to appear seventeen times], which over fifty years has established itself as a national institution with a very large, very diverse audience [and President Trump's appearing regularly on Fox]. When Bill Clinton's candidacy hung by a thread in 1992 following revelations of sexual hijinks, where did Bill and Hillary Clinton go? They went to *60 Minutes.* Fox, on the other hand, purports to be a journalist outfit; that's highly dubious. It is clearly and increasingly perceived as straight propaganda with an agenda that may come, frankly, from Rupert Murdoch—its motives, its function, its purpose. CBS and *60 Minutes* hold a place in our history that is very different from *Fox & Friends.*

MEDFORD: Of course, if you're billing yourself as a populist president, you are going to embrace those networks where you think the common man is more likely to tune in. There is that idea that there are elitist organizations and there are those that cater to the average American. Whether or not that's true, that's the perception that the common man has. . . . If you are a Donald Trump and you are trying to identify with those folks, then you're going to go where you think your audience is. He knows that he is going to have support in those areas.

[As for President Trump's use of Twitter] well, you've got Lincoln who was using the telegraph to communicate with his generals and to stay in touch with what's happening in the field. You've got McKinley who is using silent film in his inauguration and was the first to be filmed. You've got FDR with his fireside chats. Eisenhower is using TV ads in his campaign, and, of course, Obama with his technological savvy in the use of social media. So, this is not new in terms of use of technology, but it may be a tad more than what other presidents have embraced.

SMITH: Yes. In some ways the great-great-grandfather of the tweet is Lincoln, who would write public letters, clearly in an effort to influence public opinion. Lincoln himself evolved as the war evolved. At the outset of the war, he tended to look upon it as a battle over states' rights and constitutional interpretation. And to his everlasting credit, he came to realize that it could only be justified—all of the blood spilled, and all the pain inflicted, and the wrenching changes to the society—as a war about human rights and, specifically, the eradication of slavery. That evolution is traced not only in formal addresses like Gettysburg, most notably, but in a series of public letters that he would write to supporters, to newspaper editors, and others. We were just becoming a nation of newspaper readers, and so they were the mass media of mid-nineteenth century. And no one has ever used it more skillfully or more memorably than Lincoln.

BRINKLEY: Theodore Roosevelt was tremendous at [connecting directly with the public]. He gave great speeches. He would tour the

President Donald J. Trump speaks at the 2018 Conservative Political Action Conference.
Credit: Gage Skidmore

country, and he'd get fifty thousand people showing up in medium-sized cities to hear a great oration. But he also cultivated the cartoonists of that era, most famously when Clifford Berryman . . . [learned about his] bear hunt in Mississippi and drew the famous cartoon—which led to the teddy bear becoming the symbol for Theodore Roosevelt. He would constantly bring cartoonists to the White House. He befriended them because he knew there was nothing more devastating than ridicule of your opponent. We see Donald Trump doing that with Twitter. In the history of presidents and how they communicate to people, Jack Kennedy was very interesting with his press conferences. . . . And then, Jimmy Carter tried to use talk radio. People forget that he operated, out of the White House, a call-in [program in March 1977 with CBS newsman Walter Cronkite called "Ask President Carter." But he only did it once]. So, I think the real question is, are you good at it?

TR was great at manipulating cartoonists. FDR was amazing at radio. Jack Kennedy was a master at the press conference. And Donald Trump has used Twitter to his great advantage. However, there may be legal ramifications for some of his tweets . . . and it has also killed his ability to grow his box office above 42, 43 percent. There are a lot of centrist Americans, what they used to call Brooks Brother Republicans, or Rockefeller Republicans, or Gerald Ford Republicans, that don't like his tweets. . . . So, I would not call him a master of the art form at this point in time.

[When you look at President Trump's relations with Congress,] he had the great virtue of being a president that came in with both a Republican Senate and House, and he was able to get some big things done. [By the end of his first two years,] Trump could say, "I got two Supreme Court justices passed, conservative ones that are going to change the face of American jurisprudence for the next fifty years," which means he got along with Congress pretty well to get both of those two done. If you reverse that question and ask, how is he in the sense of working across the aisle in a bipartisan fashion? He flunks. So, he is really an all-or-nothing kind of figure. . . .

MEDFORD: Even [coming in] with the advantage of having his party control both houses of Congress, he still seemed to be more likely to go it alone alone. . . . So, we saw that real drive for executive action rather than working closely with congressional leaders. And besides that, the party leaders are not always sure what he wants, so they are reluctant to reach across the aisle and to make any kind of deals with the Democrats because he might change his mind.

SMITH: One area where there really is no comparison [is in assembling his White House staff]. Certainly, you can go back to the first term of Andrew Jackson and see turmoil in the cabinet over the Peggy Eaton affair, or that sort of thing. But in the modern era, you always have, with the State Department and Pentagon, built-in institutional rivalries, and that's not always a bad thing. But in terms of chaos as a governing strategy deliberately, persistently pursued, it's turning on the head every conventional theory of how to run a White House, of how to run an administration. Like so much about the Trump experiment, it may work in the short run, but it may also very well contain the seeds of its own destruction. . . .

But if we've ever had a president attacking members of his own cabinet day after day after day, exploiting those divisions, contributing to the polarization that already exists, I can't think of one. Andrew Johnson had a secretary of war in Edwin Stanton that he desperately wanted to remove and that factored into the impeachment of the president. But that was one instance. This is a governing philosophy—if you want to dignify it as such. But I think it's unprecedented.

MEDFORD: Andrew Jackson was really a consummate politician, and he certainly knew how to get rid of people, even if it hurt other innocent folk. With the Peggy Eaton affair, he is using that unfortunate incident as a way of getting rid of a cabinet that he could not trust, that he couldn't rely on to always support him when he needed them to. And so, although he was very fond of Peggy Eaton and her husband, he allowed them to be the scapegoats. . . . In that way we talk about who Trump compares with most closely, and we know that he is very fond of Andrew Jackson. In a lot of ways, he is like Andrew Jackson. He is able to use folks who are around him to his advantage, in terms of what he is trying to get done. He also surrounds himself with family members, people that he can rely on. So, this is a president who really does feel that he has to have a certain kind of person in place close to him that he can trust. That is very similar to what Andrew Jackson did as well.

BRINKLEY: I agree with that. Andrew Jackson would be the most apt comparison, but the problem of the modern presidency, for Donald Trump, there is no White House that has as many leaks as the Trump White House. It's part of this hurly-burly, reckless style of Donald Trump. It doesn't engender loyalty. It might scare some people into staying loyal, but in the end it is the bureaucracy of the White House [responding to the turmoil] in the amount of leaks that are coming out that are damaging to him; there are cascading leaks out of this administration. It belies the idea that bullying is a governable strategy for a president because people just leak to the press.

There's a professor of history at Yale University named Joanne Freeman who has a book on the history of duels in Congress and how people, if your honor was bruised, would either cane each other or have a pistol duel. We often think it was just an isolated incident with [the caning of Senator] Charles Sumner, but she documents many such incidents in politics of defending one's honor. I think that we're in a problem now where honor has left American politics. You have a Congress with an 18 percent approval rating. We have a president with historic lows. The American public is sick of Washington, DC, and American politics. It's kind of a pox on both sides. There is a clamor for an independent, a third-party wave, but you need a billion dollars to run a third party. And so, it's not very pleasant now. It's kind of a neo–Civil War going on with a lot of dysfunction and a lot of name calling. Donald Trump has been called every name in the book, and he calls everybody else a name, but with the media cycle, it sticks more. It's not one insult a year. It's an insult a day going on now, and the net effect is a lot of people are turned off from both Democrats and Republicans.

MEDFORD: Yes, but incivility has always been there in American politics. We sometimes look back to the past, and we think, "Oh, we are in a different place now. We're so very uncivil to each other, and that never happened before." In reality it has always been with us. It's a part of American politics. But when scandals occurred in the past, in many instances, these administrations simply ignored what was being said, or tried to ride it out. What's happening now is there is a real pushback because so much is at stake, a presidency is at stake. And so . . . the incivility is going to continue. I don't see that changing at any time. And it's spilled out now into the American public, so it's not just a political thing. It's right there in our communities on a daily basis.

BRINKLEY: But Barack Obama was a relatively scandal-free president, and I think that we can have a higher standard in office with presidents that aren't in regular scandals. Unfortunately, Bill Clinton and Donald Trump have dominated our lifetimes with their scandals. You can do good governance, but you have to lead a life that's transparent, that's open. And you can't live on a sense of paranoia or hiding of past deeds. You've got to be an open book.

MEDFORD: Oh sure, you can. I agree with that wholeheartedly. But the incivility will always be there, especially now that we are so divided. The political tribalism is here to stay for the foreseeable future, I believe. As long as we believe that there is "us" and then there is the "other," we're going to have these problems.

SMITH: I would say that what sets Donald Trump apart from virtually all of his predecessors, first of all, I don't think you can exaggerate the reality TV element. To Trump, this is all a performance, and every episode is a news cycle. It isn't that he has long-term vision that he wants to implement. He wants to win the day. Beyond that, and inseparable from that, is the fact that unlike virtually every president, this is someone who defines himself by his enemies and who seems curiously deflated if he doesn't have a foil to play off. And that, like so much of this presidency, may work in the short term. None of us is a prophet, but it's hard to believe that it's a formula for a successful governance.

Postscript: The Presidency, National Identity, and the Pursuit of Equal Justice

Edna Greene Medford

Americans take great pride in our exceptionalism. We think of ourselves as the guardians of democracy, the citizens of a nation without parallel, more moral and infinitely more humane than the rest. We explain away contradictions to our self-image as simply anomalies. But history suggests otherwise. It reminds us that seeds of inequality and injustice took root alongside the love of liberty, that this counter narrative reflects American political and cultural traditions as much as the notion that we are a land of opportunity and a defender of the rights of all.

This "inconvenient truth" pervades the history of the presidency. From the time of George Washington, the national executive embodied the country's image of itself. Washington represented strength and determination at a time when America sought to secure its sovereignty. His military bearing and experience suggested that the infant nation stood prepared to meet any challenge, whether at home or abroad. His personal ownership of more than one hundred enslaved men and women and his management of many more did not hinder his political ambition in a nation ostensibly committed to freedom. In our own time, he receives high marks in national surveys of the presidency because he shepherded the country through one of its most vulnerable periods. But when ranked alongside other presidents in the single category of pursuing justice for all Americans, today's sensibilities prevent him from finishing among the top ten.

For better or worse, presidents both reflect and shape national identity. Sometimes they champion America's espoused egalitarian beliefs, but just as often they act in the interests of one segment of the population. For instance, John Adams supported legislation that expanded the time to citizenship, authorized the deportation of immigrants critical of his administration, and sanctioned the arrest of American citizens for the same offense. This betrayal of the American creed came at a time when two political factions (the Federalists and the Democratic-Republicans) competed for the chance to determine whose vision would prevail in the new nation. The "bloodless" revolution of 1800, which ushered in the presidency of Thomas Jefferson, proved that America could peacefully transfer power from one political faction to another. Yet, women and people of color continued to be excluded from the body politic.

No better example of this contradiction can be found than in the administration of Andrew Jackson. Jackson's ascendancy to the presidency coincided with the expansion of the electorate and a changing political culture. A son of the frontier, where population growth reflected increasing economic opportunities, Jackson embodied the supposed egalitarian impulse of the era and the region. But the Tennessean symbolized another national inclination as well, one tethered to an ignoble tradition. During his presidency, he championed the removal of the Native American population from the southeastern part of the country, thus making valuable lands available to increasingly impatient white farmers who felt constrained by Native American landownership. The relocation began during Jackson's administration and continued after he left office, culminating in the transport of tens of thousands of native people. Remembered today as the "Trail of Tears," some groups lost a quarter of their population along the way. The history of injustices perpetrated against Native Americans continued as one president after another sanctioned, either tacitly or directly, the subjugation of these groups through broken promises, abandoned treaties, and genocidal warfare.

In general, the nineteenth century posed a serious challenge to America's image as protector of the defenseless. In addition to Indian removal, the first half of the century witnessed the regionalization of slavery as the North gradually abandoned the institution and the South attempted to expand it. The institution gained such acceptance that eight presidents owned enslaved laborers while serving in office. The actions of the abolitionists throughout the antebellum period, and Abraham Lincoln after 1863, helped to shape America's national identity in ways still experienced today. Lincoln envisioned an America true to the principles of the Declaration of Independence. While he may not have embraced social equality, he nonetheless recognized that all Americans should have the opportunity to improve themselves. His defense of African American freedom, as much as his championing of the Union, enabled him to secure the number one ranking in nearly all modern surveys of the American presidency.

Unfortunately, the presidents who succeeded Lincoln in the decades before the close of the century did little to build on his legacy. Andrew Johnson vetoed legislation intended to facilitate the transition of African Americans from slavery to freedom and withheld support for the Fourteenth Amendment. The Civil Rights Act of 1875, which aimed to eliminate discrimination, momentarily gave African Americans cause for optimism, only to have it dashed in 1883 when the Supreme Court overturned the measure. In the decision's wake, racially inspired violence, disenfranchisement, and Jim Crow legislation prevailed, primarily in the South, with little if any pushback by those who occupied the White House. And in the last quarter of the nineteenth century, immigrant groups, especially those from China and Japan, met resistance from American-born laborers who resented the willingness of these newcomers to work for lesser wages. The campaign to exclude them proved successful as one president after another bowed to the will of the people.

In the meantime, the nation reversed its stance on women receiving fuller participation in the political system. After many decades of struggle for equal access to the ballot, they achieved victory when the Nineteenth Amendment guaranteed their voting rights. Theodore Roosevelt had supported women's suffrage in the 1912 presidential campaign, and Woodrow Wilson, who won the election, expressed support during his first term but did little to move the cause along. During his second term, however, in response to the added pressure brought by women who reminded the country of their sacrifice during World War I, Wilson championed their cause. Within a year, the nation recognized its daughters as worthy partners in government "of the people, by the people, and for the people."

If women's suffrage represented a bright moment in the history of equality and justice in America, the internment of Japanese Americans during World War II represented one of the darkest periods since the abolition of slavery. Bowing to pressures exerted after the surprise attack on Pearl Harbor in 1941, Franklin Roosevelt issued Executive Order 9066, which authorized military commanders to designate "exclusion zones" on the West Coast that ultimately led to the internment of persons of Japanese descent, many of them American citizens. The men, women, and children placed in remote camps in the desert remained interned there for the duration of the war.

The Roosevelt administration also faced challenges in its response to African American demands for equal treatment during the war years. Exasperated by the continuing discrimination in employment and in military service, civil rights activist and labor leader A. Philip Randolph threatened to organize a march on Washington. Unwilling to fight a war over inequality at home while attempting to scotch fascism abroad, Roosevelt issued an executive order, which acknowledged that a democracy can be defended only with the help of all its citizens. The order established the Committee on Fair Employment Practices, which sought to eliminate racial discrimination in the defense industry. Discrimination and segregation in the military continued, but Roosevelt's authorization of the training of black military pilots served as an important step toward African American inclusion. In 1942, he expanded opportunities for women, as well, by signing legislation that created the Women's Army Auxiliary Corps.

The emerging civil rights movement of the war years grew in intensity in the postwar period and encouraged the presidents of the latter half of the century to move the country forward in its commitment to justice and equality. Harry Truman commissioned two studies, one targeting discrimination in civilian life and the other in the military. In response to the two reports the commissions submitted, he issued executive orders that established an antidiscrimination policy for military personnel and desegregated the federal workforce. His efforts led ultimately to the establishment of a permanent Civil Rights Commission and a civil rights division of the Justice Department. Lyndon Johnson's efforts on behalf of the Civil Rights Act of 1964 (proposed by the Kennedy administration) and his "Great Society" initiatives, aimed at the elimination of racial injustice and poverty, sought to aid the most vulnerable Americans by improving education and medical care and by addressing deteriorating conditions in inner cities and rural communities.

The conservative response that followed these efforts, exemplified in the administration of Ronald Reagan, represented a vision of America that embraced individualism and limited government. His record on the pursuit of justice and equality reflected that political philosophy. Reagan's support of legislation that cut social services left certain groups vulnerable, and his veto of the Civil Rights Restoration Act on the grounds that it abridged the rights of states and businesses won him few supporters in minority communities. In the area of women's rights, he received credit for nominating the first woman Supreme Court justice and for supporting an initiative designed to eradicate state statutes and federal laws discriminatory to women. However, his opposition to the Equal Rights Amendment led many women to question his commitment to gender equality.

Conversely, the Obama administration touted an increased role for government in addressing social problems. Barack Obama's support for equal pay for women reflected a recognition that one-half of the American population still suffered economic discrimination despite the essential role they played in the workforce. His commitment to LGBTQ rights (including marriage equality for same-sex couples and the repeal of the military's "Don't Ask, Don't Tell" policy) confirmed his vision of a society with a broad commitment to inclusivity, not just one that addressed racial disparities. The signature legislation of his administration, the "Affordable Care Act," sought to ensure that every American, regardless of income or previous health status, had access to medical care.

The Trump administration's pursuit of equal justice for all is still unfolding. But its stance thus far on immigration, tax reform, health care, race relations, and other issues relevant to the American public has left many concerned that it is initiating a dangerous departure from American values and is creating a new national identity that undermines America's claim to exceptionalism. As with all things, history will ultimately render its judgment.

For now, the past teaches us that America has always experienced the tension between egalitarian ideals and inegalitarian realities. American presidents have represented and perpetuated both, sometimes simultaneously. After all, presidents are a reflection of who America is—or is becoming—as a nation. Hence, while the current climate understandably elicits serious concerns, it is hardly unprecedented in the challenge it presents to America's national identity.

Appendix I

Historians' Survey on Presidential Leadership

TOTAL SCORES AND OVERALL RANKINGS

President's Name	2017 Final Scores	Overall Rankings		
		2017	2009	2000
Abraham Lincoln	907	1	1	1
George Washington	868	2	2	3
Franklin D. Roosevelt	855	3	3	2
Theodore Roosevelt	807	4	4	4
Dwight D. Eisenhower	745	5	8	9
Harry S. Truman	737	6	5	5
Thomas Jefferson	727	7	7	7
John F. Kennedy	722	8	6	8
Ronald Reagan	691	9	10	11
Lyndon B. Johnson	687	10	11	10
Woodrow Wilson	683	11	9	6
Barack Obama	669	12	NA	NA
James Monroe	646	13	14	14
James K. Polk	637	14	12	12
William J. Clinton	634	15	15	21
William McKinley	627	16	16	15
James Madison	610	17	20	18
Andrew Jackson	609	18	13	13
John Adams	604	19	17	16

President's Name	2017 Final Scores	Overall Rankings		
		2017	**2009**	**2000**
George H. W. Bush	596	20	18	20
John Quincy Adams	590	21	19	19
Ulysses S. Grant	557	22	23	33
Grover Cleveland	540	23	21	17
William Howard Taft	528	24	24	24
Gerald R. Ford	509	25	22	23
Jimmy Carter	506	26	25	22
Calvin Coolidge	506	27	26	27
Richard M. Nixon	486	28	27	25
James A. Garfield	481	29	28	29
Benjamin Harrison	462	30	30	31
Zachary Taylor	458	31	29	28
Rutherford B. Hayes	458	32	33	26
George W. Bush	456	33	36	NA
Martin Van Buren	450	34	31	30
Chester A. Arthur	446	35	32	32
Herbert Hoover	416	36	34	34
Millard Fillmore	394	37	37	35
William Henry Harrison	383	38	39	37
John Tyler	372	39	35	36
Warren G. Harding	360	40	38	38
Franklin Pierce	315	41	40	39
Andrew Johnson	275	42	41	40
James Buchanan	245	43	42	41

Appendix II

US Presidents in Chronological Order

1. George Washington: 1789–1797
2. John Adams: 1797–1801
3. Thomas Jefferson: 1801–1809
4. James Madison: 1809–1817
5. James Monroe: 1817–1825
6. John Quincy Adams: 1825–1829
7. Andrew Jackson: 1829–1837
8. Martin Van Buren: 1837–1841
9. William Henry Harrison: 1841–1841
10. John Tyler: 1841–1845
11. James K. Polk: 1845–1849
12. Zachary Taylor: 1849–1850
13. Millard Fillmore: 1850–1853
14. Franklin Pierce: 1853–1857
15. James Buchanan: 1857–1861
16. Abraham Lincoln: 1861–1865
17. Andrew Johnson: 1865–1869
18. Ulysses S. Grant: 1869–1877
19. Rutherford B. Hayes: 1877–1881
20. James A. Garfield: 1881–1881
21. Chester A. Arthur: 1881–1885
22. Grover Cleveland: 1885–1889
23. Benjamin Harrison: 1889–1893
24. Grover Cleveland: 1893–1897
25. William McKinley: 1897–1901

26. Theodore Roosevelt: 1901–1909
27. William Howard Taft: 1909–1913
28. Woodrow Wilson: 1913–1921
29. Warren G. Harding: 1921–1923
30. Calvin Coolidge: 1923–1929
31. Herbert Hoover: 1929–1933
32. Franklin D. Roosevelt: 1933–1945
33. Harry S. Truman: 1945–1953
34. Dwight D. Eisenhower: 1953–1961
35. John F. Kennedy: 1961–1963
36. Lyndon B. Johnson: 1963–1969
37. Richard M. Nixon: 1969–1974
38. Gerald R. Ford: 1974–1977
39. Jimmy Carter: 1977–1981
40. Ronald Reagan: 1981–1989
41. George H. W. Bush: 1989–1993
42. William J. Clinton: 1993–2001
43. George W. Bush: 2001–2009
44. Barack Obama: 2009–2017
45. Donald J. Trump: 2017–

Complete List of Featured Books

LINCOLN (Chapter 1) Harold Holzer, *Lincoln President-Elect: Abraham Lincoln and the Great Secession Winter 1860–1861*, Simon and Schuster, October 21, 2008.

WASHINGTON (Chapter 2) Ron Chernow, *Washington: A Life*, The Penguin Press, October 5, 2010.

ROOSEVELT, FRANKLIN D. (Chapter 3) Doris Kearns Goodwin, *No Ordinary Time: Franklin and Eleanor Roosevelt, The Home Front in World War II*, Simon and Schuster, 1994.

ROOSEVELT, THEODORE (Chapter 4) Douglas Brinkley, *The Wilderness Warrior: Theodore Roosevelt and the Crusade for America*, Harper Perennial, July 28, 2009.

EISENHOWER (Chapter 5) William I. Hitchcock, *The Age of Eisenhower: America and the World in the 1950s*, Simon and Schuster, March 20, 2018.

TRUMAN (Chapter 6) Aida D. Donald, *Citizen Soldier: A Life of Harry S. Truman*, Basic Books, October 2, 2012.

JEFFERSON (Chapter 7) Willard Sterne Randall, *Thomas Jefferson: A Life*, Henry Holt and Co., August 15, 1993.

KENNEDY (Chapter 8) Robert Dallek, *Camelot's Court: Inside the Kennedy White House*, Harper, October 8, 2013.

REAGAN (Chapter 9) Lou Cannon, *President Reagan: The Role of a Lifetime*, Simon and Schuster, April 1, 1991.

JOHNSON, LYNDON B. (Chapter 10) Robert A. Caro, *The Passage of Power: The Years of Lyndon Johnson*, Alfred A. Knopf, May 1, 2012.

WILSON (Chapter 11) A. Scott Berg, *Wilson*, G. P. Putnam's Sons, September 10, 2013.

OBAMA (Chapter 12) David J. Garrow, *Rising Star: The Making of Barack Obama*, William Morrow, May 9, 2017.

MONROE (Chapter 13) John Ferling, *Apostles of Revolution: Jefferson, Paine, Monroe, and the Struggle Against the Old Order in America and Europe*, Bloomsbury Publishing, May 15, 2018.

POLK (Chapter 14) John Seigenthaler, *James K. Polk*, Times Books, January 4, 2004.

CLINTON (Chapter 15) David Maraniss, *First in His Class: A Biography of Bill Clinton*, Simon and Schuster, March 6, 1995.

MCKINLEY (Chapter 16) Robert W. Merry, *President McKinley: Architect of the American Century*, Simon and Schuster, November 7, 2017.

MADISON (Chapter 17) Noah Feldman, *The Three Lives of James Madison: Genius, Partisan, President*, Random House, October 31, 2017.

JACKSON (Chapter 18) Mark R. Cheathem, *Andrew Jackson, Southerner*, LSU Press, October 7, 2013.

ADAMS, JOHN (Chapter 19) Gordon S. Wood, *Friends Divided: John Adams and Thomas Jefferson*, Penguin Press, October 24, 2017.

BUSH, GEORGE H. W. (Chapter 20) Jeffrey A. Engel, *When the World Seemed New: George H. W. Bush and the End of the Cold War*, Houghton Mifflin Harcourt, November 7, 2017.

ADAMS, JOHN QUINCY (Chapter 21) James Traub, *John Quincy Adams: Militant Spirit*, Basic Books, March 22, 2016.

GRANT (Chapter 22) Ronald C. White, *American Ulysses: A Life of Ulysses S. Grant*, Random House, October 4, 2016.

CLEVELAND (Chapter 23) H. Paul Jeffers, *An Honest President: The Life and Presidencies of Grover Cleveland*, William Morrow, May 30, 2000.

TAFT (Chapter 24) Jeffrey Rosen, *William Howard Taft*, Times Books, March 20, 2018.

FORD (Chapter 25) James Cannon, *Time and Chance: Gerald Ford's Appointment with History*, HarperCollins, January 1, 1994.

CARTER (Chapter 26) Michael J. Gerhardt, *The Forgotten Presidents: Their Untold Constitutional Legacy*, Oxford University Press, April 1, 2013.

COOLIDGE (Chapter 27) Amity Shlaes, *Coolidge*, Harper, February 12, 2013.

NIXON (Chapter 28) Evan Thomas, *Being Nixon: A Man Divided*, Random House, June 16, 2015.

GARFIELD (Chapter 29) Kenneth D. Ackerman, *Dark Horse: The Surprise Election and Political Murder of President James A. Garfield*, Da Capo Press, June 2003.

HARRISON, BENJAMIN (Chapter 30) Charles W. Calhoun, *Benjamin Harrison*, Times Books, June 6, 2005.

TAYLOR (Chapter 31) Elbert B. Smith, *The Presidencies of Zachary Taylor and Millard Fillmore*, University Press of Kansas, August 5, 1988.

HAYES (Chapter 32) Ari Hoogenboom, *Rutherford B. Hayes: Warrior and President*, University Press of Kansas, January 27, 1995.

BUSH, GEORGE W. (Chapter 33) James Mann, *George W. Bush*, Times Books, February 3, 2015.

VAN BUREN (Chapter 34) Michael Douglas Henderson, C-SPAN's *American Presidents* series, May 3, 1999, www.c-span.org/video/?122988-1/life-portrait-martin-van-buren.

ARTHUR (Chapter 35) Scott S. Greenberger, *The Unexpected President: The Life and Times of Chester A. Arthur*, Da Capo Press, September 12, 2017.

HOOVER (Chapter 36) Richard Norton Smith, *An Uncommon Man: The Triumph of Herbert Hoover*, Simon and Schuster, 1984.

FILLMORE (Chapter 37) Edna Greene Medford for C-SPAN's *American Presidents* series, June 8, 1999, www.c-span.org/video/?124795-1/president-millard-fillmore.

HARRISON, WILLIAM HENRY (Chapter 38) Ronald G. Shafer, *The Carnival Campaign: How the Rollicking 1840 Campaign of "Tippecanoe and Tyler Too" Changed Presidential Elections Forever*, Chicago Review Press, September 1, 2016.

TYLER (Chapter 39) Edward P. Crapol, *John Tyler, the Accidental President*, The University of North Carolina Press, October 9, 2006.

HARDING (Chapter 40) John W. Dean, *Warren G. Harding*, Times Books, January 7, 2004.

PIERCE (Chapter 41) Peter A. Wallner, *Franklin Pierce: New Hampshire's Favorite Son*, Plaidswede Publishing, October 2004.

JOHNSON, ANDREW (Chapter 42) David O. Stewart, *Impeached: The Trial of President Andrew Johnson and the Fight for Lincoln's Legacy*, Simon and Schuster, May 12, 2009.

BUCHANAN (Chapter 43) Robert Strauss, *Worst. President. Ever.: James Buchanan, the POTUS Rating Game, and the Legacy of the Least of the Lesser Presidents*, Lyons Press, October 1, 2016.

TRUMP (Historians' Perspectives on President Donald J. Trump), C-SPAN podcast interview with Douglas Brinkley, Edna Greene Medford, and Richard Norton Smith, August 31, 2018.

Acknowledgments

Many people have contributed to the creation of this book. This list, while not exhaustive, highlights those with major roles.

The *presidential historians and biographers* who have taken part in C-SPAN programs over the past forty years. Forty-three of them are featured here, but they number in the many hundreds, all contributing their scholarship to further public understanding of American history and the presidency. In addition, we thank the more than one hundred historians who have participated in each of the three Historians Surveys of Presidential Leadership, which serve as the organizing principle for this book.

Special thanks to the three historians, Douglas Brinkley, Edna Greene Medford, and Richard Norton Smith, who have helped us greatly with this project, serving as *academic advisers* for all three presidential leadership surveys and contributing original material.

Our *internal editorial team.* Katie Lee and Rachel Katz line edited the chapters; Zelda Wallace and Anthony Davis were fact checkers. Rachel Katz also served as production coordinator, selected illustrations, and wrote chapter introductions. Ellen Vest and Leslie Rhodes assisted with photos.

Rob Kennedy, C-SPAN co-CEO, and Dr. Robert X. Browning, executive director of the C-SPAN Video Archives, served as *statistical analysts* for the three presidential leadership surveys. Rob Kennedy also wrote the survey summaries headlining each chapter.

Our *marketing and social media teams,* led by vice presidents Marty Dominguez and Peter Kiley with assistance from Howard Mortman, Jeremy Art, Robin Newton, Ed Aymar, Christina Whirl, Katie Lee, and Vanessa Torres.

The *website team,* with special thanks to Richard Weinstein, Vice President of Digital Media, Stephen Harkness, Tony Laboy, and Alan Cloutier.

The *Q & A, Booknotes,* and *American Presidents editorial and technical teams* over the years—especially current *Q & A* producer Nikhil Raval—led by Programming Vice President Terry Murphy and Programming Operations Vice President Kathy Cahill, who created the original content which forms the basis for our chapters.

The staff of *PublicAffairs,* our longtime publisher, including our friend Peter Osnos, company founder; executive editor Benjamin Adams, who has edited our last several books; publisher Clive Priddle; the publicity team of Jaime Leifer and Brooke Parsons; and the marketing team of Lindsay Fradkoff and Miguel Cervantes.

C-SPAN *Counsel* Bruce Collins, who helped with contract and copyright issues.

And, finally, our *board of cable CEOs* who provide ongoing guidance, and our partners at the nation's cable, satellite, and telecommunications companies who support our network operations through their affiliate fees and marketing support—a special thank you to you all, on our network's fortieth anniversary, for making C-SPAN possible.

Index

Brian Lamb is C-SPAN's founding CEO and chairman and longtime on-camera interviewer. His forty years of C-SPAN interviews have been the basis for eight prior books with PublicAffairs.

Susan Swain is C-SPAN's co-CEO and has been an on-camera host for C-SPAN for more than thirty years, interviewing public officials, historians, and journalists. This is her tenth book project with PublicAffairs.

PublicAffairs is a publishing house founded in 1997. It is a tribute to the standards, values, and flair of three persons who have served as mentors to countless reporters, writers, editors, and book people of all kinds, including me.

I. F. Stone, proprietor of *I. F. Stone's Weekly*, combined a commitment to the First Amendment with entrepreneurial zeal and reporting skill and became one of the great independent journalists in American history. At the age of eighty, Izzy published *The Trial of Socrates*, which was a national bestseller. He wrote the book after he taught himself ancient Greek.

Benjamin C. Bradlee was for nearly thirty years the charismatic editorial leader of *The Washington Post*. It was Ben who gave the *Post* the range and courage to pursue such historic issues as Watergate. He supported his reporters with a tenacity that made them fearless and it is no accident that so many became authors of influential, best-selling books.

Robert L. Bernstein, the chief executive of Random House for more than a quarter century, guided one of the nation's premier publishing houses. Bob was personally responsible for many books of political dissent and argument that challenged tyranny around the globe. He is also the founder and longtime chair of Human Rights Watch, one of the most respected human rights organizations in the world.

. . .

For fifty years, the banner of Public Affairs Press was carried by its owner Morris B. Schnapper, who published Gandhi, Nasser, Toynbee, Truman, and about 1,500 other authors. In 1983, Schnapper was described by *The Washington Post* as "a redoubtable gadfly." His legacy will endure in the books to come.

Peter Osnos, *Founder*